Italy's Sea

Empire and Nation
in the Mediterranean, 1895–1945

Transnational Italian Cultures 5

Transnational Italian Cultures

Series editors:
Dr Emma Bond, University of St Andrews
Professor Derek Duncan, University of St Andrews

Transnational Italian Cultures will publish the best research in the expanding field of postcolonial, global and transnational Italian studies and aim to set a new agenda for academic research on what constitutes Italian culture today. As such, it will move beyond the physical borders of the peninsula as well as identifying existing or evolving transnational presences within the nation in order to reflect the vibrant and complex make-up of today's global Italy. Privileging a cultural studies perspective with an emphasis on the analysis of textual production, the series focuses primarily on the contemporary context but will also include work on earlier periods informed by current postcolonial/transnational methodology.

Italy's Sea

*Empire and Nation
in the Mediterranean, 1895–1945*

Valerie McGuire

LIVERPOOL UNIVERSITY PRESS

First published 2020 by
Liverpool University Press
4 Cambridge Street
Liverpool
L69 7ZU

British Library Cataloguing-in-Publication data
A British Library CIP record is available

ISBN 978-1-80034-800-4 cased

Typeset by Carnegie Book Production, Lancaster
Printed and bound by CPI Group (UK) Ltd, Croydon CR0 4YY

For Jason and Elsa.

Contents

List of Illustrations   ix

Acknowledgments   xiii

Introduction: Europe's Southern Question   1

  1. Nationalists and the Mediterranean in the Liberal Era   37

  2. Touring Italian Rhodes   89

  3. Belonging in the Archipelago: Nation, Race, and Citizenship   141

  4. Everyday Fascism in the Aegean   195

Conclusion: Postcolonial Returns   247

Bibliography   263

Index   285

List of Illustrations

From Giorgio Roletto, *Rodi: La funzione imperiale nel Mediterraneo Orientale* (Milan: Istituto Fascista dell'Africa Orientale, 1939) p. 108 © National Library of Florence. xvii

Figure 0.1: Photograph from above of Porto Lago (today Lakkhi), a model city built for the Italian navy base © *Islands of Exile: The Case of Leros* (www.leros-project.com). 5

Figure 0.2: Former Italian aviators' barracks in Lakki (*Caserma Avieri*), Leros, later a mental sanatorium, and repurposed as a refugee camp from 2014–18 © *Islands of Exile: The Case of Leros* (www.leros-project.com). 6

Figure 1.1: Cover illustration of *La Domenica del Corriere*, June 7–9, 1912. The caption says, "The events of the Italo-Turkish War: the arrival in Naples of Italians, especially workers, expelled by Turkish reprisals" © Biblioteca Marucelliana. 73

Figure 2.1: Rhodes shoreline circa 1930 © Archive Touring Club Italiano. 102

Figure 2.2: Governor's Palace in Rhodes, circa 1928 © Archive Touring Club Italiano. 103

Figure 2.3: Palazzo Ducale, Venice, Italy. Photo: Valerie McGuire. 103

Figure 2.4: Promotional image of the New Market © Archive Touring Club Italiano. 105

Figure 2.5: New Market and the Palace of the Knights of St. John in
vertical communication and juxtaposition © Archive Touring
Club Italiano.   106

Figure 2.6: Architectural drawing of the Kalithea Baths © General
State Archives of Greece, Department of Rhodes.   110

Figure 2.7: Interior of the Bath of Soliman, circa 1928, Rhodes, Greece.
Photo: General State Archives of Greece, Department of Rhodes.   111

Figure 2.8: "Le capitali del mondo: Isole dell'egeo RODI." Cover of a
1926 guidebook featuring Turkish monuments in the background
© Archive Touring Club Italiano.   114

Figure 2.9: At the port of Rhodes, a fisherman retrieves the cross and
emerges from the sea; festival of the Benediction of the Waters
© Archive Touring Club Italiano.   117

Figure 2.10: "The characters of a village of inner-Rhodes" ("Le
personalità di un villaggio nell'interno di Rodi"), p. 395 of
Le colonie, Rodi, e le isole italiane dell'Egeo © Archive Touring
Club Italiano.   118

Figure 2.11: The Jewish Quarter with Ottoman-era balconies
© Archive Touring Club Italiano.   120

Figure 2.12: Inside the monumental zone of Rhodes, interior view
of the medieval city gates, as seen from the Turkish quarter, after
Italian renovation and reconstruction circa 1930 © Archive
Touring Club Italiano.   120

Figure 2.13: Local Greek woman in Rhodes encounters Italian tourist,
circa 1927 © Archive Touring Club Italiano.   123

Figure 2.14: "Peasant woman of Rhodes" ("*Contadina rodiota*").
Photo: Ardito Desio and Giuseppe Stefanini, *Le colonie, Rodi, e le
isole italiane dell'Egeo* (Turin: Unione Tipografico Editrice, 1928),
p. 405 © Archive of the Touring Club Italiano.   123

Figure 2.15: Stills from "Il quartiere turco," *Rhodes*, 1924–31,
produced and distributed by Istituto Nazionale LUCE. Photo
at 19:08–20:10 © Archivio LUCE.   124

Figure 2.16: A Turkish woman replaces her veil at the request of the
filmmaker, *Rhodes*, 1924–31, produced and distributed by Istituto
Nazionale LUCE. Photo at 20:10–20:20 © Archivio LUCE.   125

Figure 2.17: The Hotel of the Roses in the Lago era © General State
    Archives of Greece, Department of Rhodes.   137

Figure 2.18: The Italian Club after the De Vecchi "purification" in
    1938. *dell'Egeo* © General State Archives of Greece, Department
    of Rhodes.   137

Figure 4.1: Page from a syllabarium, Vittorio Mancus. *I miei primi passi:
    Sillabario illustrato e Prime letture ed essercizi ad uso delle scuole
    delle Isole Egee*. Rodi: Tipografia "Rodia," 1926.   213

Figure 4.2: The Empire of Work: Italian Fascists oversee construction
    of the port in the Island of Kalymnos © Archive Touring Club
    Italiano.   237

Acknowledgments

It goes without saying that with a book of this kind there are many different institutions and people to acknowledge, without whom this book never would have been. Throughout the completion of this book, I was fortunate enough to receive external support from several charitable foundations supporting the humanities. For undertaking the original oral testimonies, I am indebted to the Fulbright foundation for the support of a year abroad in Greece. I must also note the financial support of the Council of American Overseas Research Centers, which supported further archival research in France, Italy, Tunisia, and Greece through a Mellon Multi-Country research grant for the Mediterranean region. For research on the Jewish communities of Rhodes and Kos, I would like to recognize the support of a Tsakopoulos Library Research fellowship in Sacramento, California for work in their collection of books and resources. These fellowships cumulatively provided me with unparalleled access to major state archives in Italy, especially the Archive of the Ministry of Foreign Affairs in Rome, but also the seemingly limitless body of archival sources in the Greek State Archives of the Dodecanese prefecture located in Rhodes. I very much owe a debt of thanks to both Ireni Toliou and Marco Clementi who were tireless in their commitment to making these unusual archival sources in Rhodes available to me. I would also like to thank here all of my oral informants from the islands of the Dodecanese who generously shared with me their time and memories of the Italian era. It is my sincere hope that with their passing this book might provide some insight and knowledge of the complexity to how a previous generation in the Dodecanese lived.

Like many academic books, this one began as a PhD dissertation. I will always be indebted to the advisor of that dissertation, Ruth Ben-Ghiat. Both her inspiring research in Italian history and culture and her unwavering view that this project was a viable and important avenue of critical inquiry have been a touchstone for me. I am also indebted to Mia Fuller who has been involved in this project since its earliest stages and has continued to provide feedback for its development over the course of many years. Further to those who supported this research at its nascent doctoral stage, there are several scholars at the European University Institute (EUI) who were important for me in an early postdoctoral one. This book would not be the same one that it is were it not for the dynamic "Empire and Nation" research seminar, led by Lucy Riall and Pieter Judson, as well as the suggestions for direction and development of Laura Downs, Ludivine Broch, Gabrielle Clark, Anna Triandafyllidou, and Eirini Karamouzi. Not far from the EUI campus in Fiesole, there are also several scholars at Villa La Pietra in Florence who provided me with important support, feedback, and hospitality: in particular, I would like to recognize Bruce Edelstein and Rebecca Falkoff of New York University for being important interlocuters at different stages of my writing.

In both Italy and New York there are far too many people whose home I either availed myself of or whose time I borrowed when seeking to build this book. I must express a huge thanks to Carla and Borje Magnusson without whom I never would have arrived in Rome and whose generosity and kindness during my first years in Italy I will never be able to forget or to repay. I must also thank my wonderful friend and first teacher of Italian culture and language, the uniquely curious, perceptive, and determined Francesca Bellino, as well as the other energetic postcolonial intellectuals of Rome, especially Igiaba Scego and Rino Bianchi, both of whom have done important work for redefining what constitutes the visual and literary memory of Italian colonialism. I must also thank Gaoheng Zhang and Paola Bonifazio for being wonderfully kind friends and readers and who every time they read this research responded with the same energy as if for the first time.

In Greece, a country that I made my adoptive home for several years, there are many people to acknowledge. I must thank Myrto Miliou for introducing me to Greece and for regular hospitality and adventure as well as the rest of the Miliou clan (Yannis, Ellen, Kostas, Despina, Eleni, and Nikos) for all their kindness and generosity over the years. For her help with reading and translating parts of the novel *Kitala*, as well as other Greek adventures in both Athens and New York, my gratitude goes to Antonia Andrioti. I would also like to recognize Sophy Downes, Seth Jaffe, Catherine Drake, and Stephanie Malia Hom as important friends in Athens, and the American School of Classical Studies in Athens for putting me in touch with both resources and a community of academics to support me during the research phase of this book. I have also benefited from the support and insight of a wonderful network of scholars and friends within the field of Modern Greek Studies. Among the people to acknowledge are Alexis Rappas, who has been a friend ever since we first met while researching in the Greek State Archives in Rhodes, Konstantina Zanou and Katherine Fleming, who have supported the ongoing reception of this project in both Greece and modern Greek studies, as well as the other folks of the insularity network, including Sakis Gekas, Antonis Hadjicyriacou, and Simon Jackson, all of whom have contributed in substantive ways to my rethinking this research as not just a work of Italian studies or even European history, but one that also speaks meaningfully to Ottoman transitions in the Aegean and the history of Greece under occupation.

Although I have been based in the United Kingdom less than a year, there are nevertheless a significant number of people in Scotland, at the University of St Andrews and at Liverpool University Press to whom I must express a debt of gratitude. An enormous thanks go to Emma Bond and Derek Duncan, the editors of the Transnational Italian Cultures series, for encouraging me to publish with this series and for their ongoing support and feedback at different stages of the book's development. Within the School of Modern Languages at St Andrews, I must thank the informal reading group, organized by Orhan Elmaz, and attended by Ramsey McGlazer, Margaret Anne Hutton, and Ted Bergman, who provided important feedback on an early draft of this book's introduction. In the School of History at St Andrews, I would like especially to recognize Kate Ferris for organizing a workshop for chapter 4 of this book, as well as the other scholars who participated in it, Grazia Schiacciatano, Josh Hall, Yannick Lengkeek, and Huw Halstead, and the important contribution they made to developing the discussion of everyday life in the Aegean under Italian rule. Finally, I want to further recognize the work of Chloe Johnson, the managing editor at Liverpool University Press, for her careful but efficient steering of this project as well as the two anonymous reviewers whose attentive reading and critical recommendations motivated the final rewrite of this book.

Finally, in Berkeley, my hometown and my home base, there are also many near and dear to thank. I owe a debt of gratitude to Caroline Knapp and Juliana Frogatt for their thoughtful editing and careful proofreading of multiple drafts of the chapters that follow. Thanks are due to journalist and storyteller extraordinaire Michael Lewis for help brainstorming an appropriate title and thinking about book market. I must also recognize that I could never have completed this book without the support of my indefatigable cheering section, my mother, Kathleen McGuire, the always outstanding and often outrageous Adeline Lassource, and the sympathetic ear of Wendy Badgley. And though it is impossible to summarize here all of his patience, reading, and rereading of this manuscript, and his stoic forbearance with my Greek island hopping, archive sifting, and zig-zagging adventures across the Mediterranean—and now more recently, in the northern archipelago of the British Isles—I must try nonetheless to thank my partner, Jason Badgley, for support, love, and his unorthodox positions on just about everything.

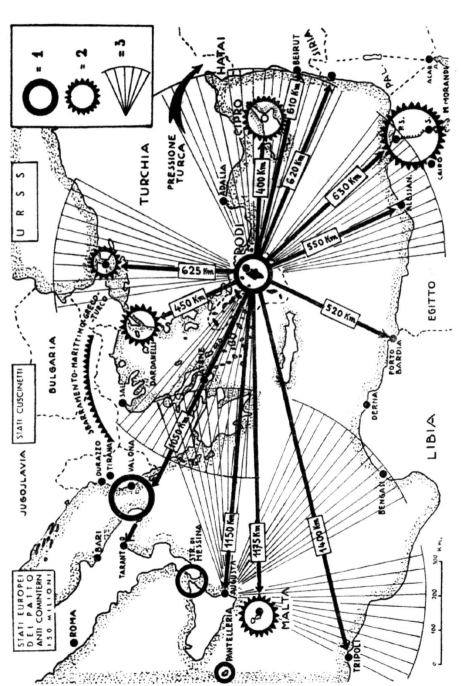

From Giorgio Roletto, *Rodi: La funzione imperiale nel Mediterraneo Orientale* (Milan: Istituto Fascista dell'Africa Orientale, 1939) p. 108
© National Library of Florence.

Introduction: Europe's Southern Question

In July 2015, a journalist for *The Guardian* visited the tiny Greek island of Leros to report on an unfolding migration crisis. Hundreds of war refugees were arriving daily from Syria. The island, along with the nearby islands of Rhodes and Kos in the southeast Aegean, had morphed into a flashpoint for debates about illegal migration. In one interview, a local explained that he and others hoped to refurbish the island's old insane asylum, closed since the 1980s, in order to process the flood of requests for political asylum. As the Leros resident crossed the threshold of the abandoned sanatorium, he referenced a little-known past. Tapping firmly on the concrete walls to emphasize their robustness, he announced, "It is Italian."[1]

Lurking not far in the background of *The Guardian* article was the larger debate about whether Greece, the black sheep of Europe's economic block (but also the nation receiving the lion's share of refugees from Syria at that time), should be receiving some form of humanitarian aid from the European Union (EU). While *The Guardian*'s international audience may have been surprised by the fact that the building was built by the Italians, that fact would have been well known to locals. What the speaker omitted was that the old sanatorium of Leros was not merely a formidable structure with the potential to house hundreds, but also a relic of the large-scale urban renovation that the Italian imperial state undertook in the second half of the 1930s, as the Fascist regime, by that time allied with Nazi Germany, prepared to conquer the whole of the Mediterranean.

The realization of *mare nostrum*, or the renewal of Roman dominance in the Mediterranean, was to be Mussolini's crowning achievement as dictator. As the home to the Italian navy's eastern operations, Leros had been

1 "The Tiny Greek Island Sinking under Europe's Refugee Crisis," YouTube video, posted by *The Guardian*, August 18, 2015, www.theguardian.com/world/video/2015/aug/18/greek-island-leros-europe-migrant-crisis-video.

renovated in the late 1930s in preparation for the eastern Mediterranean as a major theater of war for the Italian state. Renovation of the island built upon a program of colonial rule that had defined the previous three decades in which the Italian imperial state, under Fascist leadership, had undertaken a massive social engineering program, courting locals while providing them with Italian citizenship and Italian-language education, and inviting them to join the Fascist party, the Fascist trade union, and the Fascist youth organization, while forcibly expelling others who resisted the Italian state.

The invocation of this historical backdrop for the purpose of managing a European refugee crisis presents interesting ironies. Not only does the rehabilitation of Italian buildings entwine with questions about Greece's status as a frontier that must use national resources to cope with EU problems, but also, for locals, such as the one interviewed by *The Guardian,* the Italian architecture seems to signify a bid for cosmopolitan hospitality toward refugees, and in the face of growing condemnation of the EU's draconian security policies in the Mediterranean—what has loosely become known as the project of Fortress Europe. Referencing a shared past with Italy underscores not only the need for European solidarity and values but also the climate of uncertainty about the viability of the European Union.

While Greece has been increasingly involved in both the enlargement and security of Europe's peripheries (it will be remembered that Greek objections have presented the strongest threat to an eventual EU inclusion of Turkey, whether liberal or illiberal), its legitimacy as one of the core member nations has strongly been questioned, most notably between 2011 and 2015 as the Greek economy collapsed under the pressure of the global fiscal contagion in the US. Earlier in that summer of 2015—only a month before *The Guardian* reported on the refugee crisis in Leros—Greece had held a referendum on whether to accept the harsh austerity measures being offered by the European troika (the European Commission (EC), the International Monetary Fund (IMF), and the European Central Bank (ECB)) in exchange for another bailout to inject lifeblood into the national economy. Although it failed to be enacted in policy, the referendum was largely viewed at the time as a referendum on Europe. The moment was rife with references to anti-Fascism in Greece. As millions of voters headed to the polls bearing signs with the word όχι! (no!), the referendum recalled for many Oxi Day, in historical parallel with another day in 1940 when the nation rejected Mussolini's ultimatum to Greece that it should capitulate to his national empire in the Mediterranean.

The invocation of Italian Fascism, in both contemporary Leros and Greece, strikes at the core of ongoing debates about Europe and European identity today. What role does the nation and national identity have today in the context of the expanding power of the European Union? How do we think about the legacies of fascism and empire in the context of European (dis) integration and in an evolving postcolonial present? And how is it that Italy can at once represent cosmopolitan Europe and be an emblem of a staunchly anti-cosmopolitan and nationalist past? As Europe integrates, often defining itself through difference with non-European others, colonial empires of the past not only remain near at hand, but they are also assigned new historical meanings. In what ways are these meanings both revealing and concealing of the project for a cosmopolitan and inclusive Europe?

Leros and thirteen other nearby islands today comprise the prefecture of the Dodecanese (as so re-named by their former Italian rulers); roughly 250,000 persons inhabit the islands with the population falling even lower during the winter months. The islands hover at Europe's most southeastern edge, fringing the Turkish coast and buffering Europe from the Middle East. While the islands are unequivocally part of Greece today, they were only integrated into it at the end of World War II. In 1947, after thirty years of Italian Empire followed by German occupation and then interim British rule, Greek national claims based on the presence of an ethnic Greek majority finally won out against an age-old tradition of the Balkans serving as a region for the informal economic and imperial expansion of European nation-states. Although it was a much-anticipated event for the islands' Greek ethnic majority, a small portion of which had fought in the 1820 Greek revolution for independence, the integration into national Greece also marked the end of the era of "multi-ethnic" imperial states in Europe and the Mediterranean.

If today the islands may be identified with postimperial and postcolonial conditions, this was also very much the case a century ago. After the 1820 Greek revolution, the islands remained for another century under Ottoman rule; until decline and collapse of the Ottoman state paved the way for another ambitious state, Italy, to absorb the islands into their overseas territory. For the Italian state, the islands were the sea-girt, insular jewel in the crown of an empire that was closely tied to the idea of the sea—and to the wealth and identity that the sea had historically brought with it. The local population and culture in the Aegean intersected with nationalist claims at home that projects of overseas empire would restore to the nation a bygone prestige and return to Italy its more illustrious reputation connected to the ancient and Renaissance periods in the peninsula. Against the threat of Greek ethnic claims to sovereignty in the islands, the Italian state mobilized in culture

and propaganda a fable about Magna Graecia and Greco-Roman Empire
in the Mediterranean: local Greeks in the Aegean were distant "cousins"
who could benefit from an economically robust Italian state.[2] This narrative
has withstood the long passage of time and is visible in ongoing myths that
Italians and Greeks traded claims that they were like *una faccia, una razza*—
or one face and one race.

As this book will demonstrate, the islands bolstered Italian discourses
of Mediterraneanism, that is, the fantasy that the Italian state would
achieve its full potential as a nation-state once it achieved an empire in the
Mediterranean.

A complex Euro-Mediterranean landscape enabled Italy to obtain
sovereignty in the Aegean. Recalling this context throws into question the
idea that European nation-states were (and are) constituted on the basis of
linguistic and ethnic homogeneity. At the end of World War I, the Italian state
integrated the islands largely on the basis that their empire was necessary there
to "protect" the minority Turkish and Jewish communities. With Ottoman
collapse these communities lost the privileges of communal civil administration associated with the *millet* system. In the large and more populated
islands of Rhodes and Kos, the minority Jewish and Turkish communities
constituted almost a third of the local population.[3] Their presence helped
Italy to undermine Greek national claims that had received a boost in
the aftermath of World War I on the basis of Woodrow Wilson's tenets
of the "self-determination" of nation-states.[4] Yet the presence of minority
communities was a boon to the ways in which Italy was to imagine its imperial
state as the reprisal of a "Mediterranean" Empire and the creation of a strong
nation-state that presided over not just Italians, but Greeks, Turks, and Jews.
Thus, it was Italian nationalism, ironically, that spearheaded a grandiose
project to imagine ethnic diversity in the Mediterranean as intrinsic to its
nation-empire.

---

2   The idea of "cousins" across different ethnic and national groups has been observed
in other parts of the Mediterranean as well. See Naor Ben-Yehoyada, *The Mediterranean
Incarnate: Region Formation between Sicily and Tunisia since World War Two* (Chicago:
Chicago University Press, 2018).
3   British Empire's Naval Intelligence Division, *Dodecanese*, 2nd ed. (London:
Geographical Handbook Series, 1943).
4   On the impact of Woodrow Wilson's principles of the "self-determination" of nation-
states, see Roberta Pergher and Marcus Payek, eds., *Beyond Versailles: Sovereignty,
Legitimacy, and the Formation of New Polities after the Great War* (Bloomington:
Bloomington Indiana Press, 2019).

Figure 0.1: Photograph from above of Porto Lago (today Lakkhi), a model city built for the Italian navy base, circa 1940, Leros, Greece © *Islands of Exile: The Case of Leros* (www. leros-project.com).

When the Italians lined the shoreline of the islands with new constructions that were clearly hybrid, architects were inspired by the notion of a shared "Mediterranean" past that shored up sovereignty—not one that erased ethnic difference but one that framed and highlighted it while placing differences into visual hierarchies and contrasts. Such exoticizing inflection of Fascist austerity is clearly visible in the monumental sanatorium on Leros that stands today as a possible sanctuary for refugees. Sleek rationalist forms inspired by Le Corbusier's modernism were adorned by art deco and Orientalist motifs to articulate a timeless imperial modernity. Yet the iconography of the architecture, with its zealous commitment to visual contrasts between "Orient" and "Occident," strove to elide a fundamental dilemma that arose from the attempt to control a space on which Italian claims of sovereignty were highly contested: Were the islands so culturally familiar as to be constituted, at least in practical administrative terms, as *already* an Italian space? Or were they so much on the periphery of Europe, in terms of culture, history, and demography, that they needed to be thought of in the colonial terms that Italy was adopting in colonies in North and East Africa? While the Italian state

Figure 0.2: Former Italian aviators' barracks in Lakki (*Caserma Avieri*), Leros,
later a mental sanatorium, and repurposed as a refugee camp from 2014–18
© *Islands of Exile: The Case of Leros* (www. leros-project.com).

was never of course to resolve this question, it bore a striking resemblance
to another issue in Italian culture, that is, to what degree the South could be
viewed as part of Italy.

Much as the Aegean stands today—as both a part of Europe and apart
from it—the Aegean was to be both part of the Italian state and apart from it.
This fundamental ambivalence was to emerge clearly within the zeitgeist of
the interwar period: within ideas of nation, race, and belonging, and within
shifting definitions of colonial citizen and subject. It would seem, then,
that the resonance the Italian Empire has today in the Aegean, as Greeks
continue to confront their role as both a southern and an eastern periphery of
Europe, is not an accident but at least in part a reflection of ongoing ambivalences about identity that are at the core of constructions of Europe and the
Mediterranean. This book will show how retrieving the history of Italian
Empire in the Aegean provides us with a remarkable case study in how the
periphery has been a productive space for European identity long before the
postwar period of European integration. It will further suggest that Italian
rule in the southeast Aegean, or Dodecanese islands, is a striking example
of Mediterraneanism within discourses of European Empire, and one that
has marked the modern Italian culture in the nineteenth, twentieth and now
twenty-first centuries.

A Colonized Sea

In a provocative article, the historians Manuel Borutta and Sakis Gekas argue that since antiquity the Mediterranean has been a colonial—or better, a colonized—sea.[5] Asking whether the Mediterranean can be still be a useful demarcation for critical inquiry in light of the colonial projects that produced the region, the authors point out that the field of Mediterranean studies, as first pioneered by Fernand Braudel, is steeped in the drama of France's imperial twilight. Braudel himself was a young teacher of history and geography in Algeria when he wrote a PhD dissertation about "unity and continuity" in the Mediterranean in the age of Phillip II. But the French historian's oft-quoted conceptions of the Mediterranean as a movement-space (*éspace movement*) and as a "connecting sea" fostering cross-cultural pollination and multicultural identities have not only survived decolonization, but today they also influence new paradigms for thinking about mobility and the overlapping histories of immigration and emigration in the Mediterranean basin.[6] But as Borutta and Gekas point out, it would be virtually impossible to separate Braudel's concept of *La Méditerranée* (Mediterranean unity) from the French geopolitical concept of *Méditerranée* (Mediterranean).

Borutta and Gekas point to some important features of *La Méditerranée* that are worth emphasizing here: tensions between the provincial and cosmopolitan, between the traditional and the avant-garde, between the colonial and the decolonized. In the period from 1798, the year of Napoleon's invasion of Egypt, which, as first noted by Edward Said, unleashed an age of European colonialism in the Mediterranean, until decolonization of the French and British empires in North Africa in the 1950s, these tensions were inherent to and defining of both governance and identity in the Mediterranean. Following World War I the Mediterranean was not just a colonized sea but also a highly contested region of feverish European expansion, an area in which the British, French, Spanish, and Italian empires competed for territories and vied for control and dominance. As these imperial mandates grew in size and scope, they were also challenged from within by a broad rise in nationalist movements, from Greek and Turkish nationalism to Pan-Arabian nationalism to the Algerian War of Independence. Gekas and Borutta argue that to

---

5   Manuel Borutta and Sakis Gekas, "A Colonial Sea: The Mediterranean, 1798–1956," *European Review of History* 19, no. 1 (2012): 1–13.
6   See Emanuela Paoletti, *The Migration of Power and North–South Inequalities* (Basingstoke: Palgrave MacMillan, 2011).

comprehend the dense entanglement of empires requires a "Mediterranean" approach, in spite of all imperial associations. The scholars advocate for an approach that is "thalassological" (from the Greek *thalassa*, or sea) in orientation—and moves beyond metropole-colony frameworks, limitations posed by area studies, and a cross-disciplinary habit of focusing imperial histories through national if not nationalist paradigms. Without such an approach, scholarship on the colonial and postcolonial Mediterranean risks fragmentation and the undervaluing of the critical possibilities of such a truly transnational approach to the region.[7]

Yet the challenges of applying such a "thalassological" framework to the Italian Empire will be obvious to anyone familiar with the issues that have surrounded the study of modern Italy and its colonial projects. Late to form a nation-state, and even later to colonial expansion, Italy's first imperial projects are understood to have been limited and provincial in ways that mirror with Italy's provincial identity at the turn of the century. In reality, Italian projects of empire align, both ideologically and temporally, with the creation of its modern nation-state; both nation and empire began in the second half of the nineteenth century, well after other nation-states in Europe had unified and also after much of Europe had achieved vast global empires and consolidated wealth and national identity through colonial and economic expansion. Italian nationalists therefore held that colonial projects would be a marker of Italy's achievement of nationhood, but their small scale in the nineteenth century served to underscore the opposite. Famously, the Italian state arrived at imperialism after the "Scramble for Africa" had nearly concluded and at the turn of the century possessed one imperial territory in East Africa, Eritrea.

These colonial projects dovetailed with debates about how to maintain enthusiasm for a unified Italian Peninsula, and the resettlement programs in East Africa were billed as a solution to economic depression and as an important means toward forging a cohesive national identity.[8] Seen as coalescing with the persistent failure to fully integrate southern Italy, colonial projects in East Africa became known as "imperialism of the poor"

7   The "thalassological" approach was pioneered by Peregrine Horden and Nicholas Purcell, *The Corrupting Sea: A Study of Mediterranean History* (Malden, MA: Blackwell, 2000).
8   See Giuseppe Finaldi, *Italian National Identity in the Scramble for Africa: Italy's African Wars in the Era of Nation-building, 1870–1900* (New York: Peter Lang, 2009); John Dickie, *Darkest Italy: The Nation and Stereotypes of the Mezzogiorno, 1860–1900* (New York: Palgrave MacMillan, 2016).

or "ragamuffin" colonialism.[9] At the time of World War I, Italy's status within European diplomatic circles was so low that it was, in the words of historian Richard Bosworth, "the least of the Great Powers."[10]

As scholars have pointed out, the marginalization of the Italian Empire follows a larger tendency to see Italy itself as less significant than other nations for the history of modern Europe.[11] It does not mean that Italian colonialism is not important for Italy, which is to say nothing of how study of it might also be important for our understanding of Europe and European empire. In the case of Italy, then, the insights of area studies and the recognition of the importance of a nationalism may in fact work together with adopting a transnational, transimperial frame for interpreting its overseas empire. Indeed, adopting a "thalassological" approach—one that transcends area studies and traditionally nationalist paradigms through a transnational and trans-Mediterranean perspective—may well provide a fresh frame for interpreting Italy's modern nation-state as at the nexus of different imperial and cultural economies that emerged in and around the Mediterranean basin during its period as a colonial sea.

This book moves to argue that study of modern Italy from the perspective of the Mediterranean reveals several important and underexplored facets of both the Italian nation-state and the eventual Italian Empire. First, revisiting Italy's colonial involvements in the Mediterranean basin helps to adumbrate the entanglement of emigration and imperialism in regions where Italy's imperial presence was unofficial and where the history of large Italian communities has traditionally been absorbed into the history of larger, more significant empires of Great Britain and France.[12] These lesser-known

---

9   Luigi Goglia and Fabio Grassi, *Il colonialismo italiano da Adua all'impero* (Rome-Bari: Laterza, 1981), 211.

10   Richard Bosworth, *Italy the Least of the Great Powers: Italian Foreign Policy before World War One* (Cambridge: Cambridge University Press, 1979).

11   Ruth Ben-Ghiat and Mia Fuller, eds., *Italian Colonialism* (New York: Palgrave and MacMillan, 2005).

12   Julia Clancy Smith, *Mediterraneans: North Africa and Europe in an Age of Migration, c. 1800–1900* (Berkeley: University of California Press, 2013); Ilham Khuri-Makdisi, *Eastern Mediterranean and the Making of Global Radicalism* (Berkeley: University of California Press, 2010); see also Benjamin Stora, *Algeria, 1830–2000* (Ithaca, NY: Cornell University Press, 2001). Italian emigration and empire in French and British North Africa, as well as Turkey, are just two areas of research that have recently opened up for investigation. Some important new examples of this research are Joseph Viscomi, "Mediterranean Futures: Historical Time and the Departure of Italians from Egypt," *Journal of Modern History* 91, no. 2 (2019): 341–79; Alessandro Pannuti, *La comunita*

settings have been overshadowed by Italian colonialism in East Africa where Italy's presence lasted almost a century in all, with a limited form of Italian sovereignty enduring in Somalia until the 1960s.[13] Related to this, second, is that by examining Italy's involvement in the Mediterranean we achieve a different perspective on how the Fascist state evolved alongside the expansion of Italy's overseas territories. It is widely recognized that the invasion of Ethiopia, which led to international sanctions and a breakdown in diplomatic relations and that arguably helped to precipitate the outbreak of World War II, also marked an important turn in the Fascist dictatorship's internal strategies of rule and geopolitics.[14] It led to the Axis alliance with Hitler and to the adoption of an official politics on race and anti-Semitism.[15] It was also the height of Mussolini's popularity in Italy.[16] But the far-reaching impact of the invasion of Ethiopia has coincided with an enduring perception that Italian colonialism was above all spurred on after the rise of the Fascist state, helping to obscure the numerous ways in which Italy's Liberal state not only invested in overseas projects of empire but the way that Liberal ideas of the nation entwined with the empire. Italian imperial rule in the Aegean shows how Italian ideas about nation and race were shifting and unstable and that the Fascist state also had to accommodate and then appropriate the Liberal-era view that Italy should aim to spread *italianità* or Italianness, not only to the South but also throughout the Mediterranean region.

Before World War I, during his brief career as a socialist, Mussolini rejected the imperialist project of the Italian Liberal state; he had even gone to prison for his opposition to the war for Libya. His eventual adoption of the imperial program was a hallmark of his compromise with the radical nationalists who would keep him in power for the entire period of his dictatorship. Yet what is remembered is not the compromise but Mussolini's unique

italiana di Istanbul nel XX secolo: Ambiente e persone (Istanbul: Edizioni ISIS, 2006); see also, Leila El Houssi, *L'urlo contro il regime: Gli antifascisti italiani in Tunisia tra le due guerre* (Rome: Carocci editore, 2014).

13   See Paolo Tripodi, *The Colonial Legacy in Somalia: Rome and Mogadishu, from Colonial Administration to Operation Restore Hope* (New York: St. Martin's Press, 1999).

14   See Bruce Strang, *Collision of Empires: Italy's Invasion of Ethiopia and its International Impact* (New York: Routledge, 2017).

15   See Fabrizio de Donno, "La Razza Ario-Mediterranea," *Interventions: International Journal of Postcolonial Studies* 8, no. 3 (2006): 394–412.

16   Robert Gerwarth, "The Axis: Germany, Japan and Italy on the Road to War," in *The Cambridge History of the Second World War, Vol 2: Politics and Ideology,* edited by Richard Bosworth and Joseph Maiolo (Cambridge: Cambridge University Press, 2015), 21–42.

penchant for braggadocio—a prime example of which was the slogan *mare nostrum*, the Roman imperial locution for the Mediterranean (meaning, "our sea"), which had become nearly synonymous with Mussolini and his Fascist dictatorship by the mid-1930s. As scholars have persuaded us of the binding link between the Fascist dictatorship and Italian Empire, the recognition that Italian ambitions for colonial rule in the Mediterranean heralded back to the unification of the country has been slower to emerge.[17]

The emphasis on Italian colonial empire as connected mainly to an authoritarian regime also elides how culture, institutions, and political and ideological practices accompanied Italian colonial policies and representations, both before and during the dictatorship, as well as after it, during the postwar period. Studying the importance of empire during the Liberal period, and the continuities between nationalism and Fascism may also stand to reveal the complexity of contemporary postcolonial Italy's relationship to its imperial past. As will be seen, a territory such as the Aegean, which is especially remembered as experiencing a more "liberal" form of Italian Empire, offers interesting examples of such continuities. To give but one salient example, the biological racism that seemingly issued from the invasion of Ethiopia was in fact many years in the making and present in debates Italian nationalists had about to what degree "white" subjects of the eastern Mediterranean should be considered part of the Italian nation, and to what degree they were so "other" as to be held in colonial formations of subjecthood and segregation. Such debates among state nationalists during the interwar period are prescient of the ways in which hierarchies of race linked to the Italian colonial past have impacted the reception of immigrants in more recent years.[18]

Adopting a "thalassological" approach that reunites the history of Italy as a nation-state with its engagement in the Aegean and eastern

---

17 On liberalism in Italy and ambitions for empire, see *The Risorgimento Revisited*, edited by Silvana Patriarca and Lucy Riall (New York: Palgrave Macmillan, 2012). On how the Italian Fascist state's policies in Italy mirrored its policies in the empire, see Philip Morgan, *Italian Fascism, 1915–1945* (New York: Palgrave MacMillan, 2004).

18 On how postcolonial attitudes about race have been directly informed by Italy's colonial past, see Valeria Deplano, "Within and Outside the Nation: Former Colonial Subjects in Post-war Italy," *Modern Italy* 23, no. 4 (2018): 395–410; Cristina Lombardi-Diop and Caterina Romeo, "The Italian Postcolonial: A Manifesto," *Italian Studies* 69, no. 3 (2014): 424–33; Stephanie Malia Hom, *Empire's Mobius Strip: Historical Echoes in Italy's Crisis of Detention* (Ithaca, NY: Cornell University Press, 2019); Guido Bonsaver, Emma Bond, and Federico Faloppa, *Destination Italy: Representing Migration in Contemporary Media and Narrative* (Bern: Peter Lang, 2015).

Mediterranean—an area at that time known as the Orient or Levant—provides a richer perspective on the extent to which empire remained a vital frontier for Italian nationalism. The "thalassological" approach also reveals how Italy navigated the impact of its own migration as it anticipated colonial projects in the region and then secured sovereignty in new areas, such as Libya and the Aegean, by making natives into Italian citizens. The "thalassological" approach also offers a fuller recognition of the diversity of colonial encounters in Italian imperial contexts, both the official ones in East Africa and the Balkans, but also the unofficial ones in Tunisia, Egypt, and Turkey, to reveal a Mediterranean frame for the Italian Empire. The chapters that follow underscore the central place that the Mediterranean had within a wide range of Italy's expansionist and nationalist goals, and also suggest that the notion of *mediterraneità*, or Mediterraneanness, was an idea that emerged in parallel with this agenda of empire in the Mediterranean. And if *La Méditerranée* cannot be uncoupled from the geopolitical empire in the case of the French Mediterranean, this book argues that this is also certainly true in the Italian version of the same. As will be seen, Italian *mediterraneità*, Mediterraneanness, shares many features with its French counterpart, especially in its concern for Latinity and the construction of a cosmopolitan identity that could internationalize the culture of a nation-state that was viewed as highly provincial.[19] But Italy's *mediterraneità* also bore distinct pressures: to traverse considerable national instability at home, navigate a "crisis of origins" that indexed an unstable national identity, and offer a solution to the desire for both homogeneity and diversity that was a core paradox of the Italian nation-state.

In this sense, Italian representations of the Mediterranean also may be seen as constituting a discourse. This Mediterraneanism was not just an imaginative geography about alterity and difference, as in the case of Orientalism, but also an imaginative geography of unity and nationhood. Mediterraneanism was as intent on imagining an overseas empire as it was on containing Italy's own national project and on distancing the clear regionalism that was troubling it. Using the concept more reflexively, to examine Italian discourses of the Mediterranean, or Mediterraneanism, is also to think about how issues such as the Southern problem, or *questione meridionale*, which have normally been seen as defining of the contours of Italy's national history, may also be repositioned and understood within new transnational frames. As

---

19   On the French concept of *Méditerranée*, see Marta Petricioli, *L'Europe méditerranéenne/Mediterranean Europe* (Bruxelles, Belgique: Peter Lang, 2008).

has become clear in recent years, the Southern Question can be productively linked to the immigrant question, and in this sense recalling the existence of Mediterraneanist discourses that also marked the twentieth century may enrich our existing portrait of modern and contemporary Italy.

Transnationalism and Modern Italy

The migration crisis in the Mediterranean has without a doubt been transformative of Italian politics as well as how scholars interpret Italian culture and history: Italy, a country that has traditionally linked itself with tourism, now faces questions about hospitality and human rights with regard to immigrants; a country that was once a sending nation is a receiving nation, and in increasing measure.

My own experience years before writing this book showed me how Italy is deceptively Janus faced: jovial and inclusive of travelers and permanent residents when they come from other Western countries, but a different face of Italy shows itself with regard to non-Western foreigners. In 2001, I moved to Rome. As a very recent and somewhat naïve college graduate, I had equally simple-minded goals: to get out on my own and to learn to speak Italian fluently. Ironically, I had been to Rome before as a child and had detested the city. At the Trevi Fountain I had even lobbed a hundred-lire coin vowing *never* to return. But as the noisy unpleasantness and muggy chaos receded into the background, Rome emerged for me as it has to thousands of travelers throughout history: urbane and provincial, decadent and austere, a novel view of the imperial, medieval, and baroque periods with each new walk through the city.

Eight months later I was fluent in Italian. To my new Italian friends, I fulfilled a stereotype about an American on a "Grand Tour" of Italy, with my right to stay in the country assured by the nationality on my passport. Yet the September 11 attacks soon disrupted this picaresque discovery of Italy. I tried at first to forestall the inevitable new world order, heartened by affirming clichés about Italy's Southernness and its propensity to resist change. As the famous line in *Il gattopardo*, a novel of the Italian unification, goes, "For things to stay as they are everything will have to change." I naively held out hope that somehow Italy and Italians would stay outside the fray of the Euro-American wars in North Africa and the Middle East that ensued. But in Italy, like everywhere else, things did change. Precisely as the War on Terror provoked a new refugee crisis in the Mediterranean, Italy passed Law 189, better known as the Bossi-Fini legislation, after the right-wing politicians who spearheaded it. When, a year after my arrival in Rome, as an *extracommunitario,* I went to renew my *permesso di soggiorno,* or residency permit, I experienced firsthand the effects of this legislation. I was not just fingerprinted but hand-, foot-, and forearm-printed, photographed, and mildly harassed by the local police. As critics have rightly noted, the legislation labeled all illegal immigrants as potential criminal threats and helped to usher in a new era of anti-immigrant sentiment in Italy.[20]

At that time, I lived in the Esquilino, or Piazza Vittorio, a neighborhood that is now synonymous with immigration. Below my apartment were a plethora of call centers where "clandestine" migrants could call home and where every so often the local news announced that a "raid" by the police had taken place. The idea that an unknown cell of Al Qaeda should be discovered in one of those call centers seemed preposterous and my housemates and I wondered aloud how long such theater could endure. But the national fixation on immigration not only continued, in many ways it went on to prove the single most defining issue in Italian politics of recent memory.

The shining example of the power of immigration in contemporary Italian political discourses has been the realignment of the Lega Nord, or Northern League—now simply the Lega—from a party whose primary position was once the radical separation of Northern Italy from the South, into a party defined by its restrictive and politicized approach to migration. The constituency of the Lega today includes many Southerners as well as Southern politicians, and its new presentation as a nationalist and populist party of borders seems, if unstably, to make the Southern Question into a relic of the past. But the ascendance of the Lega and its leader, Matteo Salvini, and the shift of border politics toward being mainstream "national" politics, has also corresponded with the party's alignment with wider global positions of the European Union. Unlike the Lega's more fringe counterpart, the Movimento Cinque Stelle, or Five Star Movement, and in spite of some pretenses toward Euroscepticism, the Lega leads Italy toward greater and greater involvement in securing Italian borders for the European Union. In fact, what has happened is that the Southern Question seems to have disappeared only to be replaced by a Mediterranean one—in ways that may not be so different, after all, from the way that the Southern Question helped to produce an Italian Empire in the Mediterranean a hundred years ago.

20   See, in particular, Alessandro Portelli, "Fingerprints Stained with Ink: Notes on 'Migrant Writing' in Italy," *Interventions* 8, no. 3 (2007): 472–83.

The Global War on Terror and the migration crisis in the Mediterranean have touched off questions about how Italy defines itself in relation to broader frameworks of power and identity in Europe and the globe. Seen from this perspective, one wonders what meaningful status the Mediterranean may have in debates about Italy's border politics. Is the Mediterranean just the epicenter of the crisis? Or is it also a way that Italians feel about migration and react to the demographic changes that have begun to permeate their borders? And in what ways do new migratory flows in the Mediterranean reproduce former well-trodden histories? As postcolonial studies of Italian culture have sought to push back against the surge in anti-immigration sentiment, many have turned to a long tradition in Italian culture of Southern thought, of *meridionalismo*, as a way to formulate an antiracist and "subaltern" position that is defiant of European border-tightening politics. Iain Chambers's *Mediterranean Crossings: The Politics of an Interrupted Modernity* is a good example of such a move. Chambers proposes the recuperation of alternate histories that took place "between shores," arguing that the politics of an "interrupted" modernity in the South can become the basis for imagining the Mediterranean as a postcolonial sea.

But the adoption of the Mediterranean as category for protesting Europe's draconian policies on its Southern frontier seems to me suspect, as it posits a move from the Mediterranean as a "colonial" sea to a "postcolonial" sea without considering the importance of decolonization—that is to say, the still-awaited and full apprehension of how Italy's colonial empire was a formative part of its history, an experience that consolidated its economy, culture, and norms about national identity and belonging. Such visions of the Mediterranean as a postcolonial sea seems almost to imply that the contemporary equivalent of *meridionalismo* should be some form of *mediterraneanismo*, an idea that some artists have in fact taken up.[21] Substituting the South with the Mediterranean risks not only denuding the Mediterranean of

---

21   See, for example, Cristina Lombardi-Diop and Caterina Romeo's discussion of artists and scholars who believe that the Mediterranean—or *meridionalità* and *mediterraneità*—might be a means of protest against Fortress Europe. They cite the words of Luigi Cazzato, who argues that "the 'intrusion' of the global south into Europe may be a chance for southern Europe to be seen as no longer a periphery, but the centre of a new creolizing world, in which the Mediterranean may retrieve its ancient role of a cultural and economic crossroads." Cazzato's language engages strong historical echoes of the language that the Fascist state used to describe the Aegean and the Mediterranean during its expansion there. See Cristina Lombardi-Diop and Caterina Romeo, "Italy's Postcolonial 'Question': Views from the Southern Frontier of Europe," *Postcolonial*

all historical specificity but also exchanging one stereotype, that of the South, for another, that of the Global South, and of making an overly simplistic equivalence between Italian attitudes toward external "others" (migrants) and toward internal "others" (Southerners).

This move also overlooks the way in which the Mediterranean may very well have been a part of nationalist and imperialist discourses in twentieth-century colonial Italy. In fact, the shift in Italy's political preoccupation from internal dilemmas to international ones (a shift expressed in the Lega Nord's rebaptism as the Lega) is perhaps not as much of a rupture as it seems at first glance.[22] In order to affirm national sovereignty in the context of increasing European integration twenty-five years ago, Italian politics revived the age-old idea of the South. As a number of historians pointed out at that time, the South has historically been represented not just as a problem but also as a place invested with symbolic richness: its picturesqueness concealed patriotism and ongoing hopes for national unity.[23] It would seem that similar dynamics are potentially at work today, as the new confrontation with immigration revives Italian claims regarding "Mediterranean" unity and demonstrates that Italy regards its own colonial past as a historical anomaly. The ill-chosen name, Mare Nostrum, for left-leaning Prime Minister Matteo Renzi's project for managing migration in the Mediterranean in accordance

Studies 18, no. 4 (2015): 367–83, 375. Iain Chambers, *Mediterranean Crossings: The Politics of an Interrupted Modernity* (Durham, NC: Duke University Press, 2008).

22   The political transformations of the past two decades reprise older ones within Italian culture and society. The rise of Salvini and the Lega may have replicated the right-leaning turn of nearly twenty-five years previous, in which there emerged an alliance between Berlusconi's Forza Italia, the Lega Nord, and Alleanza Nazionale. As Pasquale Verdicchio noted with reference to the 1994 elections, "The search for national stability by turning emphatically to the right, pointed to issues that indicated a certain parallelism between Italian unification and European unity. The spring 2000 regional elections made the divisions clear. While in 1994 the gains of the Left in the South might have been veiled by the size and specificity of some of the parties, in the 2000 elections they could not have been more evident. The Left that gained the support of the PCI, but rather a Left-party rooted in the local as its point of departure." Pasquale Verdicchio, "Introduction," in Antonio Gramsci, *The Southern Question*, 7–26, trans. Pasquale Verdicchio (Toronto: Guernica, 2005), 19–20.

23   See in particular, Robert Lumley and Jonathan Morris, *A New History of the Italian South: The Mezzogiorno Revisited* (Exeter: Exeter University Press, 1997); Nelson Moe, *The View from Vesuvius: Italian Culture and the Southern Question* (Berkeley: University of California Press, 2002); Jane Schneider, *Italy's "Southern Question": Orientalism in One Country* (Oxford: Berg, 1998).

with human rights law is ample proof that serious consideration of Italy's colonial past seems to be out of reach.[24]

Similar efforts to bring a postcolonial or Mediterranean lens to bear on a new "migrant" literature in Italian culture over the past twenty years have met with obstacles that likewise underscore both a lack of critical vocabulary concerning colonialism and an unwillingness to squarely confront Italy's own colonial past. The terms "global" (*globale*) or "worldly" (*mondiale*) have had a much larger presence than the idea of the transnational within Italian literary criticism.[25] Elided in this emphasis on the global or the worldly are the fundamental tension between the local and the global of both colonial and postcolonial identities, as well as the critical and symbolic possibilities of being in-between, suspended both temporally and geographically. Anglophone criticism has paid more careful attention to how a transnational approach can be productive for understanding modern Italian culture as shaped by a history of overlapping mobilities and inherently transnational identities. Teresa Fiore has suggested, for example, the similarities and correspondences between emigrant writers in North and South America and immigrant writers in Italy, and maps new geographies of belonging that deterritorialize the Italian nation-state. Likewise, Rosetta Giuliani Caponetto has revealed the strain of "hybridity" that characterized Fascist discourses, even if such hybridity was eventually, after the invasion of Ethiopia, constituted as dangerous.[26]

---

24   As Alessandro Carrera rightly questions, "Does 'Mediterranean' signify anything for North African populations? ... Has there ever been a moment in their history when they could have considered it *mare nostrum*? ... Until we seriously propose these questions we should put the concept of Mediterranean in a parenthesis." "*Ma che cosa significa "Mediterraneo" per i popoli del Nord Africa? Non essendo mai stati, dopo i Fenici, in primo luogo potenze navali, hanno mai avvertito l'aura romantica del nome? C'è mai stato un momento nella loro storia in cui avrebbero potuto considerarlo anch'essi un mare nostrum?*" Alessandro Carrera, "Idola mediterranei," in "Il mondo visto da sud e *La prima volta*: Una conversazione con Franco Cassano," edited by Massimo Lollini, special issue, *California Italian Studies* 4, no. 2 (2013): 9–14, 11. On the *mare nostrum* project, see also S.A. Smythe, "The Black Mediterranean and the Politics of Imagination," *Middle East Report*, no. 286 (2018): 3–9.

25   Emma Bond, "Toward a Trans-national Turn in Italian Studies?" *Italian Studies* 69, no. 3 (2014): 415–24. Bond insists on the form "trans-national," arguing that the hyphenated word better connotes this state of suspension or in-betweenness; in this book I use the more conventional "transnational" in an effort to emphasize dialogue with the field of European history.

26   Ruth Ben-Ghiat and Stephanie Malia Hom, *Italian Mobilities* (Abingdon, VA: Routledge, 2016); Teresa Fiore, *Pre-occupied Spaces: Remapping Italy's Transnational*

And Barbara Spackman's recent work *Accidental Orientalists* shows that, despite the clear preoccupation in the nineteenth and twentieth centuries with internal geographies, particularly with North–South dualism, there was nonetheless a tradition in Italian culture of experiencing an "encounter" in an Ottoman land, a tradition that trafficked in East–West dualities akin to Edward Said's original formulation of Orientalism.[27]

Such transnational approaches to Italian culture are still required, however, for the imperial context itself. The vastly important studies of Giorgio Rochat, Richard Pankhurst, Angelo Del Boca, Claudio Segre, and more recently, Nicola Labanca, which in many ways mapped the field of Italian colonial studies, have more or less relied on a metropole-colony framework and have above all emphasized the Italian investment in African colonialism.[28]

Newer studies of Italian colonialism have helped to underscore how there has been, alongside internal North–South geographies, a persistent undercurrent of concern over Italy's peripheral status as not quite European, as "subaltern within" Europe.[29] Mark Choate has innovatively shown that African colonialism was constitutively linked to emigration to North and South America. Recent Italian colonial studies have continued to expand on Choate's insights by reconnecting the political preoccupation with

Migrations and Colonial Legacies (New York: Fordham University Press, 2018); Rosetta Giuliani Caponetto, *Fascist Hybridities: Representations of Racial Mixing and Diaspora Cultures under Mussolini* (New York: Palgrave MacMillan, 2015).

27 Barbara Spackman, *Accidental Orientalists: Modern Italian Travelers in Ottoman Lands* (Liverpool: Liverpool University Press, 2017); Edward Said, *Orientalism* (New York: Vintage Books, 1978); Karla Malette, *European Modernity and the Arab Mediterranean: Toward a New Philology and a Counter-Orientalism* (Philadelphia: University of Pennsylvania Press, 2010); Roberto Dainotto, *Europe (In Theory)* (Durham, NC: Duke University Press, 2007); Natalie Hester, *Literature and Identity in Italian Baroque Writing* (Burlington, VT: Ashgate, 2008); Charles Burdett, *Journeys through Fascism: Italian Travel Writing between the Wars* (New York: Berghahn Books, 2007).

28 Richard Pankhurst, *Education in Ethiopia during the Italian Fascist Occupation* (New York: African Publishers, 1972); Angelo Del Boca, *Gli italiani in Africa orientale* (Rome: Laterza, 1976); Giorgio Rochat, *Il colonialismo italiano* (Turin: Loescher, 1973); Claudio Segre, *Fourth Shore: The Italian Colonization of Libya* (Chicago: University of Chicago Press, 1974); Nicola Labanca, *Oltremare: Storia dell'espansione coloniale italiana* (Bologna: Il mulino, 2002).

29 Dainotto, *Europe (In Theory)*. As Bond writes, "In another aspect of specificity, Italy can also be seen as a marginal case within the supranational context of Europe, thanks to its southern-most, peripheral position, and has even been theorized as representing 'the subaltern within' due to its position on the interior borders of an orientalizing European space." Bond, "Toward a Trans-national Turn in Italian Studies," 421.

the Southern problem to the resettlement programs in East Africa and in Libya.[30] This possibility of multiple Souths—that is, not only the Italian South, but also Italy-as-the-South, and further, Italy as an emigrant nation—complicates the dynamics of power understood as operating in European imperialism. If the presence of these multiple Souths may have helped to foreclose or "preclude" the emergence of a postcolonial consciousness in Italy, it is worth considering how recognition of them might also open up our understanding for Italy's diverse colonial and imperial settings.[31] As the philosopher Roberto Esposito has eloquently stated, "Italy is a country on the frontier, not only in a geographic sense, but also culturally, between different worlds, between Europe and the Mediterranean, between North and South. Italy is traversed but in a certain sense it is constituted by this fracture."[32]

Such fractures of *italianità* were certainly experienced within Italy's colonial and imperial imaginaries. Indeed, as Silvana Patriarca describes, the concept of *italianità*, or Italianness experienced its first major upsurge in 1881 when the French annexed Tunisia, where a large Italian emigrant community resided.[33] A linkage emerged at that time between Italianness, imperial ambitions, and victimhood—a linkage that would become fully apparent in the aftermath of World War I, when the phrase *vittoria mutilata* (mutilated victory) would come to define the attitude of the Italian nationalists toward the "betrayal" of the secret treaties that had enticed Italy to the side of the French and British. It is also clear that, as an important and

---

30   Mark Choate, *Emigrant Nation: The Making of Italy Abroad* (Cambridge, MA: Harvard University Press, 2008). On the Southern Question and Libya, see Stephanie Malia Hom's magisterial new book on how the colonial past in Libya intersects with contemporary migration politics in Italy; Stephanie Malia Hom, *Empire's Mobius Strip* (2019). On the Southern Question and East African resettlement, see Rhiannon Noel-Welch, *Vital Subjects: Race and Biopolitics in Italy* (Liverpool: Liverpool University Press, 2016); on the enduring postwar legacies of Italy's transnational empire, see Pam Ballinger, *The World Refugees Made* (Ithaca, NY: Cornell University Press, 2020).

31   See Pasquale Verdicchio, "The Preclusion of Postcolonial Discourse," in *Revisioning Italy: National Identity and Global Culture*, edited by Beverly Allen and Mary J. Russo, 191–212 (Minneapolis: University of Minnesota Press, 1997).

32   Timothy Campbell and Anna Paparcone, "Interview with Roberto Esposito," *Diacritics* 36, no. 2 (2006): 49–56, 49.

33   Silvana Patriarca, *Italian Vices: Nation and Character from the Risorgimento to the Republic* (New York: Cambridge University Press, 2010). See also Gabriele Montalbano, "The Making of Italians in Tunisia: A Biopolitical Colonial Project, 1881–1911," *California Italian Studies* 9, vol. 1 (2019): 1–21.

revitalizing fantasy about the Roman imperial lineage of the Italian nation, *mediterraneità*, or Mediterraneanness, also circulated in order to mend the fractures of *italianità*. It eventually acquired a racial connotation and permeated new anthropological theories about race that emerged within a growing discourse of social Darwinism. Against the argument that there were two "races" in the Italian Peninsula—an idea pioneered by the criminologist Cesare Lombroso—alternative accounts of race in Italian culture posited an intrinsic *mediterraneità*, or Mediterraneanness for a diverse, yet still homogeneous, and more importantly, imperial peninsula.

As this book discusses, Greece and the Aegean acquired a special significance in the context of these late-nineteenth-century ideas about Italians as belonging to a "Mediterranean race." In order to re-privilege the Roman Empire and the triumph of the Latin world—against the increasing popularity of theories of Aryanism in Europe—it was necessary to recall a prehistoric Aegean and to return to Virgilian narratives about Roman Empire as the phoenix that rose from the ashes of a collapsed Hellenic world. These early ideas of biological *mediterraneità* were important for later constructions of race in the second half of the 1930s; the circulation of Italianness-as-Mediterraneanness helped to distinguish Italians racially from African colonial subjects—it "whitened" the Italian nation—while also securing an idea of the Italian nation-state that included the South.[34] But ideas of racial *mediterraneità* also intersected with uneasy debates about race and difference between Italians and imperial subjects in the Mediterranean.

It is the similarities rather than differences, however, that have been indexed in commonplace understanding of Italian rule in the Aegean, that is, the idea that Italians and locals traded claims that they were like *una faccia, una razza* or "one face, one race." Social and potentially racial proximities

---

34   As Gaia Giuliani and Cristina Lombardi-Diop have argued, the circulation of racial ideas of *mediterraneità* was a first stage in the "whitening" of the entire Italian nation. This process would be completed after more than a decade of Fascist social engineering projects and the invasion of Ethiopia: "*Il significato di italianità-come mediterraneità in modo da distinguerla dall'identità razziale dei colonizzati (mediterranei ma africani) facendo altresì appello ad una romanità (biologico-storico-culturale) che ne sbiancava il carattere. Questa operazione permise, da un lato, l'inclusione discorsiva di tutte le cosiddette differenze razziali interne al popolo italiano in un'unica identità razziale nazionale e, dall'altro, al Meridione di divenire più di una semplice parte costituiva di tale unità, ma la culla stessa del nuovo cittadino modello*"; Giuliani and Lombardi-Diop, *Bianco e nero*, 24.

among Italians and locals in the Aegean were doubtless strengthened by numerous social similarities and in shared conditions of diaspora and marginalization within discourses of Europeanness. Like their Italian rulers, locals of the Aegean archipelago had spread as migrants throughout the world, and like their Italian rulers, Greeks were privy to a cultural memory of a much more illustrious history in comparison with the condition of their modern nation-state. Eleftheros Venizelos, who helmed the nationalist movement in Greece in the same time frame, premised his leadership on a restoration of the Byzantine Empire's borders in the Aegean. As Konstantina Zanou has recently shown, Italian and Greek nationalism in the early nineteenth century was intrinsically interconnected and the similarities of these early national movements reinforced one another through parallel conditions of diaspora in the Mediterranean.[35]

An important further reading of the expression *una faccia, una razza*, then, is that it speaks to a "multicultural" unity among Greeks, Turks, Jews, and Italians, under the aegis of Fascist imperial nationalism, one with the ability to mitigate the intercommunal tensions that also certainly existed. What this expression veils, of course, are the anti-Semitic and anti-Levantine policies that defined Italian rule in the islands after the invasion of Ethiopia. On an even broader level, the idea that Italy has an intrinsically Mediterranean culture—if not character—with its natural affinities with other countries on Europe's periphery, whether these affinities are linguistic (Spain) or cultural (Greece)—seems to have helped to obscure an awareness of some of the dangerous forms of colonial empire. These forms of empire certainly compete with British and French projects for dominance in the Mediterranean, both in brutality and ambition. But Italian Empire in the Aegean also recalls other "imperial" settings where widespread migration for economic opportunities had already created instability concerning the concept of national identity. As in the United States, where the legend that the country is a "melting pot" and a "nation of immigrants" has helped to disguise more troubled histories of integration and assimilation—reifying categories of race while holding the slave and colonial past in abeyance—the

---

35   See Konstantina Zanou, *Transnational Patriotism in the Mediterranean, 1800–1850* (Oxford: Oxford University Press, 2018). See also, Paschalis Kitrolimides, *Eleftheros Venizelos: The Trials of Statesmanship* (Cambridge: Cambridge University Press, 2013); Richard Clogg, *A Concise History of Greece* (Cambridge: Cambridge University Press, 2013); Mark Mazower, "The Messiah and the Bourgeoisie: Venizelos and Politics in Greece, 1909–1912," *The Historical Journal* 35, no. 4 (1992): 885–904.

myth of Italy's Mediterranean culture seems to have helped to sustain an ongoing lack of critical seriousness about Italy's colonial past. Investigating the various forms of Mediterraneanism that existed within Italian rule over the Aegean, then, stands to reveal a wider cultural history that is relevant for how not only how Italy positions itself with regard to the rest of Europe but how Greece does as well.

Rethinking Italy's Aegean Islands

In 1911, as Italy celebrated its fiftieth anniversary as a nation-state, it launched an attack on the provinces of Cyrenaica and Tripolitania where the Ottoman state had weakened. The attack on North Africa, which was undertaken by the Liberal government under the pressure of the radical nationalists of the Italian Nationalist Association, eventually led to the annexation of the Aegean islands. The Triple Alliance, with which Italy was still allied, at that time regarded Rhodes and its neighboring islands as so far to the east as to be beyond the Ottoman Balkans. The islands were viewed, technically speaking, as part of Asia.

But if the islands' status as part of Asia rather than Europe is what had freed the islands up for occupation, it was the historical traces of Italy's own illustrious history in the Mediterranean that provided the rhetorical motivation for continuing sovereignty after a tentative peace had been reached with the Ottoman Empire. Italian nationalist writings almost anticipate Braudel, emphasizing the merchant imperial expansion of Venice and Genoa in the medieval and Renaissance periods, and on the Christian Crusaders, who attempted to infiltrate even Constantinople with economic expansion, establishing the Italian colony of Galata at the center of the city. As Braudel acknowledged, the empires of Venice and Genoa were so powerful at one time, with colonies from Corfu to Tinos and Astypalea, that the Aegean Sea and its islands have for most of its history simply been known by their Italian name, that is, as *l'arcipelago,* or the Archipelago.[36]

36   Fernand Braudel, *The Mediterranean and the Mediterranean World in the Age of Philip II,* translated by Sian Reynolds (New York: Harper & Row, 1976), 109, 115. For an intriguing commentary on the idea of the *arcipelago* as a metaphor for the nation-state, see Massimo Cacciari, *Arcipelago* (Milan: Adelphi, 1997) as well as John Foot's recent magnus opus of postwar Italy, *The Archipelago: Italy since 1945* (London: Bloomsbury, 2019).

Colonies in the Mediterranean were an issue around which both left-wing and right-wing nationalist views coalesced, in no small part, because the belief that Italy should acquire some form of empire reached back at least to the 1850s. As Donna Gabaccia has suggested, the imagery of the Risorgimento, the revolutionary movement that spurred the unification of the peninsula, is itself a watery metaphor, "a bubbling forth of the creative powers of the deep spring of the Italian nation."[37] Leading nationalists of the nineteenth century, including Giuseppe Mazzini, the democratic nationalist who believed that the entire peninsula should be unified and liberated from foreign rule—against the grain of his more conservative and elitist counterparts—had no problem with imperialism when it was with an overseas space in mind. Mazzini and other Italian nationalists believed that a colony in Tunisia, with its large community of Italians, would be a logical outcome of the Italian unification.[38] But following the unification, thanks to a preemptive annexation of Tunisia by the French Empire, Italy achieved no such formal colony in Tunisia. During the second half of the nineteenth century, Italian migration throughout the Mediterranean basin nevertheless increased. In ways that mirror the informal process of migration across the Mediterranean into North Africa that prepared the way for French imperial rule in the Maghreb, Italians by the tens of thousands migrated to North Africa, especially following the collapse of the economy of Southern Italy, which occurred following the 1861 national unification and under the pressures of integration with the industrial North. It was the French annexation of Tunisia in 1881 that had galvanized the Italian move into Eritrea in 1883.

The "loss" of Tunisia to the French would eventually align in nationalists' minds with the "loss" of hundreds of thousands of Italians to the transatlantic migrations to North and South America. As Gaia Giuliani and Cristina Lombardi-Diop have noted, emigration disrupted the anthropological project to "make" Italy and to establish a monolithic cultural and linguistic identity for the Italian nation.[39] The regionalism that Italy suppressed at home proved useful abroad and many of the associations

<hr />

37 Donna Gabaccia, *Italy's Many Diasporas* (New York: Routledge, 2013), 35.

38 Maurizio Isabella, "Liberalism and Empires in the Mediterranean: The Viewpoint of the Risorgimento," in *The Risorgimento Revisited*, edited by Silvana Patriarca and Lucy Riall, 232–54 (New York: Palgrave Macmillan, 2012).

39 See Gaia Giuliani and Cristina Lombardi-Diop, *Bianco e Nero: Storia dell'identità razziale degli italiani* (Florence: Le Monnier, 2013).

active in supporting Italian emigrants and national identity were tied to specific regions and provinces of Italy. The result was a more flexible form of Italian identity, one often linked to the idea of the rural, the regional, the environmental, one that aligned with a growing belief about the essential *mediterraneità* of the Italian nation that was linked to imperial settings among Italian emigrants in North Africa and the eastern Mediterranean. Although this more flexible Italianness did not get applied to Southerners at home—where they remained a continuing site of alterity for Italians— the larger idea of *mediterraneità* was transformative for representation of the South, and to some degree, Southernness.

While studies have frequently noted how following the Italian unification, with a view to development and modernization, national energies centered on growing the economy of the industrial North, it is also true that emigration, while noted as a corollary to the *questione meridionale*, or Southern problem, was considered to be an equally important source of economic wealth through remittances.[40] Moreover, while scholars have long debated the nature and the contours of the Southern Question—and whether, for example, it was, as Antonio Gramsci eventually argued, itself a form of internal colonialism—they have paid less explicit attention to how Southernness in the North African setting was also a site of rich cultural encounter and cosmopolitanism.[41] It is clear that if the 1861 unification of Italy was followed by the political isolation of the South, widespread civil unrest, if not civil war, resistance to state centralization, and doubts, which have proved enduring, about the viability of a unified Italian national project, the memory of Roman Empire in the Mediterranean has frequently served as a talisman against the disintegration of the national project. As Pasquale Verdicchio has remarked, the Italian Peninsula has been unified only once before in its history, during Roman colonization of the Mediterranean.[42]

40   See in particular Mark Choate's discussion of how the views of emigration espoused by nationalists included thoughts on not only the important place of remittances but also national and cultural identity. Mark Choate, *Emigrant Nation: The Making of Italy Abroad* (Cambridge, MA: Harvard University Press, 2008).

41   Mark Choate, "Tunisia, Contested: Italian Nationalism, French Imperial Rule, and Migration in the Mediterranean Basin," *California Italian Studies* 1, no. 1 (2010): 1–20; Antonio Gramsci, *La questione meridionale* (Rome: Editori Riuniti, 2005).

42   See Pasquale Verdicchio, "The Preclusion of Postcolonial Discourse," in *Revisioning Italy: National Identity and Global Culture*, edited by Beverly Allen and Mary J. Russo, 191–212 (Minneapolis: University of Minnesota Press, 1997), 195.

The decision to go to war against the Ottoman Empire occurred alongside a broader campaign led by the political right, the Italian radical nationalists, for expansion into Trento and Trieste—the latter a powerful port on the Mediterranean Sea with access into central Europe.[43] By cutting across tensions between center and periphery, between regionalism and unity, the Mediterranean presented itself as a mirage of both national and colonial possibility, a fantasy that sustained the project of the nation throughout the crisis of the unification that endured until World War I and that would eventually result in Mussolini's projects for the creation of Eurafrica in the 1930s.[44] Although many Italian nationalists in 1911 were maintaining that Italy should continue to "turn toward the Alps," to paraphrase the oft-noted words of Alfredo Oriani (*"alzandosi sulle Alpi, guardava l'Europa"*)—and align itself as it had in the past with other developed nations in Europe—a pivot to the south, and toward the Mediterranean Sea, also occurred during the Liberal period, as a path toward affirming prosperity and a unified Italy.[45] It therefore comes as no surprise that following the annexation of Cirenaica and Tripoli, the Italian state saw Libya, renamed after the Roman name for Africa, as the key to a long-term strategy of Mediterranean Empire.[46] The ongoing occupation of the Aegean would similarly allow the Italian state to tie together nationhood with migration and empire and after World War I and the collapse of the Ottoman Empire, Italy acquired an official mandate there on the grounds that Italy, too, as one should have a "sphere of influence"—so as to better protect its emigrant communities in the region in the "Orient," or eastern Mediterranean region.

---

43 Alexander De Grand, *The Italian Nationalist Association and the Rise of Fascism in Italy* (Lincoln, NE: University of Nebraska Press, 1978); Christopher Seton-Watson, *Italy from Liberalism to Fascism, 1870–1925* (London: Meuthen, 1967), 376–77.

44 Ruth Ben-Ghiat, "Modernity Is Just Over There: Colonialism and Italian National Identity," *Interventions* 8, no. 3 (2006): 380–93.

45 Alfredo Oriani, *Fino a Dogali* (Bologna: Gargagni, 1912), 405.

46 Barbara Spadaro, *Una colonia italiana: Incontri, memorie, e rappresentazioni tra Italia e Libia* (Milan: Mondadori, 2013); Ingrid Terre, "Managing Colonial Recollections: Italian–Libyan Contentions," *Interventions: International Journal of Postcolonial Studies* 17, no. 3 (2015): 452–67; Ali Abdullatif Ahmida, *Forgotten Voices: Power and Agency in Postcolonial Libya* (Hoboken, NJ: Taylor & Francis, 2013); Nicola Labanca, *La guerra italiana per la Libia, 1911–31* (Bologna: Il mulino, 2012); Maurice Roumeni, *The Jews of Libya: Coexistence, Persecution, Rehabilitation* (Brighton: Sussex Academic University Press, 2008); and Pam Ballinger, "Colonial Twilight: Italian Settlers and the Long Decolonization of Libya," *Journal of Contemporary History* 15, no. 4 (2016): 813–38.

The Aegean does not squarely fit into the resettlement paradigm that has dominated Italian colonial studies; Italians were resettled there during only a brief period, between 1935 and 1940, and Italian nationalists never envisaged the islands as a destination for large-scale resettlement as they did for African colonies. Administered by the Ministry of Foreign Affairs rather than the Ministry of the Colonies, moreover, the Aegean also seems to elide conventional definitions of "colonialism" and "imperialism."[47] Yet examining the Italian presence in the Aegean stands to better reveal the complex interactions between Italy's campaigns in Africa and those closer to home, in the northeastern borderlands, in the Balkans, and in the southern half of the peninsula, as well as the shifting and unstable definitions of race that accrued within Italy at home as the state expanded so as to shore up the project of the nation.

As Roberta Pergher has shown in her recent book, *Mussolini's Nation-Empire*, if Italian imperialism is brought productively into dialogue with its wider historical and European context, programs of resettlement can be understood—not as a solution to demographic problems in Italy (e.g., overpopulation in the South, mass unemployment)—but as a means to claim sovereignty in uncertain imperial times.[48] As Pergher and others have emphasized, World War I is far from marking the end of the age of empire, as theorized by Hobsbawm; in fact, the resulting collapse of the Ottoman and Austro-Hapsburg empires unleashed a new scramble for imperial expansion, especially in the Balkans and the Middle East, where European nation-states had already been extending themselves through informal economic expansion for more than a century.[49] It is against this backdrop that Italian

---

47   Italian rule clearly has much more in common with Italy's colonial projects in Africa than it does, for example, with the Italian concession in Tientsin, although the time period is analogous with Italian rule in the Aegean. See Sabina Donati, "Italy's Informal Imperialism in Tienjin during the Liberal Epoch, 1902–22," *The Historical Journal* 52, no. 2 (2016), 447–68; and Alessandro Di Meo, *Tientsin: la concessione italiana, Storia delle relazione tra Regno d'Italia e Cina, 1886–1947* (Rome: Ginevra Bentivoglio Editoria, 2015).

48   On Italian colonialism as a response to Italian demography, see Carl Ipsen, *Dictating Demography: The Problem of Population in Fascist Italy* (Cambridge: Cambridge University Press, 1996) and Roberta Pergher, *Mussolini's Nation-Empire: Sovereignty and Settlement in Italy's Borderlands, 1922–1943* (Cambridge: Cambridge University Press, 2019).

49   Pergher's phrase "nation-empire," like Bond's preference for "trans-national," uses a hyphen to indicate the ways in which nation and empire in Italy were both geograph-ically and temporally linked. Roberta Pergher, *Mussolini's Nation-Empire* (2019). On

colonialism in Libya and Italian nation-building in the Triestine borderlands, or the Alto Adige region—and additionally, Italian Empire in the Aegean—can be situated.

As Pergher shows, the program that Mussolini was forced to adopt when he allied himself with the imperialists (who were also in Italy's case, revealingly, the nationalists) entrenched the dictator in a paradox: although Mussolini rose to power on the promise of national homogeneity—that is, the achievement and then celebration of *italianità*—his twenty years of rule were to be strongly defined by Italy's growing diversity in its borderlands and in its empire. Over the course of his rule the number of non-Italians who were subject to the state would exponentially increase, as would accordingly a fixation on ethnic purity. This paradox resulted in a complex set of strategies of governance in Italy's nation-state, which, when seen together with colonialism reveal both an alliance between imperialism and Italianness, and the similarities between strategies of nation-building at home and strategies for sovereignty in the *oltremare* or overseas empire.

The Aegean can be set into this post-World War I context, but the territory nevertheless presents its own set of questions, which, although similar to the ones that defined colonial strategies in both the Balkans and Libya, relate to the unstable ways in which Greece and the Levant were already operating within Italian travel imaginaries and within Italian discussions of national identity from the Risorgimento onwards—as well as to the ways in which Italy's Southernness (not just its Southern Question) shaped its beliefs about what imperialism would eventually do for Italians, both economically and culturally. As will be seen, Southernness could operate productively in the context of a Greek or Levantine expansion, allowing Italian actors to simultaneously imagine "Mediterranean" familiarity while retaining their European cultural superiority. Indeed, Greece not only provided Italian colonial actors with an additional sense of otherness that could compete with and deflect the otherness of the South, but also reproduced and stabilized the threat of

the legacies of imperial collapse in the Balkans, see Tara Zahra, *Great Departure: Mass Migration from Eastern Europe and the Making of the Free World* (New York: W. W. Norton, 2017), and Isa Blumi, *Ottoman Refugees, 1878–1939: Migration in a Post-Imperial World* (London: Bloomsbury, 2015). On Italian Empire in a transnational vein see Silvana Patriarca and Lucy Riall, *The Risorgimento Revisited: Nationalism and Culture in the Nineteenth Century* (Basingstoke: Palgrave and MacMillan, 2011), as well as Maurizio Isabella and Konstantina Zanou, *Mediterranean Diasporas: Politics and Ideas in the Long Nineteenth Century* (London: Bloomsbury, 2016).

internal fragmentation, activating fantasies about restoring the Greco-Roman alliance of antiquity.

In this regard, Italian views of the Aegean sharply differ from what Maria Todorova has called "Balkanism," which emerged in Europe with the decline of the Austro-Hapsburg and Ottoman empires in the nineteenth century, to create a buffer between Eastern and Western Europe.[50] The Italian adoption of Mediterraneanism in the Aegean, on the other hand, suggests a prolific expansion of the nation-state, one that inevitably led to the assimilation projects that characterized the administration of the islands under Cesare Maria De Vecchi. But such Mediterraneanism was also to impact ideas about race: the expansion of the nation into the "familiar" Orient would also mean demarcating symbolic borders through ethnicity, and, eventually, would lead to the exclusion of "Oriental" Jews.

The recent discovery and cataloguing of a special secret police archive, previously closed until 2014, has revealed the extent to which the Aegean was a periphery that nevertheless motivated the presence of a strong central government. Italy's surveillance over the local population has enabled a new chapter in the history of the Holocaust while offering researchers documentation on the Italian collaboration with the German deportations of the islands' Jewish community in 1944, after the armistice.[51] These revelations have disrupted the longstanding perceptions that Italian rule in the Aegean was in some way soft or "light," as in the ubiquitous myth of Italians as *brava gente* or "good people."[52] The existence of this archive also testifies to the extent of Italy's surveillance over the local population, with a little over 140,000 files for the islands' 120,000 inhabitants at the time.

Given the absence of the Dodecanese from the wider historiography of Italian and European Empire, studies have tended to promote a view of Italian rule as a sui generis nature. These have profited from these archival resources available in Rhodes, both the recently catalogued surveillance archive and the administrative archive of the Italian government as well as the materials available in the Italian Ministry of Foreign Affairs in Rome.

---

50   Maria Todorova, *Imagining the Balkans* (New York: Oxford University Press, 1997), 3–20.

51   See Marco Clementi and Ireni Toliou, *Gli ultimi ebrei di Rodi: Leggi raziali e deportazioni nel Dodecaneso italiano, 1938–1948* (Roma: DeriveApprodi, 2015).

52   David Bidussa, *Il mito del bravo italiano* (Milan: Il Saggiatore, 1994); Angelo Del Boca, *Italiani, brava gente: Un mito duro a morire* (Vicenza: Neri Pozza, 2005); Nicola Labanca, "Colonial Rule, Colonial Repression and War Crimes in the Italian Colonies," *Journal of Modern Italian Studies* 9, no. 3 (2004): 300–13.

Luca Pignataro's three-volume study of Italian rule in the Dodecanese is a good example of how much of that archival material there is to mine, while Nicholas Doumanis's study of the collective memory of Italian rule demonstrates how an approach "from below" can challenge the ways we think about how Italy presented itself in relationship to a local population. More recently, transnational approaches have invigorated investigation revealing that the Dodecanese can be brought into comparison with the British rule of Cyprus, while also showing Italy's genius with respect to courting consent through inclusion with the local population.[53] To a certain extent, this book treats Italian rule in the Dodecanese as a case study that has to be examined separately from other Italian colonial contexts. But it also commits to showing that Italian rule in the Aegean, as well as perceptions of the Italian state among the local population, were always tied to wider imperial questions, and were strongly impacted by both Italy's transnational experiences of migration and the colonial project in Africa.

53   Luca Pignataro, *Il Dodecaneso italiano, 1912–1947* (Chieti: Solfanelli, 2011) and Nicholas Doumanis, *Myth and Memory in the Mediterranean: Remembering Fascism's Empire* (New York: St. Martin's Press, 1997). These two works have stressed the favorable point of view the locals took of the Italian state (Doumanis) and vice versa (Pignataro). On how debates in the field have polarized around the question of whether Italy's occupation of the Dodecanese was colonial, see Alexis Rappas, "The Domestic Foundations of Imperial Sovereignty: Mixed Marriages in the Fascist Aegean," in *New Perspectives on the History of Gender and Empire: Comparative and Global Approaches*, edited by Ulrike Lindner and Dörte Lerp, 31–58 (London: Bloomsbury Academic Press, 2018). Interestingly, in documenting the influence of the Italian administration of the Dodecanese on British imperial Cyprus, Rappas attends less to how the former was influenced by the British; this is perhaps a testament to the novel and innovative nature of Italian governance and is a further call for rethinking Italy as offering a "minor" contribution to the history of European Empire. Alexis Rappas, "The Transnational Formation of Imperial Rule on the Margins of Europe: British Cyprus and the Italian Dodecanese in the Interwar Period," *European History Quarterly* 45, no. 3 (2015): 467–505. And while one would expect the discussion of Italian rule in the Aegean to be more abundant in the Greek language historiography, it is not, and is a subject that is mostly dealt with by local historians, of which the best is Zacharias N. Tsirpanlēs, *Italokratia sta Dōdekanēsa, 1912–1943: Allotriōsē tou anthrōpou kai tou perivallonto* ("The Italian Occupation of the Dodecanese, 1912–43"), prologos Ēlia E. Kollia (Rodos: Ekdosē Grapheiou Mesaiōnikēs Polēs Rodou, 1998).

Methodology and Chapter Overview

The imperial formation of Mediterraneanism was not only about crafting an appropriate form of governance within the Aegean, but also functioned as a means to simultaneously hold both similarity and difference. Mediterraneanism was consolidated through the idea of imperial nostalgia, a longing to return home (to the Roman, Crusader, or Venetian empire) that ultimately ensured that the Italian "home" was always located unstably in an elsewhere better able than the peninsula to accommodate the shifting needs and realities of imperial rule.

The chapters that follow move horizontally, that is, chronologically, starting in the era of Crispi's campaigns for the colonization of East Africa and moving through the period of World War II and to postwar legacies of the Italian Empire in the Aegean. But they also engage in vertical movement while aiming to reveal the diverse nature of the colonial encounter in the Aegean. Italy's program of rule in the islands involved not just a military, but culture, institutions, and economies, as well as creative strategies of administration. All of these aspects are visible in the Italian state's pivot from a form of "temporary" sovereignty, from 1912 to 1923, to a full-blown expansion of the Italian nation after 1935. This transformation was not as abrupt as it has sometimes been remembered, but was a gradual process and a negotiation of sovereignty that required both representation and rule.

This interdisciplinary approach is in recognition of the insights of subaltern studies, which have emphasized how colonial histories reside not only in administrative archives, but also in a wide variety of sites and materials. Seen thus, the colonial past reveals itself as a complex and tangled enterprise of institutions and identities that extends well beyond the bureaucratic—colonial fantasies exist in photography, literature, and film.[54] My analysis within this expanded sense of the colonial archive is moreover not just "extractive": what follows is not an assemblage of sources that prove the extent to which Italy invested in remaking the Aegean. Building upon Ann Stoler's insight that colonial documents are "epistemological experiments

---

54   Ania Loomba points out that the virtually limitless terrain of colonial and postcolonial studies calls for precisely that recognition of multiple levels of culture and institutions implicated by its ideologies: "The point is not that we need to know the entire historical and geographic diversity of colonialism in order to theorise, but rather, that we must build our theories with an awareness that such diversity exists." Ania Loomba, *Colonialism/ Postcolonialism: The New Critical Idiom*, 2nd ed. (New York: Routledge, 1998), xvi.

rather than sources," this book's examination of various literary productions, tourism artefacts, architecture and urban planning, case-by-case discussions of the legal status of the occupied subjects, and finally, oral histories pays as much attention to form and tactics as it does to content.[55] I attend further to the ways that objects, political documents, and the built environment may have circulated within frameworks of ethnographic and colonial examination, so as to better illuminate the complex ways that Italian colonization constituted itself not just through a hegemonic discourse but also through local interactions. This latter attention to the local environment and to local interactions, I suggest, offers important insights into the legacies of empire and the continuing influence of this imperial past on Italian national identities as well as on local Greek or "insular" identities in the Aegean.[56]

This interdisciplinary approach also aims to account for the ways in which the Aegean acted on Italian culture, first symbolically and politically, then geopolitically. By the late nineteenth century, the Aegean had emerged as a third term that could mediate ideas of race and nation that the Italian campaigns for colonialism in Africa engendered. The Aegean encompassed a fantasy about Greece and the Levant, and was a site of erotic otherness, a wellspring of possible imperial strength, and an archipelagic landscape that encapsulated, almost as a synecdoche, the Mediterranean Sea as a whole. After 1912, the Aegean also consolidated the potential for Italy's further expansion in the Balkans and eastern Mediterranean.

The peculiarities of the treaties that resolved the collapse of the Ottoman Empire at the end of World War I helped to ensure that the Aegean would continue throughout the interwar period to be a site of "unadulterated cultural significance," to use Edward Said's famous turn of phrase. In the Aegean, while establishing Turkey as the legacy of the once-sprawling Ottoman state, the British Empire orchestrated a population exchange of approximately 1.5 million Orthodox and Muslim former Ottoman subjects—the "unmixing of the peoples" as Lord George Curzon, the British Secretary of

---

55 Ann Laura Stoler, "Colonial Archives and the Arts of Governance," *Archival Science* 2 (2002): 87–109. On oral histories together with archival documents, see Alessandro Portelli, *The Battle of Valle Giulia: Oral History and the Art of Dialogue* (Madison, WI: University of Wisconsin Press, 1997).

56 Jacqueline Andall and Derek Duncan, *National Belongings: Hybridity in Italian Colonial and Postcolonial Cultures* (New York: Peter Lang, 2010). As Andall and Duncan rightly describe, postcolonial interpretive frameworks that account for encounters between settlers and locals provide tools for thinking about legacies and influences of the colonial period.

State, famously referred to it. This Aegean population exchange was the first of its kind, but it was to set a precedent for later population exchanges adopted by the British Empire during decolonization.[57] Because Italy had already occupied the islands since 1912, the Dodecanese were, however, exempt from the population exchange. The islands of Rhodes and Kos, with their large minority populations of Muslims and Jews, thus became an anachronistic specimen of the old multiethnic world of Ottoman cosmopolitanism after the empire's collapse. As Roberta Pergher has remarked, one important feature of Italian Empire was that it was attempting to be "imperial" in a world that, post-Versailles, promoted colonial rule as a form of trusteeship presenting eventual emancipation.[58] This book's examination of continuing representations of the Aegean as a site of Levantine otherness during the interwar period provides an important map for understanding Italian decisions about its rule, as well as the ambiguous legacies of Italian imperialism, both within Italy and locally.

It almost goes without saying that the book's methodology owes much to *Orientalism*. As Edward Said powerfully showed, empire was not just an economic project but also a cultural one that remade institutions and identities, and that guaranteed the legitimacy of political hegemony through representation of the colonial subject. Said's appropriation of Gramsci's concept of hegemony to show the legitimizing effects of culture for empire has moreover proved an enduring concept in subaltern studies. But most importantly, when confronting the myriad cultural productions that accumulated around Rhodes and the Aegean as a site of a bygone "Oriental" world, it would be impossible not to turn to Said's original formulation of Orientalism, especially the concept of the Levant, that is, the "familiar" Orient. But lest I exchange one stereotype for another, that is to say, replace the Gramscian "South" with the Saidian "East," the book also takes into consideration the critique, launched by Dennis Porter and Homi Bhaba, that Said's theory, while revealing undeniably true dualisms—between Occident

---

57   See Dirk A. Moses, "Cutting out the Ulcer and Washing away the Incubus of the Past: Genocide Prevention Through Population Transfer," in *Decolonization, Self-Determination, and the Rise of Global Human Rights Politics*, edited by A. Dirk Moses, Marco Duranti, and Roland Burke, 153–78 (Cambridge: Cambridge University Press, 2020); Renée Hirschon, ed., *Crossing the Aegean: An Appraisal of the 1923 Compulsory Population Exchange between Greece and Turkey* (New York: Berghahn Books, 2003). See also Bruce Clark, *Twice a Stranger: The Mass Expulsions that Forged Modern Greece and Turkey* (Cambridge, MA: Harvard University Press, 2009).

58   Pergher, *Mussolini's Nation-Empire*, 2.

and Orient, self and other, modern and backward, and so on—is itself dualistic.[59]

The chapters that follow therefore give room to the possibility of ambivalence and to the instability intrinsic to imagining the local population in the Aegean as "familiar others." The ample evidence of this instability reinforces the ongoing historical critique that imperial contexts were ultimately highly unstable, contested by both the periphery and the center, challenged by the occupied populations as well as by the very project of empire, which was costly, mutable, and draining of the metropole's resources, definitions, and energies.[60]

Chapter 1 seeks to uncover how the view of the Aegean as an important Mediterranean periphery of the Italian nation-state, one that brought home the memory of Roman Empire, had its roots in the postunification and Liberal eras. But this sense of the Aegean as an ancestral homeland was accompanied by the dangerous shadow of Levantine alterity, and the chapter also traces how the hardline policies of race enacted after 1936 drew upon older cultural precedents among Italian nationalists. The five nationalists whose writing the chapter describes—Gabriele D'Annunzio, Giuseppe Sergi, Edmondo De Amicis, Enrico Corradini, and Luigi Federzoni—have all, in much debated ways, been linked to the right-leaning swerve in nationalism in early twentieth-century Italy, which created the cultural backdrop for and heralded the rise of fascism in Italy. The chapter focuses on how their concern with the nation was channeled into an obsession with the exotic. In their writings, the frontiers of an imagined "Greece" and "Levant" emerge as spaces that enrich the cultural possibilities associated with the Italian Empire and the colonial resettlement of Africa. While travel literature has been much studied to provide evidence of Orientalism, this chapter shows how the stance of "going native," even of having an erotic experience of the "Orient," which in some ways went against the grain of a program of imperial superiority, was also able to reinforce the unique mission of spreading Italian state's Mediterranean

---

59 Dennis Porter, *"Orientalism* and Its Problems," in *Colonial Discourse and Post-colonial Theory: A Reader,* edited by Patrick Williams and Laura Chrisman, 150–62 (New York: Columbia University Press, 1994). See also, Homi Bhaba, *The Location of Culture* (London: Routledge, 2004).

60 Frederick Cooper and Ann Laura Stoler, *Tensions of Empire: Colonial Cultures in a Bourgeois World* (Berkeley: University of California Press, 1997). On this issue in the Aegean more specifically, see also Marc Aymes, *A Provincial History of the Ottoman Empire* (London: Routledge, 2013); Antonis Hadjikyriacou, *Islands of the Ottoman Empire* (Princeton, NJ: Markus Wiener Publishers, 2019).

culture abroad. In fact, the long history of Italian travel in and exploration of the Mediterranean as well as more recent Italian emigration there became the premise for a new project of colonial modernity, one that set itself in direct juxtaposition to French, British, or even Greek ideas about nationalist empire in the Mediterranean.

As chapter 2 demonstrates, the invention of organized leisure tourism to Rhodes went hand in hand with a celebration of *mediterraneità*. It further encouraged the refashioning of the South as *mediterraneità*, a touchstone of the forgotten cosmopolitan, expansive history of Italy. State-sponsored Mediterranean tourism was carried out by key organizations of the regime, such as the Opera Nazionale Dopolavoro, the Fascist trade union. These institutions did not eschew the image of Italians as subaltern migrants but rather exploited it to suggest that Italians could easily adapt to "Levantine" environments. Tourists testified that Rhodes was the perfect specimen of the Orient—the best of both worlds—with its colorful local population framed by the modernizing constructions of the Italian state. The "armchair travelers" who visited the Aegean vicariously through guidebooks, photography, documentary film, and travel writing partook of the idea that Fascist imperialism was benevolent and, precisely because Italy was also a Mediterranean country, able to support the regeneration of ex-Ottoman regions. Though the project for heritage and cultural tourism in the island was extensively revised after the invasion of Ethiopia, when the association between Italians and the picturesque, exotic, and Levantine was purged, the Mediterranean remained a unifying aesthetic theme of the new touristic cultural landscape.

Chapter 3 explores how Italian state actors envisioned their permanent sovereignty in the islands as a form of expansion of the Italian nation that would be inclusive of their "cousins" in the Aegean. The islands' Jewish and Turkish minorities were initially embraced within the Italian nation's enlargement of cultural and linguistic—if not ethnic—definitions of belonging in the Aegean. Only later, after the Italian invasion of Ethiopia, were these communities the targets of colonial policies of race and subjected to the rule of colonial difference. A strong sentiment of ethnic affinity with the local Greek population—thanks to theories of *mediterraneità*—was enhanced by the Italian state's existing imperial practices, which saw emigration as a potential virtue for the empire. Like their Italian colonizers, the local community in the islands had spread throughout the world as economic migrants, from Chicago to Kinshasa to Italian colonies in East Africa, as well as to places where Italy hoped to further develop the presence of its empire, such as Egypt. However, the proximity of the islands to both Africa and the Orient had been present in the project for empire in the Dodecanese from the outset and was connected to the complex ways in which Italian culture and theories of race had dealt with the issue of the Semitic (in the sense of both Jews and Arabs). The chapter emphasizes the shifting nature of Italy's administration, in contrast with Davide Rodogno's theory that the Aegean operated as the "small space" or an intermediary zone between the Balkans and Africa, and attends to how the shift from Liberalism to Fascism saw a split in the Italian state's views of the population, with the Greek ethnic majority brought into assimilation programs while the Jewish and Turkish minorities became subject to reprisal, repression, and expulsion.[61]

Finally, chapter 4 takes up the issue of practical Mediterraneanism and analyzes how local nationalism and everyday life adapted to Italian Empire.[62] In local memory, the period of De Vecchi's rule in the islands is registered as "Fascism" in its most repugnant and authoritarian form. What goes unacknowledged in that memory is that De Vecchi's ambitious administration, however unrealized its goals—and with the vantage of hindsight, however unrealistic—was built upon two decades of a more moderate and "liberal" approach to empire, which was equally concerned with the issue of assimilating the local population. The chapter points out how such binary memories of Fascism among the local community may in fact share many traits with the Italian Peninsula in its handling of memories of Fascism.[63] While underlining how the Dodecanese were strongly brought into the scheme of empire as a form of national-imperial expansion, it examines how the local community has retrospectively thought about this national expansion, and charts to what extent stereotypes of *mia fatsa, mia ratsa* (the Greek translation of "one face,

---

61   In his study of Italian plans for expansion in the Balkans and Africa after the alliance with Hitler and the declaration of war, Davide Rodogno has argued that the Dodecanese was to be the "small space" of the Fascist Empire in Europe, and that the Dodecanese "determined the constitutional framework of the territories conquered after 1940 and influenced the organization of their governments and administrations." Davide Rodogno, *Fascism's European Empire: Italian Occupation during the Second World War* (Cambridge: Cambridge University Press, 2006), 42.
62   For "Practical Mediterraneanism," see Michael Herzfeld, "Practical Mediterraneanism: Excuses for Everything from Epistemology to Eating," in *Rethinking the Mediterranean*, edited by W.V. Harris, 45–63 (Oxford: Oxford University Press, 2005).
63   Paul Corner, *The Fascist Party and Popular Opinion in Mussolini's Italy* (Oxford: Oxford University Press, 2012).

one race"), may also reflect a local reappropriation of Fascist strategies of rule in the islands. Mediterraneanism as a lived, practical experience may imply both positive and negative memories of Italian rule, silences and conclusions about the Fascist past that work together to create collective memories. The chapter draws on both archival documents and oral testimonies to explore how issues such as citizenship, education, religious reform, mixed marriage, and popular protest reflect the local community's recognition of both the strengths and weaknesses of the Fascist state.

In asking what Italy's imperial experiences meant for Italian ideas of nationalism and national identity, and indeed, the very concept of the nation that lay at the core of the project to expand that nation overseas, this book intends to underscore that Italy in every way participates in what postcolonial scholars call the "reciprocal" condition of empire—that is to say, that its overseas projects were as much about making the nation at home as they were about the conquest of new markets abroad.[64] At the same time, this study is conscious of the fact that the process of remaking Italian identity through Mediterraneanist discourse was defined not just by discursive encounters and fantasies of the exotic but also by very real interactions between the Italian state and the local population. The conclusion of the book reflects on what both the "top–down" and the "bottom–up" approaches to the Italian Empire can tell us about colonial inertia: the desire to preserve the period of Italian Empire within both local and global identities that find recourse to the concept of the Mediterranean. It asks how nostalgia for a cosmopolitan and Levantine world of "Greeks, Turks, and Jews" that is sanctioned in the new touristic consumption of the Mediterranean, may revive notions of *mediterraneità* for the purpose of imagining "post-national" European Empire.

---

64 Cooper and Stoler, *Tensions of Empire.*

CHAPTER ONE

Nationalists and the Mediterranean in the Liberal Era

In her powerful study of the intersection of sex, race, and imperialism, Ann McClintock argues that a "crisis of origins" lies at the heart of the European voyages of colonial discovery.[1] McClintock's claim that "the inaugural scene [of discovery] is not only redolent of male megalomania and imperial aggression but also of male anxiety and paranoia" is a provocative rereading of travel literature that reveals the gendered and racialized geographies of difference that were to define not just the colonial setting but the nation-states that helmed these projects. As McClintock argues, this "crisis of origins" can tell as much about ideas of gender and race at home as it can reveal to us the attitudes that would come to define colonial projects.[2] The potential consequences of McClintock's theory for the Italian context are extraordinarily rich. Italian nation-building and colonial expansion followed a twinned course, aligned in time frame, but also in its ideology of "Mediterraneanism." A "crisis of origins" unfolded in colonial narratives—from voyages of discovery to archaeological excavations to travel reportage—and dovetailed with the crisis of origins that occurred at home as Italy sought to forge unity and "make" Italians against an unforgiving backdrop of regionalism, local resistance, and disappointment with national unity.

This first chapter considers Italy's engagement with colonial geographies of the Mediterranean during the immediate post-unification period. While much attention has been placed on representations of the South following the unification, as well as, to a lesser extent, representations of Africa in the late

---

1 Ann McClintock, *Imperial Leather: Race, Gender and Sexuality in the Colonial Contest* (New York: Routledge, 1995), 28–29.
2 Ann McClintock, *Imperial Leather,* 26.

nineteenth century, less attention has been paid to Italy's engagement in the Balkans, the Adriatic, and Aegean at this time.[3] As will be discussed, these areas, alongside East Africa, became areas of vibrant intellectual interest and activity among Italian nationalists. Travel narratives and voyages of "discovery" produced knowledge of the Aegean (in the Foucauldian sense) and set the stage for later colonial projects that Italy adopted there after World War I. Indeed, the recovery of the Aegean was necessary to create a greater geography of difference between Italy and the wider Mediterranean precisely as the nation-state first began, under the leadership of Francesco Crispi, to experiment with the idea that Roman Empire could provide a coherent narrative about a unified peninsula.

Although Italian emigration to the eastern Mediterranean was surpassed by the massive transatlantic migrations, it steadily increased throughout the second half of the nineteenth century.[4] The communities of so-called Italians in the Orient (*italiani nell'Oriente*) helped to commit Italy to a policy of expansion in the region. Yet even fairly recent studies still tend to downplay Italy's ambitions in the Balkans within this period.[5] But Ottoman territories represented important frontiers of cultural and economic expansion for the Italian nation-state; significantly, all were regions where Italians had been explorers, emigrants, colonists, and

---

3   See Giuseppe Finaldi, *Italian National Identity in the Scramble for Africa: Italy's African Wars in the Era of Nation-building, 1870–1900* (New York: Peter Lang, 2009); John Dickie, *Darkest Italy: The Nation and Stereotypes of the Mezzogiorno, 1860–1900* (New York: Palgrave MacMillan, 2016) as well as Nelson Moe, *The View from Vesuvius: Italian Culture and the Southern Question* (Berkeley: University of California Press, 2002); Jane Schneider, *Italy's "Southern Question": Orientalism in One Country* (Oxford: Berg, 1998). There are many fewer studies of Italy's interest in the Balkans than of Italian colonialism in Africa. With a few important exceptions, such as Roberta Pergher's comparative study of Italian projects in Libya and the Alto-Adige, the studies that do exist tend not to include Italian interests in the Balkans within the analytic frame of studies of Italy's overseas colonies, but instead understand them as part of a history of European empires in the Balkans. See Roberta Pergher, *Mussolini's Nation-Empire: Sovereignty and Settlement in Italy's Borderlands, 1922–1943* (Cambridge: Cambridge University Press, 2019).

4   See Angelo Pellegrino, *Verso oriente: Viaggi e lettere degli scrittori italiani nei paesi orientali* (Milan: La vita felice, 2018); Pietro Maravigna, *Gli italiani nell'Oriente balcanico, in Russia e in Palestina, 1915–19* (Rome: Stab. Poligrafico per l'amministrazione della guerra, 1923).

5   Isa Blumi, *Ottoman Refugees, 1878–1939: Migration in a Post-Imperial World* (London: Bloomsbury, 2015).

merchants in the Mediterranean. In fact, at the turn of the century, Italian was still the lingua franca in the Balkans, in a legacy of centuries of economic penetration by the Venetian and Genoese republics.[6] Finally, if ambitions for Italy after the unification centered on achieving greater political recognition in Europe, and on aligning itself with Northern Europe both economically and geopolitically, this inevitably meant that Italy was also very much concerned with the so-called Eastern Question— or what would be the effect on the global economy of an eventual collapse of the Ottoman Empire.[7]

It comes as no surprise, then, that the writings about the Aegean and Levant discussed in this chapter substantiate the argument that the nineteenth and twentieth centuries mark the Mediterranean as a "colonial sea," an area in which archaeological discovery and scientific knowledge helped to create a cultural justification for colonial mandates.[8] And yet, Italian representations of the Mediterranean and the Aegean do more than to suggest correspondences between representation and rule—what Edward Said described as Orientalism's power to be "a Western style for dominating, restructuring and having authority over the Orient."[9] Early representations of the Aegean within it also reveal the fundamental paradoxes, dislocations, and anxieties that haunted Italy's nostalgic engagement with the Mediterranean as both an ancient home and a site of "contamination" by other cultures. To adopt

6 Mark Mazower, "Travellers and the Oriental City, c. 1840–1920," *Transactions of the Royal Historical Society* 6, no. 2 (2002): 59–111.

7 Competition for markets and sovereignty in areas of Ottoman decline would eventually lead to the outbreak of World War I. While Italy is still to some extent viewed as at the margins of competition among the European powers for sovereignty and the expansion of liberal markets in the Balkans, the idea that the Italo-Turkish War in 1911 helped to precipitate the Balkan Wars of 1912–13, and in turn, the collapse of the Balkan region by 1914 is increasingly accepted. See Dominic Geppert, William Mulligan, and Andreas Rose, eds. *The Wars before the Great War: Conflict and International Politics before the Outbreak of the First World War* (Cambridge: Cambridge University Press, 2016); Nicola Labanca, "The Italian Front," in *The First World War*, edited by Jay Winter, 266–96 (Cambridge: Cambridge University Press, 2013); Cyrus Schayegh and Andrew Arsen, eds., *The Routledge Handbook of the History of the Middle East Mandates* (London: Routledge, 2015). See also Christopher Seton-Watson, *Italy from Liberalism to Fascism, 1870–1925* (London: Meuthen, 1967), 376–77.

8 Manuel Borutta and Sakis Gekas, "A Colonial Sea: The Mediterranean, 1798–1956," *European Review of History* 19, no. 1 (2012): 1–13. See also, Timothy Mitchell, *Colonising Egypt* (Berkeley: University of California Press, 1988).

9 Edward Said, *Orientalism* (New York: Vintage Books, 1978), 3.

the Orientalist paradigm differently, the Mediterranean was at once foreign territory for Italy and its fabled homeland, both a powerful symbol of the nation and a sign of its "underground self."[10] This issue emerges with clarity within the representation of the Aegean as a miniature Mediterranean. This sea within the sea encompassed both the creative and "regenerative" possibilities of reconnecting with the Greco-Roman past—the primordial homeland of the Italian nation—and the "unhomely" possibilities of being rootless and without a strong nation-state to support the project of imperial expansion.

As will be evident in the discussion that follows, anxieties about masculinity and about the loss of boundaries concerning the self accumulated in the travel setting to reveal a "crisis of origins," as defined by McClintock, that entwined with fears about the vitality and racial integrity of the Italian nation. These fears were consonant with the postunitary crisis that, as has been much discussed, increasingly posited the South as a backward region of Italy to be colonized itself.[11] But the writers discussed below show novel ways of imagining "backwardness" as linked to Ottomanization and Oriental decline. Simultaneously, these writers move to perpetuate the Risorgimento view of ancient Greece as linked to the early Italian nation-state in its form during a Roman rule in the Mediterranean. The Aegean evokes to them strong imagined cultural—and eventually, racial—links between the ancient Hellenistic and Roman empires. But these representations of the Aegean also activate gendered and racialized patterns and show that recuperating Greco-Roman and Mediterranean heritage of Italy would be fraught by fears of dangerous and contaminating encounters with the Orient and Africa.

The presence of Orientalism in Italian culture has largely been discussed in reference to the South and the *questione meridionale*, or Southern Question, and it has only more recently examined how Italy may have engaged with external Orientalisms, and to study how images and representations of the Levant and the Balkans may have constituted another "significant other" within Italian culture.[12] In this regard, Fabrizio De Donno's *Italian*

---

10   Edward Said, *Orientalism*, 3.

11   On Orientalism as a paradigm for understanding Italy, see Jane Schneider, *Italy's "Southern Question": Orientalism in One Country* (Oxford: Berg, 1998); Moe, *The View from Vesuvius*; Dickie, *Darkest Italy*; and Maria Petrusecwiz, *Come il meridione divenne una questione* (Soveria Monelli: Rubettino, 1998).

12   My use of the term "significant other" comes from Anna Triandafyllidou, *Immigrants and National Identity in Europe* (London: Routledge, 2001).

Orientalism as well as Barbara Spackman's *Accidental Orientalists* have offered important new directions for inquiring as to how Italian travel encounters in the Ottoman Empire navigated complex imaginaries of an elsewhere, and how a strain of Italian culture negotiated constructions of self and other by means of representations of the "Orient."[13] These studies underscore that even as Italian travelers sought to inscribe the Orient with difference, the search for an identifiable yet labile idea of home persisted in their representations. As Spackman argues, the political instability of home led to a "heightened volatility of identity abroad," one that suggests an alliance between processes of Orientalization and those of Italianization.[14] Put simply, the journey to the Orient often brought nationalists into an uncomfortable recognition of a lack of home. The response to such a recognition was often none other than to sound an even more urgent call for an empire, held by many nationalists to be a the one viable route toward achieving an economically robust and healthy nation-state.

In the same time frame as the Italian state waged a campaign for the colonization of the Horn of Africa, the Aegean began attracting scholarly interest and drawing Italian nationalists to its shores. This fact suggests how the campaigns to colonize in East Africa, while often viewed as motivated by the *questione meridionale*—and seen as a resolution to the crisis of unemployment and poverty in the South—occurred as Ottoman decline engendered a new "scramble for Africa" in the much more culturally and economically familiar areas of the Balkans and eastern Mediterranean. Indeed, Crispi justified his disastrous campaigns in East Africa on the basis that it would help Italy to obtain a colony in the much more desirable area of the Mediterranean basin.[15] By the turn of the century, the Aegean was furthermore a place of vibrant archaeological activity. In 1900, Arthur Evans completed his famous excavations of Knossos. Evans's project ensured that Greek antiquity became fully uncoupled from Roman Empire, replaced by an image of Greece as the cradle of enlightened, liberal, and European democracy.[16] The Italian nation-

---

13   Fabrizio De Donno, *Italian Orientalism: Nationhood, Cosmopolitanism, and the Cultural Politics of Identity* (New York: Peter Lang, 2019); Barbara Spackman, *Accidental Orientalists: Modern Italian Travelers in Ottoman Lands* (Liverpool: Liverpool University Press, 2017).

14   Barbara Spackman, *Accidental Orientalists*, 7.

15   William Kidston McClure, *Italy and North Africa: An Account of the Tripoli Enterprise* (London: Constable, 1913).

16   See Cathy Gere, *Knossos and the Prophets of Modernism* (Chicago: University of Chicago Press, 2009).

alists whose writings this chapter explores, on the other hand, reinscribe a Greco-Roman narrative onto the Aegean, endowing it with a special and privileged status as a site of Italian national belonging, a place of the origins of an Italian ethnic "stock" or *stirpe* that led to the establishment of Roman Empire.[17]

In this regard, Italian encounters in the Aegean traverse different subject positions and identities and their accounts of it are typical of the European encounter with the Levant. Since its first publication, Edward Said's theory of Orientalism has been widely criticized for its excessive reliance on a monolithic and almost universalizing idea of the Orient as constructed by the West.[18] While Italian nationalists no doubt invested the Orient with an "unadulterated cultural, geographical, and historical significance" and in ways that mirror Orientalism in representations of the South at this time, position Italian culture and identity as of moral superiority, they also luxuriate in the exoticism of the Aegean and Mediterranean, and celebrate their Southernness.[19] Nationalist writers assert both familiarity with and distance from the Aegean. They recuperate its Italo-Greek heritage, but while shunning Greece's Ottomanization they also identify with it. All the authors discussed here are self-conscious about the fact that their position within European imaginaries of the Levant is one of Italian provincialism and they recognize that they represent a relatively weak empire and navigate what is for them a new frontier of Ottoman decline. And yet, each of these writers, when confronting the Levant as a startling image of difference, will mobilize the South as a site of virility and power. It is not only that these travel narratives presage fantasies about the renewal of *mare nostrum* to mitigate the historic role of the South as a signifier of Italy's backwardness;[20] it is also that travel through the Aegean allows these authors to study, to scrutinize, and to

17   Fabrizio de Donno, "Routes to Modernity: Orientalism and Mediterraneanism in Italian Culture, 1810–1910," *California Italian Studies Journal* 1, no. 1 (2010): 1–23.
18   As Dennis Porter has argued in his critique of *Orientalism*, the genre of travel literature can allow for multiple readings and is often "of sufficient complexity to throw ideological processes into relief and raise questions about their fictionalizing processes." Dennis Porter, *"Orientalism and Its Problems,"* in *Colonial Discourse and Post-Colonial Theory: A Reader,* edited by Patrick Williams and Laura Chrisman, 150–62 (New York: Columbia University Press, 1994), 153.
19   Said, *Orientalism*, 84.
20   Nelson Moe, *The View from Vesuvius: Italian Culture and the Southern Question* (Berkeley: University of California Press, 2002).

articulate the Orient as the uncanny but familiar Other—the unhomely homeland—of Italian culture.

So, if the project of these authors is essentially nostalgic—one that seeks within the idea of empire a homecoming to Italy's great heritage—discussions of the Aegean also traverse the troubled project of nationalism at home. The very fragmentation that a monolithic representation of the Mediterranean attempts to conceal returns in the description of the Eastern elsewhere. The Aegean thus becomes the site of a productive negation that explores the ambivalent location of the Mediterranean within Italian nationalism, and to a certain extent, Italian national identity. These narratives also reveal the paradox of race in the Italian case—a view of itself as both white and other, both European and Oriental—a paradox that is visible as authors put themselves into a position of colonial encounter. In what follows, only Giuseppe Sergi's treatise regarding the Mediterranean race does not strictly conform to the genre of travelogue, but he clearly considers his research to be the result of his extensive travels throughout the broader Eastern world and the Black Sea, and is navigating a complex set of associations about the Italian South thanks to his place in positivist debates about race in Italy at the time and his relationship to the writings of Cesare Lombroso. The other authors discussed in this chapter—Gabriele D'Annunzio, Edmondo de Amicis, Enrico Corradini, Luigi Federzoni, and Orazio Pedrazzi—are furthermore all regarded as important nationalists and, to varying degrees and in complex and much-debated ways, as cultural and ideological predecessors to the Fascist state.[21] For all these nationalist writers, then, representing the Aegean is not just a question of imagining it and inscribing it with cultural and geographic significance but of creatively reworking it to make it into a potential homeland and an affirmation of both the Italian nation and the Italian Empire.

Similarly, while there is significant literature on the construction of Greece in the European, and especially British, cultural imagination, no equivalent interrogation exists for how Italians constructed Greece in the eighteenth and nineteenth centuries. The period of Grand Tour travel to the Ottoman Empire and Greek national revolution produced a rich and often romantic engagement with Greece—with notable examples such as Lord Byron who famously died as a revolutionary fighting in the Greek war of independence. Although Italy was not a major imperial player at this time,

21   Barbara Spackman, *Fascist Virilities: Rhetoric, Ideology and Social Fantasy in Italy* (Minneapolis: University of Minnesota Press, 1996).

nor even yet a nation-state, an image of Greece, but a very different one, had operated in nineteenth-century Italian discourses of the nation; nostalgic memories of Magna Graecia were present in Risorgimento rhetoric.[22] It is therefore perhaps difficult to imagine how Italy might have adopted a set of crypto-colonial or quasi-Orientalist discourses about how Greece was unlike Europe—still a place of Turkish despotism—while also like Europe, mainly because of the presence of Christianity.[23] The Italian engagement with Greece thus looks very different from the "straightforward attitude, usually negative, but rarely nuanced" described by Maria Todorova in her well-known discussion of the Balkans as a "place of unimaginative concreteness" in the European cultural imagination.[24] In turn-of-the-century Italian accounts, on the other hand, Greece and the Aegean proves a highly charged space that offers enrichment of the Italian national project and prefigures a long-awaited epic homecoming—as in the literal translation of the word *nostalgia*, a longing to return home—one that in the Homeric tradition is intimately intertwined with representations of an Odyssean journey by sea.

The first part of the chapter addresses a performative and emblematic tour of the Aegean by Gabriele D'Annunzio, one overtly invested in recovering the narratives of Homer and the memory of the ancient Greeks. True to D'Annunzio's form, the poet unites the confessional genre with the Odyssey, rewrites Homer as a voyage of self-discovery, and represents the Aegean Sea as a site of erotic plenitude from which he can source his own potential as an Orientalist and imperialist. Carrying forward D'Annunzio's notion of a Greco-Roman "stock," the chapter turns to how Giuseppe Sergi invests in reconstructing a Greco-Italian ethnic heritage in the Aegean as he searches for the primordial homeland of the Roman people. The latter half of the chapter addresses, on the other hand, how travel narratives across the Aegean and into Rhodes, following the 1912 conquest, translate the nostalgic homeland of the Mediterranean into an imperial frontier. These post-conquest authors—Enrico Corradini, Luigi Federzoni, and Orazio Pedrazzi—were major nationalists who had championed the invasion of

22   See Lucy Riall, *Garibaldi: Invention of a Hero* (New Haven, CT: Yale University Press, 2007), 19–32. See also Roberto Dainotto, *Europe (In Theory)* (Durham, NC: Duke University Press, 2007) and Konstantina Zanou, *Transnational Patriotism in the Mediterranean, 1800–1850* (Oxford: Oxford University Press, 2018).

23   Maria Todorova, *Imagining the Balkans* (Oxford: Oxford University Press, 1997), 62–88.

24   Todorova, *Imagining the Balkans*, 14.

Libya and who would go on to have important careers as nationalists and as leaders of Italian foreign policy during the Fascist dictatorship. Their narratives belie the notion that the Italian state ever entertained any notion of returning the islands to the Ottoman Porte, as the Italian state promised to the Turks at the Treaty of Ouchy in 1912. More importantly, these authors mine the question of how to think about their Greek "cousins" now that some form of empire in Greece was a *fait accomplit*. In all of these cases, the South and Southernness play a pivotal role in shielding Italians from the moral turpitude and decadence of the Orient.

Gabriele D'Annunzio's Uncanny *Oikos*

In July 1895, with an advance from his editorial house, Gabriele D'Annunzio purchased an enormous yacht and plotted an extravagant cruise across the Aegean. Having just completed *Le vergini delle rocce* (*The Virgins of the Rocks*), his fourth novel, which was inspired by his encounter with the writings of Nietzsche, D'Annunzio was on the cusp of literary stardom; he settled on a plan that would bring these new ideas into a vivid personal reality, which would embody the principle of *vita e arte*, or the living of life as if it were a work of art. D'Annunzio spent the months prior to his departure writing to his friends who were part of the journal *Convito*—which D'Annunzio had established in 1895 to restore "the sovereign dignity of the spirit" and the glory of the Risorgimento—to convince them to join him on a tour that would enact these ideals.[25] There was no better index of this ambition than the name of the yacht itself: *La fantasia*, or *The Fantasy*.

Accompanying him on *La fantasia* eventually were Edoardo Scarfoglio, a young journalist (and with whom D'Annunzio had purchased the yacht), Pasquale Mascantonio, an ambitious young politician, Guido Boggiani, a painter and ethnographer, who a few years later would by killed by natives while on expedition in Paraguay, and lastly, Georges Hérelle, the French translator of D'Annunzio's novels. The sailing tour was to follow a Homeric route in reverse: rather than head from Turkey home to a symbolic Ithaka in Italy, the yacht would depart from Puglia, sail past the Ionian archipelago, across the Aegean and through the strait of Bosporus to Constantinople,

---

25   Cited in Elena Borelli, *Giovanni Pascoli, Gabriele D'Annunzio, and the Ethics of Desire between Action and Contemplation* (Madison, WI: Fairleigh Dickinson Press, 2017), 96.

inaugural city of the Orient. The tour would attempt to navigate toward the East, and while establishing the Aegean (as well as the Adriatic) as a frontier for Italian expansion, it would commit D'Annunzio to a lifelong obsession with recuperating the memory of the ancient Greeks.

D'Annunzio's tour of the Aegean aligned perfectly with the national moment: the crew of literati headed to the East exactly as the Crispi campaigns to colonize East Africa were reaching their treacherous peak. Six months after the *Fantasy*'s tour of the Aegean, Italy experienced unmitigated defeat by the Ethiopian army. In his 1885 novel of scandal, *Il Piacere*, the decadent hero and D'Annunzio's alter ego, Andrea Sperelli, had scoffed that the disastrous Dogali battle in East Africa, in which around four hundred outnumbered Italian soldiers were slain by an Ethiopian army, deserved no more than a fleeting thought.[26] But on board the yacht the African question was never far off.[27] The poet's abandonment of the cruise seems to have proleptically rehearsed Italy's defeat and rapid military retreat from the Horn of Africa, as well as to suggest D'Annunzio's decadent rejection of the virile campaign to colonize new African territories for the Italian nation.

Indeed, the journey to affirm Italy's imperial program was to result in exactly the sort of crisis that Ann McClintock has described as so typical of the colonial geography of discovery. Once aboard the yacht D'Annunzio began to complain bitterly of nausea and seasickness; he objected to the stultifying atmosphere of modern Greece. He showed no interest in keeping his promise that on board they would harness the energy of intellectual camaraderie and revive the spirit of Greek antiquity—along the lines of the English Romantic poets Byron and Shelley—but revealed himself as above all interested in making lewd jokes and carousing with local prostitutes. Somewhere around Cape Sounion, southeast of Athens, a minor storm blew in and D'Annunzio made an early return to Italy with Scarfoglio.[28] In Hérelle's recollection, the

---

26   "All for four hundred brutes, who died brutally!" D'Annunzio had included his disdain for the African campaigns despite editorial objections that he should cut the reference to the massacre in order not to offend the public. Quoted in Gabriele D'Annunzio, *Pleasure*, translated by Lara Gochin Raffaeli (New York: Penguin, 2013), xxi.

27   "*I discorsi che accompagnarono il loro viaggio furono in gran parte riservati a scambiarsi vicendevolmente le impressioni e i ricordi di esplorazioni precedenti. Herelle parlava della Spagna, Scarfoglio dell'Oriente e della questione africana*"; Raffaele Giglio, *Per la storia di un'amicizia: d'Annunzio, Herelle, Scarfoglio, Serao: documenti inediti* (Naples: Lofredo, 1977), 20.

28   Paolo Alatri, *D'Annunzio* (Turin: Unione Tipografico-Editrice Torinese, 1983), 162.

voyage proved that the poet was no more than a caricature of himself. "There really is something puerile about Gabriele D'Annunzio," commented Hérelle some years later.[29]

After his premature return, however, D'Annunzio published a further trilogy of works that was to affirm his literary fame, all of which bore the sign of a new fixation on Greek culture.[30] By no accident the *Fantasy* eventually became synonymous with the poet's quest to embody a Nietzschean superhuman beyond all good and evil. An engraving of D'Annunzio aboard the yacht eventually adorned an early edition of his memoirs.[31] The yachting tour was not only reported on in the tabloid media at the time, but was to follow D'Annunzio for the next thirty years and to inhabit various cultural productions associated with his image as an archangel (*l'arcangelo*). All of D'Annunzio's major biographers treat the cruise as an important juncture in D'Annunzio's life, philosophy, and career. John Woodhouse argues that the cruise and the possibility of self-transformation associated with it would obsess D'Annunzio for at least a decade after it.[32] Lucy Hughes-Hallett describes that eight years later when he wrote his modern epic, *Maia*, "the visit to a Patras brothel which Hérelle found so sordid, appeared transmuted into a half comic, half profoundly sorrowful episode in which Helen of Troy symbolizes the transience of the pleasures of the flesh."[33] D'Annunzio's self-styled transformation was noted by close observers at the time: Francesco Paolo Michetti, a famed painter and friend of D'Annunzio,

29   Quoted in John Woodhouse, *Gabriele D'Annunzio: Defiant Archangel* (Oxford: Clarendon Press, 1998), 133; D'Annunzio was *"capace di commettere un crimine per soddisfare la sua passione e perfino la sua curiosità,"* according to his French translator, Georges Hérelle. See Georges Hérelle, *Notolette Dannunziane: Ricordi, Aneddotti, Pettegolezzi,* edited by Guy Tosi (Pescara: Centro Nazionale di Studi Dannunziani, 1984).

30   Between 1895 and 1903, D'Annunzio completed *Le vergini delle rocce* (1895), *La città morta* (1898), and *Maia* (1903). See Centro nazionale di studi dannunziani e della cultura in Abruzzo, ed., *Verso l'Ellade: Dalla Città morta a Maia: 18. Convegno internazionale: Pescara, 11–12 maggio 1995* (Pescara: Ediars, 1995).

31   See Federico Vittore Nardelli, *L'Arcangelo* (Rome: Alberto Stock, 1931); Gabriele D'Annunzio, *Taccuini,* edited by Enrica Bianchetti and Roberto Forcella (Milan: Mondadori, 1965), 1230.

32   "The sometimes bizarre journey and its consequences would divert D'Annunzio's literary attention and ambitions for the next decade." Woodhouse, *Gabriele D'Annunzio,* 127.

33   Lucy Hughes-Hallett, *Gabriele D'Annunzio: Poet, Seducer, and Preacher of War* (New York: Alfred A. Knopf, 2013), 20.

made a new portrait of D'Annunzio on his return, remarking that pastel is certainly the first portrait of D'Annunzio as "superman."[34] In 1897, just two years later, D'Annunzio ran successfully for a seat in the Italian Chamber of Deputies.

D'Annunzio's brief career in formal politics was characterized, famously, by his switch from far right to far left and his eventual defeat when he ran for reelection as a socialist. This, as well as his position as a fierce nationalist and irredentist, leader of the march to capture Fiume in Croatia for Italy, and his views that expansionism could be an artistic expression of the avant-garde have inextricably linked him to Fascism and to the ideological and cultural revolution swept across Italy in 1919–20 and led to Mussolini's dictatorship, which began in 1923. As Barbara Spackman has pointed out, however, D'Annunzio's actual contribution to Fascism would be minimized by his decadence, which interfered with the strict gender binary that the Fascist state incorporated into its rhetoric of virility and martial values.[35] Yet D'Annunzio's rhetoric of virility is all the same germane to an understanding of how the Fascist revolution eventually appropriated nationalism for its an ambitious design to colonize the minds of the Italian people.

D'Annunzio's discovery of the Aegean works to convert liberal, Risorgimento-era values into colonial and imperial ones. While the poet inverts the strict binaries between self and other, Italy and Orient, and exchanges virile masculinity for homoerotic desire, it is precisely this inversion that allows D'Annunzio to convert the crisis of origins—the recognition that the Orient is a place of terrifying Otherness—into an occasion to recuperate the ideas of ancient Greece, Magna Graecia, and Greek masculinity as models for Italian nationalism. D'Annunzio's fragmentary record of the cruise makes clear that the failure to cross the Aegean was not as total, nor as unintentional, as it may have appeared at the time.[36] Rather, the cruise was

---

34   "*Ora, il Gabriele D'Annunzio rappresentato da quel pastello è un uomo tutto nuovo che sembra non avere più niente in comune con i ritratti precedenti. In questi ultimi, l'insieme della fisionomia è dolce, lo sguardo un po' abbassato, i baffi modesti, con un sorriso vagamente malinconico. Al contrario, nel pastello, i tratti sono duri, i baffi si sollevano come lunghi uncini, la barbetta a punta minaccia, gli occhi sono aggressivi, le sopracciglia un po' aggrottate. Quel pastello è certamente il primo ritratto di D'Annunzio 'superuomo'.*" Cited in Paolo Alatri, *D'Annunzio*, 164.

35   Spackman, *Fascist Virilities*, 16–24.

36   D'Annunzio's record of the voyage of the *Fantasy* became available posthumously, with a critical edition of his journals, first published by Mondadori in 1965. D'Annunzio, *Taccuini*, 31–71.

an exploration and a stage for the poet's own rebirth and transformation into a national figure, one whose political career would be an extension of his artistic production.

At first blush, D'Annunzio's narrative of crossing the Aegean is almost clichéd: Greece is decidedly picturesque, a landscape at the crossroads of the ancient and the decadent, of Homer and the inflated *dracma*. But D'Annunzio's poetics of decadence, sickness, and homoerotic regeneration deliberately disrupt the Odyssean travel economy of nostalgia.[37] Rather than return safely to the *oikos*, or home, and restore a phallic hierarchy, D'Annunzio assumes the position of illness, figured as nausea, and avoids passing through a vaginal entrance to the Orient, here imagined as the feminizing strait of Bosporus. Instead, the poet retreats further and further into the safe confines of the womb-like yacht, itself also a phallic symbol.

While there is no exit from D'Annunzio's tour—in the true embodiment of utopia, the *Fantasy* seems bound for nowhere—failure to arrive in Constantinople marks the commitment to navigation by sea as a form of spiritual rejuvenation. He writes, from sea, "It seems to me I am already on the brink of a purification. It's incredible to me how profound this sentiment of estrangement from all the things I have left behind me, even after just a few hours of navigation" (*Mi sembra già di essere a traverso una purificazione. È incredibile quanto sia in me profondo il sentimento di distacco di tutte le cose lasciate dietro di me, pur dopo alcune ore di navigazione*).[38] D'Annunzio's nausea, moreover, is accompanied by "a sort of sleepiness illuminated from time to time by indistinct flashes of thoughts and dreams" (*"una specie di sonnolenza illuminata di tratto in tratto da bagliori indistinti di pensieri e di sogni"*), one that sounds suspiciously similar to the male birth fantasy found in Marinetti's 1909 *Mafarka il futurista*, in which the protagonist Mafarka gives birth, thanks to virile powers of philosophy and alchemy, to

---

37 As Georges Van Den Abeele has remarked, "Away from home, Odysseus encounters 'other' women, who remain, at least for him, alluring and/or menacing, seductive and/ or castrating," whereas the return home marks the restoration of the proper phallic order. Georges Van den Abbeele, *Travel as Metaphor: From Montaigne to Rousseau* (Minneapolis: University of Minnesota Press, 1992), xxv. "One need go no further than the prototypical travel narrative that is the *Odyssey* to find a modeling of the sexual division of labor: the domestic(ated) woman, Penelope, maintains the property of the home against would-be usurpers while her husband wanders about."; see also, Teresa de Lauretis, *Technologies of Gender: Essays on Theory, Film, and Fiction* (Bloomington: Indiana University Press, 1987).

38 D'Annunzio, *Taccuini*, 38.

Gazourmah, a black-faced child who will grow up to be a Nietzschean-styled *Übermensch*.[39]

In this case, however, D'Annunzio does not give birth; rather, in the ultimate expression of the "giant who kills his own creator," D'Annunzio disposes of his former decadent self in order to regenerate as a new imperial man for whom the ship, and the act of crossing the Adriatic (if not the entire Aegean) are his central raisons d'être.[40] Departure from Pescara in 1895, amid marital and extramarital crises, with his second marriage, to his former lover Maria Gravina, on the brink of ending, correlates to D'Annunzio's commitment to excising women from the poet's maritime universe. As D'Annunzio imagines himself fearless in his penetration of foreign harbors, his spirit of conquest is spurred on by an erotic and uninhibited attraction to antiquity. Although D'Annunzio partially represses the personal reasons for setting off on an extended holiday, his failed marriage to Gravina is the backdrop for his construction of departure as an escape from an effeminized Italy in search of a masculine Greece.

Shortly after departing, the poet confesses to his joy in being released from "such a long cohabitation" (*"una convivenza cosi lunga"*) with a woman he describes as so "tenderly oppressive" (*"teneramente oprimente"*).[41] His "eviration," the loss of virility that marked his repressive bourgeois homelife in Pescara, fades away as he finds himself in this rejuvenating maritime world, and in close proximity to men. He delights at the "sweetness of great naval freedom" (*"la dolcezza della gran libertà navale"*).[42] The yacht is simple but elegant, he remarks, and so is the room he shares with Guido Boggiani. Within a few hours of departure, the deck of the *Fantasy* is the scene for a "surrogate birth" in which D'Annunzio is born a new man. In this delivery *without* women, he recovers both his masculinity and an erotic pleasure in the male body:

> Excellent bath in the clear deep sea. After it, a sailor throws a bucket of fresh water over me to wash the salt off. The pleasure I feel while remaining naked is intense, so is the confidence as I move, the total lack of physical shame. I feel truly as if I have been penetrated by Hellenism

---

39   D'Annunzio, *Taccuini*, 36. On male birth fantasies, see Christine Kanz and Adam Cmiel, "Ex-Corporation: On Male Birth Fantasies," *Imaginations* 2, no. 11 (2011): 54–67.
40   Christine Kanz and Adam Cmiel, "Ex-Corporation: On Male Birth Fantasies," 59.
41   D'Annunzio, *Taccuini*, 31.
42   D'Annunzio, *Taccuini*, 33.

to my marrow, and that I should have been born in Athens, exercising in the gymnasiums of youthfulness.

Eccellente bagno nell'acqua fresca limpida e profonda. Un marinajo, dopo, mi getta addosso un gran catino di acqua dolce per lavarmi del sale. Al piacere vivo che provo nel rimanere ignudo, alla mia disinvoltura nel muovermi, alla mancanza assoluto del pudore fisico, sento che veramente io sono penetrato d'ellenismo fino alle midolle e che avrei dovuto nascere ad Atene, esercitare nei ginnasi di giovinezza.[43]

D'Annunzio's departure from his "evirating" home allows the poet to experience liberation through his entrapment in the yacht, and the exoticism of the Aegean in turn becomes the premise for his rebirth.[44] With each progressive movement toward the East, the poet retreats further into a maritime universe of his own imagination—a universe where women are no longer alluring nor threatening. As the *Fantasia* sails past phallic lighthouses and stretches of land compared to elongating tongues, the yachting tour stakes its claim as an Odyssey. References to Homer litter the text, and phantasmatic images of antiquity appear on the horizon and then recede from it and, as in Homer, the song of the sirens can be heard. But this time the song does not take the form of a woman's voice; rather, it seems to emanate from the vibrations of the yacht's ropes, which produce an uncanny and human-sounding song.[45]

The ship may resemble an erect phallus—one plowing through an erotic and feminine sea—but it is also a fetish that protects D'Annunzio from the threat of castrating sirens. The Orient, for D'Annunzio, is an uncanny landscape, both deeply strange and deeply familiar, and in a turn that strikes a Freudian chord, a reminder of woman's horrifying lack.[46]

43   D'Annunzio, *Taccuini*, 34.

44   This type of travel would seem to have the power to enact "the paradoxical play of entrapment and liberation evinced by critical thought"; Georges Van Den Abbeele, *Travel as Metaphor*, xx.

45   D'Annunzio, *Taccuini*, 38.

46   In the Freudian paradigm, the "uncanny," reflects a deep-seated anxiety about the unfamiliar that is linked to the female organ. The idea of woman's eerie otherness is also present in Freud's essay on the Medusa, a figure that will shortly make an appearance in D'Annunzio's as well. Sigmund Freud (1919), "The Uncanny," *The Standard Edition of the Complete Works of Sigmund Freud*, vol. 17, 217–56 (Stanford, CA: Stanford University Press, 2001; first published in 1919). See also Hélène Cixous's famous

Except for Hérelle, the party had brought along their tuxedo suits with the expectation of amorous encounters at port. But revealingly, Greek women are represented mostly as prostitutes and D'Annunzio describes these as to be avoided at all costs. The crew decidedly avoids the sex tourism it had planned to undertake. A visit to one prostitute causes D'Annunzio to recoil with horror and make a swift return to the yacht: "We avoided this disgust— let's thank the gods! (*"un disgusto evitato—ringraziamo i dei!"*).[47] Although D'Annunzio figures the sea as a feminine body and erogenous zone to be penetrated and conquered, he also uses this trope so as to underscore that his crew must avoid the "contamination" and potential for "degeneration" caused by entering into a "contact zone" where colonial boundaries will be lost.[48] Instead of in romantic, or even just sexual, entanglements with local women, erotic pleasure is located within the contours of the yacht itself—a perfectly shaped image of the phallus.

Before D'Annunzio moors in Patras, he describes the mainsail of the *Fantasy* as full blown with his pleasure, in what is an unmistakable metaphor for an erection:

> The ship zooms superbly, inclined on its side, in a furrow of fervent foam. The mainsail is blown up with joy and transmits its pleasure. I stretch out along the bow, so that the large bowsprit seems an extension of my body: an enormous phallic extension that gives me a strange sense of powerful virility. Pointed toward a rocky mountain, the bowsprit goes straight, almost without oscillation.

> *La nave fila superbamente, inclinata sul fianco, in un solco di schiume fervide. La randa è gonfia di gioja e ci comunica la sua felicità. Mi distendo a prua, così che il gran bompresso sembra un prolungamento del mio corpo: un mostruoso prolungamento fallico che mi dà uno strano senso di virilità possente. Appuntato contro la montagna rocciosa, il bompresso va diritto, quasi senza oscillazioni.*[49]

reading of Freud's essay in a feminist lens, Hélène Cixous, "Fiction and Its Phantoms: A Reading of Freud's *Das Unheimliche* (the Uncanny)," *New Literary History* 7, no. 3 (1976), 525–46, 619–45.

47   D'Annunzio, *Taccuini*, 48.

48   Mary Louise Pratt, *Imperial Eyes: Travel Writing and Transculturation* (New York: Routledge, 2008).

49   D'Annunzio, *Taccuini*, 42.

Yet a dangerous and destructive undertow haunts the arrival in Patras—the crossing of the boundary between Italy and Greece threatens death by asphyxiation: "A torrid and suffocating wind, like the exhalation of a thousand ovens, hits us, and steals our breath" ("*Un soffio torrido, soffocante, simile all'esalazione di mille fornaci, c'investe mozzandoci il respiro*").[50] Although his "powerful virility" comes to his aid precisely as the yacht lands, D'Annunzio asks if he has not, in fact, arrived in the Red Sea: "This is our first breath of Greece, desiccated and enervating. Are we in Patras or in front of Aden?" ("*Ecco il primo alito della Grecia, disseccante e snervante. Siamo d'avanti a Patrasso o d'avanti a Aden?*").[51] The loss of all sense of orientation drives a revealing comparison of the Aegean to the Red Sea—where the Italian state was focusing its colonial energies at the time. In stark contrast to his aspirations for a virile Hellenic rebirth, D'Annunzio experiences Greece as not a buffer but as the threshold of the Orient, a backward, decadent, and Ottomanized East, a place so nauseating that it (almost) cannot be survived.

The metaphor of Hellenic rebirth, that drew him from home so that he could recover himself at sea, paradoxically, also places him at the precipice of disaster. When the crew arrives in Patras, the land is replete with harsh displays of death and, not without irony, decadence. D'Annunzio describes a face "more yellow than saffron" as a funeral procession passes him bearing an uncovered corpse. Greece proves a landscape of the worthless drachmae and a place of Eastern decadence where one can spend entire days smoking in mute contemplation.[52] These descriptions of Greece are not unlike D'Annunzio's own images of the Dalmatian coast in his early *Novelle della Pescara*, a spurious imitation of Giovanni's Verga's *verismo* style in his short stories dedicated to Sicily.[53] D'Annunzio's weak (national) virility will require him to turn away in horror and turn back from the exploration of unknown waters. But the decadence and disorderly nature of the Aegean eventually commits D'Annunzio to carrying "home" Greek masculinity—one is tempted to call it

50   D'Annunzio, *Taccuini*, 42.

51   D'Annunzio, *Taccuini*, 42–43.

52   D'Annunzio, *Taccuini*, 44.

53   In D'Annunzio's short story "La vergine Anna," for example, the protagonist's father sails back and forth between Italy and the Dalmatian coast, the latter that he describes as a landscape "inhabited by monkeys and men from India" ("*abitata dalle scimmie a da uomini dell'India*"); Gabriele D'Annunzio, "La vergine Anna," in *Tutte le novelle* (Milan: Mondadori, 1992), 133. See also Barbara Spackman's discussion of this short story in *Decadent Genealogies: The Rhetoric of Sickness from Baudelaire to D'Annunzio* (Ithaca: Cornell University Press, 1989), 105–51.

a talisman for a future when the poet will lead the march on Fiume to annex Croatia for the Italian state.

The aesthetic culmination of the tour takes place with its arrival not in Constantinople but in Olympia, with a visit there to a sculpture of a young Hermes from the fourth century BC, by Praxiteles. Hermes—the god who represented, in the Odyssean tradition, male youth, agility, and speed—thus becomes the perfect example of Hellenic youthfulness, or *giovinezza*, able to transmit to D'Annunzio the virility that he clearly needs in order to survive in the Aegean.[54]

> Life flows through all his body parts. Seen from the front, the statue has a character of incomparable grace and an almost feminine softness. The belly and pubis have—on sight—the elasticity of flesh; the torso breathes. Seen from the side, this grace is strengthened, it appears more robust and more virile. [...] Everything is perfection. Here is the ideal image of Hellenic youthfulness.

> *La vita fluisce in tutte le membra. Vista di fronte, la statua ha un carattere di grazia incomparabile e quasi una mollezza femminea. Il ventre e il pube hanno—alla vista—l'elasticità della carne; il torace respira. Vista di fianco, questa grazia si afforza, appare più robusto e più virile. [...] Tutto è perfezione. Ecco la perfetta immagine ideale della giovinezza ellenica.*[55]

D'Annunzio celebrates the sculptor's ability to bring forth the image of perfection—the sculpture is a fine example of a Hellenic boy—by correcting nature and moving beyond the limitations of mimetic referents. As Charles Bernheimer interprets Oscar Wilde's famous words on art: "Art is woman as corrected through male invention, 'our spirited protest, our gallant attempt to teach Nature her proper place.' Masculine protest motivates the fetishization of art by denying its mimetic referent to nature."[56] Praxiteles's Hermes is made more virile by correcting that "almost feminine softness" that is natural

---

54   From a new Italian translation of the Odyssey: "*Hermes, il dio della bacchetta d'oro, simile a un giovane cui fiorisce sul mento la prima barba, splendente di grazia è la sua giovinezza*"; Omero, *Odissea*, translated by Maria Grazia Ciani (Venice: Tascabili Marsilio, 2000), 153.

55   D'Annunzio, *Taccuini*, 51.

56   Charles Bernheimer, "Fetishism and Decadence: Salome's Severed Heads," in *Fetishism as Cultural Discourse*, edited by Emily Apter and William Pietz (Ithaca, NY: Cornell University Press, 1993), 64.

to youth, but that is transmuted and made robust by the sculptor's powerful hand. Praxiteles's Hermes exerts a bold erotic attraction, but one so remote that it seems to D'Annunzio to surpass all prior encounters with Hellenic youth and "to enclose for all eternity the secret of Joy" (46). In a lengthy passage, one that bears retranscription here, D'Annunzio concludes that it is the dramatic landscape of the Aegean that led the ancient Greeks to make their bold leap toward art and conquest over the natural world:

> The Greek spirit formed through the continuous reaction of man against the precise and imposing *personality* of things. There is no landscape more stimulating to me than this one, composed almost entirely of the violent forms of the cliff and olive tree. So proud and singular is every figure here, that it all imposes itself almost *like an abuse*. There is—it seems to me—a dominating line in these things. They are always lean, raw, precise, very determined, perfectly clear in the sun. It is not possible to escape their dominion, to ignore them, to not consider them. These things impose themselves imperiously. And in turn, they engender an energetic man with instinctual reactions. This man wants to be *stronger than things*. And this is how the magnificent personality of the ancient Hellenes formed. The landscape they inhabited was a continual stimulation, continually inspired energy and will.

> *Lo spirito greco si formava nella continua reazione dell'uomo contro la precisa e imponente* personalità *delle cose. Non v'è per me un paesaggio più eccitante di questo, composto quasi tutto dalle forme violente degli olivi e delle rupi. Così fiera e singolare è qui ogni figura, che s'impone allo spirito quasi come un soppruso. V'è—mi sembra—nelle cose una linea dominatrice. Esse sono sempre magre, scarne, precise, ben determinate, chiarissime nel sole. Non è possibile sottrarsi al loro dominio, trascurarle, non considerarle. Esse s'impongono prepotenti. Allora nasce nell'uomo energico un istinto di reazione. Egli vuol essere* più *forte delle cose. Ed ecco come si formano le magnifiche personalità degli antichi Elleni. Il paese ch'essi abitavano era per loro un continuo stimolo, un continuo suscitatore di energie e di volontà.*[57]

In marked contrast to his own decadent lived experience of travel, D'Annunzio is able to imagine that this violent landscape dominated those who lived within it, "almost like an abuse" ("*quasi come un soppruso*"), but

---

57 D'Annunzio, *Taccuini*, 56–57; italics in original.

that it engendered a man who was himself, in turn, capable of domination. If the Aegean is so bewildering that the poet must turn away in horror, retreat into the safety of the yacht, take shelter in the museum, and ultimately abandon the tour altogether, the same vision of the Aegean convinces him that the ancient Hellenes had an altogether superior spirit. D'Annunzio's nationalist ideas regarding the Italian "stock" (*stirpe*) will emerge with greater clarity later, yet here already D'Annunzio implies that the Romans, as the direct descendants of the ancient Greeks, were the inheritors of a bold and unrelenting superiority. D'Annunzio rewrites Nietzsche: the birth of the "magnificent personality of the ancient Hellenes" occurs through their ability to dominate—one dares say, to colonize—their surroundings. D'Annunzio has reinterpreted Nietzsche's "will to power" as not so much a release from the slave mentality of Judeo-Christian morality as a colonial moment in which the will to dominate the "natural" or feminine (and feminizing) landscape of the Orient results in a "continual stimulation" and a "continually inspired energy and will," and the rebirth of masculinity.

D'Annunzio concludes his account of the Aegean with a fragmented description of a visit to a museum in Eleusi near Athens on his return trip (meanwhile Hérelle, Scarfoglio, and Boggiani continued on to Constantinople) that reinforces the gendered and racial hierarchies that underpin the entire tour. There, D'Annunzio observes a "lifeless" sculpture of three women who remind him of snakes on the head of Medusa, who turned to stone any man who gazed at her, in what Freud contended was a metaphor for an erection. But as these snakes multiply before D'Annunzio's eyes, the image leaves D'Annunzio limp and flaccid.[58] Indeed, this sculpture stands in stark counterpoint to the erotic worship of masculine perfection in the description of the Hermes by Praxiteles. For D'Annunzio, these women appear as demonic: grotesque, and deformed into improbable positions, contorted into poses that render them "against nature," as in the subject of Huysman's great decadent novel *Au rebours*. Their phantasmagoric appearance recalls to D'Annunzio lesbian queens, one of whom holds a commanding scepter, are "encircled by slaves," and dominate through deviance; they are "against nature" in terms of their sexuality and in terms of their dominance over men. D'Annunzio calls the sculpture (and

---

58   On the various interpretations of the Medusa throughout history, see Marjorie B. Garber and Nancy Vickers, *The Medusa Reader* (New York: Routledge, 2003). Of all of them, Freud's is certainly the most well-known. See also Bernheimer, "Fetishism as Decadence," 62–83.

his sketch of it) "caricatures" of Asia Minor, and reveals—had the idea not emerged clearly enough already—that D'Annunzio's terror of the Orient is linked to a terrorizing and deviant femininity, to a horrifying lack of virility, or, as in the Freudian theory of fetishism, a horrifying lack of the male member.

D'Annunzio thus correlates Greece with the possibility of finding an uncanny homeland where women are either absent or "corrected" into men through art, and where men are "free" to recuperate a dominant spirit of conquest. If D'Annunzio is unable to arrive in this imaginary and idealized version of Greece, because he remains thwarted by the decadent and feminine realities of an Ottomanized Greece, his homoerotic sea still presages his transformation after World War I into just such a dominant man, a public figure well known for his embrace of the crowd and for his exhortatory speeches to galvanize his troops during the siege of Fiume.

Before leaving Pescara, D'Annunzio had charged Hérelle, whom he had met only once before, with finding specific editions of Thucydides in Paris to bring on the cruise. Not long after embarking, D'Annunzio, standing at the prow, reads aloud from it "an example of military eloquence," an exhortatory speech from the Athenian attempt to dominate Syracuse and annex Sicily into the Hellenistic Empire.[59] He remarks that "the prose of Thucydides gives us a sense of clarity and force that is even more powerful *(potente).*"[60] Similar to the ways in which he has reversed the Homeric poetics of a return home to enable him to "return" to being an even more virile man, D'Annunzio declaims Thucydides to write a new page in ancient history— one with clearly very modern implications for Italian national identity. As he grandiloquently recites the words of an Athenian general on a mission to Hellenize the Italian South, D'Annunzio not only anticipates the classical phase in his writings that ensued after his return from Greece—as well as his speeches at Fiume—but he claims the South as in some way *already* Greek; he unites his Southern identity with the ancient imperial order of Magna Grecia.

---

59   On the evolution of D'Annunzio's ideas about "race" or "stock" and their connection to the Nietzschean and classical context see Jared M. Becker, *Nationalism and Culture: Gabriele D'Annunzio and Italy after the Risorgimento* (New York: Peter Lang, 1994).
60   *"Propongo di leggere qualche pagina di Tucidide. Leggo la meravigliosa narrazione di una battaglia navale nel porto di Siracusa, intramezzata dalle concioni dei capitani. La concione di Nicia è un esemplare di eloquenza militare. L'aria è limpida ma la prosa di Tucidide ci dà una sensazione di limpidità e di forza anche più potente."* Gabriele D'Annunzio, *Taccuini*, 24.

It is worth considering briefly here the parallels between D'Annunzio's notions of Magna Grecia and the birth of Mussolini's *mare nostrum*, and his new "imperial man" after the invasion of Ethiopia. D'Annunzio's 1895 voyage to Greece marks him as establishing his identity as a man from the *imperially* Hellenized landscape of Pescara and the Adriatic. As D'Annunzio compares Ottomanized Greece to the picturesque maritime landscape of Pescara and Puglia (in ways that mirror the same dynamics in *Le novelle di Pescara*), the Italian South retrospectively becomes a "familiar" place that is replete with historical echoes of Magna Graecia and adjacent to the birthplace of the ancient Hellenes. D'Annunzio eviscerates all sense that Puglia is a place of national failure or compromise. As a native of the Hellenized South, D'Annunzio is a man for whom an imperial Greece is the roots of his identity. His voyage to Greece thus marks the conversion of a decadent fetishism of the past (*passatismo*) into a futurist and colonial representation of the ancient past. And though the search for an *oikos* in Greece largely turns inward on itself—and reverses when it encounters the uncanny in an Ottomanized Greece—the journey also equates Greece with a "powerful virility" that will come to his aid during the conquest of the Adriatic. Thus, like Mussolini would do some years later in his rhetoric of *mare nostrum*, empire refers not just to the possibility of wealth or the markets to be obtained through overseas colonization, but more importantly to the rebirth of culture and identity at home.

Giuseppe Sergi's Afro-Mediterranean *Urheimat*

At about the same time that D'Annunzio attempted a spiritual rebirthing on the deck of a yacht cruising through the Aegean, Giuseppe Sergi was studying prehistoric skulls from the same region in hopes of identifying the original "stock," or race, that had arrived in Italy after populating the Aegean and wider Mediterranean region. In 1895, Giuseppe Sergi published *Origine e diffusione della stirpe mediterranea*, introducing a theory of *mediterraneità*, or Mediterraneanism into Italian culture. *Mediterraneità* would endure until the Fascist regime adopted the concept of *romanità* in 1938 as a way to define a clear line on Italy's racial politics with respect to Hitler's Germany, but *romanità* arguably owes much of its architecture to Sergi's earlier theories of a Mediterranean race. Translated into English and published five years after the Italian edition as *The Mediterranean Race*, the book not only received wide international recognition for its research but also marked a distinctly imperial turn in debates among Italian anthropologists about the racial identity of Italians.[61]

Sergi's theory responded to positivist and criminal anthropologist theories of race in the Italian postunification context as well as to the increasing anxieties caused by competing arguments that multiple, very different, "races" had populated the Italian Peninsula in prehistoric times. Cesare Lombroso, perhaps the most well-known author of this positivist school, argued, famously, that Northern and Southern Italy had been populated by different races and that Southerners were more prone to criminality due to a combination of atavism and racial degeneration encouraged by the South's proximity to Africa.[62] Against this backdrop, Sergi posits a primordial unity that can nevertheless accommodate racial diversity. His multiethnic ideal of the ancient Mediterranean, as will be seen, was important not only for thinking about the Italian Peninsula as a place that was originally inhabited by multiple ethnicities and yet remained unified, but also for thinking about how the whole of the Mediterranean constituted a regional unity in ancient history. In *The Mediterranean Race* Sergi further locates the origins of the ancient Etruscan civilization in East Africa and directly links the birth of ancient Rome to a prehistoric race that had once had as its cradle the Horn of Africa. Like D'Annunzio's tour of Greece, then, Sergi's genealogy has obvious connections to the overarching political context of Crispi's East African advance and closely unites a prehistoric and speculative colonization of Africa and the Mediterranean with Italy's expansionist goals at the time.

Sergi recenters the origin of civilization along an East African, Libyan, and eastern Mediterranean axis, in ways that are doubtless prophetic of Italy's expansionist goals, but also revealing of how Italian expansionism aligned with issues and debates about Italian national identity. The national-imperial goals that underpin Sergi's theory of *mediterraneità* also directly respond to the international climate and to the predominance of theories of Aryanism, or Indo-Europeanism, which had helped to diminish the importance of Roman history. As Martin Bernal has shown, until the mid-nineteenth century, scholars had taken for granted the Egyptian and Levantine origins of ancient Greek civilization. But with the rise of Indo-Europeanist theories of Aryanism, linguists, archaeologists, and classicists had abandoned the

---

61   De Donno, *Italian Orientalism*, 200.

62   See Mary Gibson, "Biology or Environment? Race and Southern 'Deviancy' in the Writings of Italian Criminologists, 1880–1920," in *Italy's "Southern Question": Orientalism in One Country*, edited by Jane Schneider, 99–115 (Oxford: Berg, 1998).

Afro-Mediterranean origins of Greece in favor of a theory that "there had been an invasion from the north—unreported in ancient tradition—which had overwhelmed the local 'Aegean' or 'Pre-Hellenic' culture."[63] Giuseppe Sergi's theory of *mediterraneità* is a rebuttal of the Indo-Europeanists who had assimilated ancient Greece into an Aryanist narrative. In other words, Sergi's theory of *mediterraneità* responds not only to a "crisis of origins" internal to debates about Northern and Southern differences, but also to the rise of Indo-Europeanism.

Sergi initiates *The Mediterranean Race* with an attack on recent claims by his colleagues that the Aryans, after populating Northern Europe, had invaded the Mediterranean basin and subjugated its population. With reference to prehistoric skull size, Sergi argues that "since it is difficult to find the Germans in their own home we cannot expect to find them as Aryan stock in Greece and Italy, subjugating the dark populations and creating the two great Mediterranean civilizations, Hellenic and Latin, also called Aryan" (*"se è difficile ritrovarli in casa loro, non possono trovarsi, come stirpe aria, nella Grecia e nell'Italia, quali soggiogatori delle popolazioni brune e quali creatori delle due grandi civiltà mediterranee, dette anche arie, l'ellenica e la Latina"*).[64] Sergi decries the so-called "Homeric evidence" advanced by a Germanist school of thought that posited that the early Greek heroes had been described by Homer as blonde:

> I cannot pass over in silence the supposed testimony to the presence of the fair type in Greece, and to its superiority over the darker population, furnished by the Homeric poems, in which, it is affirmed, the heroes and gods are described as of the fair type with blue eyes.

> *Ma non posso passare in silenzio ciò che si afferma come argomento della presenza del tipo Biondo in Grecia e della sua superiorità sul Bruno, la testimonianza che si stima ricavare dai poemi omerici, nei quali, si afferma, gli eroi e gli dèi sono descritti come tipi biondi con occhi cerulei.*[65]

---

63   Martin Bernal, *Black Athena: The Afroasiatic Roots of Classical Civilization* (New Brunswick, NJ: Rutgers University Press, 1987), 2.

64   Giuseppe Sergi, *The Mediterranean Race: A Study of the Origins of European People*, edited by Philip Lamantia (New York: Scribner and Sons, 1909), 18; Sergi, *Origine e diffusione della stirpe mediterranea* (Rome: Dante Alighieri Society, 1895), 19–20.

65   Sergi, *The Mediterranean Race*, 18. Sergi, *Origine e diffusione della stirpe mediterranea*, 20.

Sergi's rebuttal of the so-called Indo-Europeanists (also known as Indo-Germanists) pivots on the meanings ascribed to the Greek words "*glaukos*" and "*xanthos.*" Sergi not only argues that to translate these words as "blue" and "blonde" respectively reduces if not perverts their meaning as Homer intended it, but also gives a long catalog of how the Homeric deities were described in all other terms but the ethnographic ones. He concludes that "in Homer none of the divinities are fair in the ethnographic sense" ("*in Omero nessuna divinità è bionda nel significato etnografico della parola*").[66] In turning to the case of the ancient Greeks—as explicitly not fair—Sergi intends to give further currency to the belief that Italians and Greeks were a "Mediterranean" people whose pigmentation may have been defined by environmental rather than biological factors.[67]

The Indo-Germanist theory of an invasion of the Mediterranean basin from the north—however distantly placed in human prehistory—was moreover an affront to one of the main rhetorical conceits of the Italian unification, that is, that the modern Italian nation-state was in direct racial lineage with the Roman Empire. Sergi himself had fought as a member of Garibaldi's army, and it is therefore not surprising that his theory of a Mediterranean race should reprise nationalist tropes of the unification. But set against the new backdrop of Ottoman decline, the memory of Roman Empire becomes infused with notions of the Greco-Roman world. Like D'Annunzio, who saw in Greece the possibility of modernist rebirth, Sergi believed it was essential to recall the ancient Greeks into discussions about the birth of modern European civilization. In Sergi's case, the role of ancient Greece in this narrative draws biology into it. His theory of *mediterraneità* pivots on his recuperation of the primordial consanguinity of the *italogreci*, or Greco-Roman stock, that had emerged as dominant, thus hewing to the social Darwinism that underpinned all theories of race (and recalls D'Annunzio's own appropriation of Nietzsche). As Sergi traces out a genealogy of a Mediterranean race that originated in East Africa, migrated northward, and then sprouted diverse and vital branches, it is with the emergence of the *italogreci*, Sergi claims, that prehistory bears witness to the first truly "modern" civilization. Again in ways quite similar to D'Annunzio, Sergi sees the Aegean

---

66   Sergi, *The Mediterranean Race*, 20; Sergi, *Origine e diffusione della stirpe mediterranea*, 20–21.

67   Discussions of skin tone in the nineteenth century, and Sergi's place within these, are admirably treated by David Forgacs in *Italy's Margins: Social Exclusion and National Formation since 1861* (Cambridge: Cambridge University Press, 2016), 103–16.

as containing the answer to the riddle of the "true" spirit that led to the rise of the Roman Empire. Claiming to combine findings from physical anthropology, archaeology, and linguistics, Sergi compares the Mediterranean to an elusive classical figure—"The Mediterranean is a sphinx with various faces, and to solve its enigma we need to know the stock or stocks that have peopled it" (*"Il Mediterraneo è una sfinge a diverse apparenze e figure, e un mezzo di soluzione dell'enigma dovrà essere la cognizione della stirpe o delle stirpi che l'hanno popolato"*).[68]

Yet, however elusive the Mediterranean may be for Sergi, it is clear that to him it was "never a homogenous nation" (*"un'identica nazione"*) in the way that his German colleagues were presenting their own prehistory at the time.[69] By pointing to the existence of the *italogreci*, Sergi gives a biological rationale for the previously accepted notion that Greco-Roman civilization had prospered precisely through cross-cultural fertilization and diversity. Indeed, Sergi's theory directly contradicts the Indo-Europeanist theories of Arthur de Gobineau, for example, who argued that a degeneration of the Latin race had occurred through miscegenation between Romans and the African and Asian subjects of the empire.[70] The heterogeneity within the Mediterranean will still, however, prove "nationally" homogenous.

In addition to reviving the notion of the vitality of the Greco-Roman world, Sergi's theory further challenges his German colleagues' discussions regarding language and the *urheimat*, or original homeland of the proto-Europeans. Sergi directs his polemic against a new school of German philologists, Franz Bopp predominant among them, who, in bringing "science" to bear on the study of language, set the stage for ethno-nationalist narratives of ethnic purity. As Edward Said has said of Bopp, "the study of language entailed its own history, philosophy, and learning, all of which did away with any notion of a primal language given by Godhead to man in Eden."[71] Yet the work of these pioneering philologists to disprove the theory of an Edenic language in turn produced the notion of "families" of languages, giving rise to debates about prehistoric tribes that mirrored both contemporary rivalries among

---

68   Sergi, *The Mediterranean Race*, 24; Sergi, *Origine e diffusione della stirpe mediterranea*, 33.

69   Sergi, *The Mediterranean Race*, 17; Sergi, *Origine e diffusione della stirpe mediterranea*, 17.

70   Fabrizio De Donno, "La Razza Ario-Mediterranea," *Interventions: International Journal of Postcolonial Studies* 8, no. 3 (2006): 396.

71   Said, *Orientalism*, 136.

nation-states and the classification of species that was rampant in the new age of Darwin. That there were "families" of European protolanguages reinforced the notion that there must be an Indo-European language that accounted for their linguistic similarities. From the existence of an Indo-European protolanguage, the nineteenth-century philologists finally speculated that the European peoples must have had a common origin, an *urheimat*, or original homeland, and that it was beyond the Ural Mountains where speakers of Sanskrit (the closest living language to this imagined Indo-European language) could still be found. As the linguist Jean-Paul Demoule has argued, the myth of an Indo-European language was no more than a recasting of a tale of origins, one ironically not very dissimilar from the biblical narrative, in the vein of science and in support of an ethno-national narrative: the search for a fabled homeland to promote a racial concept of the nation.[72] Hence emerged the German claim, derived from Indo-Europeanism, that a mythic Aryan tribe had migrated across the steppes of Asia, originating from somewhere beyond the Ural Mountains, before conquering and dominating the rest of Europe.

If Sergi refutes the idea of an Aryan conquest in the Mediterranean, he invests nevertheless in modeling his own version of that narrative and proposes that an early migration by an Afro-Mediterranean tribe originally populated the Aegean and then Italy. In turn, he brings to these debates about philology and early migrations a uniquely Mediterraneanist perspective that seeks to reinforce the idea of Italian ethnicity or "stock" while rejoining it to the earlier narrative of a Greco-Roman world that had been vitiated in the move toward scientific Aryanism. Sergi closely reproduces the notion of an *urheimat* but assimilates it to the new coordinates of Italian expansion into the Mediterranean and East Africa. Indeed, the alternative that he offers to Indo-Europeanism, or Aryanism, is a Mediterraneanism that echoes the ethno-nationalism of the Aryanists, while locating the *urheimat* of the Roman Empire in East Africa, in exactly the region that the Italian state was attempting to conquer at the time. He supplants the notion of Aryan conquest, however, with the peaceful diffusion of the Mediterranean "stock" afforded by environmental factors. Envisioning the islands of the Aegean acting as miniature bridges to enable the early civilizations to cross from one to another, he imagines a great primordial migration across the Mediterranean Sea:

72   Jean-Paul Demoule, *Mais où sont passés les Indo-Européens: Le mythe d'Origine de l'Occident* (Paris: Editions du Seuil, 2014).

Bathed by the waters of the Mediterranean, Europe is separated from the two great continents with which it forms the basin, on the east by the Hellespont, and on the west by the Straits of Gibraltar, but these waters are no obstacles to the progress of migration, nor are the more ample waters of the whole Mediterranean, since the innumerable islands scattered over it serve as bridges or stations, and the peninsulas stretch out their arms towards Africa as though to welcome it. The emigrants had the sea before them, and the evidence shows that at various points they passed over it. It seems that from Egypt, before yet Egypt was known in history, African colonists passed over to Greece by the islands, perhaps first of all Crete; from the region of Numidia they probably crossed over into Sicily, Sardinia, Southern, Central, and Northern Italy, Southern France.

L'Europa bagnata dal Mediterraneo è separata dalle acque dai grandi continenti che con essa formano il bacino, a oriente dall'Ellesponto, a occidente dallo stretto di Gibilterra; ma queste acque non sono ostacolo al progredire delle emigrazioni, come non lo sono le acque più ampie di tutto il Mediterraneo, dove a guisa di ponti o di stazioni sono sparse innumerevoli isole, e le penisole protendono le loro braccia all'Africa, quasi per accoglierla. L'immigrazione della stirpe aveva il mare davanti, e i documenti che abbiamo dimostrano che lo valicò in diversi luoghi. Pare che dall'Egitto, quando ancora non era l'Egitto conosciuto nella storia, i coloni africani siansi trasferiti in Grecia passando per le isole, in Creta prima forse; dalla regione che fu Numidia passarono in Sicilia, Sardegna, Italia meridionale, centrale, setten-trionale, Francia meridionale.[73]

In Sergi's narrative, not only does Europe "welcome" the emigrants coming from Africa and the Levant, who "had the sea before them," but this early migration in fact populates the entire southern rim of Europe. This reorientation not only casts East Africa as the origin of European populations, in alignment with the campaigns in East Africa at this time, but it also suggests that a "natural" emigration of peoples across the Mediterranean preceded the founding of the Roman Empire.

It is worth briefly considering how Sergi's vision of a prehistoric migration and colonization of the Mediterranean coheres with larger political debates

---

73   Sergi, *The Mediterranean Race*, 158; Sergi, *Origine e diffusione della stirpe mediter-ranea*, 64.

at this time. By claiming the Mediterranean as an "anthropological unit" and the "center of civilization and dispersion," Sergi creates a prehistoric locus that mirrors the great migrations also happening at this time, especially those emigrations from Southern Italy, some of them directed across the Atlantic to North and South America, but many of them radiating throughout the Mediterranean. As Mark Choate has shown, the Italian state imagined the massive emigration to North and South America as a form of "pacific" colonialism, with Italian culture spreading through language, settlement, and commerce, rather than through imperial conquest.[74] Choate has also demonstrated that Italian emigration in North and South America encouraged the project to cultivate national identity, prompting the Italian state to disseminate *italianità* both at home and abroad. If Sergi's primordial northward diaspora is thus the imaginative foundation for Roman civilization, it also implies that contemporary Italian migration into Africa could constitute a "return" to a primordial homeland. In other words, Sergi's theory of *mediterraneità,* or Mediterraneanism, folds biological ideas of race into larger constructions of national identity and mobility at the time, arguably linking the Mediterranean with the propensity of Italians to migrate.

Seen from this perspective, Sergi's theory also reveals itself as closely aligned with Italian agricultural programs to resettle in East Africa the landless peasantry from the South. While just a few years later—namely in *Arii e Italici* (1898), or *The Aryans and the Ancient Italians*—Sergi will make concessions to the Indo-Germanist claim that the Italian Peninsula may have experienced an invasion from the north (and hence, concede the idea that there may have been inherent racial differences between the Northern and Southern populations of the Italian Peninsula), in *The Mediterranean Race* Sergi remains intent on identifying a strain of heterogeneity in the origins of the Italian civilization within the Mediterranean, but one that also has decisive racial difference with sub-Saharan Africans. As Cristina Lombardi-Diop and Gaia Giuliani have argued, Sergi was influential in shaping an idea of the Italian race that was heterogeneous but not "contaminated" by African stock—that is, Mediterranean but not black.[75] Sergi is therefore grouped with Lombroso as one of the early racialist thinkers who anticipate the "racist" turn in the Fascist state after 1936; however, this grouping elides that Sergi has much in common with the more "liberal" nationalist thinkers in the

---

74 Choate, *Emigrant Nation.*
75 Gaia Giuliani and Cristina Lombardi-Diop, *Bianco e nero: Storia dell'identità razziale degli italiani* (Florence: Le Monnier, 2013), 21–32.

same time period who also saw colonization of Africa as the best alternative for the South's "moral, economic, and political regeneration." As Rhiannon Noel-Welch has demonstrated, the liberal humanist projects of the *meridionalisti* (Southernists) to improve the life of peasants in Italy's South—such as those espoused by persons such as Pasquale Villari, Leopoldo Franchetti, Sidney Sonnino, and Giustino Fortunato—have much in common with the explicitly racialist writings of figures like Sergi.[76] The point of Sergi's writings is precisely the way in which they are able to unite concerns about promoting nationalism and the nation-state in Italy through the project of empire: the metaphor of the Mediterranean (or *mediterraneità*) had the power to suggest that Italians were potentially returning "home" to East Africa (through Italy's colonial projects) and firmly tethered empire to nation.

Sergi's apparent embrace of Southernism has in the past attracted many scholars' interest, especially for how his theories of Italian race both corroborate and disrupt the Lombroso vision of two races in Italy. Yet Sergi ultimately follows Lombroso in his insistence that Italy was marked by several phases of migrations—not northern (Aryan) and southern (African) migrations, however—but one from the South, and one from the east, or Levant, that occurred after the first civilized world developed in the Aegean. Sergi embraces an apparently "liberal" attitude about the level of civilization of ancient societies in Africa by suggesting that it was also "branches" of the Mediterranean (or Italo-Greek) stock that may have populated North Africa in prehistoric times, thus making North Africans superior to sub-Saharan Africans, and opening up the potential for some biological similarities with Italians. His anthropological theories ultimately rehearse the late-nineteenth-century obsession with the division of Africa and the eastern Mediterranean among tribes, protectorates, "spheres of influence," and nation-states, all of these deserving of autonomy in ratio to their level of civilization. His taxonomy of the Egyptian and Libyan "families" of the Mediterranean race, in particular, indicates the wider European view that, with the Ottoman Empire weakened, the moment was ripe for a "soft" expansion into North Africa.

It is Sergi's contribution to Mussolini's biological ideas of race, however, that has made him the subject of critical scrutiny in recent years.[77] His

76   Rhiannon Noel-Welch, *Vital Subjects: Race and Biopolitics in Italy* (Liverpool: Liverpool University Press, 2016), 54.

77   See Lucia Re, "Italians and the Invention of Race: The Poetics and Politics of Difference in the Struggle over Libya, 1890–1913," *California Italian Studies* 1, no. 1

hypothesis that there was, in prehistoric times, a Eurafrican population that went on to populate the Italian Peninsula and to found Rome has striking resonance with the rhetoric of empire that followed the 1936 invasion of Ethiopia, when Mussolini claimed that Eurafrica was now an economic and national project and commenced work on a trans-African railway that started in Tripoli.[78] A key part of this discursive "whitening" of the Italian character in Sergi's vision of Eurafrica occurs through his return to the idea of Greece and the revival of the status of Greek culture within the Roman Empire. After describing the Egyptian and Libyan "families," Sergi goes on to indicate the names of the three "families" that populated Europe: the Iberians, the Ligurians, and the Pelasgians. This last of these is first mentioned in Homer, and was said to have originated in the Aegean and to have given birth to the ancient Homeric and then Hellenic civilizations, before arriving in the Italian Peninsula as Etruscans. Sergi says that, like his Mediterranean Sphinx, the Pelasgians have been shrouded in mystery, but their full examination and emergence will ultimately resolve the whole riddle of the Italian question:

> The solution of the Pelasgian problem will also be the solution to the Etruscan problem, for the relation of the Etruscans to the Pelasgians is no longer doubtful. [...] The Etruscans are western Pelasgians, while the Pelasgic family chiefly extends between Greece and Asia Minor.[79]

In returning to the idea of the Pelasgians, Sergi shows himself again to be committed to older theories about the origins of civilization while contending that Greeks and Italians are not just part of the same Mediterranean race, but members of the same "family" within it. Indeed, in referring to these fabled Pelasgians as the *italogreci*, he consolidates their prehistoric consanguinity

(2010): 1–59; Gaia Giuliani, "L'Italiano Negro: The Politics of Colour in Early Twentieth-Century Italy," *Interventions* 16, no. 4 (2014): 572–87; Giovanna Trento, "From Marinetti to Pasolini: Massawa, the Red Sea, and the Construction of 'Mediterranean Africa' in Italian Literature and Cinema," *Northeast African Studies* 12, no.1 (2012): 273–307.

78   Ruth Ben-Ghiat, "Modernity Is Just Over There: Colonialism and Italian National Identity," *Interventions* 8, no. 3 (2006): 380–93, 389.

79   Sergi, *The Mediterranean Race*, 165–66. Sergi's ideas on the Pelasgians are not included in the Italian edition of *Origini e diffusione della stirpe mediterranea*. However, they can be found in his earlier work, *Etruschi e Pelasgi* (Rome: Nuova Antologia, 1893). In *Origini e diffusione della stirpe mediterranea*, Sergi notes, "*Il ramo della stirpe mediterranea che creò la civiltà egea, fu senza dubbio il pelasgico*," 103.

linguistically. If Sergi attacks his Germanist colleagues for their desire to imagine a "homogenous nation," his ideas of heterogeneity through cross-Mediterranean fertilization restore the traditional routes of the Roman world extending particularly their connection to the eastern Aegean. This earlier narrative was of course a deeply familiar one and one told by none other than by the poet laureate of the Roman Empire, Virgil himself.

Unlike many of Sergi's Germanist colleagues, moreover, for whom the new science of race was rooted solely in Darwinian selection and biology, Sergi still clings to an older tradition that invoked the idea of a noble lineage, or *stirpe* ("stock"). By not abandoning the idea of "stock" entirely, refusing to exchange it for the newer, more scientific idea of race, or *razza*, Sergi helps to ensure the preservation of the notion of direct lineage from antiquity, and, indeed, his text can be interpreted as an attempt to adapt older narratives of the ancient world within the new science of race. Sergi uses the two terms interchangeably; *stirpe* and *razza* tend to be "mobile signifiers" in the Italian language, and to this day they do not carry the same biological connotations of genetic difference that their corresponding terms usually do in English.[80] For Sergi, then, the idea of "race" needs to be reconceived so that it can still hew closely to a version of history that posits the modern Italian nation-state as the direct descendant of Roman antiquity. What sets the Pelasgian (or Italo-Greek) family apart from the other "families" of the Mediterranean race is that it was the one to produce "modernity" and to endure into the present day.[81] It is also, according to Sergi, the Mediterranean that "produced the most favorable conditions for the development of a more cosmopolitan civilization" (*"Il Mediterraneo ha presentato le condizioni più favorevoli allo svolgimento della civiltà, e d'una civiltà più cosmopolita che non fosse quella nata e sviluppata nelle valli dei grandi fiumi"*).[82]

Sergi's Mediterranean "cosmopolitanism" is an ethnically pure one. Although the author is intent on casting East Africa as the original cradle of a "Eurafrican" civilization, the Mediterranean stock's departure from East

---

80   Noel-Welch, *Vital Subjects*, 127–29. See also Re, "Italians and the Invention of Race," 1–59.

81   Sergi maintains that "a differenza della civiltà latina che ancor vive, più o meno trasformata, nella vita sociale odierna," *Origini e diffusione della stirpe mediterranea*, 41.

82   *The Mediterranean Race*, 30; *Origini e diffusione della stirpe mediterranea*, 41. On environment and Sergi's myth of the Mediterranean, see Fedra Pizzato, "How Landscapes Make Science: Italian National Narrative, The Great Mediterranean, and Giuseppe Sergi's Biological Myth," in *Mediterranean Identities: Environment, Society and Culture*, edited by Borna Fuerst-Bjelis, 79–98 (Rijeka: Croatia in Tech, 2017).

Africa proves an almost total abandonment of it. He maintains that the lightness of skin of the Eritrean and Ethiopian may be the result of "mixing" between the Mediterranean and "negroid" races during prehistoric times. This concession to the superiority of Eritreans and Ethiopians, because of some prehistoric contact with the progenitors of the Italo-Greeks, was consonant with wider beliefs about racial hierarchies in Africa at the time.[83] But elsewhere in the colonial project, the notion of racial "mixing" helped to promote the view that expansion was a necessity. Cesare Correnti, an early missionary in Italian East Africa and the eventual founder of the Italian Geographic Society, said that Africa's influence on the Mediterranean was the reason that Italy should be involved in African colonization: "It is our destiny. This mysterious horizon [Africa] locks us in, makes the Mediterranean semi-barbaric, and puts Italy at the outer edge of the civilized world."[84] The "return" of the Italo-Greeks to East Africa that is implicit in Sergi's narrative is one that finally rests on the idea of restoring racial hierarchies.

Like D'Annunzio's journey through Greece, Sergi's ideas of the *italogreci*, or Greco-Roman race, seek to "restore" and "regenerate" not merely Italian nationalism, but the ethnic lineage and purity of the Italian nation. The Dannunzian poetics of a surrogate birth at sea, followed by a dangerous recognition of decline and decadence, are visible in Sergi with regard to the larger question of whether African colonial "returns" could restore the biological and moral health of the Italian nation (while redirecting emigrants to national spaces), or whether it would unmake Italians. Such views perhaps reflect a long tradition of thinking about Italy as a bridge to Africa, of which "Africa begins at Naples" is the most stereotypical expression.[85] Against such

---

83　See Forgacs, *Italy's Margins*, 105.

84　"È una predestinazione. Ci sta sugli occhi da tanti secoli questo libro suggellato, quest'orizzonte misterioso, che ci chiude lo spazio, che ci rende semibarbaro il Mediterraneo, che costringe l'Italia a trovarsi sugli ultimi confini del mondo civile." The quotation appeared in a 1940 exhibition about nineteenth-century African missionaries that commemorated the creation of Italy's colonial empire. It may be remembered that another quotation by Correnti opens Angelo Del Boca's monumental history of Italian colonialism in East Africa. Angelo Del Boca, *Gli italiani in Africa orientale* (Rome: Laterza, 1976).

85　As Pasquale Verdicchio has noted, this stereotype was intimately connected to Italy's own diaspora and it was certainly influential on Italian debates about African expansion in the late nineteenth century. Pasquale Verdicchio, *Bound by Distance: Rethinking Nationalism through the Italian Diaspora* (Madison, NJ: Fairleigh Dickinson Press, 1997).

a viewpoint, both D'Annunzio and Sergi, Greece represents the possibility of positive, revitalizing memories of the Mediterranean. They desire a "Latin Renaissance," a nostalgic position, one that longs for a *nostos*, or a return home by sea.[86]

Reading these two texts together thus reveals Greece as already a third but essential term within Italy's nineteenth-century projects for empire in Africa. The Aegean, the archetypal setting of ancient Greece, mediates the racial negotiation at stake in an Italian advance into Africa. Greece allows both these authors to invest in the ideas of Mediterranean unity and Latin regeneration, yet also to efface potential anxieties about national and racial degeneration within Italy. In both cases, the literary testing of these colonial waters precipitates failure—a turning back from the Orient in D'Annunzio's case, and an unresolved picture as to what degree the generative powers of the Mediterranean sea had insulated the Italian people against the threat of "contamination" posed by Africa in Sergi's theory.

Much later, when the conquest of Ethiopia led Mussolini to officially declare empire in 1936, and then, while visiting Libya in 1937, to proclaim himself the leader of the Muslim world, theories of a Mediterranean race would disappear from circulation and be replaced with *romanità*, or Romanness. As chapters 2 and 3 will explore in full, *romanità* was a racial as well as aesthetic theory that was anti-Semitic (as well as anti-Levantine), asserted Italian supremacy over conquered peoples, and eschewed any suggestion of cultural or ethnic intimacy with the eastern Mediterranean region. Sergi's sense of *mediterraneità* is a clear ideological precedent for many of the views that Italian state actors eventually espoused in the campaign to integrate the Aegean islands, at least partially, into the Italian nation-state. Unlike Lombroso, who at times considered Jews as members of the Italian race, Sergi was unequivocal that the Mediterranean race was not a Semitic one.[87] While the introduction of policies of biological racism and anti-Semitism has often been viewed as a moment of rupture, one linked to the formation of the Axis alliance, scholars have increasingly called for racial laws' contextualization within Italy's demographic campaigns both at home and abroad. This

---

86   On D'Annunzio and Sergi's mutual concern for a "Latin Renaissance," see Fabrizio De Donno, "Routes to Modernity: Orientalism and Mediterraneanism in Italian Culture, 1810–1910," *California Italian Studies Journal* 1, no. 1 (2010): 1–23.

87   Lombroso, of course, was himself Jewish. See Paul Knepper, "Lombroso's Jewish Identity and its Implications for Criminology," *Australian and New Zealand Journal of Criminology* 44, no. 3 (2011): 355–69.

close interrogation of D'Annunzio's Sergi's texts further reveals the degree to which myths of racial and cultural *mediterraneità*, of restoring a Greco-Roman world of Magna Grecia, circulated during the era of the African campaigns. Such discussions also paved the way for an eventual colonization in the Mediterranean that began in 1911–12 with the Italo-Turkish War.

Rhodes: A New Pompei

While the issue of Italian emigration is absent in D'Annunzio, and remains latent in Sergi, it is clearly visible in discussions of empire in the Mediterranean by 1912, when Italy advanced on the Aegean to shore up its conquest of North Africa. Immediately following the taking of the Dodecanese in 1912, Luigi Federzoni and Enrico Corradini, the two firebrand leaders of the Italian Nationalist Association, which had championed the Libyan campaign, traveled across the Aegean to report on the Italian action there. In his account, Federzoni proclaimed Italy's sweeping victory by ventriloquizing it in the thick, syncopating dialect of a Neapolitan. He made clear, in his paraphrase of a gunner identifying Constantinople as Italy's next territory of conquest, that Italy's victory was one championed for and also by the South:

> "Rhodes to us ... Do you want to give it to us? The prisoners hurried to cede Rhodes to us." The gunner, crossing his arms and staring at each one of them in their eyes, spit out the syllables: "Constantinople for us" ... a rush of dismay swept over the crowd of listeners ... These Italians are becoming truly insatiable!"

> *"Rodi a nuie ... Ci 'a vulite dà? I prigioneri intimoriti si affrettano a cedere anche Rodi." Allora il cannoniere, incrociando le braccia e fissandoli a uno a uno negli occhi, spiccica le sillabe: "Custantinopule a nuie" ... un moto di sgomento corre nella folla degli uditori ... Questi italiani sono diventati davvero incontentabili!"*[88]

When the Italian navy captured Rhodes and the twelve other Dodecanese islands it provided Italy with a strategic maritime blockade to thwart cabotage, or the trafficking of arms from Anatolia into North Africa. More

---

88 Luigi Federzoni [Giulio de Frenzi, pseud.], *L'Italia nell'Egeo* (Rome: G. Garzoni Provenzani, 1913), 108.

importantly, the seizing of the islands also acted as a pressure point on the Turks regarding reprisals toward Italian emigrant communities in Constantinople and the eastern Aegean. These were being widely reported in the Italian media at the time (see figure 1.1: cover of a 1912 issue of *La Domenica del Corriere*).

The major theme in nationalist writings at this time in support of the conquest was to be the vindication of Italy's emigrant masses in the Mediterranean—in Turkey, but also Tunisia. As scholars have already noted, the approximate 4.5 million Italians who emigrated between 1870 and 1924 were largely from rural backgrounds, and in many ways, emigration was deeply entangled with the economic depression that had ensued in the South following the unification of Italy.[89] While the vast majority of this migration was directed toward North and South America, Italians by the hundreds of thousands had also emigrated throughout the Mediterranean basin into North Africa and other areas of Ottoman decline.[90]

Capture of the Dodecanese forced the Turks to consent to the Treaty of Ouchy, in which Italy agreed that the Italian state would return the islands to the Ottoman Empire only when all Turks had evacuated North Africa. The agreement was virtually impossible to uphold and assured that Italy would, a decade later, be in a position to annex the islands permanently.[91] Yet conquest in the Aegean in 1912 also served a far more important purpose: it helped to dissuade the public from a perception that the war for North Africa was on its way to failure. Continuing resistance by the Senussi tribes in Libya had prolonged the Italian campaign there. With the memory of defeat in East Africa all too recent, the chronicles of victories in the Aegean by Corradini and Federzoni were certainly meant to shift the public's attention away from the difficult invasion of Libya, and toward a long-held value of Greece as regenerative for the Italian national project. Thus, Federzoni assured the public that even Neapolitans were feeling triumphant in Rhodes, that Italian humiliations as peasants, laborers, and emigrants—many of them under the rule of the French and British empires in the Mediterranean—were ending,

89   See Donna Gabaccia, *Italy's Many Diasporas* (New York: Routledge, 2013), 35–128.

90   Alessandro Pannuti, *La comunita italiana di Istanbul nel XX secolo: Ambiente e persone* (Istanbul: Edizioni ISIS, 2006); Francesco Pongiluppi, *La Rassegna Italiana: Organo degli interessi italiani in Oriente: Giornale Ufficiale della Camera di Commercio Italiana di Constantinopoli* (Istanbul: Edizioni ISIS, 2015).

91   Richard Bosworth, "Britain and Italy's Acquisition of the Dodecanese, 1912–1915," *The Historical Journal* 13, no. 4 (1977): 683–705.

Figure 1.1: Cover illustration of *La Domenica del Corriere*, June 7–9, 1912.
The caption says, "The events of the Italo-Turkish War: the arrival in Naples of Italians, especially workers, expelled by Turkish reprisals" © Biblioteca Marucelliana.

and that a new era of empire that would revive Italy's historic cultural and political preeminence in the Mediterranean was beginning.

Federzoni's enthusiastic assurance that the occupation of Rhodes would lead Italy further into the Ottoman Empire was not without precedent and built on previous travel writings by celebrated authors such as Edmondo De Amicis, a nationalist widely considered one of the most significant writers of the Italian postunification. De Amicis's *Cuore* (*Heart*), published in 1886, which chronicles the adventures of a young Italian boy in Turin, is to this day a textbook in the Italian elementary classroom. A few years before the publication of *Cuore*, in 1881, De Amicis, who was also a celebrated journalist, published an illustrated travelogue, *Constantinopoli*, which prominently featured several descriptions of encounters with Italians in that city. It includes a lengthy discussion of Galata, the neighborhood in Constantinople originally founded by the Genoese merchant community, that exhibits the same patriotic themes of *Cuore* but places these in the context of Turkey. In moves that were to characterize later Italian representations of Rhodes, De Amicis described the pristine and picturesque Italian qualities that could still be perceived underneath Galata's more recent decline.[92] Ali Bedhad has argued that in the late nineteenth century and early twentieth, French travelers to the eastern Mediterranean began to experience the Ottoman Empire with belatedness, already seeing it through the memory of the eighteenth century, when the French Empire was at its height, and with the view that both France and the empire might already be in decline.[93] For these Italian nationalists, on the other hand, there is no belatedness: the picturesque is a "geographic poetics" that signifies the time was ripe for the restoration of the Italian character of these communities and neighborhoods abroad.[94]

De Amicis wanders through Galata, stopping in at an Italian café called Bella vista, and hears Greeks and Turks communicating with one another in Italian barbarisms. It is his description of a chance encounter with a young Italian family that reveals the inextricable link between emigration, the South, and the fantasy of the "picturesque" Levant:

92   Edmondo De Amicis, *Constantinopoli* (Milan: Fratelli Treves, 1881).

93   Ali Behdad, *Belated Travelers: Orientalism in the Age of Colonial Dissolution* (Durham, NC: Duke University Press, 1994).

94   The idea of a "geographic poetics" is explored by Nelson Moe in relation to Verga's Sicilian short stories. As Nelson Moe shows, embraced both a romantic and pessimistic view of the South, which aligned with the political debates about the South in Northern circles at this time. Moe, *The View from Vesuvius*, 250–63.

At that moment a smiling woman came up, carrying a baby in her arms, who told me that she was from Pisa, the wife of a Livorno marble-cutter, that she had lived eight years in Constantinople, and this was her son. If this good woman had been a handsome matron, with a turreted crown upon her head, and a mantle over her shoulders, she could not have represented Italy more vividly to my heart and eyes.

In quel punto mi s'avvicinò una donna con un bimbo in collo, tutta sorridente, e mi disse che era pisana, moglie d'uno scalpellino livornese, che si trovava a Costantinopoli da ott'anni, e che quel ragazzo era suo figlio. Se quella buona donna avesse avuto un bel viso di matrona, una corna turrita sulla testa e un manto sulle spalle, non avrebbe più rappresentato più vivamente l'Italia ai miei occhi e al mio cuore.[95]

De Amicis's clear reference to *Italia turrita*—the allegorical personification of Italy, appearing as a woman with a turreted crown and mantle over the shoulders—takes on a new rhetorical meaning here, and in the context of De Amicis's colorful descriptions of Constantinople, refers also to the Levantine costume worn by its European inhabitants. This woman's humble appearance, with a babe in her arms, similarly evokes the representation of the South at this time, especially as presented in the works of Giovanni Verga, whose romantic and fictionalized representation of the South would do considerable work in the construction of the South as a space to be redeemed for the national project.

In embracing the resurgence of Italians in the Mediterranean, Federzoni, De Amicis, and Corradini sought to vindicate the hundreds of thousands of Italians living in the region and laboring under the flags of the French and British. To a certain extent, these writers applied this same idea to some of Italy's Greek "cousins." Of the two possible resolutions to the Balkan question in the Aegean—the expansion of Italy's Mediterranean Empire or the integration of the Aegean into an expanding Greek nation-state—it was obvious to Federzoni that the former was preferable, to both Italians and Greeks. The Greek nation-state was far too weak to hold the Aegean against the Ottoman Empire, Federzoni asserted, and Italy would be an ideal ruler, uniquely positioned to understand and reinstate the importance of Greece's ancient past. Federzoni replaced D'Annunzio's ambivalent reaction

95 Edmondo De Amicis, *Constantinople*, translated by Stephen Parkin (London: Hesperus Classics, 2005), 47; Edmondo De Amicis, *Costantinopoli*, 83.

to Greece from 1895 with enthusiasm over the possibility that the war effort in Greece was giving Italy a renewed sense of its national mission and preeminence. But condescending views that modern Greece was a far cry from its prior glory persist. As Federzoni traveled throughout the Aegean on his way to Rhodes to pay homage to the soldiers who had "liberated" the island from Ottoman domination, he described these Greek "cousins" as persons to be pitied rather than disdained: "We reached Greece prejudiced against these poor cousins of ours who try to advance as best they can the enormous weight of their unproductive ancient glory."[96]

Following the topos of a return home by sea, along the lines of Sergi and D'Annunzio, it is in Rhodes that Federzoni finally finds himself at home. His arrival in the island marks the end of his travelogue to Greece and the beginning of a return to Italian soil. He describes how landfall on Rhodes caused the troops with him to feel, in his words, "delight that we had not felt in Tripoli or in any other of the conquered Libyan territories," because of the island's "instinctive sense of the epic." Rhodes was "like an antique jewel of the family" that Italy had unexpectedly come to repossess thanks to its vital spirit of adventure. Beneath these imaginaries of Rhodes was also the sense that Italy's new frontier in the Mediterranean was a restoration of Latin and Roman Catholic tradition. As Federzoni described, "The whole history of Latin and Christian Rhodes is imprinted with our glories."[97] These affected descriptions of the island helped to set the stage for the eventual urban renovation projects—discussed in more detail in chapter 2—that would turn on restoring the island's Christian Crusader cultural heritage as part of the "Italian" identity of the island.

As Enrico Corradini made port in Rhodes, he echoed Federzoni, describing the "joy of national conquest," and linked this excitement to the invigoration of finding himself on an important frontier in the East: "that joy was so much more intoxicating because the island was beautiful and splendid with the purest spirit of air and with the most radiant sunshine of the Orient."[98] Corradini expands nostalgia for a Mediterranean world, to

---

96   "Noi siamo giunti in Grecia mal prevenuti contro questi poveri nostri cugini che cercano di portare come meglio possono il peso enorme della loro antica gloria improduttiva"; Federzoni, *L'Italia nell'Egeo*, 76.

97   Federzoni, *L'Italia nell'Egeo*, 113–14.

98   "Tanto più inebriante quella gioia, perché l'isola era bella e splendida nel più puro spirito dell'aria e nel più radioso sole d'oriente"; Enrico Corradini, *Sopra le vie del nuovo impero: Dall'emigrazione in Tunisia alla guerra nell'Egeo* (Milan: Fratelli Treves, 1912), 82.

include memories of previous Italian expansion into the Ottoman Empire. When passing Lepanto, the site of a sixteenth-century victory of the Venetian Republic against the Ottoman Empire, Corradini exclaims that any Italian who navigates toward Rhodes relives Italy's most beautiful history.[99]

But this sentiment of homeward return was also distinctly tied to the view that ongoing Italian emigration in the Mediterranean basin mandated an imperial solution for national questions about the status of Italians in the world. In Corradini's discussion of the Aegean, the conquest of Rhodes was an eloquent solution to this question of Italy as a nation paradoxically held together by its emigrant identity. Unlike many of his Liberal nationalist counterparts, Corradini viewed Italian emigration negatively, and had proven himself outspoken in his call for African colonialism as a means to stop this "blood-letting" of the Italian nation through emigration.[100] Yet his portrait of Italy's 1911–12 action, *Sopra le vie del nuovo impero: Dall'emigrazione in Tunisia alla guerra nell'Egeo* (*Along the roads of the new empire: From emigration in Tunisia to the war in the Aegean*), looks to the Aegean, rather than Libya, as a place that might finally vindicate and "resolve" the question of the hundreds of thousands of Italians laboring in Tunisia under the flag of the French Empire.

As Silvana Partriarca has described in her magisterial study of *italianità*, notions of the "Latin character" of Italians emerged in the 1880s in concert with widespread disappointments about Italy's failure to annex Tunisia.[101] After its annexation of Tunisia in 1881, France instituted a policy that remained in effect into the early twentieth century, mandating that all Europeans living there should naturalize to a local French nationality (informally known as *tunisienne*), thus fomenting fears that Italian emigrants abroad were losing not only their sense of Italian identity but also their civic and legal ties to the peninsula. Chapter 3 will discuss how the Italian state's struggle with the French Empire in Tunisia would directly impact some of the legal and diplomatic strategies used in the Aegean to consolidate sovereignty there. It is not by chance that Corradini's 1912 account of the conquest of the Aegean also discusses France's project to assimilate Italians in Tunisia: his argument links the demographic rationale for empire with

99   "Poichè l'italiano che naviga verso Rodi, rivive la più bella storia d'Italia"; Corradini, *Sopra le vie del nuovo impero*, 84.

100   See Tullio Pagano, "From Diaspora to Empire: Enrico Corradini's Nationalist Novels," *Modern Language Notes* 119, no. 1 (2004): 67–83.

101   Silvana Patriarca, *Italian Vices: Nation and Character from the Risorgimento to the Republic* (New York: Cambridge University Press, 2010), 80–81.

the need for greater Italian Empire so as to protect the perilous existence of *italianità*, or Italianness in the Mediterranean. According to Corradini, France lacked demographic strength in Tunisia and the Italians there had resisted French claims on them:

> In their African empire the French suffered from the tragic effects of their diminishing European population there: although they wanted to Frenchify Africa, they did not have enough people to work and populate it. So the Italians came, especially from nearby and exuberant Sicily, and they worked and populated it: but though the French attempted to assimilate them, [the Sicilians] would not have it.

> *I francesi pativano nel loro impero affricano gli effetti tragici del loro diminuire di popolazione in Europa: avrebbero voluto francesizzare l'Affrica, ma non avevano gente per lavorarla e popolarla. Venivano allora gli italiani, specie dalla prossima esuberante Sicilia, e la lavoravano e popolavano; ma tentando i francesi di assimilarseli, quelli non ne volevano sapere.*[102]

Corradini was not wrong in his assessment that the migration of Sicilians had transformed the European demographic in Tunisia and undermined French authority in North Africa. In the second half of the nineteenth century, the Italian population of Tunisia is said to have increased threefold, bringing it to almost one hundred thousand people; up until World War II the Italian population in Tunisia outnumbered not only the Italian settlement population in Libya but also the French population in Tunisia. In some accounts, French residents referred to the seasonal onslaught of Sicilian fishermen as an "invasion."[103] As recent studies show, the annexation of Tunisia by the French Empire had taken place precisely to preempt any possible claims by the large, wealthy, and landowning Italian community for an eventual Italian mandate there. The growing Italian community presented a potential threat to French rule in Algeria, and the ways in which Italy saw Tunisia as an extension of its national project precipitated a view among French state actors that Tunisia was in some way "French."[104]

---

102   Corradini, *Sopra le vie del nuovo impero*, 16. The English translation is my own.
103   Julia Clancy Smith, *Mediterraneans: North Africa and Europe in the Age of Migration, c. 1800–1900* (Berkeley: University of California Press, 2013).
104   Mary Dewhurst Lewis, "Geographies of Power: The Tunisian Civic Order, Jurisdictional Politics, and Imperial Rivalry in the Mediterranean, 1881–1935," *Journal*

Likewise, it would seem that Corradini and others like him were quite ready to see the Aegean as "Italian." The Italian war for Libya took place in the context of these increasingly strident nationalist claims to sovereignty in the Mediterranean. Like others, Corradini championed the conquest of North Africa as a necessity for "economic expansion, emigration, giving the South its hinterland in North Africa."[105]

Yet it is in Rhodes and the Aegean that Corradini unites the imperial war with the truly national character of Italian expansionism, and where Italy's status as a "subaltern" immigrant-sending nation might be reframed as the premise for greater migration and empire in the Mediterranean. Echoing D'Annunzio's desire for youthful vitality and Federzoni's Neapolitan gunner, Corradini remarks that the style of the Italian troops who advanced on Rhodes has a "youthful character" and that their war effort is an act of vitality that likens them to Romans.[106] Corradini looks back not only to the Roman Empire but also to the unification of Italy and compares the conquest of Rhodes to a Garibaldi maneuver: "quick and effective, ardent, concluding with the completed fact."[107] Indeed, for Corradini (like D'Annunzio), there is an uncanny familiarity to the landscape of Rhodes that can reawaken memories of Italy's magisterial past. The bucolic landscape of the island recalls the Sicilian countryside. The panorama of the medieval city reminds him of the towers of San Gimignano in Tuscany; its louvered windows and stone alleyways are a new Pompei. To be sure, we are tempted to read this new Pompei in Rhodes as one that will also vindicate the one in Campania and transform the Neapolitan "race" into a conquering nation.

This new Pompei stands like a fortress against the surrounding decadence of the Aegean as a Levantine Sea. The same fears of decline and degeneration that haunt the representation of the eastern origins of Italy in D'Annunzio and Sergi also punctuate Corradini's otherwise elated view of the Aegean. The *mediterraneità* of Rhodes is evident: he declares it is possible to detect traces of "the ancient stock" that once inhabited the island.[108] But Corradini

---

of Modern History 80, no. 4 (2008): 791–830. The Italian government did not formally recognize the French mandate in Tunisia until after World War II.

105 "Espansione economica, emigrazione, dare il mezzogiorno il suo hinterland nell'Africa settentrionale"; Corradini, *Sopra le vie del nuovo impero*, 222.

106 Corradini, *Sopra le vie del nuovo impero*, 166, 109.

107 Corradini, *Sopra le vie del nuovo impero*, 185.

108 *"I pavimenti a mosaico dinanzi alle porte risvegliano i nostri ricordi classici e fanno pensare che tali piacessero agli abitatori dell'antica stirpe"*; Corradini, *Sopra le vie del nuovo impero*, 89.

will echo D'Annunzio in his disgust and contempt for the island's Oriental side when describing a certain immoral decadence there, likening Rhodes to its African counterpart in Libya. Both the city of Rhodes and Tripoli stand outside time, abandoned by the modern world, backwaters of modernity: they are "dead cities" of the Orient. Corradini describes the filthy Levantine quality that joins Rhodes to Tripoli. The island's "cesspit" (*cloache*) of different ethnicities causes Corradini to feel an unmistakable nausea:

> Wherever these nations have found themselves together, like the Turk, the Arab and the Jew in Tripoli, or the Turk, the Arab and the Jew in Rhodes, all and each one of them incapable of modernizing and transforming themselves, they have proliferated in their ancient and centuries-old immobility. Like beasts sitting in their manure these people have covered themselves with their proliferation. And the conditions of their existence are precisely their economic, civil, and moral stagnation, their ethnic separation, and filth. When from one of our modern cities we pass to one of these stables of proliferation of the old races, we feel as though we have stumbled back in time, and a huge nausea overwhelms us.

> *Ovunque questi popoli si ritrovarono insieme, come il turco, l'arabo e l'ebreo a Tripoli, o il turco, l'arabo e l'ebreo a Rodi, impotenti tutti e ciascuno di loro a rinnovarsi e trasformarsi, prolificarono nella loro immobilità secolare e millenaria. Come bestie giacenti del loro sterco così essi si ricoprirono delle loro prolificazioni. E le condizioni della loro esistenza sono appunto la immobilità economica, civile, morale, la loro separazione etnica, la sozzura. Quando da una delle nostre città moderne passiamo in uno di questi stallaggi di prolificazione e delle vecchie stirpi, e subito naturalmente sentiamo di aver fatto un salto a picco nel passato, una grande nausea ci assale.*[109]

As in D'Annunzio, the possibility of restoring (national) health cannot be uncoupled from the Orient's bewildering shadow, its moral turpitude, and cultural decline. Here in Rhodes the nostalgia for ancient glory and Mediterranean Empire exists along with—and dangerously close to—another past, that of the old and bygone world of the Ottoman state. Corradini repeatedly makes reference to the way that prolonged Ottoman rule had spelled the end of the vitality, knowledge, and pragmatism that were the profound legacy of Roman civilization.

---

109   Corradini, *Sopra le vie del nuovo impero*, 102.

But in a surprising turn, Corradini also suggests that though this encounter with the Orient might nauseate, for the same reason, it can exert an undeniable charm—a charm that is, paradoxically, rooted in its profound Ottomanization and reminiscent of an Italian past. Corradini finally concludes that this combination of ancient nobility and Ottoman decline can motivate the Italians to take hold of the opportunity and forge a Mediterranean Empire that will both preserve and restore to Rhodes its ancient centrality. It is precisely Italy's "subaltern" status as an empire that can evoke the Mediterranean:

> Rhodes, so stuck in the past, was all the same a sovereign seat of poetry, an unexpected marvel of the Mediterranean. Would it be like this, had it fallen into the hands of European nation? But we Italians will be the delicate but powerful nation that will know best how not to deform Rhodes, but renovate it, restore to it a mission, in the Mediterranean, between Europe, Asia, and Africa, to which it is conjoined.

> *Rodi, così rimasta indietro nel tempo, era pure una sede sovrana di poesia, un'inaspettata meraviglia nel Mediterraneo. Sarebbe così se fosse venuta in mano di un popolo europeo? Ma noi italiani saremo il popolo delicato e potente che saprà il meno possibile deformare Rodi, rinnovandola, restituendole una missione, nel Mediterraneo, tra Europa, Asia e Africa, a cui è congiunta.*[110]

Corradini's tour of Rhodes therefore points to the new economies of representation in the Aegean that emerged with annexation of the islands and that underscored the Aegean's role to act as a tableau for the consumption of both Mediterranean and Levantine history. Rather than to completely recoil from the decadent Orient (in the spirit of D'Annunzio), Corradini suggests that a new, more subtle apprehension is possible: Italians can immerse themselves in the Oriental setting of the Aegean while also celebrating their own Italian national history and culture in the Mediterranean. This intersection of multiple histories (Greek, Roman, Crusader, Venetian, Ottoman) within the specific, contained, and insular space of Rhodes is the chronotope that was to unify the architectural vernacular of *mediterraneità* that designers adopted in the new cultural landscape for the island. Indeed, Corradini's views anticipate the way that

---

110   Corradini, *Sopra le vie del nuovo impero*, 106.

the massive reconstruction and cultural heritage projects that were soon to characterize Italian rule in Rhodes in the 1920s pivoted on making the island into a place for the consumption of Mediterranean regional histories. It almost goes without saying that in these new cultural heritage projects the Italian Empire, both past and present, was meant to represent the greatest periods in the history of the Mediterranean. Yet, as the next chapter discusses, preservation of the Ottoman past was just as central as restoration of Roman and Crusader heritage within the local administration's plans to transform the island into a luxury tourist destination. By restoring—and in several instances embellishing—the sense of the "Oriental," the Italian administration encouraged tourists to apprehend the subtle hierarchies of difference that early nationalists, from D'Annunzio and Sergi to De Amicis, Federzoni, and Corradini, had "discovered" and embraced during their tours of the Aegean.

Posing as Levantine

Representation of Rhodes, then, insisted on the need for the island's domestication. Organized leisure tourism soon provided the economic motive for the making of the island into a *domus* (Latin for "home") that signified Italy's dominion in (and domination over) the Levantine Sea. But the issue of domestication with regard to the Greek community was more ambiguous. As earlier described, Italian nationalist authors of the Liberal era celebrated the familiarity—and consanguinity—among Greeks and Italians within their proposals for "Latin renaissance," and within their rhetoric of reviving antiquity. But such rhetoric did not easily square with the actual practice of colonial governance and the need to subjugate the Greek ethnic majority to the rule of the Italian state. One answer to this riddle was naturally to emphasize Greek Ottomanization and to link the island of Rhodes more fully with eastern decadence.

Orazio Pedrazzi, in his 1913 travel memoir of the Aegean, *Dalla Cirenaica all'Egeo*, presents such a picture of local Greeks as strange, backward, and Levantine. He finds Greek Orthodox churches charming and bizarre in equal measure ("Nothing more picturesque than this strange cathedral!"), and their religious ceremonies are a source of curious if perverse fascination.[111] But

---

111   Orazio Pedrazzi, *Dalla Cirenaica all'Egeo* (Rocca San Casciano: L. Cappelli, 1913), 265.

these "sights" also become "sites" domesticated by virtue of Pedrazzi's colonial position and authority. As Pedrazzi gestures toward the potential for spiritual and emotional transformation through an experience of the Levant, he embodies the rhetoric of Italy's transformative, nostalgic empire in the Mediterranean.

Orazio Pedrazzi went on to have an illustrious career in the Fascist state. He would support D'Annunzio as his director of press relations during the siege of Fiume, be a member of Parliament during the Fascist dictatorship, and eventually hold appointments in the consular offices of Jerusalem, Prague, and Tunis. His speeches to Parliament on Italian plans for the Dodecanese and further expansion in the eastern Mediterranean, eventually anthologized as *L'Italia e l'Oriente Mediterraneo*, were a veritable blueprint for the role of the Dodecanese in upholding the Italian imperial project in the midst of criticism after World War I that ethnic majorities in the Balkans had the right of self-determination and could not be held under European imperial rule.

Pedrazzi's experience of "posing" as a Greek pilgrim, when visiting the small village of Kremastò in 1913, anticipates the rhetoric that will hold Greeks in the islands ambivalently. It also foreshadows the massive subsequent projects to renovate Rhodes, with their vision of making the Aegean more "Mediterranean" through a double-pronged program that committed to both an exotic and domesticated cultural landscape, detailed in the next chapter. As Barbara Spackman describes in her study of accidental Orientalists in the nineteenth century, the trope of "posing" as a Muslim in order to make the holy pilgrimage to Mecca features regularly in Orientalist literature among Italian travelers in Ottoman lands. In adopting this trope, but adapting it to the Greek Orthodox setting of Rhodes, Pedrazzi's memoir rehearses the exoticization of Greeks that would occur alongside that of the Muslim minorities on the island. While the Italian Empire had not arrived all the way to Mecca by 1912, Pedrazzi's reprisal of the idea of "male masquerade in Mecca" intimates the fantasy of an empire that would reach the furthest corners of the Middle East.[112]

Although Pedrazzi lightheartedly mocks the idea of encountering his exotic alter ego as he takes up the dress and style of an Orthodox religious pilgrim, his experience of a religious festival in a small village not far from the port of Rhodes is central to the way that he will reprise both D'Annunzio and the Italian Orientalists who came before him. Making recourse to the idea of his ancient soul as a justification for his temporary conversion and

112 Spackman, *Accidental Orientalists*, 90–153.

asking the gods—playfully using a pagan plural—for forgiveness (*"chiedo umilmente perdono agli Dei del mio paese se mi sono convertito per un giorno ed una notte alla religione ortodossa"*), he suggests that his seeming conversion is both masquerade and a perversion of his nationalist commitments.[113] But because the masquerade is only temporary—and is concluded by his safe return to the port of Rhodes—the episode reinforces both his national identity and his virility. His journey to Kremastò provides a synecdoche for his journey to the Aegean islands. The experience will end by affirming his nondecadent and Italian superiority ("The day after the party it began again at dawn for nine days. I, however, had given my resignation as a pilgrim"), but via a circuitous route.[114] His immersion in the strange Other through a masquerade as a pilgrim allows him to better identify himself as a European.

Choosing to be a committed pilgrim, he decides to give up the comfortable carriages he has made use of in the port of Rhodes, and to travel by mule for the occasion. He soon discovers that to do so he must ride sidesaddle. The mule thus becomes a means to undo both his European identity and his masculinity, and yet it is precisely by this self-conscious act of undoing that Pedrazzi claims the label of the European traveler in the Orient. Not by chance does gender play a role: Pedrazzi seems to pose like an Egyptian queen during his parodic tour of Greek village. But in posing he also reminds his readers of his virile power:

> It was the true animal of a pilgrim, a little dirty, a bit lame, very ugly in short. But on that mount, I felt right. I tried to put myself in the saddle in the European way, but the saddle was too large and the stirrups, which sawed my legs, impeded me, and therefore I placed myself in the saddle to one side like a woman, and it became an armchair, the mule at the first kick gave a shake, on the second he took a step and made a couple kicks, on the third he started to trot off toward the road to Kremastò.

> *Era il vero animale da Pellegrino, un po' sudicio, un po' zoppo, molto brutto inzomma. Con quella cavalcatura mi sentii a posto, provai a mettermi a cavallo secondo l'uso europeo, ma la sella troppo larga e le assicelle che mi segavano le gambe me lo impedironi, e allor mi collocai a sedere da un lato come le donne, la sella doventò poltrona, il mulo ad una prima legnata si*

113   Orazio Pedrazzi, *Dalla Cirenaica all'Egeo*, 266.
114   Orazio Pedrazzi, *Dalla Cirenaica all'Egeo*, 271.

scosse, alla seconda mosse un passo e tirò una coppia di calci; alla terza cominciò a trottellare verso la strada di Kremastò.[115]

Interestingly, this trope of exploring the island of Rhodes by mule is not unique to Orazio Pedrazzi's travel memoir of the Aegean but can also be found in an earlier memoir by the French travel writer Eugène Flandin, translated and published in Italy as Eugenio Flandini, *L'Isola di Rodi e le Sporadi* (Milan: Fratelli Treves, 1912).[116]

The conversion to an effeminate, Greek Orthodox "schismatic" pilgrim who arrives by mule is short-lived; the religious rituals horrify him and reaffirm his position as Western outsider. Initial excitement passes into confusion and dismay over the incense that lends an impure and yellow haze to the scene inside the church. Not unlike D'Annunzio, who is nauseous and overtaken by the sights and smells of the Orient—even if that nausea will be a precursor to his rebirth as a virile ancient Greek—Pedrazzi comments how his own body, which is modern and healthy, feels sick when it encounters the display of decadence inside the church:

A spectacle to horrify you; the unfortunate patients who would have done well with a little clean air and light spent nine days so asphyxiated by the church, by the yellow light a smoke of the candle, breathing the air corrupted by all of the things that were being done inside there, and from the breath of those people packed in their like sardines. We, who are healthy and svelte, felt awful.

Era uno spettacolo da fare orrore; le disgraziate pazienti cui avrebbe fatto bene un poca di luce e di aria pura passavano le nove giornate nel tanto asfissiante della chiesa, alla luce gialla e fumosa delle candele, respirando l'aria corrotta da tutte le cose che si facevano là dentro, e dal respiro della gente assiepata come le sardine. Noi, sani e svelte, ci sentivamo male.[117]

Unlike D'Annunzio, Pedrazzi finds that the act of "posing" as a pilgrim gives him the power to affirm his difference from the locals, and to inscribe his

---

115 Orazio Pedrazzi, *Dalla Cirenaica all'Egeo*, 268. The translation is mine.
116 As Edward Said has noted, "Every writer on the Orient (and this is true even of Homer) assumes some Oriental precedent, some previous knowledge of the Orient, to which he refers and on which he relies." Said, *Orientalism*, 20.
117 Orazio Pedrazzi, *Dalla Cirenaica all'Egeo*, 276.

judgment of them with a notion of realism and the idea that it is in some way "a true representation of life" (*"una vera rappresentazione della vita"*).[118] The festivities following the mass prove a true spectacle of sexual agitation and excitement. A dance spills into the street and threatens to upset the boundaries between public and private, between ordered and disordered worlds: "the faces were lit up with excitement and indigestion, the crowd was happy, chatty, with a crazy will to get agitated and to scream" (*"le facce erano accese di eccitazione e di indigestione, le folla era allegra, chiacchierona, con una matta voglia di agitarsi e urlare"*).[119] This bacchic frenzy is nevertheless visceral to Pedrazzi, who concludes that it is "a dance full of desires and repulsions" (*"piene di desideria e repulse"*).[120]

Pedrazzi's careful positioning of himself as an invisible tourist and outsider—who can be mesmerized temporarily, but not permanently bewitched—strengthens his position as a colonizing visitor. It can be no coincidence, either, that similar religious festivals commonly took place in Southern Italy—the so-called *sagre*, where men and women were known to go into trances for days on end. By making the Greek Orthodox religion appear alien and spectacular, and at the same time showing an arrogant familiarity, Italian travelers like Pedrazzi asserted a moral and cultural authority over the Aegean in a double discourse of intimacy and difference.

Pedrazzi thus achieves what D'Annunzio could not: he is able to experience and accept modern Greece in all its decline and all its glory. One is tempted to argue that it is precisely the intervening conquest of the Aegean that had made possible such a comfort with discomfort and decadence. Pedrazzi's narrative, however, does illustrate a further problem that was soon to be fully crystallized in governance: how could Italians simultaneously imagine that Greeks were ancient "cousins" and at the same time assert a moral and political distance that assured a colonial hierarchy and a civilizing mandate? One way that this issue would finally be resolved was, of course, in linking the Aegean fully to the Italian South, a region with which nationalists already had considerable practice in simultaneously exercising romantic views of inclusion and pessimistic views of exclusion. As the next chapters show, it would also be important to retain these exotic spectacles so as to allow future travelers to renegotiate the definition of both Italy and its Mediterranean Empire. Finally, that notion of the uncanny—a place that was almost like home but

118   Orazio Pedrazzi, *Dalla Cirenaica all'Egeo*, 276.
119   Orazio Pedrazzi, *Dalla Cirenaica all'Egeo*, 276.
120   Orazio Pedrazzi, *Dalla Cirenaica all'Egeo*, 271.

not quite—became a necessary component of the imperial identity of Italian Rhodes. If Italy recognized itself in the Aegean, its fabled history and its tradition of voyages to the Orient, the double gesture of its ethnographic practices also allowed it to distance itself from the islands' familiarity. The next chapter will show how travelers who visited Rhodes during the period of Fascist rule reinscribed the island with signs of Italy's dominance, not only through reference to past imperial markers, such as Venice and Rome, but also through the careful planning, staging, and witnessing of the Levant within local tourism and folklore.

CHAPTER TWO

Touring Italian Rhodes

In March 1926 the popular culture magazine *L'illustrazione italiana* ran on its cover a photograph of Mario Lago, the newly installed Fascist governor of the Dodecanese, costumed as a medieval knight.[1] Photographed as he crossed the threshold of the recently restored castle of Rhodes, Lago presided over a groundbreaking ceremony that meant to herald in a new era for Rhodes as a celebrated tourist destination. The event was said to be a "superb reevocation of other times," and to speak to the island's voluminous history.[2] But though the governor's masquerade as a Christian knight intended to evoke the island's storied past, it clearly strove also to intimate even more celebrated colonial futures. The local newspaper reported that an English division of the Knights of St. John in attendance had left admiring "the order, cleanliness and general courtesy of the city and its inhabitants."[3]

Lago's appearance on the cover of *L'illustrazione italiana* marked the inauguration of a master plan to remodel the island, providing the port city with both new architecture and state-of-the-art amenities, while also conserving the rich cultural heritage of the entire Dodecanese and creating a dedicated museum of archeology from the Hellenistic, Roman, and Christian Crusader periods. A feverish tide of new public works in the islands was underway and these would soon transform the island into a veritable summer resort, a *stazione balneare*, which could appeal to a broad, international set

---

1 "Una caratteristica cerimonia a Rodi," *L'illustrazione italiana*, no. 15, April 11, 1926. *L'illustrazione italiana* had represented and supported the Italian colonial project for several decades. See John Dickie, *Darkest Italy: The Nation and Stereotypes of the Mezzogiorno, 1860–1900* (New York: Palgrave MacMillan, 2016) as well as Nelson Moe, *The View from Vesuvius: Italian Culture and the Southern Question* (Berkeley: University of California Press, 2002).

2 "Una caratteristica cerimonia," 379.

3 "I cavalieri gerosolimitani d'Inghilterra investono S.E. il Governatore delle insegne dell'Ordine," *Messaggero di Rodi*, March 24, 1926.

of leisure tourists—and not only Italians—but well-to-do Europeans from Egypt and other areas of the eastern Mediterranean. In ways that mirrored the Fascist regime's commitment to restoration and modernization of cities on the Italian Peninsula, the colonial government committed both to creating new infrastructure and modernizing Rhodes and undertaking restoration projects that would underscore the island's significant culture heritage.[4] The goal was to make Rhodes into a "world capital": to trade up the island's reputation as a run-down, dirty city of the Orient—a *borgo levantino*, as Enrico Corradini had called it—for one as a meeting place for elegant and cosmopolitan leisure travelers.[5] But while modernization and cultural conservation were ostensibly the goals of the island's renovation, the urban redesign marked an unstable project to redefine the island's colonial identity and to bring it into line with the shifting temporalities of Mussolini's Fascist regime.

The master plan took more than ten years to complete and it was stylistically revised a second time after the invasion of Ethiopia and Mussolini's declaration of empire. But by 1936, the urban overhaul of Rhodes had effectively brought its built environment into line with the rebuilt historical centers of cities in the Italian Peninsula.[6] The touristic makeover of the island also brought the port of Rhodes into aesthetic harmony with the capital cities of other Italian colonies: it paralleled the construction of hospitality economies in colonial Libya and anticipated the introduction of tourism in Italian-occupied Albania after 1939. The reinvention of Rhodes as tourist destination is evidence of what Stephanie Malia Hom, with reference to Said, has called Italy's "preposterous transition from text to practice," that is, the shift from imagining imperialism in the Aegean to enacting it in colonial geographies of consumption and tourism.[7]

4   Medina Lasansky, *The Renaissance Perfected: Architecture, Spectacle and Tourism in Fascist Italy* (University Park, PA: Pennsylvania State University Press, 2004). As Lasansky shows, the Fascist regime was not only obsessed with the Roman past, but it also maintained a keen interest in the medieval.

5   Enrico Corradini, *Sopra le vie del nuovo impero: Dall'emigrazione in Tunisia alla guerra nell'Egeo* (Milan: Fratelli Treves, 1912), 106. See my discussion of Corradini's visit to Rhodes in chapter 1.

6   As Mia Fuller observes, "In the 1920s, under the governorship of diplomat Mario Lago, [Rhodes] saw the development of a tourist destination, archaeological and museum projects, and the creation of technical and institutional infrastructure on a par with those in the metropole." Mia Fuller, *Moderns Abroad* (New York: Routledge, 2007), 33.

7   Stephanie Malia Hom, "Empires of Tourism: Travel and Italian Colonial Rhetoric in Libya and Albania, 1911–43," *Journal of Tourism History* 4, no. 3 (2012), 281–300, 282.

But though the tourism project in Rhodes resembled projects undertaken in the same time frame in both the Italian Peninsula and the overseas colonies, the ambiguity of the islands' status within the empire resulted in a corresponding ambiguity about its representation in colonial geographies and tourist propaganda. Viewed as neither a colony nor one of Italy's borderlands, the Aegean was held in a space of ambivalence. In Rhodes, different possible readings of the island's "Mediterranean" history accrued and proved an issue around which the administration shifted its position over the course of its rule, in ways that finally mirrored the ambivalence about the racial *mediterraneità* of Italians (as discussed in the previous chapter). Indeed, the "preposterous transition" to *romanità*, or Romanness, that Hom demonstrates as at the core of the tourism projects in Libya and Albania was, in Rhodes, arguably overshadowed by an aesthetic vernacular of *mediterraneità*, and the belief that the island's value was in no small part located in its history as an important cultural crossroads in both the early modern and modern periods. The checkered and creolizing history of the island was productive for the Fascist colonial designers and architects who were brought in to design the new built environment, but also undergirded the local administration's commitment that the island should be an emblem of colonial and Fascist modernity in the Levant.

In many ways, this ambivalence about the symbolic geographies of the Aegean was consonant with ambivalences that characterized Mussolini's approach to modernity. The multiple layers of history present in the island seemed to embody Mussolini's call for a Fascist culture that was "traditionalist and at the same time modern, [one] that looks to the past and at the same time to the future."[8] Yet how these different historical epochs should be showcased within the urban overhaul was open to considerable interpretation. As Jeffery Schnapp has observed, ambiguity about the representation of the past was perhaps inherent to Italian Fascism itself: "Did the triumph of fascism entail a decisive break with Italy's past or, instead, the recovery of a lost origin (for instance, of the glory of Imperial Rome)? Or, as Mussolini had implied, did it mark both rupture and return, at once the reassumption of a historical legacy and the transcendence of that very legacy?"[9] Schnapp observes that this

8   Mussolini's speech to the Academy of Fine Arts in Perugia, "Arte è civiltà," delivered on October 5, 1926, reprinted in *Benito Mussolini Opera omnia* (Florence: La Fenice, 1951–63), 22: 230.
9   See Jeffrey Schnapp, "Epic Demonstrations: Fascist Modernity and the 1932 Exhibition of the Fascist Revolution," in *Fascism, Aesthetics, and Culture*, edited by Richard Golsan, 1–31 (Hanover, NH: University Press of New England, 1992), 2.

unresolved contradiction can perhaps explain the "surfeit of signs" that was a hallmark of the Fascist state and helped to conceal an unstable ideological core. Likewise, in Rhodes, a proliferation of such signifiers would eventually lead the port to feel like "an open-air museum," but one denuded of all real historical context.[10] It is arguably this overly renovated and resort-like atmosphere that has led Rhodes to acquire status in the postwar period as an emblem of postmodern Greek island tourism in the Aegean. Despite the recent attempts of the local municipality to have the island included within cultural heritage itineraries in Europe, Rhodes' reputation continues to be one of short-stay and budget mass tourism.[11]

In 1926, the Italian state's goals for the port of Rhodes centered on the possibility that mass tourism could modernize and help bring the island from the periphery to the center, although while also remaining peripheral to the actual center of the empire that was, of course, to be in Rome. Tourism was argued to be able to bring the island to enjoy a role that it had not enjoyed since antiquity and the Renaissance, but the re-acquisition of this status would make it into a popular destination for resort tourism and well-to-do European travelers in the Orient. The Italian state also maintained that tourism constituted a developmental economy that would provide jobs to locals and that anticipated the development of agrarian and industrial economies in the islands (about which more is said in chapter 4).[12] Lastly, reconstructing and celebrating Rhodes' *mediterraneità* within the tourism economy brought the islands into the body of the national, and by celebrating Italian mobility as linked to imperial formations, tourism also encouraged

---

10   "Indeed, Italians seem to have regarded the entire city as primarily an archaeo-logical and touristic site (a fact that is confirmed by archival sources), rather than one where they had to accommodate citizens' Otherness. In other words, Italians' view of Rhodes as 'historic'—a view that in Tripoli or Benghazi was counter-balanced by Italian perceptions of local ethnicities and religions—outweighed its other characteristics, leading to Italian activities that left the city resembling an open-air museum by the end of Italian rule"; Fuller, *Moderns Abroad*, 79.

11   In 2017, the local government of Rhodes made a bid to become one of Europe's "cultural capitals" but lost the competition to Matera in Italy and Plodiviv in Bulgaria. See my own, "Italian Identity, Global Mediterranean: Heritage and the Cultural Politics of Tourism in the Aegean," in *Transcultural Italies: Mobility, Memory and Translation*, edited by Charles Burdett, Loredana Polezzi, and Barbara Spadaro (Liverpool: University of Liverpool Press, 2020), 75–99.

12   As Nicola Labanca has remarked, the Italian overseas spaces never succeeded in generating more income than the state's investment into them; Nicola Labanca, *Oltremare: Storia dell'espansione coloniale italiana* (Bologna: Il mulino, 2002).

the continued linking of emigration and empire. As during the Liberal era, when the Italian government sought to ensure that emigrants did not lose the culture, language, and identity of the homeland—that they maintained a sense of *italianità* from abroad—introducing tourism in Rhodes ensured that the colonial periphery also obtained a sense of the national. This was discreetly imagined as *mediterraneità* and denoted a feeling of belonging that could apply to the wider imperial peripheries of Italy.[13]

As much as the stakes of the tourism project seemed intent on promoting the nation and on "domesticating" the Aegean landscape, another strand in government plans reveals that such a commitment promoted colonial ambivalence and the idea that the islands should be at once "Italian" and "Levantine." Internal discussions about developing tourism frequently referenced the possibility of also locating a second potential market among other cosmopolitan or "Levantine" communities in the Mediterranean—that is, Europeans from Egypt, Africa, and Palestine who might make the island into a regular summer outpost. Moreover, the Levantine and "Levantineness" acted as further elements that were regrafted in new architecture and urban planning alongside (and in conjunction with) an aesthetic of Mediterraneanness. Unlike the Mediterranean, which represented to both designers and state actors their colonial futures (in both the metropole and the islands), the concept of the Levant allowed for a sustained engagement with nostalgia for the Ottoman past and enabled the production of continuing Orientalist hierarchies.

In what follows, this chapter discusses how the aesthetics of *mediterraneità* was as an extension of what Josh Arthurs has aptly called the Fascist regime's chronopolitics—"a set of transcendent, eternal values as well as a tangible, moldable physical space" that could embody Fascism's unique brand of socialist modernity. *Mediterraneità* was also paradoxically an aesthetic regime that could re-establish the colonial hierarchies that it vitiated in the spirit of creating a sense of shared Mediterranean histories.[14] As in the previous chapter's discussion of early nationalists' colonial encounters, the Aegean continued to represent to the Italian state a picturesque and yet also uncanny frontier, one that was to be viewed with familiarity and disdain, as intimate and familiar as strange. Venice was to be the natural symbol of

---

13   Mark Choate, *Emigrant Nation: The Making of Italy Abroad* (Cambridge, MA: Harvard University Press, 2008).

14   Josh Arthurs, "The Excavatory Intervention: Archaeology and the Chronopolitics of Fascist Italy," *Journal of Modern European History* 13, no. 1 (2015), 44–58, 47.

this new empire, with its architectural history of incorporating Ottoman motifs into Italian Renaissance architecture.[15] After the invasion of Ethiopia, however, the Italian state would purge much of the exoticizing symbolism that had decorated its government buildings, hotels, and public *palazzi*. In official discourse this second layer of renovations was the replacement of *mediterraneità* with *romanità*, or Romanness, with the latter having already defined the urban and touristic landscape in Libya for at least a decade. But it is much more accurate, this chapter will argue, to examine all the revisions to the built environment vis-à-vis the concept of "Levantineness," that old bygone world of the Orient, outside of time and central to colonial ideology, which centered both designers' and the state's commitment to appropriating the local into representations of Fascist modernity in the island of Rhodes.

Framing the Sign: The Walled City of Rhodes

Cultural heritage projects and conservation commenced immediately following capture of the Aegean islands in 1912.[16] Within the first year of occupation, the Italian state undertook the restoration of the island's impressive moated medieval city. Between 1912 and 1915, the Italian administration first refurbished the Hospital of the Knights, one of the oldest original buildings of the medieval period, erected during the Fourth Crusade; it next began a project to entirely rebuild the medieval palace that had once surged above the port. The medieval fortifications as well as the castle, both of which had helped to defend the island against the expansionist advances of the Ottoman state until 1522, had obvious correspondences with the Italian state's civilizing and Christianizing mission in the region. As an early historiographer of the island explained, in the robust fortifications one "could truly find the memory of the heroic knights who defended them, of the great captains who with so much self-sacrifice and courage collected the sword fallen from the hands of the crusaders and slowed by two centuries, together with Venice, the definitive triumph of the crescent

---

15 Venice also was for the Italian nation-empire in the Adriatic. Maura Hametz, "Replacing Venice in the Adriatic: Tourism and Italian Irredentism, 1880–1936," *Journal of Tourism History* 6, nos. 2–3 (2014): 107–201.

16 On the ambitious renovation of Rhodes as an experiment in vigorous urban planning during the Liberal occupation of Rhodes, see Leonardo Ciacci, *Rodi italiana, 1912–23: Come si inventa una città* (Venice: Marsilio, 1991).

[Islam]."[17] State actors imagined conservation of the medieval city and the castle of Rhodes as an important metaphor for their own role as colonizers in the Aegean; they were doing no less than reprising the forgotten mission of the Crusaders and Venetians, while now under the aegis of empire by the Italian nation-state.

The urban renovation of the rest of the city, inaugurated in 1926, two years after Italy officially obtained the islands through the second treaty of Lausanne, was an expansion of this earlier conservation program. It centered on shaping the city into both a capital and a resort, providing Italy with an administrative center for its rule over the Aegean and creating a setting that could attract international tourism. City planning decisions sought to transform the capital of Rhodes into a "garden city," an English idea in vogue at the time, and hence to showcase colonial programs of hygiene, renewal, and urban development, as well as Italy's status as equal if not superior to the English Empire's presence in the Aegean region (in Cyprus). The master plan was allegedly to perform a *risanamento*, an urban renewal that would clear out Ottoman additions to the medieval city of Rhodes, which were perceived as decrepit architectural pollution that obscured the Crusader masonry. During the Ottoman period, the Turkish rulers not only made significant alterations to the city fortifications, but also converted many Byzantine churches into mosques and renovated further buildings to include the enclosed balconies typical of Ottoman architecture, the so-called *mashrabiya*, where one can obtain a good view of the street without being seen, and often intended for use by elite women.

The Italian master plan ostensibly aimed to reverse much of the Ottoman redesign of the medieval city. It realigned the streets of the old city in an alleged return to the ancient plan of the city as drafted by Hippodamus of Miletus.[18] It also included new zoning laws that demarcated a colonial city distinct from areas where locals lived. The plan called not only for the restoration of the medieval city but also for the creation of an elite neighborhood for the colonial administration and their families—in the

17 "Si trovano veramente le memorie degli heroici Cavalieri che le hanno difese, dei grandi Capitani che con tanta abnegazione e con tanto coraggio raccolsero la spada caduta dale mani dei Crociati e ritardarono di due secoli, insieme a Venezia, il trionfo definitivo della Mezzaluna"; Eugenio Flandini, *L'Isola di Rodi e le Sporadi* (Milan: Fratelli Treves, 1912), 18.

18 Simona Martinoli and Eliana Perotti, *Architettura coloniale italiana nel Dodecaneso, 1912–1943* (Turin: Fondazione Giovanni Agnelli, 1999).

Greek-inhabited area, known as the Neochori, or New Village—and of a tourist zone and colonial administration center called the Foro Italico. The master plan ensured that, upon disembarking on Rhodes, the typical traveler would behold two cities, one colonial-modern and one medieval and Crusader. As a traveler described in 1933, "There is a long beach with two ports, defended by an enormous tower. Behind the first is an even bigger one, severe in its presence, and from which emerges imposing fortifications, white minarets, palm leaves, and windmills: it's *old Rhodes*, home of the Knights-Crusaders. Along the second port, on the other hand, is a long stretch of superb modern buildings surrounded by elegant villas and flowering gardens. This is *new Rhodes*, Italian Rhodes."[19]

The master plan to create a new colonial city encircling the old medieval town was a strategic framing: it drew the visitor's attention to the Crusader past and justified Italian expansion on the basis that it was a "return" to Christian dominance of the Orient. Inside the medieval city, however, was a further framing: the medieval fortifications were to enclose an Ottoman past, which was in turn "preserved" so as to provide an experience of the "picturesque" and "Oriental" on an international tourist itinerary. On one side of the medieval city Italian "conservation" focused entirely on restoring Christian masonry and fortifications, while on the other side of the city Ottoman architecture was left intact. Many of the Ottoman additions and decorations that were stripped from the medieval city were eventually grafted onto the new colonial city that was erected adjacent to it—this regrafting was to form the basis of an aesthetic of *mediterraneità*. Architects involved in the redesign made bold claims about "harmonizing" East and West and appropriating "native" architectural practices as they placed decorative motifs that originated with Ottoman or other "exotic" architectures in deliberate juxtaposition with the art-deco and rationalist structures. New colonial buildings in their striking cubic and monumental frames formally dominated the Ottoman and Orientalist flourishes that adorned them; such designs reproduced the colonial hierarchies that were already present in the framing of the old city of Rhodes.

---

19 Original Italian: "*Ecco lungo la spiaggia due porti, difesi da una torre gigantesca. Dietro il primo, il più grande, sta una città murata, severa nell'aspetto, da cui si ergono imponenti fortificazioni, bianchi minareti, ciuffi di palme e mulini a vento: è* Rodi vecchia, *quella dei Cavalieri crociati. Lungo il secondo porto invece si ammira una distesa di superbi edifici moderni e un ameno contorno di graziose ville e di giardini fioriti. Questa è* Rodi nuova, Rodi italiana." Camillo Sarti, *Un viaggio in Oriente* (Varese: Nuova Italia, 1936), 88–89. Italics in original.

The local administration further committed to restoring many of the island's most important Ottoman monuments. It eventually commissioned an engineer to assist with an archaeological survey of the island's Ottoman period, and between 1930 and 1934, Hermes Balducci stayed on Rhodes to study monuments of Islamic and Ottoman heritage.[20] Although the resulting monograph by Balducci, *Architettura turca in Rodi*, reflects a sentiment of moral superiority typical of the Italian state's attitudes to the Turkish inhabitants, it also shows a remarkable attention to the Ottoman heritage of the island.[21] One way that designers worked with this heritage was by emphasizing the history of Venetian Empire in the colonial architecture of the so-called "new" city, thus re-grafting the Ottoman past onto the urban redesign, while reproducing the Venetian Empire's own appropriation of Ottoman design and architecture during the Renaissance. This engagement with the Ottoman legacy contrasts strongly with a view, expressed elsewhere, that the Byzantine heritage of the island was of little importance.[22] To be sure, emphasizing the Crusader and Venetian past (and ignoring the Byzantine one) helped to distance Greek national claims on the islands. This strategy mirrored the rhetoric adopted in Libya and Albania where the Italian administration invoked Roman precedent—the idea of *romanità*—to justify and concretize its rule.[23] But by restoring the Ottoman monuments, the Italian administration also ensured that the touristic atmosphere contained a lively sense of the Oriental, and to maintain the notion that the island was "scholastically speaking, in Asia."[24]

---

20   Luca Orlandi, "An Italian Pioneer on Ottoman Architecture Studies in the Dodecanese Islands: Hermes Balducci (1904–1938)," in *Proceedings of the 14th International Congress of Turkish Art*, edited by Frédéric Hitzel, 531–41 (Paris: Collège de France, 2013).

21   The architectural historian Hermes Balducci completed a survey of all the mosques in the island in 1932; Hermes Balducci, *Architettura turca in Rodi* (Milan: Ulrico Hoepli, 1932).

22   Italian touring books played down the significance of Byzantine architecture in Rhodes: *"Il periodo bizantino ha scarsa importanza per Rodi per quanto duri otto secoli. È un periodo oscuro. [...] Solamente qualche chiesetta dalla caratteristica cupola a tamburo, qualche mosaico e qualche cadente muro di torri costiere attestano la lunga dominazione di Bisanzio"*; Touring Club Italiano, *Rodi: Guida del turista* (Milan: Bestetti e Tumelli, 1928), 12.

23   See Fuller, *Moderns Abroad*, 39–62, as well as Brian McLaren, *Architecture and Tourism in Italian Colonial Libya: An Ambivalent Modernism* (Seattle: University of Washington Press, 2006).

24   *"Scolasticamente in Asia."* The words are from a 1912 study of the islands; Goffredo Jaja, *L'Isola di Rodi* (Rome: Società Geografica Italiana, 1912), 5.

By 1926, when the Fascist government broke ground on the master plan for Rhodes, it was already established that the medieval city and the Ottoman monuments were the two main signifiers of the Italian colonial discourse about the island. The development of organized leisure tourism in the island leveraged these signifiers further making them into the inspiration for a very specific cultural and imperial itinerary. In what follows, the rest of this chapter will describe how the architectural redesign of Rhodes eventually brought a diverse and eclectic range of architectural motifs to bear on the cultural landscape that departed from these signifiers—so as to continually suggest the "Eastern" identity of the island while also investing in the idea that the islands were particularly hospitable to tourism because of their rich Western history as well. Designers eventually sought to use traces of Italian history, not only from the periods of the Knights of St. John, but also the classical periods of Hellenistic and Roman antiquity and of the Venetian and Genoese maritime expansions in the Mediterranean, to emphasize and advertise a new colonial style of the Mediterranean. The linking of Rhodes with Venetian rule, and islands such as Corfu and Crete, also well-known repositories of Italian maritime history, would influence famous writers, such as Carlo Emilio Gadda, who visited Rhodes in 1929.[25] However, as the renovation project succeeded in collapsing Mediterranean history and drawing equivalencies between the Crusader and Venetian pasts and contemporary expansion in the Mediterranean and Africa, it also suggested a close entanglement between Western modernity and Eastern exoticism in ways that also served Fascism's attempt to engage in new political temporalities and to link modernity with tradition and a return to the rural, even when that past was an Ottoman or "Oriental" one. Ironically, while the administration believed that modernization programs could make the Levantine setting into the premise for a luxury experience of Fascist modernity, it struggled to convince many foreign states of the same. The fact that the Aegean was understood abroad as a colony and not part of Italy prevented the administration from obtaining the high prices that they asked of travelers and undermined the development of tourism.[26]

As completion of the master plan continued into the late 1930s, renovations focused on bringing the island into closer correspondence with urbanization in the peninsula. Parts of the medieval, walled city of Rhodes eventually closely replicated the historical center of an Italian city on the peninsula. When information about the original construction of buildings in the medieval city

---

25   Carlo Emilio Gadda, *Il Castello di Udine* (Florence: Edizione Solaria, 1934), 141–49.
26   GAK, 1486/1935.

was missing, architects turned to Italian buildings of a similar era for models. In some instances, new constructions obviously evoked settings that would be recognizable to Italian visitors. The Bank of Italy at the foot of the Avenue of the Inns, for example, closely resembles edifices in Viterbo, the seat of the papacy in the tenth and eleventh centuries.[27]

But the duality of Rhodes identity, both Italian and Levantine, remained. In ways that reprised representations of the South in the nineteenth century—where the "picturesque" implied both a place of great beauty and of great despair—the representation of Rhodes alternated between celebrating the island's exoticism and citing it as reason for further programs of hygiene and "regeneration."[28] A coupling of the exotic with the familiar was executed with exceptional reliability throughout the island's various urban and tourist frames and it produced slippage, a productive ambivalence about whether the island of Rhodes was "Western" or "Eastern," that travelers by the tens of thousands commented upon.[29] This encounter was not just for those who made the physical journey to the island, but also, following the lead of scholar Ali Bedhad, available to the "armchair travelers" who experienced Rhodes vicariously by consuming material culture linked to the production of tourism.[30] As urban rehabilitation projects conspired to create a very specific encounter with the "local" for travelers to Rhodes, visitors mined differences between themselves and the occupied population. Popular travel literature thus became a site where Italians rehearsed metropolitan identities as well as a larger story about Italy as a nation of explorers and pioneers in the Mediterranean. But these impressions of Rhodes were mediated by the carefully constructed urban landscape that sought to represent Rhodes as a "home away from home," a locale that was both Italian and other, both bourgeois and traditional, modern and yet also anti-modern.

27   See Vassilis Colonas, *Italian Architecture in the Dodecanese Islands, 1912–1943* (Athens: Olkos, 2002), 33–34.

28   See Nelson Moe, "The Geographic Poetics of Verga," in *The View from Vesuvius: Italian Culture and the Southern Question*, 250–97 (Berkeley: University of California Press, 2002).

29   "Last year more than 50,000 tourists visited the island." "Rhodes a Changed Island," *Egyptian Gazette*, June 8, 1935. GAK DOD, Envelope 1486(2)/1935.

30   Ali Bedhad, *Belated Travelers: Orientalism in the Age of Colonial Dissolution* (Durham, NC: Duke University Press, 1994). On the new literature of travel that was generated throughout the Fascist years in parallel with Italian colonial expansion, see also Charles Burdett, *Journeys through Fascism: Italian Travel Writing between the Wars* (New York: Berghahn, 2007).

Mediterraneanness

As the principal architect of the Aegean from 1926 to 1928, Florestano Di Fausto (also the lead architect in Italian colonial Libya) theorized a vision of the Mediterranean that not only defined new constructions on the islands of Rhodes, Kos, and Leros, but also shaped a growing discussion about new constructions in all Italian colonies. Di Fausto's work was instrumental to mapping the "twinned courses of Italian colonialism and *mediterraneità*," as Sean Anderson has described.[31] Di Fausto maintained that new constructions in the Dodecanese Islands and Libya should have stylistic continuity with existing structures and even derive inspiration from local building practices. Yet choices as to when and how to appropriate "native" architecture reveal a definite program of staging colonial power. The "Mediterranean" vernacular, *mediterraneità*, resolved a dilemma between the apparently antithetical categories of modern and traditional that permeated debates about new constructions during the years of Fascist rule.[32] This vernacular provided a way to appropriate a large body of architectural styles and themes and absorb an emergent flow of exotic signifiers from the colonial space. As Anderson explains, "the Mediterranean is ... a filter through which architects like Di Fausto and others generated a new Italian architecture in the colonies," and through which they could appropriate motifs and styles from a whole range of exotic cultural landscapes, from North African to Slavic architecture.[33]

The appropriation of extant motifs and styles became a key strategy of the urban redesign in part because it allowed Italy to reproduce a well-known European encounter in the Ottoman Orient. But new architecture in Rhodes strove tell the story of Europeans in the Orient in a specifically Italian way. Fusing diverse epochs and the "antithetical" styles of the West and the Levant, the Mediterranean vernacular operated as a chronotope that discreetly signified Italy's "return" to imperial dominance in the Orient while bracketing previous "Italian" journeys to the Ottoman Empire.[34] Importantly,

31   Sean Anderson, "The Light and the Line: Florestano di Fausto and the Politics of *Mediterraneità*," *California Italian Studies Journal* 1, no. 1 (2010): 1–13, 3.
32   See Mia Fuller, "Building Power: Italy's Colonial Architecture and Urbanism," *Cultural Anthropology* 3, no. 4 (1998): 455–87.
33   Anderson, "The Light and the Line," 2–3.
34   As Fuller has shown of Italian colonial architecture in Libya, architects there justified the appropriation of local forms on the basis that these forms were in essence

the medieval architecture of the Knights of St. John was one of the first signifiers of the Christian past of the island that Italian architects were eager to reappropriate. Buildings in the Foro Italico made use of a red-orange porous stone called *finta pietra* (fake stone) to replicate the masonry of the Knights.[35] Restorers in the old city likewise used this to create further correspondences with constructions in the new city.[36]

Also in the Foro Italico, Di Fausto designed a large esplanade adapted to mass political gatherings, which were as much part of the cultural life of Rhodes under Fascist rule as they were in mainland Italy. Along the shoreline, he planned for an imposing edifice of brick that would command the attention of travelers arriving in the harbor. The shoreline promenade was designed to closely resemble the one in Libya and to create a set of mimetic correspondences between the two "facing" shores of Italy's colonial Mediterranean. The new shoreline, which contained the major Italian public buildings including the post office, the Bank of Italy, the Catholic Cathedral of St. John, and the Italian Club, embodied the latest in Italian architectural fashion, including the trends of rationalism and Novecento (see figure 2.1: Rhodes shoreline circa 1930). These *finta pietra* buildings were an important way in which the new architecture cultivated a sense of pleasant "familiarity" for travelers and linked the island more closely to metropolitan Italy.

Yet these same buildings contained embellishments and eclectic decorations that celebrated Rhodes' Eastern identity and underscored Italy's history of maritime expansion in the Mediterranean. The centerpiece of the Italian shoreline—and the example par excellence of his hybrid Mediterranean vernacular—was Di Fausto's ingenious Palazzo del Governo.[37] This highly unusual building recalibrates a variety of stylistic influences, including Renaissance, baroque, and neo-Gothic. The bottom colonnade in a neo-Gothic style recalls the medieval architecture of the Knights

Roman: "Here the 'real' basis for using Libyan building as a model was that the latter was actually Roman"; Fuller, "Building Power," 472.

35   Anthony Antoniades, "Italian Architecture in the Dodecanese: A Preliminary Assessment," *Journal of Architectural Education* 38, no. 1 (1984): 18–25.

36   Restoration plans called for the use of *"intonaco cementizio impermeabile con terre colorate, per il muro dal parte del Museo, dosato con kg. 400 di cemento per mc. di sabbia, compreso lo scrostamento del vecchio intonaco e le impalcature necessarie";* GAK DOD, Envelope 144.2/1928.

37   See Medina Lasansky's discussion of the Palazzo del Governo in *The Renaissance Perfected*, 196–97, as well as Fuller's analysis of Mediterraneanness in *Moderns Abroad*, 39–62.

Figure 2.1: Rhodes shoreline circa 1930 © Archive Touring Club Italiano.

of St. John. The top is rationalist, with smooth, light-colored, geometric surfaces. Decorative elements appropriate motifs from Arabic architecture, including latticed balconies and Moorish window treatments. The very shape and positioning of the building intimates the return of the "thalassocracy," or maritime empire, in the Mediterranean. As one architectural historian has aptly described it, the enlarged portico that wraps around the base of the building gives the impression that the Palazzo del Governo is "emerging from the sea" (see figure 2.2).[38] Finally, the clear visual and architectural allusion to the Palazzo Ducale in Venice announces that Italian rule in Rhodes builds upon the Venetian tradition of economic and military expansion in the Islamic world (see figure 2.3).

On the other side of the Palazzo del Governo, walking distance from the administrative center, Di Fausto designed and erected the main buildings of a tourist zone that brought together decorative motifs of the Orient with forms from rationalist architecture. The Navy Club, the La Ronda Sea Baths, the Hotel of the Roses, and, at the northernmost tip of the island, the aquarium were constructed in soft pastel yellows and beiges, a palette

38   Colonas, *Italian Architecture of the Dodecanese Islands*, 46.

Figure 2.2: Governor's Palace in Rhodes, circa 1928 © Archive Touring Club Italiano.

Figure 2.3: Palazzo Ducale, Venice, Italy. Photo: Valerie McGuire.

that Italian designers, following Le Corbusier, claimed was suited to the Mediterranean. Many of the buildings were rationalist and inspired by Le Corbusier's modernism, but they had unusual, iconoclastic decorative elements.[39] Their embellishments borrowed "arabisances," or elements of Islamic architecture, and included curving rooftop parapets that suggest undulating waves, Moorish window treatments, and, in some instances, minarets and large domes. The architecture on Rhodes followed the same route as that of other colonial powers in reappropriating earlier manifestations of Orientalism in Western architecture.[40] While Di Fausto freely borrowed from a variety of architectural traditions, he was clearly committed to replicating familiar Italian architectural themes that would, by contrast, heighten the exoticism of the new built environment. And though Le Corbusier was an influence on Di Fausto's work the Italian city constructed on the island of Leros, which was much closer to realizing Le Corbusier's vision of the modernist city, in Rhodes the architect chose to integrate familiar medieval structures and eclectic motifs into the built environment of the tourist resort. This choice mimicked the efforts at conservation of the medieval and Ottoman past that were simultaneously taking place within the walled city of Rhodes.

Di Fausto's designs imported distinctive themes of Islamic architecture from other colonial settings. At the other end of the shoreline, adjacent to the entrance of the medieval city, was his New Market (see figure 2.4). He fashioned this grand hexagonal building after the Great Mosque in Kairouan, Tunisia. The New Market became a model for later constructions in Asmara (Eritrea) and Barce (Libya) and is perhaps the clearest reference to Italy's other colonial projects in North and East Africa. On its upper level, facing the shoreline, were to be the apartments of resident Italian officials and their families.

The center of the courtyard interior was appointed with a large gazebo with a copper dome, where local farmers and fishmongers were to gather to trade in produce and foodstuffs. The selling of local food products near

39   The rationalist school of architecture disavowed decoration; see Le Corbusier, *Towards a New Architecture* (London: Architectural Press, 1946).
40   "For the Italians did not essentially incorporate elements from local tradition but drew inspiration exclusively from their own heritage. In fact, however, architects did not need to study the local architectural tradition of neighboring countries for elements of 'Islamic' architecture, since cultural exchange between the East and the West in Italian art dates back to the Renaissance"; Colonas, *Italian Architecture of the Dodecanese*, 51.

Figure 2.4: Promotional image of the New Market
© Archive Touring Club Italiano.

this dome was included within a later documentary film about Rhodes' renovation suggesting the ways in which the Italian colonial government exercised "respect" for local customs.[41] When the New Market opened in 1926, the Italian administration heralded it as a watershed event and called for the immediate removal of all merchants still selling food or other goods in the medieval city.[42] Where the old market had stood in the walled city, the local administration had other plans: it promised to establish "one of those characteristic oriental bazaars" for the resale of artisanal products to tourists.[43] Thus, the local practice of a farmer's market was reframed within colonial modern architecture and a "bazaar" that could better enhance the

---

41　"Rodi Splendori di civiltà italica nell'Isola dei cavalieri. Le terme di Calitea e l'albergo delle rose," Giornale LUCE B0329 (1933), Istituto LUCE.

42　*"Disseminato nella città murata, senza la possibilità di un accurato controllo, quasi dovunque privo di acqua abondante, in locali non suscetibili di miglioramenti e di addattamenti, non rispondeva più alle specifiche condizioni della Rodi moderna, incamminata ormai sicuramente e fermamente sulla via di un meraviglioso e promettente sviluppo"*; Messaggero di Rodi, August 10, 1926.

43　*"Dopo l'apertura del Nuovo Mercato: Tentativo frustrato e illusioni cadute— Erbivendoli di occasione. Una opportuna ordinanza—contro gli abusi"*; Messaggero di Rodi, August 18, 1926.

Figure 2.5: New Market and the Palace of the Knights of St. John
in vertical communication and juxtaposition © Archive Touring Club Italiano.

touristic consumption of the Ottoman heritage in the island. As the reverse
image of the open-air market sanctioned by the Italian state, the "Levantine"
bazaar reinforced the links between colonial modernity and tourism.

The New Market was in a strategic position along the shoreline of the
port, both where visitors first landed and directly underneath the imposing
Palace of the Knights of St. John. Its position contributed to the carefully
crafted Mediterraneanness called for by Di Fausto in his 1926 master plan.
The view from the harbor and shoreline placed the New Market and Palace
in direct vertical communication with one another (see figure 2.5). This
relationship created a sharp, visually exciting contrast and suggested the
renewal of the two main symbols of the Italian intervention: Christian
medieval and colonial-modern (or Mediterranean). The effect was much the
same as in French Algeria where "the Casbah was locked behind the solid
row of French structures … engrav[ing] the power relations of the colonial
order onto the urban image."[44] And yet what distinguished the Italian case
in Rhodes from the French one in Algeria is that, although the design clearly
strove to accentuate hierarchies and economies of difference between the
local and the colonial, the Italian state also laid claim to the entanglement of
these histories as part of the new touristic experience of the island.

---

44   Zeynep Celik, *Urban Forms and Colonial Confrontations: Algiers under French Rule*
(Berkeley: University of California Press, 1997), 35.

Sights/Sites

In calling for Rhodes' transformation into a tourist destination, designers and planners built upon the island's existing cultural capital. By the mid-nineteenth century, Rhodes already enjoyed a reputation as an off-the-beaten-track detour for adventurous Grand Tour travelers in pursuit of the sights and smells of the Orient. Some of the island's more noteworthy visitors were, in effect, well-known, nineteenth-century Orientalists such as Gustave Flaubert, who visited Rhodes in 1850. Flaubert remarked "the bazaars are bright and open, and they do not have an Oriental character anymore" and that "it feels like a Greek grocery" (*"Les bazaars sont clairs et n'ont plus le caractère oriental—ça sent l'épicier grec"*).[45] In contrast with Flaubert's impression that Rhodes was already clean and losing some of its Oriental flavor, both hygiene and the restitution of an Oriental character remained priorities of the Italian state.[46]

As Jonathan Culler has wryly observed in his analysis of tourism, "The tourist is interested in everything as a sign of itself, an instance of a typical cultural practice: a Frenchman is an example of a Frenchman, a restaurant in the Quartier Latin is an example of a Latin Quarter restaurant, signifying 'Latin Quartier Restaurantness.'"[47] Following Culler, one might observe that, in Rhodes during the interwar period, the various tourism sites that Italy created during its occupation of the island sought to accentuate the island's "Levantineness" and to make the island into an emblem, once again, of the "Near East" or "familiar Orient."[48] As Edward Said first remarked, the tension between the "familiar" and the "Other" has always characterized Orientalist representations of the Levant. It was not merely that by conserving

---

45 Gustave Flaubert, "Rhodes" (1850), in *Voyage en Orient*, 320–36 (Saint-Amand: Gallimard, 2006), 322.

46 As Ali Bedhad argues, by the nineteenth century many travelers like Flaubert expressed such a sentiment that the Orient was already "vanishing" with the century of France's greatest expansion having already passed. Bedhad, *Belated Travelers*.

47 Jonathan Culler, *Framing the Sign: Criticism and Its Institutions* (Norman, OK: University of Oklahoma Press, 1988), 155.

48 "The Orient was therefore subdivided into realms previously known, visited, conquered, by Herodotus and Alexander as well as their epigones, and those realms not previously known, visited, conquered. Christianity completed the setting up of main intra-Oriental spheres: there was a Near Orient and a Far Orient, a familiar Orient, which René Grousset calls '*l'empire du Levant*,' and a novel Orient"; Edward Said, *Orientalism* (New York: Vintage Books, 1978), 57.

the Ottoman that Italy emphasized the local Turkish community as a figure of cultural alterity, but also that, by domesticating and "familiarizing" parts of the island and framing its heritage for touristic consumption, the Italian state implied that Rhodes was in many ways a "familiar Orient," part of Asia and not Europe. As Culler has observed, there is a semiotic process at work in tourism, and that "the proliferation of markers or reproductions confers an authenticity upon which may at first seem egregiously inauthentic."[49] By subtly hinting at the "Levantineness" of the setting, new tourism frames made the traveler's encounter with the local culture and inhabitants into an "authentic" one.

Perhaps the best example of this quest to establish a subtle form of exoticism that could link the island to Orientalist histories is the Kalithea Baths. Located just outside Rhodes, the baths are the most fully articulated of the eclectic projects of Pietro Lombardi, who replaced Di Fausto as the Dodecanese resident architect in 1928. They were built to promote the possibility of health tourism to the islands, for persons wishing to undertake mineral water cures. Lombardi brought together diverse stylistic influences in planning the design: "elements of classical composition, Arabesque detailing, and International Style disposition."[50] Constructed upon the site of the Italian landing in Rhodes in 1912, the baths operated as a symbol of the transformation of Rhodes into a new outpost for colonial tourism in the Italian Mediterranean. Their overall design reflected the seasonal nature of tourism and each of the components of the buildings, including the double-chambered bathing pool, adjacent semi-circular building, and gazebo-entrance, allowed for natural ventilation that was to be pleasant during the summer months. The idea that the Kalithea Baths also embodied—corporally and physically—the Fascist regime's discourse of "regeneration" (or *bonifica*) was not lost on state actors and after the site's completion, Lago directed his administration to solicit medical organizations in Italy for help with promoting long stays at the baths as a source of palliative medicine for patients.[51]

The main building of the site was a large, concrete cupola with a small bathing pool that acted as a visual focal point for the baths' function to provide mineral therapy for tourists. The decorative elements adopted by the cupola represented Italian fantasies that their rule in the island was a "return"

49   Culler, *Framing the Sign*, 160.
50   Antoniades, "Italian Architecture in the Dodecanese," 19.
51   GAK DOD, Envelope 216[1]/1935. On Fascist advertising and propaganda and its entanglement with the corporal, see Karen Pinkus, *Bodily Regimes: Italian Advertising under Fascism* (Minneapolis: University of Minnesota Press, 1995).

to Roman Empire, but while subtly framing that return in a creolizing way—to suggest not only *romanità* but also exotic, Mediterranean difference. Although the large cupola evoked a Greek Orthodox church, any allusion to Byzantine architecture was discouraged by the cupola's isolation from adjoining structures. The cupola itself bore a Fascist-sounding promise to rejuvenate the visitor through the national discourse of a welfare state. Half of a Latin hexameter verse on the imposing cupola proclaimed a message about health being the reward brought to those who engaged in hard labor: "For the ailing [person,] not for the lazy [one,] I open my gifts of [good] health." The monumental size of the cupola and its openings for natural ventilation seem clearly to link the building to the Pantheon and ancient Rome. Lombardi placed additional Arabic decorative elements at the base of the cupola to enhance the overall allusions to Turkish religious architecture as well as to the Turkish *hammam*, or public bathhouse. The diamond-shaped openings of the ceiling are in an Islamic style and suggest his dictum that new architecture should be dressed in "Muslim attire" (see figure 2.6). The resulting complex of the site intimates multiple overlapping histories; but mixing these diverse referents to a pastiche-like effect also removes any sense of historical specificity. As one visitor declared, the success of the Kalithea Baths as a "paradise-like landscape" rested on the fact that the "architecture is completely in harmony with the vagueness of the place."[52]

The vagaries of the Kalithea Baths were also possible because of other choices the local administration was making about the "preservation" of Ottoman heritage in the island. The Kalithea Baths would not have expressed their full semantic meaning as a marker of "Levantineness" were it not for the presence of "authentic" Ottoman bathhouses that the typical traveler might also be able to visit. Not far from the medieval palace of the Knights of St. John where Lago inaugurated the master plan to renovate Rhodes was the so-called Turkish Quarter, where the island's minority Turkish and Jewish communities resided. Against the backdrop of a program to rapidly "Italianize" the island and make Rhodes into a modern tourist destination suited for a "cosmopolitan crowd" (*"folla cosmopolita"*), the local administration undertook the restoration of more than thirty Turkish mosques on the islands.[53] These

---

52 Maria Benzoni, *Oriente Mediterraneo: Memorie di una crociera* (Milan: La Prora, 1935), 144.

53 As a headline for the Messenger of Rhodes declared, *"La stagione balneare a Rodi: Le cure marine, climatiche, idropiniche; La folla cosmpopolita; Nobili famiglie italiane; Occorrono alberghi,"* Il Messagero di Rodi, October 8, 1929.

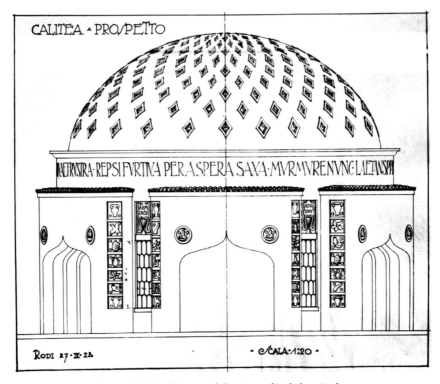

Figure 2.6: Architectural drawing of Kalithea Baths
© General State Archives of Greece, Department of Rhodes.

restorations were coupled with efforts to consolidate the old Ottoman world
as one of the island's main tourist attractions. In one corner of the medieval
city, Lago's administration even converted a mosque into a *hammam*, the
Bath of Soliman, intending it to service and promote the culture of the local
Turkish community. The administration ordered specially adapted "carpets"
and attire from Turkey to enable the "preservation of Oriental costume for
persons employed at the Bath" (see figure 2.7).[54] The reconstruction of the
Bath of Soliman also provided tourists with an additional spectacle and an
"authentic" experience of the Orient—one that confirmed both Italian culture
and their ethnic difference with the local population. As one traveler observed,

54 Lago also asked that at least *"due bagni-masseur di età superiore ai venti e inferiore ai
50 anni, moralmente e fisicamente sani e provetti nella tecnica del bagno turco"* always be on
hand; General State Archives of the Prefecture of the Dodecanese, GAK DOD, Envelope
121[4]/1928.

Figure 2.7: Interior of the Bath of Soliman, circa 1928, Rhodes, Greece.
Photo: General State Archives of Greece, Department of Rhodes.

the architecture of the Bath of Soliman was highly intriguing, but she herself would never deign to make use of it: "Those human bodies smeared with sweat seem like people about to suffer a Dantean punishment" ("*ma nell'interno, quei corpi umani colanti sudore sembran di gente che stia per subire una pena dantesca*").[55]

Not only were Turkish baths a touchstone among architects studying autochthonous constructions, but they also embodied Ottoman practices in everyday life that defined locals as different from Italians. Hermes Balducci called the local baths found in the island "particularly characteristic" of the Ottoman period because the Turks had been unable to adapt existing buildings from the period of the Knights of St. John and had hence needed to construct original models.[56] Balducci's description of the use of a *hammam* reveals a mixture of familiarity and fascination with the strange. As he dwells on the differences between Turkish bathing practices and Roman ones (from which they may have originated, at least in part, although Balducci made no note of this fact), he emphasizes the Turkish "reluctance" to use a bathtub

55   Maria Benzoni, *Oriente Mediterraneo*, 138.
56   Balducci, *Architettura turca in Rodi*, 37.

or swimming pool.[57] New public works such as the Kalithea Baths, then, invited Italians to enjoy the merits of the island in terms of Italian programs of hygiene, modernization, and urban renovation, while renovations like that at the Baths of Soliman drew visitors into the Orientalist fantasies that underpinned Italian colonial modernization. Conservation and Ottoman "preservation" worked together with the Fascist regime's temporalities of the colonial Mediterranean. It was the combination of both types of bathhouses that was best situated to express to travelers the view that Rhodes was at once traditional and modern, picturesque and cosmopolitan.[58]

Touristic appropriations of the local therefore rested on the idea that modernization did not serve to erase but to enhance the encounter with the exotic Ottoman past. When the first edition of the Touring Club Italiano's (TCI's) *Guidebook of the Colonies and Possessions* appeared in its signature red canvas format, with Rhodes and the Dodecanese as the first chapter, it offered precautionary suggestions about special dress for inland excursions and warned that Italians "of even the most modest means" would not feel comfortable in accommodations used by the local Orthodox community on the interior of the island. At the same time, the TCI laid claim to the idea that "nothing to meet the needs of tourists is lacking."[59] It was not just that

57 Balducci writes at length about the *hammam*, noting that "the prescriptions of the Quran in fact admit the bath as aspersion [sprinkling] and not immersion, and the Turk conceives of the operation of the bath as not only an act of cleaning but also a method of pastime. If then according to this concept it approximates in a certain sense the Roman bath [...] the modalities of the Turkish bath present themselves as wholly original in our view because of their strong reluctance regarding the use of the swimming pool or the common bathtub"; Balducci, *Architettura turca*, 37–38.

58 "*Il periodo bizantino ha scarsa importanza per Rodi per quanto duri otto secoli. È un periodo oscuro. [...] Solamente qualche chiesetta dalla caratteristica cupola a tamburo, qualche mosaico e qualche cadente muro di torri costiere attestano la lunga dominazione di Bisanzio*"; Touring Club Italiano, *Rodi: Guida del turista* (Milan: Bestetti & Tumminelli, 1928), 12. See also Colonas, *Italian Architecture of the Dodecanese*, 41–42.

59 "*Nulla le manca per soddisfare le esigenze dei turisti: facilità da sbarco e brevità delle operazioni doganali e sanitarie che vengono eseguite con speciale cortesia; alberghi di lusso e di primo ordine sul mare e in montagna; musei e biblioteche; estrema pulizia della città e facilità di poterla visitare in ogni dove; numerosi pubblici Giardini in cui le rose fioriscono*"; L.V. Bertelli, ed., *Guida delle Colonie e Possedimenti* (Milan: Touring Club Italiano, 1929), 75. The role of the Touring Club Italiano in creating momentum for tourism to Rhodes should not be underestimated. See Simona Martinoli, "Il ruolo del Touring," in *Architettura coloniale italiana nel Dodecaneso, 1912–1943*, edited by Simona Martinoli and Eliana Perotti, 43–57 (Turin: Fondazione Giovanni Agnelli, 1999). A 1926 obituary of Luigi Vittorio Betarelli, the founder of the Touring Club Italiano, aptly describes how Betarelli elevated tourism

the tourist could find luxury accommodation within the city of Rhodes, but more importantly, that a visitor's needs and expectations about the "colorful variety of ethnicities and languages" would be met during their stay on the island.[60] Mary Louise Pratt's concept of "imperial eyes" is appropriate here—that is, "the strategies of representation whereby European bourgeois subjects seek to secure their innocence in the same moment as they assert European hegemony."[61] Italian travelers who described the local population as "cosmopolitan" in fact tended to underscore the very modern and cosmopolitan regard they had for their own Italian culture. As one travel journalist for the Touring Club Italiano enthusiastically described, Rhodes was a microcosm of sorts: "Almost every evening I went to one of these coffee shops to observe all the different characters—Turks, Jews, Greeks, Levantines, Europeans, sometimes joined by a uniformed marine or one of our soldiers—and I listened to this sort of Tower of Babel of the many languages spoken in this tiny sliver of Mediterranean land."[62] Revealing of the new iconography of Italy's colonial cosmopolitanism is the cover of an early guidebook from the Touring Club Italiano: while it announces Rhodes with the words, "world capital of the Aegean" running as a celebratory banner, the image below features a lush scene of Ottoman minarets and palm trees that is suggestive of colonial difference and colonial fantasies of the Orient (see figure 2.8).

These staged encounters with the local population in the island also underscore how colonial display intersected with efforts to secure Italian sovereignty. Mario Lago's administration took care to ensure that throughout

to a religion of the nation: *"Luigi Vittorio Betarelli seppe elevare il turismo a religione di Patria; seppe, attraverso la descrizione e la valorizzazione delle bellezze naturali ed artistiche del nostro paese, insegnare agli italiani ad amare l'Italia e seppe dimostrare agli stranieri che l'Italia è il più bello paese che occupa uno dei primi posti nella scala della civiltà e del progresso";* Messaggero di Rodi, January 22, 1926. On the larger role of the Touring Club Italiano in Italian national and imperial politics, see also, Stephanie Malia Hom, *The Beautiful Country: Tourism and the Impossible State of Destination Italy* (Toronto: Toronto University Press, 2015).

60   "In the internal part of Rhodes (with the exception of Trianda and Sàlaco) and Kos and the other islands, there are only hotels and restaurants managed by Orthodox, visited by the local clientele, and it will be difficult for the Italian tourist, even of the most modest means, to find himself at ease here"; Bertelli, *Guida delle Colonie*, 18.

61   Mary Louise Pratt, *Imperial Eyes: Travel Writing and Transculturation* (New York: Routledge, 2008), 7.

62   Giotto Dainelli, "Rodi dei cavalieri," *Le vie d'Italia: Rivista mensile del Touring Club Italiano*, no. 3 (1922): 234–40, 236.

Figure 2.8: "Le capitali del mondo: Isole dell'egeo RODI." Cover of a 1926 guidebook featuring Turkish monuments in the background © Archive Touring Club Italiano.

the calendar year, all of the religious holidays and their attendant festivals took place and that these were advertised in the colonial newspaper, *The Messenger of Rhodes*. As Orazio Pedrazzi demonstrated during his visit to the village of Kremastò during Greek Orthodox Easter (discussed in the previous chapter), religious festivals were not accidentally a source of peculiar fascination for Italians: these had the potential to displace discursive constructions of nation and race that represented Greeks as a link to Italy's ancient roots in the Mediterranean as well as to draw the Aegean into the larger Orientalist representations. But the Italian imperial state's appropriation of local religious festivals also marked the integration of the islands into the Italian nation-state under Fascism; as has been documented, folkloric festivals were an important way in which the Fascist state entered into the everyday life of Italians.[63] Indeed, the Italian colonial administration usually referred to local religious festivals as *sagre*, the word for popular folkloric festivals in Italy. The office of propaganda and tourism on Rhodes annually published a list of festivals and events that were to take place throughout the year. By sponsoring and overseeing sporting events such as regattas and horse races, as well as religious festivals such as Greek Orthodox celebrations of the Dormition on August 15, the annual benediction of the waters on January 6, and the festivals of St. John (patron saint of the island) and St. Silvano (patron saint of the forest), and for the Muslim community, the festivals of Ramadan and Bairam, local religious expression entwined with the presence of a Fascist state in the islands.

As a further benefit, these festivals could in turn help to build up the island's profile as offering a considerable list of local festivities for international touristic consumption. The sponsoring of festivals helped affirm the idea that Fascist rule in the islands presented benevolent dictatorship. One example was the benediction of the waters, which took place on Epiphany, a "suggestive and picturesque Orthodox ritual" that Italy promoted as one of the key festivals for tourists to attend during the calendar year. In comparison with the interwar period, the Italian government had suppressed Greek Orthodox Festivities during the years of informal occupation (1912–23) when these became occasions for protest and displays of nationalism and had several times precipitated uprisings against the Italian regime.[64] Yet

---

63   See Stefano Cavazza, *Piccole patrie: feste popolari tra regione e nazione durante il fascismo* (Bologna: Il mulino, 2003) and Kate Ferris, *Everyday Life in Fascist Venice, 1929–40* (Basingstoke: Palgrave Macmillan, 2012).
64   See Cesare Marongiù Buonaiuti, *La politica religiosa del fascismo nel Dodecanneso* (Naples: Giannini, 1979), 18.

under Lago's rule, the festival revived; a short description of it by an Italian bureaucrat reveals how this event elided all potential for nationalism and confirmed rather the view that the locals were apolitical:

> Very picturesque procession thanks to the lavish hangings carried by the clergy, preceded by the flags, banners, and lights, and followed by the populace, they gather while singing chants at the gates of the Mandraki, the ancient port of the galley ships, where a crowd waits on the benches, in a great orgasm, a multitude of sailors and fishermen that fill up dozens of boats that form a sort of quadrant around the gates.

> *La processione assai pittoresca per i fastosi paramenti del clero, preceduta dagli stendardi dai labari e dai fanali e seguita dal popolo, si reca salmodiando al pontile del mandracchio, l'antico porto delle Galee, dove attende la folla sulle banchine, in grande orgasmo, una moltitudine di marinari e di pescatori che gremiscono moltissime barche che formano una specie di quadrato intorno al pontile.*[65]

As had been the case among Italian elites with regard to Southern Italy in the nineteenth century, the optic of the "picturesque" helped to enforce the view that peasants in Rhodes and the Dodecanese were apolitical subjects who did not oppose the Italian state. This description of an almost animalistic crowd, chanting, gathered together in great (orgasmic) agitation at the Mandraki pier in central Rhodes framed the main event when, after the patriarch threw the cross into the sea, sailors and fishermen dove in to retrieve it. A photograph by the Touring Club Italiano shows the successful fisherman emerging from the sea and climbing scaffolding to return the cross to the patriarch. His muscular bared body at the center of the photo seems to invoke a scene of Christ's passion; although the ceremony is Greek Orthodox, the image of it, when disseminated to Italians at home, is a particularly Catholic one (see figure 2.9). The photo conveys what Homi Bhaba would call colonial mimicry, which "appropriates the Other as it visualizes power."[66] Such mimicry is necessarily ambivalent: it disavows its attempt to reproduce power through representation. The photo encapsulates the logic of Italian governance under Lago, which disavowed the project to "colonize" or "assimilate" the local population while imagining the population as apolitical.

---

65   GAK DOD, 1935/216/1.
66   Homi Bhabha, *The Location of Culture* (New York: Routledge, 1994), 122.

Figure 2.9: At the port of Rhodes, a fisherman retrieves the cross and emerges from the sea; festival of the Benediction of the Waters © Archive Touring Club Italiano.

It is also worth noting that Lago's choice to re-stage these festivals for touristic consumption, apparently without any fear of inspiring nationalism or revolt, speaks to the repressive institutions that were in place at this time.

Mirroring the entanglement of East and West found in the architectural and urban *mediterraneità* described previously, guidebooks and travel itineraries commissioned by the Italian state supplemented this ambivalence with corresponding ideas about ethnicity and race. The large-format guidebook *Le colonie, Rodi, e le isole italiane dell'Egeo*, coauthored by the legendary mountain climber, explorer, and cartographer Ardito Desio, contained vivid photographs of the local communities of the Aegean islands and emphasized the colorful "Mediterranean" diversity of the landscape.[67] Rather than to speak of the cultural and linguistic differences separating Italians from the local population, the guidebook insisted on cultural stereotypes about Mediterraneanness and claimed that local Greeks revealed through their dialect the profundity of previous Venetian rule in the archipelago: "The sea-faring people even retain the Venetian sing-song in their manner of speech, and almost all of the terms to do with the sea

---

67 Ardito Desio and Giuseppe Stefanini, *Le colonie, Rodi, e le isole italiane dell'Egeo* (Turin: Unione Tipografico Editrice, 1928).

Figure 2.10: "The characters of a village of inner-Rhodes" ("Le personalità di un villaggio nell'interno di Rodi"), p. 395 of *Le colonie, Rodi, e le isole italiane dell'Egeo* © Archive Touring Club Italiano.

are Venetian or Genoese" (*la gente di mare ha talora la cantilena veneziana persino nel tono del discorso; e quasi tutti i termini marinare sono veneti o genovesi,*" 393–94). Adding that local Greeks had quickly apprehended the language of their rulers ("many by now speak Italian"), the guidebook depicted local Greek culture as uncannily similar to the "Mediterranean" character of Italians: "[The Greek] loves conversation and passes long hours at the café, playing cards, and above all, chatting about politics" (393–94). A picturesque scene of Greek "personalities" meeting at the coffee shop might easily have described a typical Italian *paese* of the same era, suggestive as it is of Italian stereotypes of the culture of the *mezzogiorno* (see figure 2.10). Such representations trafficked in stereotypes of Greeks and Italians as "one face, one race," and sought to reclaim an earlier colonial history in which Venice had dominated the Aegean and brought its culture and religion to Greek-speaking peoples.

But this Mediterraneanism also depended on subtle hierarchies and on a subject-splitting that located alterity in the idea of the Levant. Descriptions of Greeks, who took after their Italian rulers in both dialect and attitude, offered a stark contrast with guidebook descriptions of the Turk, who was "different, perhaps not so much physically—though he has almond-shaped eyes, full lips, and a drooping moustache that allows him to be easily recognized—as morally different" ("*Diverso è il tipo turco, ma forse non tanto fisicamente—per quanto la forma un po' a mandorla degli occhi, le labbra carnose, i spioventi lo lascino abbastanza spesso riconoscere—quanto moralmente*" [394]). The description of this Turk's almost grotesque physiognomy was indicative of his links to an Oriental and bygone way of life. Desio's *Le colonie, Rodi* described the Turk as generally immobile and sedate except when prey to irrational fits of emotion: "The Turk has nearly always a calm attitude, of a great philosopher, as he is for the most part. He doesn't say much; he's tranquil, but should he get irritated, he becomes violent" ("*Il turco ha quasi sempre un'aria paccata, di gran filosofo, che del resto lo è. Non fa molte parole; è tranquillo, ma se arriva ad irritarsi diventa violento*" [394]). The spiritual racism that labels the Turk a "great philosopher" barely disguised the fact that the Turk is viewed as a non-speaking and therefore apolitical subject (*non fa molte parole*). Furthermore, the guidebook rehearses the well-worn cliché of Oriental decadence: "He is certainly not a great one for work: he likes to sit and smoke the narghile, in mute contemplation" ("*Non è certo un gran lavoratore e gli piace molto starsene seduto a fumare il narghile, in muta contemplazione*" [394]).

Such a subject-splitting between "Levantine" inhabitants, on the one hand, and "Mediterranean" ones, on the other, was also ingrained into the recommended touristic itineraries of Rhodes. Complementing the master plan's new routes through the city of Rhodes, guidebooks suggested that travelers visit the new city first, take in its modernizing constructions, and then wander through the medieval city where they might discover the unexpected: "some small corner that makes your own personal sensibility vibrate" (*Rodi: Guida del turista*, 52). The guidebook explained how such a coordinated ambulation would make tourists into the heirs of a long tradition of poets who had visited Rhodes in the centuries after the island fell to the Turks and became a "sleepy" outpost of the Levant (54). The lingering residue of the Ottoman past, in other words, stood to generate for travelers a productive encounter with their own fantasies. Such a notion led to prosaic notions that the Italian traveler might welcome the ghost of an armored knight, or instead cross paths with an infirm or veiled Turk: "In certain alleys completely of stone and louvers, while you would expect to meet a knight clanking in iron, here comes silently an ass that carries a man hunched over by his fluttering turban, or here disappears into the distance the dark phantasms of veiled women. There is a lot of silence in this Daedalus of ancient alleyways. The Turkish population is restrained of voice and gestures" (55). Ottoman-era additions, such as common fenestration with an extended balcony, or *mashrabiya*, were left intact in the Jewish and

Figure 2.11: The Jewish Quarter with Ottoman-era balconies
© Archive Touring Club Italiano.

Figure 2.12: Inside the
monumental zone of
Rhodes, interior view
of medieval city gates,
after Italian renovation
and reconstruction circa
1930 © Archive Touring
Club Italiano.

Turkish areas of the medieval city (see figure 2.11). The Jewish and Turkish quarters designated as inside the monumental zone, or green belt, of the city that was particularly important to tourism (see figure 2.12). The Turkish and Jewish quarters—and more importantly, their inhabitants—came to constitute an essential part of the Fascist tour of Rhodes. Such historical preservation also justified expropriations to confiscate the property of Turks and Jews, enclosing these communities in one corner of the medieval city.

Rural Returns

By the late 1920s, the obsession with promoting "Levantineness," if only to give tourists a fuller sense of the "authentic" when visiting the Aegean, began to intersect with the anti-modernist turn in Fascist culture that took place in the same time frame. The *strapaese* movement, which took as its objectives a return to the rural and agricultural, the valorization of peasant culture, and the cultivation of provincial identities, became visible within photographic and filmic representations of the island, and, eventually, it marked a first turn toward excising the cosmopolitan and the Levantine—a turn that would be fully completed following the invasion of Ethiopia. In collaboration with the Touring Club Italiano, the local administration established a photographic archive to promote further international publicity of the island in 1926. As *The Messenger of Rhodes* described, the archive was dedicated to capturing "monuments, landscapes, events, costumes" that "illustrate Rhodes and the other islands under our rule in its most characteristic aspects."[68] Many of these photographs were destined for the pages of the guidebooks that tourists carried with them to Rhodes, but others appeared in coffee-table books that were clearly meant for consumption at home.[69] Frequently captured on film were the pastoral rituals (e.g., annual harvests), religious festivals, and traditional celebrations, supporting the local administration's efforts to promote folklore and religious and rural holidays within the island.

68   "*[Il Gabinetto fotografico] provvede a raccogliere e diffondere le fotografie di monumenti, di paesaggi di avvenimenti, di costumi, che, in forma squisitamente artistica, costituiscono il nucleo di una serie di pubblicazioni che illustrano Rodi e le Isole Egee sottoposte al nostro dominio nei loro aspetti più caratteristici*"; *Messaggero di Rodi*, March 25, 1926. I owe many thanks to Luciana Senna at the Archive of the Touring Club Italiano in Milan for making me aware of their photographic archive.
69   On the consumption of Italian colonial culture at home, see also Valeria Deplano, *L'Africa in casa: propaganda e cultura nell'Italia fascista* (Florence: Le Monnier, 2015).

Photographs of members of the local Turkish, Jewish, and Greek communities invariably show them in traditional dress, and to emphasize their contrast with Italian modernity, with new Italian architecture often in the background. An unusual photograph seems an attempt to highlight such contrasts between rural (Rhodes) and modern (Italy) in its capture of an encounter between a Greek local and an Italian visitor (see figure 2.13). The parallels and contrasts in this photograph are all the more striking in the details: the Italian woman wears the height of 1920s fashion while the Greek woman is in traditional peasant dress; the reins of the donkey are at the same level as the Italian cigarette. These contrasts are aligned to such a degree that they almost seem to point to parallels and equity, and a dangerous loss of colonial hierarchies and ideas of ethnic difference—indeed, despite their ostensible difference in costume the two women appear unfazed by the recognition of their cultural difference. But when the photograph was finally published the editors had excised the image of Italian tourist (see figure 2.14). If the unedited photograph documented the grand-scale tourism project that the local administration wanted to champion, it also contained the problematic figure of an Italian woman who within a few years would become a symbol of urban degeneration ("*la donna crisi*"). The final published photograph seems to mark what Lara Pucci has described as "the rejection of the self-obsessed urban woman in favor of the maternal peasant" that was central to the ideology of the *strapaese* movement and to its presentation of "the rural as antidote to the homelessness of modernism."[70]

These same excisions and inclusions are visible in film representations of the island. In 1928 a documentary filmmaker arrived from the LUCE Institute in Rome to film the island, with the commission to create cinematic footage that would complement the other promotional materials of Rhodes. An abbreviated version of the images he shot appeared as a three-minute newsreel representing the diverse communities of Rhodes—Greek, Jewish, Turkish, and Italian—through a series of processions.[71] The film traffics the same tourist clichés as guidebooks: as local Greek peasants parade through the cobbled streets of the old town of Rhodes, cosmopolitan Italian tourists wander through the new Italian constructions—the Hotel of the Roses and the Kalithea Baths—intimating the usual cliché that the island sat at a

70   Lara Pucci, "Remapping the Rural," in *Film, Art, New Media: Museum Without Walls?*, edited by Angela Dalle Vacche, 178–95 (New York: Palgrave MacMillan, 2012), 186.
71   "Rodi Splendori di civiltà italica nell'Isola dei cavalieri. Le terme di Calitea e l'albergo delle rose," Giornale LUCE B0329 (1933), Istituto LUCE.

Figure 2.13: Local
Greek woman in Rhodes
encounters Italian tourist,
circa 1927 © Archive of
the Touring Club Italiano.

Figure 2.14: "Peasant
woman of Rhodes"
("*Contadina rodiota*").
Photo: Ardito Desio
and Giuseppe Stefanini,
*Le colonie, Rodi, e le isole
italiane dell'Egeo* (Turin:
Unione Tipografico
Editrice, 1928), p. 405
© Archive of the Touring
Club Italiano.

crossroads of unique temporalities of modernity. A longer version of the film,
however, includes scenes that reveal greater intimacy, such as one in which
an Italian colonist (identifiable by his cork helmet) takes part in a Greek
festival, likely a "bride bazaar," in the village of Embona, joining the locals
during a ritual circle dance. The scene intimates the commonplace—but still
taboo—event of marriages between members of the Italian army and local
women. As Ruth Ben-Ghiat has described, "empire films also evoke other

Figure 2.15: Stills from "Il quartiere turco," *Rhodes*, 1924–31, produced and distributed by Istituto Nazionale LUCE. Photo at 19:08–20:10 © Archivio LUCE.

histories, fraught and forbidden, unrealized or unrepresentable, addressing the spectator through allusions and references flashed onscreen."[72]

But in locating such social intimacy into an appropriately rural and ritualistic context, the film also reinforces colonial hierarchies and implies that Italian colonists are leading the charge in returning to both the land and to tradition. Representations of the Turkish community likewise imply a return to an old Ottoman world held together by ritual and tradition. In a chapter of the documentary entitled *"Il quartiere turco,"* long pans show Turks in traditional Ottoman dress, including the fez, smoking lethargically, traversing the medieval city slowly on donkeys, and taking part in apparently rambling philosophic conversations (figure 2.15). The Turk reappears in the film "like a great philosopher, which for the most part he is," and steals the viewer's gaze with his Oriental costume, tranquility, and habitual smoking.[73]

---

72   Ruth Ben-Ghiat, *Italian Fascism's Empire Cinema* (Bloomington: Indiana University Press, 2015), xxii.
73   Desio and Stefanini, *Le colonie, Rodi*, 393–94.

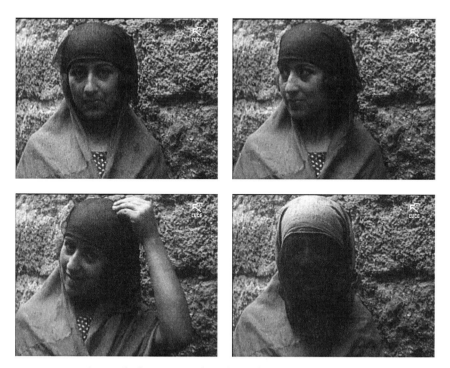

Figure 2.16: A Turkish woman replaces her veil at the request of the filmmaker, *Rhodes*, 1924–31, produced and distributed by Istituto Nazionale LUCE. Photo at 20:10-20:20 © Archivio LUCE.

In these scenes, the Turkish Quarter becomes the site of an Ottoman land that no longer exists, but that is being restored by the Italian state. With the collapse of the Ottoman Empire at the end of World War I, much of the eastern Mediterranean was now a region of increasing nationalism and nation-states, and the rise of Kemalist Turkey meant that just a few miles away from Rhodes, a different regime of modernization and modernity was underway. In one clip from the feature-length LUCE documentary, the viewer witnesses a Turkish woman respond to the filmmaker who, from offscreen, asks her to replace her veil; she seems to do so willingly, even briefly flashing a conspiratorial smile (figure 2.16). As this film fulfills the viewer's fantasy about an essentialized Orient on Rhodes, the viewer is brought into the narrow space of contact and intimacy with the colonial subject in ways that closely replicate the architectural project to bring the traveler safely into an encounter with the Ottoman. It is worth noting, moreover, that this action presents a reversal of the European colonial gesture as traditionally understood. As Frantz Fanon once argued, it has been the West's mandate to bring progress to the Orient, an idea that is most fully articulated in its insistence upon the unveiling of Muslim women.[74] Here we find the opposite, that is, an interest in keeping the Orient hidden behind the veil, in what seems perhaps a visual representation of the desire to include the Turkish community within the "local" in the same way that the Greek community was presented as a return to the rural.

But the gazing at the veiled woman, which the very apparatus of cinema reinforces, like that of bathing at the *hammam*, helps to reinscribe the Levantine into a space imaginary of the islands. By re-placing the veil (and by watching that act as a voyeur), the film affirms the rule of colonial difference, and the ongoing imperative to rule over the separation of ethnicities, to create hierarchies of difference, and to craft a civilizing mission that did not "modernize" so much as hold the local population as "picturesque" and different. In the meantime, the idea of the traditional and rural habits of the population clearly moved to promote the viewpoint that the local population was in some way familiar, and therefore part of the Italian imperial body politic. If both traditional and modern could work together in the terms of Mussolini's chronopolitics and discourse of dictatorship as an anti-modern modernity, it is less clear the degree to which these two apparently antithetical terms could work with regard to the praxis of rule and with regard to governing the local population. The question of whether locals in Rhodes and the other Aegean islands "belonged" in any meaningful way to the Italian state is an issue that the next chapter takes up at length.

Cosmopolitanism Italian Style

As the local government transformed Rhodes into an idealized touristic setting, hoping to offer the best of both "Western" and "Eastern" worlds, the Italian state advertised this project for mass consumption—both nationally in Italy and internationally in Europe and to other European communities in the eastern Mediterranean. Among the tens of thousands of tourists who visited the island of Rhodes in the 1920s and 1930s, many arrived there under the aegis of cruises organized by the Fascist trade union, the Organizzazione Nazionale Dopolavoro (OND), as well as by the Dante Alighieri Society, the

---

74   Frantz Fanon, "Algeria Unveiled," in *Decolonization: Perspectives from Now and Then*, edited by Prasenjit Duara, 42–55 (London and New York: Routledge, 2004), 55.

Società Geografica Italiana, the Naval League, the Italian Tourism Company, the Society of Italian Navigation, and the Fascist Colonial Institute. As Victoria De Grazia has shown, the OND was a key institution through which Italian Fascism entered into Italian civil society and manufactured consent for the party.[75] The involvement of the OND and other Fascist institutions in cruise tourism doubtless helped to produce an image of Rhodes as an extension of the peninsula. Guidebooks, photography, and documentary film as well as travel literature by both minor and major writers permeated everyday Italian life and captured consumers at home. As discussed in chapter 1, travel literature traverses many possibilities of alterity; in the Liberal era it indexed nationalism's complex engagement with the idea of the Mediterranean as both the noble origins of the Italian nation and a potentially dangerous colonial future. The following section discusses how travelers and organized tourism to Rhodes during the Fascist era also navigated the complex relationship to the Mediterranean and helped to secure colonial identities "at home," as the regime increasingly pointed to the overseas empire as its most significant accomplishment.

While the European colonial project had produced numerous noted French and British novelists and authors in the nineteenth century—from Gérard de Nerval to T. S. Eliot—major Italian authors had not yet participated in a central way in the Orientalist project.[76] New opportunities to witness and describe the experience of travel in the Orient—and to be published on the topic—were thus further signs that the Fascist revolution could also make Italians into a more "cosmopolitan" nation. When Carlo Emilio Gadda wrote about his visit to Rhodes in the early 1930s, he described an idyllic experience of the Orient thanks to the high standards of cleanliness found on the island. Gadda focused on the public works that had taken place between 1926 and 1930, when the master plan commissioned by Lago and designed by Florestano Di Fausto had dramatically and swiftly altered the port of Rhodes.

---

75 Victoria De Grazia, *The Culture of Consent: Mass Organization of Leisure in Fascist Italy* (New York: Cambridge University Press, 1981). Stephanie Malia Hom has further demonstrated how tourism was an important part of Fascist organization of leisure time; Stephanie Malia Hom, *The Beautiful Country: Tourism and the Impossible State of Destination Italy* (Toronto: University of Toronto Press, 2015).

76 Although, as Barbara Spackman has now evidenced, Orientalism did produce any number of "minor" writers in Italian culture. *Accidental Orientalists: Modern Italian Travelers in Ottoman Lands* (Liverpool: Liverpool University Press, 2017).

The work of Italian hands, the streets, large and good, that throughout the island make a tour by car a joy and that we were able, two days later, to compare these to the disastrous back alleyways of Corfu. Also by Italy are the buildings of the schools, the hotels, the stadium, the gorgeous church, military barracks, the governor's residence: it is lovely, the work of Italy in this cleanup and restoration of the masonry of the Knights-Hospitaller.

Opera di mano italiana le strade, larghe e buone, che per tutta l'isola fanno la gioia dell'auto e che potemmo, due dì dopo, paragonare con le sconquas-sa-budelle di Corfù. Opera italiana gli edifici delle scuole, degli alberghi, dello stadio, dalla bellissima Chiesa, delle caserme, della Residenza: e amoroso lavoro d'Italia la ripulitura e il riòrdino degli edifici cavallereschi.[77]

For Gadda, there was a clear difference between even Corfu and Rhodes: while Corfu had traces of Italianness and Venetian cities, it was in Rhodes, under Italian occupation, that the true vitality of the Italian state could be witnessed. Gadda had followed what was a typical cruise itinerary for Italian travelers of the Mediterranean, exploring Southern Italy first (with an emphasis on port cities and maritime spaces) and then traveling on to Rhodes and the Aegean. His essays on this experience appeared in various Italian newspapers throughout the 1920s, and then were later published as an anthology in 1931.

This new route through the Mediterranean followed by Gadda and others reprised but redefined the romantic journey to Italy—taken by Byron and Goethe, to name only two important Northern European travelers—but also rewrote the narrative of the peninsula as a cultural oddity. Grand Tour travelers tended to focus on the ancient ruins of Rome and to represent modern Italy, by contrast, as a nation of thieves and backward idolaters. This focus on the ancient past had helped to exclude Italy from the cosmopolitan and interna-tionalist movements of nineteenth-century Europe.[78] New tourism strategies, on the other hand, were positioned to change this perception of Italy as a nonmetropolitan nation. The image of a well-heeled Italian indulging in excursions through the eastern Mediterranean could signify Italy's emergent bourgeoisie and colonial cosmopolitanism and presents an image of Italy's

---

77 Carlo Emilio Gadda, "Approdo alle zattere," in *Il Castello di Udine* (Florence: Edizione Solaria, 1931), 144.

78 Joseph Luzzi, *Romantic Europe and the Ghost of Italy* (New Haven, CT: Yale University Press, 2008).

national resurgence under Mussolini. Rhodes became a mandatory stop for all cruises—and when an Italian cruise ship failed to port into the harbor, Lago would issue a stark reprimand to the Ministry of Foreign Affairs in Rome and ask that measures be taken to prevent this.[79]

Cruises organized by the state in turn resulted in a prolific production of travel literature. Memoirs of cruise journeys through the Mediterranean practically constitute a "whole new literature" foregrounding exoticism and Italian colonial empire, and they index a "collective experience" of touring the Mediterranean region.[80] Such an intersubjective literature aligned with the nationalist ideology of fascism. Accounts of the tour proclaimed that Italians had a natural affinity for travel and represented the Mediterranean as innate to the very definition of Italianness. In some instances, it was minor writers, like Maria Benzoni (described below), who made the tour of Rhodes; but major writers like Gadda and Franco Ciarlantini, an ideologue with the Italian Fascist state, also visited Rhodes and wrote fervent accounts celebrating the empire. Their accounts of the island of Rhodes as a restorative interlude that brought the individual back to health were a clear metaphor about how empire was restoring both health and pride to Italy. Ciarlantini, for example, observed that Italians were natural sailors. He equated his own journey with Italy's previous expansionist glories: "The Italian, when he leaves the coast of the peninsula and navigates toward the Levantine Sea, has the sensation (which corresponds to a profound reality) of navigating on natural routes, toward fated destinations, whose name echoes with greatness and glory."[81]

This travel literature reprised the myth of Greece as the return to an original homeland that had so strongly characterized earlier nationalist

---

79   In 1935, for example, Mario Lago inveighed against a cruise sponsored by the Italian Navigation Association that was to travel instead to the island of Patmos, which was "certainly notable as a curiosity, but in any case, not comparable to Rhodes." GAK DOD, 216/1935.

80   As Charles Burdett has observed, "The eastern Mediterranean was a common destination for many of the well-established writers of the interwar years." Lesser-known Italian writers who published their memoirs contributed to the formation of a "whole new literature" that was both generic and original: "the most striking feature of the accounts of the journeys to the eastern Mediterranean, whether written by Italian tourists or by travel writers following a tourist itinerary, is not the individual but the collective nature of the experience they record." Burdett, *Journeys through Fascism*, 24–25. See also Charles Burdett and Derek Duncan, *Cultural Encounters: European Travel Writing in the 1930s* (New York: Bergahn Books, 2002).

81   Franco Ciarlantini, *Viaggio nell'Oriente Mediterraneo* (Milan: Mondadori, 1936), 45.

depictions of the Aegean. The first stops in cruises to Rhodes were often other Italian maritime cities, often Genoa and Naples and the coastal cities in Apulia and Sicily, where travelers not only witnessed signs of Roman rule but also recuperated the memory of Mediterranean civilization. Maria Benzoni, in her own tour memoir, wrote that Syracuse was a city where "Greece and Rome had met one another, and where the refinement of one culture had given way to the power of the other."[82] Visits to the archaeological excavations of Magna Graecia gave travelers a narrative of fabled, cultural connection between the two ancient civilizations. They also bore witness to the fact that Fascism's modernity was committed to excavating a broader imperial past in Italy, as well as to expanding throughout the Aegean and the Mediterranean.[83] These traces of Roman rule in the Mediterranean thus provided travelers a sense of Italy's imperial heritage that went beyond the Italian Peninsula.

Such imperial heritage was also racially encoded and pointed back to the discursive constructions of the Mediterranean, along the lines of Giuseppe Sergi, as a place where the Roman stock had finally emerged to spread the seeds of Roman civilization. Camillo Sarti, for example, exclaimed over what he saw in Pompeii as the history of the emergence of Roman racial dominance: "The population of Pompeii for many centuries was a mix of ethnic groups; then the Roman element prevailed. At first, the city was a place for commercial exchange and traffic; then, with the Roman occupation, Pompeii became a center for holidays, fun, and the pleasure of rich Romans."[84] The colorful terms that Sarti used to describe Pompeii were also applied to Rhodes, where Sarti likewise encountered rich "Romans" on holiday. Travelers would eventually discover that in Rhodes, as Ciarlantini put it, the ashes of a great civilization were being gathered and reignited through the numerous public works undertaken by the Fascist regime.

Travel literature also corresponded to the new role of women to be protagonists of the Fascist regime's ideological goals.[85] Maria Benzoni, who

---

82   "Grecia e Roma s'incontrarono e la raffinitezza sapiente dell'una cedette alla potenza sapiente dell'altra." "Il pennacchio del Vesuvio ci saluta da lontano [...] Napoli non è per noi meta, ma semplice sosta per imbarcare passeggeri"; Benzoni, Oriente Mediterraneo, 39–45.
83   Josh Arthurs, *Excavating Modernity: The Roman Past in Fascist Italy* (Ithaca, NY: Cornell University Press, 2016). See also Giovanna Bandini, *Lettere dall'Egeo: Archaeologhe italiane tra 1900–1950* (Florence: Giunti, 2003).
84   Camillo Sarti, *Un viaggio in Oriente* (Varese: Nuova Italia, 1936), 24.
85   See Victoria De Grazia, *How Fascism Ruled Women, 1922–45* (Berkeley: University of California Press, 1992); Luisa Passerini, *Fascism in Popular Memory: The Cultural Experience of the Turin Working Class* (Cambridge: Cambridge University Press, 1987).

traveled to the eastern Mediterranean two times on cruises with the Italian Geographic Society, confessed at the outset of her sentimental narrative, *Oriente Mediterraneo*, that she was barely able to write about her experience because the exotic was just too ineffable for words. But this position of denying her authority, a typically feminine one, also acted as a pretense to sound the nationalist and patriotic spirit of tourism, its power to transcend the individual's experience of travel. Indeed, Luigi Orsini, the well-known poet and operettist, who provided an introduction (likely because Benzoni, as a woman, required a preface), explained that the memoir not only offered cultural and artistic interest but also made a valuable political contribution.[86] The book's epitaph further cites D'Annunzio, from whom she borrowed many literary devices, as her inspiration for setting sail to the colonies and, in the spirit of Fascist temporalities, she equated Italy's journey to the Orient as one that had brought the nation to a new dawn.[87]

Benzoni's appropriation of D'Annunzio enables this female author to write herself (and presumably her female readership as well) into the tradition of great men discovering new worlds. Like D'Annunzio, she opens her memoir with a confessional device, but uses it to assert the authenticity of her experience: her voyage has revealed land without limits, an incessant path of discovery, an eros too sensual for words. But once back home, Benzoni reports that by some extraordinary miracle she has been able to recall each and every precise detail of her voyage. She tells her readers that she has a photographic memory and that it has enabled her to recall her journey in perfect vividness: "And yet, with the distance of time, all the spectacles that seemed to be confused forever in a superimposition of the most variegated colors, uncertain contours, images and landscapes—which were continually new and different—become miraculously, clear again in the mind."[88] Benzoni describes to her readers a journey as a cinematic experience, comparing it to a never-ending film (*"cinema inesauribile"*).[89]

She also navigates carefully her subject position vis-à-vis the South. Visits to maritime cities in Southern Italy are precursors to the "true Orient" and disrupt any sense of Italian backwardness in connection with their position as Southern Europeans. If Benzoni personifies the Italian landscape and describes Vesuvius as a sleeping giant, she also takes care to note that Naples

---

86   Benzoni, *Oriente Mediterraneo*, 9.
87   Benzoni, *Oriente Mediterraneo*, 11.
88   Benzoni, *Oriente Mediterraneo*, 14.
89   Ben-Ghiat, *Italian Fascism's Empire Cinema*.

is a point of departure and not the final destination. After visiting the coast of Southern Italy and Sicily, travelers like Benzoni often sailed to Egypt, Lebanon, and Cyprus, while often disparaging these destinations as no more than delusions. European travel literature had misled travelers to expect in these capitals the grand cosmopolitan cities of French and British imperial rule. Instead, Benzoni endured the dingy doldrums of an Alexandria that "no longer has any trace of the splendor of a Hellenic or Roman civilization."[90] She summed up Cyprus in a word, "Disappointing!" and attributed its dilapidation to English rulers who were interested merely in the island's strategic importance and indifferent to its cultural value.[91]

Experiencing Rhodes as a superior destination in comparison with the degraded territories of the French and British empires recurs as a motif within Italian travel writing about the eastern Mediterranean. Ciarlantini disavowed any connection to the Orientalist cosmopolitanism that had inflected so much of nineteenth-century travel writing about Egypt.[92] He cited famous lines from Baudelaire (*"luxe, calme et volupté"*) as misleading and remarked that "docking at Alexandria was little more than a disordered scene of a caravansary."[93] Rhodes, on the other hand, was the sole place in the Orient that Italian travelers proclaimed one would never want to leave, a place one could call "home." The island was a true spectacle of Italy's regeneration of the Mediterranean, with its new public works, such as the Italian-administered schools, industries, and sanitation.[94] Rhodes provided a virtuous moment within the tour, one that enabled "the restoration of the spirit and of body, like an Oasis in the hot Levantine cities."[95] As in Sarti's Mediterranean itinerary, Rhodes was often a stop that travelers made when returning to Italy after having visited other cities of the eastern Mediterranean, making the island

90   Benzoni, *Oriente Mediterraneo*, 46.

91   Benzoni, *Oriente Mediterraneo*, 128.

92   For that matter, the descriptions of the eastern Mediterranean by Ciarlantini, Benzoni, and Sarti differed from earlier Italian depictions of Egypt. See Lucia Re, "Alexandria Revisited: Colonialism and the Egyptian Works of Enrico Pea and Giuseppe Ungaretti," in *A Place in the Sun: Africa in Italian Culture from the Post-unification to the Present*, edited by Patrizia Palumbo, 163–96 (Berkeley: University of California Press, 2003).

93   Ciarlantini, *Viaggio nell'Oriente Mediterraneo*, 6.

94   On spectacle and Fascist Italy, see Simonetta Falasca-Zamponi, *Fascist Spectacle: The Aesthetics of Power in Mussolini's Italy* (Berkeley: University of California Press, 2000).

95   Ciarlantini, *Viaggio nell'Oriente Mediterraneo*, 96–104.

part of a passage home after a journey through the bewildering Orient. An abundance of advertising followed up on this theme of homecoming with the claim that any traveler who visited Rhodes would feel compelled to return a second time.

And yet, travelers still insisted upon the erotic and Orientalist possibilities that the island also offered. In words that only thinly conceal a metaphor of seduction, Ciarlantini declared that "only he who loves and knows how to understand the Orient" would appreciate the fantastic architecture, tapestry of colors, and clamor of sounds and smells that made Rhodes a port of call. Likewise, Benzoni, in one of her many descriptions affirming that the regime had effected a masterful reshaping of the island, commented upon the profound excitement that beckoned the visitor to explore. "Do you want to get another view?" she asks her readers rhetorically, "it's enough to wander (*"penetrare"*) into the animated streets of the bazaar and the Jewish quarter where the people are noisy, happy, and live, you might say, 'in the heart of the people,' in courtyards and in open houses."[96]

The relationship between the erotic nature of "exploration" and colonial conquest has been widely explored, especially by Ann McClintock. As in the previous chapter's discussion of Gabriele D'Annunzio's voyage to Greece, it was present in representations of Greece despite the fact that these same imaginaries introduced an image that was the inverse of difference: the notion of the *italogreci* and primordial "cosanguinity" within the Mediterranean. During the interwar period, travel writers, while appropriating these earlier notions, insisted that the Fascist state had been able to resolve the paradox inherent in these contrasting representations of Greece. The intricate cultural landscape designed by the Italians that was "picturesque as well as cosmopolitan," as Benzoni explained, was consumable, precisely because a program of colonial hygiene had made it so.[97] The Italian state had made the Jewish quarter into a "marvel along with the cleanliness of the old quarters: empty streets and beautiful houses that have recently been whitewashed: nothing appears of the Oriental dirtiness," and yet it was not dispossessed entirely of its charming and Oriental character either.[98] Benzoni declared that it was distinctly Italian (and by implication Fascist) to have achieved such a harmonious integration

---

96   "Volete mutare quadro? Basta penetrare nelle animate vie del Mercato e del quariere israelita dove la gente è chiassosa, allegra, e vive, si può dire 'coram populo' nei cortile e nelle camera aperte." Benzoni, *Oriente Mediterraneo*, 137.

97   Benzoni, *Oriente Mediterraneo*, 134.

98   Benzoni, *Oriente Mediterraneo*, 138.

of the Orient's exotic (and erotic) possibilities and its domestic (and colonial) comforts: "only Italy, heir to Rome, could reach such an exact measure of expansion, and give such a noble aspect to new Rhodes."[99]

It might be easy to dismiss, as mere imperial touring propaganda, travel memoirs insistence as clichéd "best of both worlds." However, beneath the veneer of touristic packaging was a local population under forceful occupation. This fact, too, was rewritten by visitors to the island. Ciarlantini, for example, declared that the ethnic diversity of Rhodes was testament to Italy's "rejoining" of the diverse societies of the Mediterranean. His metaphor was quite similar indeed to that of Fascism itself as the rejoining of the Latin fasces. The notion that Rhodes was a "multicultural" and "multiethnic" island, one of the last surviving spaces of its kind from the once sprawling Ottoman Empire, came to be within the service of the Fascist state:

> In its closed circle a variety of languages are spoken: Italian among metropolitans, Turkish among the Muslims, Greek among the Orthodox, and the Spanish dialect among the Jews; and all these citizens, of different languages and customs, live in their respective quarters, which are animated and clean, in perfect concordance, in lively respect for the observations of religion, to which they are extremely attached. The Muslims celebrate on Friday, the Israelites on Saturday, the Christians on Sunday; attending the mosque, the synagogue, the Orthodox and Catholic churches, according to their confession, each one has his own civil and personal status and life carries on in full harmony, one would be tempted to say idyllically.

> *Rodi è un esempio perfetto, molto in piccolo si capisce, della pacifica convivenza di razze e di civiltà diverse. Nella sua ristretta cerchia si parlano le più svariate favelle: l'italiano dai metropolitani, il turco dai mussulmani, il greco dagli ortodossi, un gergo spagnolo dagli ebrei; e tutti questi cittadini di lingua e di costume così diversi, vivono nei loro rispettivi quartieri animati e puliti, in perfetta concordia, in vicendevole rispetto delle costumane e delle religioni cui sono attaccatissimi. I musulmani festeggiano il venerdì, gli israeliti il sabato, i cristiani la domenica; frequentando la moschea, la sinagoga, la chiesa ortodossa o cattolica, a seconda della confessione, ognuno ha un suo statuto civile e personale, e la vita si svolge in piena armonia, si sarebbe tentati di dire idillicamente.*[100]

99   Benzoni, *Oriente Mediterraneo*, 134.
100 Ciarlantini, *Viaggio nell'Oriente Mediterraneo*, 114.

Very often these invocations of diversity trafficked the notion of renewing a *pax romana* and the idea that the Mediterranean would become a utopia under renewed "Roman" dominion. Yet Ciarlantini's words do in fact indicate the way this "idyllic" coexistence depended upon the separation of ethnicities, via the creation of ethnic neighborhoods, symbols, religious days, individualized civil statuses, and, finally, a keen sense of ethnic otherness. This lively sense of otherness, latent and productive in designers' and state actors' ambitions for the island during the first decade of Italian Fascist rule, fully revealed itself following the invasion of 1935–36 invasion of Ethiopia.

Beyond Mediterraneanness

Up until the end of Rhodes' occupation in 1943, when Italy signed an armistice with the Allies and promptly lost the islands to German control, the regime maintained that introducing tourism in Rhodes had been one of its major colonial success stories, and central to the way the Fascist state was able to spread Italian culture through imperialism. Gabriele D'Annunzio's early travel narrative presaged many of these representations with his fantasy that colonizing Greece meant returning to Magna Graecia. Travelers who visited Rhodes during the period of Fascist rule reprised many of the same tropes that nationalists such as D'Annunzio of the Liberal era had applied to the Aegean, although now they united these under the metaphor of *mare nostrum*. Where they differentiated themselves from the Liberal-era nationalists is that they began to see Rhodes and the Aegean as almost like home. Securing Italian sovereignty in the islands seems to have meant, at least to a certain extent, that Italians imagined the "Orient" as safe for consumption. The different touring frames the local administration brought into the urban landscape pivoted on the notion that the Ottoman past could be brought into line with the rhetoric of Fascist modernity as both the rise of a modern bourgeois class and the return to traditional values and folkloric culture.

Yet there remained an unequivocal ambivalence to these imaginaries casting the island as simultaneously Western and Eastern. These haunted and undermined Fascist efforts to cast Rhodes as a symbol of Italy's national regeneration in the Mediterranean. And while the tension between "Eastern" and "Western" identities was at the core of the project between 1926 and 1936, the appeal of Rhodes' dual status became unsustainable after the invasion of Ethiopia. In the context of urgent demands for hierarchies of race and difference, both the image of Oriental exoticism—what this chapter has called the expression of "Levantineness"—as well as the regime's official embrace of Mediterraneanness, which had been so carefully produced for consumption, became targets for Fascist programs of hygiene and "purification." After 1937, under the influence of heightened anxieties about race, the local government overhauled the built environment of Rhodes yet again, this time removing its own exoticizing stamp. Cesare De Vecchi, who presided in Rhodes as governor from late 1936 to 1940, initiated a major intervention to "cleanse" the architecture constructed in the 1920s of its Islamic-style decorations, calling for an aesthetic regime of *romanità* to replace that of *mediterraneità*. Hermes Balducci, who had earlier embraced the Ottoman heritage of Rhodes, declared, "We should accept that domes and minarets convey an image that is anything but characteristic of the city. We believe that one of the primary duties of architecture in an occupied territory is to express the personality of the conqueror tangibly over a long term. The art of modern construction in Rhodes systematically must be purely Italian inspiration and sentiment; it must promote the stamp of *romanità*."[101]

A turn toward a more rationalist aesthetic for new constructions aimed to make the Knights of St. John into the unifying referent for all Italian architecture. Further land expropriations expanded the city of Rhodes, yet another restoration of the walled city of the Knights-Hospitaller was undertaken, and new buildings were commissioned in a monumental, neo-medieval style. De Vecchi further called for "purification" of many of the Islamic decorations that had defined the aesthetics of *mediterraneità*. One of the most dramatic interventions was the stripping of the chamfered arches of the Hotel of the Roses, and their replacement with Roman-style arches similar to those of the Palazzo della Civiltà, the so-called Square Coliseum in Rome's EUR district, which was built in 1940 to commemorate the enactment of Italian Empire. The chamfered arches in the hotel's original formation recall other Mediterranean resorts, including the Excelsior Hotel at the Lido in Venice. After their removal, the Hotel of the Roses was further replastered with *finta pietra* so as to give the hotel the same neo-medieval style that characterized the other new building projects (see figures 2.17 and 2.18).

The "purification," with its interventions upon the walled city to strip its Ottoman monuments and restore its medieval, Crusader aesthetic, expanded the emphasis on the Crusader period already present in the original 1926

---

101 As cited in Colonas, *Italian Architecture of the Dodecanese*, 56.

Figure 2.17: The Hotel of the Roses in the Lago era
© General State Archives of Greece, Department of Rhodes.

Figure 2.18: The Hotel of the Roses after the De Vecchi "purification" in 1938.
© General State Archives of Greece, Department of Rhodes.

master plan. It also included a second major renovation of the Palace of the Knights of St. John, now the seat of the governor, to reinforce the martial and imperial character of the most important landmark of the island. Renovators used Hellenistic-era mosaics and Roman-era statuary, taken from the nearby island of Kos, to decorate the palace, underscoring the classical heritage of the islands. Interestingly, this "purification" of the built environment made the island look less like a picturesque version of Italy and more like its counterparts in colonial Africa.[102] Mia Fuller notes that the later emphasis on the "historic" character of Rhodes, together with the increasing mania for preservation, led to the transformation of the island into a museum piece that could conceal the colonial program while linking the island to Italy's campaigns in Africa. The novelist Lawrence Durrell, while stationed on Rhodes during transitional British rule of the island from 1945 to 1947, commented on the "hideous archness" of the renovation, calling it a brash testament the Fascist ideology of Italian colonial rule.[103]

As Derrida has noted in his well-known lectures on hospitality, in ancient Greek the word for "guest" is the same as the word for "foreigner," *xenos*, and hence *xenophilia* (hospitality) and *xenophobia* share the same root.[104] Fantasies about friendship and making the strange familiar are forever bound to anxieties about the foreigner. In constructing a tourism economy for Rhodes, the Italian regime claimed to be reviving the ancient Mediterranean traditions of hospitality and "modernizing" and "domesticating" the Orient when, in fact, tourism also sought to keep alive the foreign and potentially dangerous stranger, by reproducing the Levant in new architecture and by incorporating the spectacle of the Muslim Turk, the Orthodox Greek, and the Sephardic Jew into the tour of the island. The tension between self and other and the oscillation between the familiar and the strange also allowed the possibility of ambivalence and encouraged the loss of difference. In the final phase of their rule, the Italians no longer imagined Rhodes as a "home away from home," but as a facsimile of a forgotten Crusader era. The focus on archaeological projects in Rhodes and Kos in the late 1930s also

---

102   See Mia Fuller, "Preservation and Self-Absorption: Italian Colonization and the Walled City of Tripoli, Libya," in *Italian Colonialism*, edited by Ruth Ben-Ghiat and Mia Fuller, 131–42 (New York: Palgrave and MacMillan, 2005), 138.

103   Lawrence Durrell, *Reflections on a Marine Venus* (London: Faber and Faber, 1963), 28.

104   Jacques Derrida and Anne Dufourmantelle, *Of Hospitality*, translated by Rachel Rowlby (Stanford, CA: Stanford University Press, 2000).

helped to bring the wider rhetoric of a new Roman Empire in Africa and the Mediterranean into the urban fabric and cultural landscape of Italy's possessions in the Aegean.

After 1937, the sense of the Aegean islands' importance for the Italian Empire still resided in the ways in which the islands reunited Italy to its history of expansion in the eastern Mediterranean. The difference was that the urban environment now emphasized the Crusader, the Roman, and to a lesser extent, the Hellenistic past as part of Italian culture and history. Such emphasis embodied the hardline regime of assimilation that characterized the Italian occupation between 1937 and 1940 when, under the rule of De Vecchi, all religious private schools and native languages were banned, Italian being the only language permitted for instruction (see chapter 4). As the next chapter discusses in greater depth, De Vecchi also attempted to expel a quarter of the island's Jewish population by deploying the anti-Semitic race laws, or laws for the defense of the race (*La difesa della razza*), against nonnative Jews of the islands during the same time frame.[105] In comparison with other Italian colonial territories, however, the idea of *romanità* ultimately arrived much later, and when it did, it insisted on the Crusader era as its signifier rather than the Roman Empire.[106] With the invasion of Ethiopia and rumors that sanctions against Italy had led to a deterioration of the situation in Rhodes, including an outbreak of malaria, international tourism declined sharply. Nevertheless, even after Italy entered World War II and the Mediterranean became a theater for major international hostilities, the local administration continued to try to promote tourism and kept careful records of the number of seasonal visitors to the island until 1942.

The De Vecchi period of *romanità* has often been labeled by locals as an aberration, a period that ran counter to the regime's commitment to

105   Marco Clementi and Ireni Toliou, *Gli ultimi ebrei di Rodi: Leggi raziali e deportazioni nel Dodecaneso italiano, 1938–1948* (Rome: DeriveApprodi, 2015); see also, Renee Hirschon, "The Jews of Rhodes: The Decline and Extinction of an Ancient Community," in *The Last Ottoman Century and Beyond: The Jews in Turkey and the Balkans, 1808–1945*, edited by Minna Rozen, 291–307 (Tel Aviv: Tel Aviv University, 2002).

106   Simona Troilo, "'A Gust of Cleansing Wind': Italian Archaeology on Rhodes and in Libya in the Early Years of Occupation (1911–14)," *Journal of Modern Italian Studies* 17, no. 1 (2012): 45–69, and Simona Troilo, "Pratiche coloniali. La tutela tra musealizzazione e monumentalizzazione nella Rodi 'italiana' (1912–1926)," *Passato e Presente* 87 (2012): 80–104, and Stephen Dyson, *In Pursuit of Ancient Pasts: A History of Classical Archaeology in the Nineteenth and Twentieth Centuries* (New Haven, CT: Yale University Press, 2006), 183–84.

modernize but also "respect" local traditions and customs. This chapter has therefore attempted to demonstrate the extent to which the commitment to modernization programs in Rhodes in the 1920s and 1930s, when the massive project to transform the island of Rhodes into a model tourist destination and to celebrate its "multiethnic" history was put to work toward creating a consumer and "cosmopolitan" culture, in fact may anticipate the shift toward *romanità*. An earlier incarnation of Fascist colonial chronopolitics was certainly mobilized through the idea of *mediterraneità* and manifest in the popular celebration of the island as at once traditional and modern, Eastern and Western. Whether one viewed Rhodes from the vantage point of the harbor, through the pages of one of the numerous guidebooks produced by the Touring Club Italiano, or from the inside of a local Turkish bath, the island continually disrupted provincial and national identities and replaced them with metropolitan and colonial ones—all the while narrowing the gap between "self" and "other," so as to further ingrain Italy's sovereignty in the islands. It was ironically precisely the imaginative possibilities of such *mediterraneità* that Italy chose to negate following the invasion of Ethiopia and the official enactment of empire.

The tourism project in Rhodes thus stands as a powerful emblem of not so much the way that Italian Fascism invested in modernization programs in its overseas colonial territories but the way in which colonial politics were, in effect, an extension of national politics and an area in which policies were subject to drastic shifting with the ideological changes of the Fascist state. As the next chapter demonstrates, a similar dynamic was to be at work in rule over the local population. The same paradox of eliding ethnic difference for the sake of securing a nation-empire, while also maintaining for the sake of ensuring the ethnic purity, eventually came to arbitrate the administration of citizenship over the local population.

CHAPTER THREE

Belonging in the Archipelago: Nation, Race, and Citizenship

Since the first colonization of Eritrea in the late nineteenth century, Italy had applied some form of civil status to all the native populations under its colonial rule. In 1919, at the end of World War I, Italy further created the first formal colonial citizenship status, for Libyans in Tripolitania and Cyrenaica (excluding the nomadic population).[1] Like the natives of French Algeria, on which the model was largely based, Libyans became Italian nationals who held local political rights but were exempted from military service and retained the "personal statute," that is, the right to conduct most judicial affairs within their religious communities and to maintain autochthonous practices of marriage. In Libya, the creation of this citizenship status for Libyans (*cittadinanza italiana libica*) corresponded with new and eventually repressive projects to Italianize the Arab part of the native population, including replacing the Koranic schools with a system of public schools in which all subjects were taught in Italian and the native language was banned.[2]

When Italy wrote into law and applied *cittadinanza italiana egea*, Italian Aegean citizenship, to all natives of the Aegean in 1924, it was therefore the newest tier in a growing economy of colonial subjectivities that were hierarchically differentiated according to race—with sub-Saharan Africans holding a lower status than Muslim natives of Libya, and Greeks, Turks, and Jews in the Aegean enjoying a status that was considered by many, both locals and

---

1   See Florence Renucci, "La strumentalizzazione del concetto di cittadinanza in Libia negli anni Trenta," *Quaderni Fiorentini Per La Storia Del Pensiero Giuridico Moderno*, nos. 33–34 (2005): 319–42.
2   See Matteo Pretelli, "Education in the Italian Colonies during the Interwar Period," *Modern Italy* 16, no. 3 (2011): 275–93.

state actors alike, to be a form of Italian nationality that guaranteed Italian sovereignty in the Aegean. Like Libyan citizenship, Aegean citizenship eventually also included the right to naturalize to full Italian citizenship through the completion of military service. But the citizenship project in the Aegean was to evolve in a very different fashion than the one in Libya. Unlike in Libya, where Italian citizenship did not include the Bedouin population, Italian Aegean citizenship applied to all natives living in the islands at the time of annexation; eventually, it would be applied to almost any person who could show some form of connection to the islands, through family or property. The project to Italianize the local population was also to look very different than the one in Libya because institutions for the dissemination of European language and culture were already in place from the Ottoman era. By 1934, not only would Italian Aegean subjects have the right to acquire full Italian citizenship, but the Italian state would also recognize the population's need for mobility, providing Italian Aegean citizenship to Dodecanese emigrants in Egypt as well as their descendants. Against the backdrop of the ending of the era of open borders, and the United States' introduction of quotas aimed at emigrants from southeastern Europe, substantial parts of the population were to find Italy's citizenship initiatives at least acceptable if not welcome.

Perhaps most revealing of the singularity of the citizenship project in the Dodecanese is the fact that of all of Italy's former colonial citizenships it is the only one still present in the postcolonial era. In ways that partly parallel the experience of the *pied-noir* communities in France, Italy's Jewish communities in former colonial territories in the southeast Aegean preserve their right to Italian citizenship in the twenty-first century. This stands in marked contrast with the lack of citizenship guaranteed to former colonial subjects of Italian East Africa and North Africa, and the significant barriers that immigrants to Italy and their children have faced in obtaining citizenship. The direct descendants of former Italian Aegean nationals have been able to acquire Italian citizenship on the basis of heritage, even in cases in which neither the applicant nor any of their parents or grandparents were born in Italy.[3] This has been even more so since 1992 when the Italian

---

3   On the Rhodesli diaspora and their adoption of citizenship ties, see Renee Hirschon, *The Jews of Rhodes: the Decline and Extinction of an Ancient Community* (Tel Aviv, Israel: Chair for the History and Culture of the Jews of Salonika and Greece, Goldstein-Goren Diaspora Research Center, Tel Aviv University), and Renee Hirschon, "Cosmopolitans in the Old Town: The Jews of Rhodes: A Story of Extinction and Survival," paper

government strengthened norms for acquiring Italian citizenship on the basis of heritage.[4]

As Daniel Gorman has shown in his innovative study of the British Empire's use of citizenship for its colonial subjects, citizenship—one of the most fundamental indicators of belonging in modern nation-states—was rife with paradoxes when it was adopted for the colonial subjects of an empire. As Gorman remarks, "in seeking to create an imperial citizenship ... they faced the challenge of developing political and cultural bonds under the aegis of an Empire which was not, in and of itself, a state."[5] The paradox that Gorman elaborates was to prove extraordinarily acute in the case of the Dodecanese where colonization was undertaken by a Fascist government whose very premise was the consolidation of strong nation-state. On the one hand, nationalism and Italian national identity entwined with the expansion of colonial territories in the Mediterranean making Italian statehood in the islands a central part of its imperial discourse; on the other hand, the Dodecanese, because of their large ethnic Greek population, could not be included as part of Italian national territory without inciting an immediate diplomatic upheaval.

Speaking to the Italian Parliament on the eve of formal annexation of the islands, Orazio Pedrazzi, who had toured the interior of Rhodes in 1913 strapped ungracefully to a donkey (chapter 1), hinted at the ambiguous terms that were to locate the Dodecanese squarely within such a paradox: the islands were to be neither a colonial project, like Libya, nor a provincial extension of the Italian nation, like Trento and Trieste:

> A province, no. Our possession [the Dodecanese] cannot be viewed as the same as a strip of national territory not only because of the political

presented at Deportation of Jews and Rhodes and Cos: 1944–2014, a Commemorative International Symposium on the Holocaust in the Aegean, Rhodes, Greece, July 22, 2104. As Hirschon points out, the diaspora of Jews of Rhodes and Kos is so expansive and multiple that later generations may hold multiple citizenships and passports, but due to the fact that the islands of Rhodes and Kos only became part of the Greek state at the end of World War II, ironically Greek nationality is not counted among the long list of national identities that the Rhodesli diaspora collectively maintains.

4   As Teresa Fiore has pointed out, the strengthening of the practice of offering citizenship for second and generation Italians occurred, in 1992, against the backdrop of expanding immigration into Italy. See Teresa Fiore, *Pre-Occupied Spaces*, 1–21.

5   Daniel Gorman, *Imperial Citizenship: Empire and the Question of Belonging* (Manchester: Manchester University Press, 2013), 2.

problems that impact and complicate its internal administration but also because of the civil status of the population. [...] A colony, no. The population of the Dodecanese is not a population of color: they do not need to be civilized but only assisted.[6]

Una provincia no. Questo possedimento non può essere considerato alla stregua di un lembo di terra nazionale non solo per gli speciali problemi che sfuggono completamente alle funzioni della politica e della amministrazione interna, ma soprattutto per le condizioni dello stato civile della sua popolazione. [...] Le popolazioni del Dodecanneso non sono popolazioni di colore, non hanno bisogno di essere civilizzate e hanno bisogno solato di essere assistite.

Pedrazzi's views on the matter, later anthologized as *Il Levante Mediterraneo e l'Italia* (*The Eastern Mediterranean and Italy*), reveal how a subtle politics of race was already beginning to work in definitions of sovereignty in the Dodecanese in the early 1920s, helping to secure the project as a colonial one even despite the "whiteness" of the local population. Even as Pedrazzi insisted on all the ways in which the Italian mandate in the Dodecanese was not "colonial," and that the islands did not have a subject population of "color," and that if the Italian state were to treat their acquisition as an "end in itself," the rest of the world would "laugh in our face" he described a grandiose future for "the Muslims, the Jews and the Orthodox, who one fine day would become Italian citizens with the same rights and obligations," but who were still not "ready" for the full rights and responsibilities of Italian citizenship.[7] As will be seen in chapter 4, this fundamental in-betweenness of the local population was to help make Italian Aegean citizens into proto-postcolonial subjects who while still under European imperial rule in the interwar period would adopt strategies of creatively reworking the colonial system that resemble our own era of transnational nation-states and global mobilities.

This chapter describes how the creation and administration of *cittadinanza italiana egea* was a key tool for navigating the Aegean islands' status as a *possedimento*, or a possession—that is, as neither a province of Italy nor a colony. Retracing Italian Aegean citizenship shows further how Italy's ideas about imperial subjectivities in the Aegean were to a certain degree tied to its own complex experiences of mobility and diaspora throughout the Mediterranean

6   Pedrazzi, *Il Levante Mediterraneo e l'Italia* (Milan: Alpes, 1925), 40–41.
7   "*I mussulmani, gli ebrei, gli ortodossi, che diventassero cittadini italiani con gli stessi diritti e doveri*"; Pedrazzi, *Il Levante Mediterraneo e l'Italia*, 40.

and more globally, to create even further questions and instability about what it meant to forge imperial rule in the Aegean. The familiarity with which Italians viewed their Dodecanese "citizens" also coexisted with the will to bring Dodecanese subjects into wider Fascist expansion schemes for empire in Africa and the Levant, and this, in turn, implied not "softness," as has been often touted, but hardline measures of repression and expulsion. The evolution of Italian Aegean Citizenship as a form of imperial citizenship therefore offers a unique window of how Italy's historic mobility has entered not into just imperial discourses or impacted its own citizens but has also been a fundamental part of the way it reconceived of race and nation in its colonial contexts.

In exploring the critical possibilities that emerge should we understand the Dodecanese islands as both one of Italy's colonies (even if its most privileged one) and one of its borderlands, I go against the grain of the existing historiography of Italian rule in the Aegean. The long-overdue international recovery of the "Italian Aegean Islands" has tended to sideline the links between the islands (and their population) and colonial expansion in Africa to understand the Dodecanese in isolation. These studies are quick to point out that the Dodecanese were not placed under the direction of the Ministry of the Colonies but under the Ministry of Foreign Affairs and that their unique status as a department reflects the fact that rule there was not "colonial" in orientation. Such a viewpoint has been built upon the recognition that tropes of *Italiani brava gente,* or Italians as "good people," have circulated within popular memory of Italian rule in the islands, an issue that the next chapter addresses more fully.[8] Yet, that the Italian state did not see the Dodecanese entirely as a colony also had the potential to mean that the islands should be brought into line with nation-building projects similar to its internal colonial ones, such as in the Pontine Marshes (Agro-Pontino), as well as on its Triestine borders and in its Balkan peripheries.[9] The desire

---

8   See Luca Pignataro, *Il Dodecaneso italiano, 1912–1947* (Chieti: Solfanelli, 2011) and Nicholas Doumanis, *Myth and Memory in the Mediterranean: Remembering Fascism's Rule* (New York: St Martin's Press, 1997). Scholars have sometimes translated this term as "department," but its more literal translation intimates how state actors saw the islands as a *possession,* underlining the islands' status as affirmation of a growing empire in the Mediterranean.

9   See Roberta Pergher, *Mussolini's Nation-Empire: Sovereignty and Settlement in Italy's Borderlands, 1922–1943* (Cambridge: Cambridge University Press, 2018); Mia Fuller, "Laying Claim: On Italy's Internal and External Colonies," in *A Moving Border: Alpine Cartographies of Climate Change,* edited by Marco Ferrari, Elisa Pasqual, and Andrea

to reintegrate the Dodecanese into its larger national-imperial context may have rendered the Italian state more—and not less—aggressive about assimilating the local population ethnically and culturally and bringing it into line with the ideology of the Fascist state. Such a possibility seems all the more worth entertaining when one also considers the fact that the islands' Greek ethnic majority entered into Italian nationalist fantasies of recuperating a Greco-Roman race in the Mediterranean and that the transnational and cosmopolitan character of the Jewish communities of Rhodes and Kos implied the existence of strong ideological ties between it and the Italian Jewish communities in the peninsula and in the larger Levant.

The discussion that follows holds that both familiarity and "otherness" were at work in sovereignty and citizenship in the Aegean. The fact that the Dodecanese islands were not a "colony" may have brought them closer to the metropole, but it nevertheless also exposed them to serious forms of colonialism. I hold a third possibility as well: instability regarding the status of the Aegean may also have helped to produce the hardline measures that defined the final years of Fascist rule in the islands, notably under Cesare De Vecchi. Moving away from representations of *mediterraneità* and *romanità* in nationalist discussions of nation and race and in tourism initiatives, this chapter asks instead how representation may have informed rule, and documents how these same concepts of *mediterraneità* and *romanità* also shaped Italian ideas about nation, race, and belonging in the Aegean. For the purposes of successful Italian governance, the Dodecanese subject was a *potential* citizen—one whose loyalty was both desired and in question, and whose diaspora provided the Italian state with new possibilities for the growth of their empire in its peripheries. At the same time, this potential citizen could also become a colonial subject, especially when, for ideological purposes, the local administration came to view a Dodecanese person or class as undesirable. If these two opposing views of the Dodecanese native unfolded chronologically, they also reinforced one another—that is, one citizen's undesirability confirmed another subject's desirability.

In the first phase of Italian occupation, Dodecanese subjects became recipients of ideas of *italianità*, or Italianness, which had marked the Liberal era's ideas of empire as achieved by disseminating Italian identity abroad.

Bagnato, 99–111 (New York: Columbia University Press, 2008); and Andreas Guidi, "Defining Inter-Communality between Documents, Tradition and Collective Memory: Jewish and Non-Jewish Capital and Labor in Early Twentieth Century Rhodes," *Southeast European and Black Sea Studies* 17, no. 2 (2017): 165–80.

This phase ended as soon as the Italian state had officially annexed the islands to the Italian overseas empire and was replaced by an administration defined by the idea of *mediterraneità,* or Mediterraneanness. Dodecanese locals were now brought into new schemes for Italian expansion, with the island's strategic positioning in the eastern Mediterranean marking them as important potential actors in expanding and propagating the empire regionally, and their propensity to migrate making them important globally. After the invasion of Ethiopia in 1936, and the Fascist regime's adoption of an official politics of race, a new administration defined by the idea of *romanità,* or Romanness, reaffirmed the idea that Dodecanese locals belonged to a great Mediterranean Empire, and, in many ways, marked the fulfilment of the radical nationalist fantasy that the Italian nation-state could offer a solution to the Balkan problem, which had heralded the conquest of the islands in 1912 (as discussed in chapter 1). Yet this phase was also marked by the Italian administration's rereading of the Lausanne Treaty to enable expulsions and the stripping of Italian Aegean citizenship from the local Jewish and Turkish minorities, and finally, by the reframing of the Dodecanese native as a colonial subject rather than as a citizen of Italy's Mediterranean peripheries.

Locals have since often referred to the latter phase of Italian rule as "Fascist," indicating the way it diverged from the administration they had known up until that point, which they designate instead as "Italian." While the distinction between "Fascist" and "Italian" is clearly erroneous (as Italian Fascism began in the Dodecanese in 1923, as it did in Italy), this legend does indicate the way the local population was perceptive about strong ideological differences within Italian attitudes toward the population. The Italian belief in *romanità,* however, emanated not only from fear of irredentism among the population, but also from the demand for racial hierarchies that could differentiate Italians from the local population, especially given the enormous size and diversity of colonial populations of the imperial state after the conquest of Ethiopia.

Throughout the legal and ideological transformations of Italian Aegean citizenship there were always ambivalences and ambiguities about the way citizenship was practiced. The fact that Italy applied Aegean citizenship to petitioners on a case-by-case basis created flexibility and encouraged ambiguity. Such ambivalences were characteristic of the time period as well.[10]

10   Gorman, *Imperial Citizenship,* 2–30.

As in other Italian colonial settings, moreover, Italy did not always practice its racist logic to the letter, a fact that has helped to preserve in postcolonial memory the idea that Italians were "good people."[11] Yet the recognition that Italy's rule in the Aegean was both colonial and national, that it has also engendered postcolonial conditions—which include the transmission of Italian citizenship to descendants of the Dodecanese diaspora—reveals the way that both race and a disavowal of it were inherent to Italy's imperial project in the Aegean. The Aegean native marked the threshold of Italy's politics of colonial difference and race; construction of that identity is therefore revealing of both the conflict and the similarities that linked the "Liberal" and "Fascist" ideologies of empire.

From Ottoman Capitulations to Italian Possession

When the Italian consul in Istanbul read, in 1922, a draft for the law for Italian Aegean citizenship, he replied tersely to Mario Lago expressing shock over the fact that in it Lago had referred to both Greeks and Turks in the Dodecanese as "Italians," when they were, above all, Greeks and Turks. Lago's claim was all the more egregious in the aftermath of the World War I and Woodrow Wilson's tenets of self-determination, and the critique of the view that the Balkans would help European empires to grow their territory, as had been initially expected before entering the war.[12] Yet the idea that Greeks and Turks in the Aegean could in some way be construed as "Italian" had arisen in the first years of Italy's interim occupation, from 1912 to 1924, when under the direction of the Liberal government, the Italian administration had actively undertaken policies to ensure that its presence in the islands would become permanent after the end of World War I. As it had in the Balkans, the Italian government had seen the dissemination of Italianness as the best way to create an imperial project in the Dodecanese. For this purpose, the idea of a more flexible form of *italianità,* one that saw

11   See Giulia Barrera, "Sessualità e segregazione nelle terre dell'Impero," in *L'Impero fascista: Italia ed Etiopia (1935–41),* edited by Riccardo Bottoni, 393–414 (Milan: Il mulino, 2008), who has noted a similar trope in the memory of the Italians thanks to the fact that the Italian state did not assiduously apply its antimiscegenation laws after 1938.

12   "Statuto di Rodi," ASMAE, Political Affairs Series, "Dodecaneso," 1919–30/983, Fascicolo 2392. See also, Pergher, *Mussolini's Nation-Empire,* 2–3.

Italian identity abroad as linked not only to ethnicity but also to national patriotism, provided both an ideological and a juridical basis for creating a long-term mandate in the Aegean.

At the time of the Italian landing in the Aegean, Greek nationalism was present but relatively weak thanks to the archipelago's distance from Athens and its proximity to Turkey. Almost a century before, a small minority within the islands' Greek population had participated in the 1821 revolution against the Turks that resulted in Greek independence. But the resulting Greek state chose to trade the Dodecanese to the Ottoman Empire in order to integrate the much larger, and closer, island of Euboea. In the terms of this exchange, the Greek communities of the Dodecanese Islands had received "capitulations" that exempted them from most Ottoman taxation. This concession was just one of the many forms of capitulation that the Ottoman Empire made to Europeans, and in granting them to the Greek communities of the Dodecanese, the empire implicitly accepted, to a degree, Greek national claims on the islands. With the rise of the Young Turks, this special situation of the capitulations ended, and, in 1908, the new, soon-to-be Kemalist regime in Turkey began levying heavy taxes and grew repressive toward the islands' Greek Orthodox majority. It was in the context of the ending of the capitulations that the arrival of the Italian army in 1912 was hailed as a liberation from Turkish tyranny. According to most accounts, the Italian taking in 1912 of Rhodes from the Ottomans lasted only a matter of hours and, in at least one battle, several Greeks fought alongside the Italian army.[13] In Luigi Federzoni's elated description, Rhodian Greeks greeted the Italian army as their long-lost "cousins," having long been inspired by Italian nationalism and the Italian unification.[14]

Versions of the conquest of the archipelago like Federzoni's, in which Greek Dodecanese appeared to be closely allied with Italians—willing to take up arms beside them—fulfilled the promise of earlier narratives about the nobility of Greeks and their consanguinity with Italians. These visions of Greeks as "cousins," as discussed in chapter 1, had helped to produce

---

13   C.D. Booth and Isabelle Bridge, *Italy's Aegean Possessions* (London: Arrowsmith, 1928); Zacharias N. Tsirpanlēs, *Italokratia sta Dōdekanēsa, 1912–1943: Allotriōsē tou anthrōpou kai tou perivallonto*, prologos Ēlia E. Kollia (Rhodes: Ekdosē Grapheiou Mesaiōnikēs Polēs Rodou, 1998).

14   Luigi Federzoni [Giulio De Frenzi, pseud.], *L'Italia nell'Egeo* (Rome: G. Garzoni Provenzani, 1913), 60. On the spread of nationalism in the Mediterranean in the nineteenth century, see Maurizio Isabella and Konstantina Zanou, eds., *Mediterranean Diasporas: Politics and Ideas in the Long Nineteenth Century* (New York: Bloomsbury, 2015).

Greece as an ideal space for Italy to territorialize as it expanded its empire in the Balkans and eastern Mediterranean. But archival documents related to Italian governance show that local Greeks soon acted to disrupt these fantasies, and that Italy faced measurable resistance to its rule. When it became clear that the Italian army intended to stay in the islands, protests ignited throughout the archipelago; these sparks of Greek nationalism are also evident in Italian representations at this time, which deny Greeks their earlier fetishized status. A Catholic missionary stationed in Rhodes in the early stage of occupation recounted that in the view of the Italian government, the Greeks had proved themselves to be "hypocrites," "untrustworthy," and "liars."[15] Far from declaring them "cousins," the Italians had concluded that they were a "brutal Greek race" (*"brutta razza greca"*).[16] A local plebiscite meanwhile declared that the islands comprised the "City of the Aegean" and should be independent from both Italian and Turkish rule.

Giovanni Ameglio, who had led the 1912 conquest of Rhodes and was acting governor at the time, attempted to mitigate these protests by giving the appearance of reinstating the old Ottoman order. He organized proportional elections among the notables in each of the ethnic communities in the islands, a practice that Lago would also maintain.[17] When the Balkan Wars in 1913 presented a further boost to Greek nationalism in the region, with the allied advance of Bulgaria, Serbia, Montenegro, and Greece against the Turkish army enabling Greece to nearly double its territorial size and to integrate many new areas of the Aegean, the Italian foreign minister at the time, Antonino di San Giuliano, declared warily in a classified memo to Ameglio, "Greece is becoming a Mediterranean state of increasing competition for us."[18] Nevertheless, directed by the Liberal regime in Rome, the Italian state was already undertaking attempts to win Dodecanese locals to the virtues of identification with Italianness, when the outbreak of World War I in 1914 led it to believe that the local mood had shifted toward

15   Corrado Prodomi, *Memorie di un missionario di Rodi-egeo, 1913–1920* (Verona: A. Bettinelli, 1937), 106.

16   Interestingly, Prodomi adds that Ameglio saw the Turkish community, on the other hand, as one that "never moved, never offended anyone—that they were honest people." Prodomi, *Memorie di un missionario di Rodi-egeo*, 105.

17   Denis Bocquet, "Rhodes 1912: Les mésaventures du Général d'Ameglio," *Cahiers de la Méditerranée* no. 68 (2004): 133–52. On the archipelago as the "City of the Aegean," see *Dodekanesiaka chronika* 4 (Athens: He Stege, 1975).

18   Telegram from San Giuliano to Ameglio, dated August 19, 1913; AUSSME, "Libia," L.8 N.62.

the Italian administration's favour.[19] A Dante Alighieri school in Rhodes soon opened for the purpose of the "permanent diffusion of the Italian language."[20]

Projects to spread the Italian language, spearheaded by organizations such as the Dante Alighieri Society, had been successfully adopted in North and South America during the phase of consolidating an imperial program through policies toward Italian emigrants.[21] This move to create institutions and framework for the expansion of Italianness to a non-Italian population was to reflect a decisive shift in Italian governance of its empire. The Italian state had also attempted such initiatives in Albania and in collaboration with the Austro-Hungarian Empire, but, as the local administration in Rhodes recalled at the time, Italian schools in Albania had failed; their Austro-Hungarian teachers had disseminated anti-Italian sentiment.[22] Given this recent history, the local administration proceeded with sacking all the French teachers who at the time held posts in Rhodes as instructors, in particular at the Freres school, with its international student body of the children of the most prominent families.[23] The initial creation of an Italian school was so enthusiastically received by the Turkish and Jewish minority communities in Rhodes and Kos that there was further demand for Italian teachers in their

19 *"Dopo l'intervento della Italia nella guerra europea, ragioni varie di carattere politico—o meglio di opportunismo politico—produssero sulla popolazione indigena di Rodi, e più specialmente nell'elemento turco e nell'elemento israelitico, una specie di movimento di simpatia, più o meno sincera, verso tutto ciò vi è qui—o vi può essere italiano."* Reserved memo dated December 6, 1915 from the General of the Occupying Forces to the Ministry of Foreign Affairs, GAK DOD, Box K.6/Envelope 37/1915–1917.

20 GAK DOD, Box K.6/Envelope 37/1915–1917. Memo dated August 30, 1913.

21 On Italy's programs to diffuse Italian language and identity among its emigrants see Mark Choate, *Emigrant Nation: The Making of Italy Abroad* (Cambridge, MA: Harvard University Press, 2008).

22 *"L'insegnamento italiano dato dai "Freres" sarà solamente un mezzo per meglio addestrare la nuova generazione a contenderci il passo nella relazione esteriori e nella esplicazione delle nostre attività. Non altrimenti fece il Governo Austriaco in Albania facilitando e sovvenendo nelle scuole cattoliche l'insegnamento della nostra lingua; affinché gli allievi, entrando poi negli affari e nella politica, potessero, consci dell'italiano, meglio combattere la nostra azione, meglio scalzare e frustrare le nostre iniziative."* Memo dated August 30, 1913; GAK, Box K.6/Envelope 37/1915–1917.

23 On the role of the Alliance Israélite Universelle in shaping the French imperial mandate in the eastern Mediterranean, see Aron Rodrigue, *Images of Sephardi and Eastern Jewries in Transition: The Teachers of the Alliance Israélite Universelle, 1860–1939* (Seattle: University of Washington Press, 1993).

religious schools. While some Turkish persons with Kemalist inclinations initially expressed resistance to the Italian school, many Turkish subjects were eager to obtain a favorable arrangement with the Italian regime. And the administration remarked with satisfaction that the Jewish community, in particular, had greeted the initiative with enthusiasm. The Jewish community saw the advantages of learning Italian for success in their business affairs—demonstrating the nationalist conviction that the Italian language was very much the lingua franca of the eastern Mediterranean, as it had once been during the Venetian merchant empire. Although only a few Greeks enrolled their children in the school, given that Italy's project for the diffusion of Italian culture was directly at odds with the nationalist campaign for integration with Greece, the administration nevertheless expressed confidence that the advantages offered by an Italian school would eventually outweigh negative attitudes toward the Italian occupation. As a further measure, the administration made plans for a technical school to attract the Greek population, who otherwise had to leave the islands for post-secondary education of any kind.

The Italian state's views of the Dodecanese population were also under the influence of the regime of the capitulations in the Mediterranean region more broadly. In the late nineteenth century—when the Italian state was pursuing policies to support emigrants in North and South America—the Italian state had also exploited the regime of the capitulations to support its Italian communities in North Africa, especially in Tunisia. The origins of the Italian community in Tunisia hailed back to the sixteenth and seventeenth centuries, when the maritime republics of Genoa, Amalfi, Pisa, and Venice had established Italian trade networks between Europe and the Ottoman Empire. After the unification of Italy, Vittorio Emanuele succeeded in reaching an agreement with the Ottoman bey of Tunis to give the Italian community a protected status, allowing them independence in civil administration and exempting them from Ottoman taxation. This was a typical form of capitulation for a European population living in the Ottoman Empire and it doubtless contributed to the community's continuing growth, as well as to the perception among nationalists that Tunisia was "a necessary possession if Italy were ever to cast itself as a credible empire."[24] After the unification, Italian migration to Tunisia spiked, bringing the Italian community to almost 120,000 by the turn of the century; it far outnumbered the French community in Tunisia for the entirety of French colonial rule. Indeed, the

---

24 Mark Choate, "Tunisia, Contested: Italian Nationalism, French Imperial Rule, and Migration in the Mediterranean Basin," *California Italian Studies* 1, no. 1 (2010): 1–20.

1881 French invasion and annexation of Tunisia as a protectorate can be read as an attempt, as Mary Lewis Dewhurst has noted, to thwart increasingly aggressive use of the capitulations by the Italian state to provide diplomatic, or Italian consular, protection to its citizens as a means of maintaining the Italian demographic strength of the community in Tunisia.[25] Italy similarly used the capitulations to "protect" Italians and expand its imperial influence in both Egypt and Turkey at this time.[26] By applying the capitulations so aggressively to Italian emigrants throughout Ottoman territories, Italy succeeded in maintaining an imperial program that could support its diaspora in the Mediterranean despite the colonial failures in East Africa that had scarred Italian imperialism so profoundly in the late nineteenth century.

It is therefore perhaps understandable that the Italian state should have turned to the European capitulations in the Dodecanese as a means to shore up its tenuous occupation of the Aegean. By 1914, the local administration determined that Italy could use capitulations to apply Italian diplomatic and consular protection to local residents of the Aegean caught abroad. By doing so, Italy eventually did persuade many Greek Dodecanese of the advantages of at least nominally accepting a preliminary form of Italian nationality. Italy's entrance into the war in 1915 engendered another advantage: Greeks could avoid conscription in both the Ottoman and Greek armies by obtaining Italian diplomatic protection. Further, equipped with Italian passports, Dodecanese natives could migrate to join relatives already abroad. While the Italian government remained guarded about viewing Dodecanese natives as Italian subjects, exceptions to this rule—such as the Dodecanese natives living in Italy's East African colonies, who were eagerly classified as Italian subjects— promoted the practice that diplomatic protection could be generously applied when it came to Dodecanese persons residing not just in the islands but also in the Mediterranean and Africa more broadly. Offering diplomatic protection also proved an effective tool to undermine the local nationalisms that were proliferating in the Aegean region in the aftermath of Ottoman collapse. The regime of diplomatic protection allowed Italian authorities to

---

25 Mary Dewhurst Lewis, "Geographies of Power: The Tunisian Civic Order, Jurisdictional Politics, and Imperial Rivalry in the Mediterranean, 1881–1935," *Journal of Modern History* 80, no. 4 (2008): 791–830. See also Choate, "Tunisia, Contested."
26 Alessandro Pannuti, *La comunità italiana di Istanbul nel XX secolo: Ambiente e persone* (Istanbul: Edizioni Isis, 2006); Joseph Viscomi, "Mediterranean Futures: Historical Time and the Departure of Italians from Egypt," *Journal of Modern History* 91, no. 2 (2019): 341–79.

censor, for example, a counsel general in Cardiff who had produced and given his consular seal to certificates of Greek "religion and race" for a handful of natives of the island of Simi.[27] And in the case of Dodecanese natives residing in Egypt, the Ministry of Foreign Affairs determined that it was necessary to view these persons as Italian subjects, lest their Hellenic "race" lead them to be accepted as Greek nationals by their local consulate.[28]

At the end of World War I, Italy's demands for the incorporation of the "unredeemed lands" (*terra irredenta*) at Italy's northeastern border, extending into the Balkans, went unmet. Known by 1919 as the *vittoria mutilata*, or mutilated victory, for the fact that Italy did not obtain most of the territories that the British and French powers had originally promised, despite the deaths of hundreds of thousands of Italian soldiers for the cause, the war's end was to have far-reaching implications, not least among them Mussolini's dramatic march on Rome. While Gabriele D'Annunzio anticipated Mussolini's rise to power and the establishment of a corporatist state with his occupation of Fiume (Croatia) in 1919–20, the Liberal government was also committed to expanding Italy's territories in the Mediterranean at all costs. Rebuffed at Versailles in 1918 over its claims in the Adriatic, Italy responded by making a bid to expand even further eastward and dispatched a part of its navy, stationed in Rhodes at the time, to occupy the eastern Aegean (or western Anatolia), successively occupying parts of the Turkish coast, from the historic port city of Smyrna to as far southeast as Antalya. The Italian move into Anatolia led the Greeks to commit to further military action as well, and under the leadership of the nationalist Eleftherios Venizelos—and with the backing of the British government, which did not want to see an Italian expansion in Anatolia—the Greek state sent its army to occupy the eastern Aegean. During the Greek nationalist advance, Italy signed secret agreements with the Turkish government ensuring that Turkey would withdraw its troops from the region (as did France). Their withdrawal from the region effectively left the Greek army to hang.[29]

The Greek setback in Anatolia eventually put Italy at an unexpected advantage with regard to the question of the empire's permanent annexation of the Dodecanese. Although it is little remarked upon in the

---

27   ASMAE, Political Affairs, "Dodecaneso," 1915–19, Box 58.

28   "Nativi del Dodecaneso nel Egitto," ASMAE, Political Affairs, "Dodecaneso," 1915–19, box 57, fascicolo 30.

29   Peter Jensen, "The Greco-Turkish War, 1920–1922," *International Journal of Middle East Studies* 10, no. 4 (1979): 553–65.

earliest commentaries on Fascism's early imperial pursuits for control of the Mediterranean, one of Mussolini's first success stories in realpolitik diplomacy was a promise of Italian sovereignty in the Dodecanese at the 1922 Lausanne convention.[30] Mussolini insisted that the Allied Powers refer back to Article 8 of the 1915 Treaty of London, which had brought Italy into the war in the first place: it contained the promise that Italy, too, as one of the victors in the war should obtain "some compensation in the East," where the Ottoman Empire had once sprawled. Mussolini therefore insisted that the British government recognize treaties that Italy had signed with the Ottoman state in 1912, when it had concluded its war for a colony in Libya, which had awarded a limited degree of sovereignty over the Dodecanese to Italy. To the dismay of the British government, Mussolini also tied the issue of the Dodecanese together with a border dispute with the British government over Somalia. Mussolini further presented Italy as in a position to safeguard Turkish interests in Rhodes and Kos, where a large Turkish minority resided, and that were linked economically to Turkey. By protecting the Turkish minority, as Mussolini explained to the British government, the Italian state would restore the peace in an area that had been consumed in the flames of ethnic violence for more than a decade:

> Given the delicate political situation in the eastern Mediterranean and the antagonistic interests that still exist today, permanent sovereignty of Italy in the Dodecanese can be the best way to guarantee peace and to avoid the outbreak of the now dormant hostilities. The Italian possession of the Dodecanese can constitute a kind of yoke against conflict between the two populations—the Turkish and the Greek—divided by both recent and ancient political and military affairs.[31]

> *É indispensabile tener presente che data la delicata situazione politica nel Mediterraneo Orientale e gli interessi antagonistici che tuttora vi esistono, la permanenza delle isole del Dodecanneso sotto la sovranità Italiana può essere il miglior mezzo per garantire la pace evitando il riaccendersi di mal sopite*

---

30   Acquisition of the Dodecanese is notably absent from Denis Mack Smith's early study of Italian imperialism, even though the study emphasizes Mussolini's commitment to empire in the Mediterranean from an early moment in his regime; Denis Mack Smith, *Mussolini's Roman Empire* (New York: Viking, 1976), 1–14.

31   Letter to S.E. MacDonald, Prime Minister of England, May 2, 1924, signed Mussolini. ASMAE, Political Affairs, "Dodecaneso," 1919–30, Box 987.

> *competizioni. Il possesso italiano del Dodecanneso viene a costituire una*
> *specie di diaframma che evita l'urto fra due popoli—il turco e il greco—divisi*
> *da recenti e antiche vicende politiche militari.*

It is unlikely that the argument that Italy was best positioned to maintain peace in the eastern Mediterranean was convincing to the British government. It did hint, however, at the ways that the campaign for empire that Mussolini had appropriated from the nationalists would eventually culminate in the idea of a *pax romana* and then later, *mare nostrum*, the rhetoric of renewing Roman Empire in the Mediterranean that would define Mussolini's Fascist Empire after the invasion of Ethiopia. Assimilating the argument of the radical nationalists before him, who had seen colonies in the Mediterranean as central to Italy's economic future—but also inverting their logic—Mussolini implied that, without the Italian state, the multicultural Mediterranean as it had been known under Ottoman rule would cease to exist.

Under Fascist direction, the expansion of the Italian nation-state to local or "native" subjects of the Aegean was soon to eclipse the nationalist idea of protecting Italian emigrant communities; however, the principle of growing Italianness (*italianità*) abroad was to persevere, and indeed would provide the basis for a regime of Mediterraneanness, in which local subjects in the Aegean were to a degree brought into inclusion within the Italian nation-state. The groundwork for this expansion of nationalist ideas of Mediterraneanism had been laid from the Aegean peripheries, and by the Liberal and "progressive" view of empire that had imagined it would be a benefit to both the locals as well as the imperial state. Italy had already extended Italian citizenship to an additional class of potential Italians with ties to the archipelago: the so-called Levantini or non-Muslims of either Christian or Jewish confession, supposedly descendants of the ancient republics of Genoa and Venice in the eastern Mediterranean.[32] By one account, at the time of formal annexation, this "Latin community of Italians" already consisted of four thousand people.[33] A draft law for the application of Italian citizenship to such persons declared that not only should ethnic criteria be brought into consideration but also determinations should be made regarding applicants' "sentiments of Italianness (*italianità*)

---

32   Sabina Donati, *A Political History of National Citizenship and Identity in Italy, 1861–1950* (Stanford, CA: Stanford University Press, 2013), 133–37.
33   Vittorio Alhadeff, *L'ordinamento giuridico di Rodi e delle altre isole italiane dell'Egeo* (Milan: Istituto editoriale scientifico, 1927), 41.

and that they offer various guarantees for contributing to the maintenance of the good name and prestige of Italy."[34]

Having secured Italian citizenship for Levantini as well as for emigrant Italians in the Aegean, it became more urgent to create a civil status that clearly ensured the rest of the local communities in the islands did not belong to either Greece or Turkey. Mario Lago, the future governor of the islands, recommended that a "small naturalization" be put into place whereby islanders could opt individually for Italian nationality. Unsurprisingly, given Lago's nationalist affiliations, the locution "small naturalization" hailed back to the nineteenth-century wars of the unification. During that era, a "small naturalization" (*la piccola naturalizzazione*) had been offered to foreigners permanently residing in Italy and, on the basis of an individual application, allowed immigrants in Italy to acquire Italian citizenship inclusive of local political rights. It was differentiated against another status known as *grande naturalizzazione* (administrative legislation) or full citizenship, which was reserved for foreign persons who had an ethnic link to Italy or who had fought for the unification. In 1924, Lago maintained that such a "small naturalization" would prove an eloquent solution to the question of competing national claims in the islands. It would serve as a "counter example" to all those persons who still rejected the Italian state's presence in the islands. He was further convinced that Italy would be successful in its mandate as long as the communities were allowed to organize among themselves, as they had under the *millet* system, and that the natives would soon see the advantages of getting an Italian education and belonging to a strong state such as Italy.[35]

Although the final version of the law for Italian Aegean citizenship had no reference in it to a "small citizenship," the earlier discussions of Aegean citizenship as a form of *piccola naturalizzazione* and the prior regime of diplomatic protection influenced both its language and its practice.[36] In many ways, Italian Aegean citizenship insisted on what was a typical paradox of European Empire—that the territory was part of the Italian nation-state

---

34 *"Disposizioni sulla cittadinanza italiana (R.decreto-legge 10 settembre 1922, n. 1387 Gazz. uff., 6 novembre, n. 259) Art. 3 abbiano dato prova non dubbia di sentimenti di italianità ed offrano varie garanzie di contribuire al mantenimento del buon nome e del prestigio italiano."* GAK CCRR, 1924 F. 75.

35 "Statuto di Rodi," ASMAE, Political Affairs, "Dodecaneso," 1919–30/983, Fascicolo 2392.

36 Donati, *A Political History*, 133–37.

while the locals who resided there were foreigners. But the unofficial adoption of the nomenclature *piccola cittadinanza,* which continued to circulate among Italian state actors and that hailed back to the unification itself, is also revealing of a view that though the locals could not be viewed as ethnically Italian, they were in some significant way being assimilated into the Italian nation-state. Having appropriated the capitulations to encourage local Aegean subjects to turn to Italy for consular protection, the Italian administration under the direction of the Liberal government had set the stage for Fascist rule, in which Aegean locals were not only considered Italian nationals, but also viewed as instrumental to the broader project of empire in the Mediterranean. Migration and habits of mobility among the population were to provide the local administration with the potential to further expand state sovereignty in the region.

Dodecanese Diaspora, Aegean Citizenship

If Italian nationalism and the politics of empire through diaspora—what Mark Choate has called the "Making of Italy abroad"—had influenced early Italian policies in the Aegean, the diaspora of the local population was to be even more transformative to how Italy understood and applied Aegean citizenship.[37] The creation and administration of Italian Aegean citizenship presented an opportunity for the Italian state to extend its power beyond the southeast Aegean, to cultivate the "sphere of influence in the East" that it envisioned, by offering Italian nationality to the thousands of Dodecanese natives living abroad at the time of Italian annexation. Whether they were emigrants in other countries or continents or were refugees of the Ottoman collapse in the Aegean, these persons represented potential new Italian subjects, and to borrow the words of Mario Lago, "a counter example" to all the locals still resistant toward Italian rule. Yet though conferring Italian nationality on Dodecanese natives abroad helped Italy to strengthen its position locally, as well as its political and diplomatic position with respect to other imperial and regional powers, it also created ambiguity about Italy's objectives for the local population within its own administration of the islands. This very same vision of remaking "Roman" Empire through nationality also raised the more problematic issue of whether locals—and if so, which locals—could in fact be understood as potential Italians. The

37   Choate, *Emigrant Nation,* 3.

expansion of Italian nationality to Aegean subjects finally risked erasing distinctions between the Italian settlers and their imperial subjects in the Mediterranean. This ambiguity was eventually "resolved" by a hardening of categories of race.

The Italian administration was visionary in its understanding of how the local community's condition as emigrants was similar to that of Italians abroad, and how state-building and public welfare projects could work together with citizenship to promote consent for Italian rule among the local population. With annexation of the islands, earlier Italian plans for the Dodecanese as an important source of labor in Italian public works projects, such as the Marmaris-Aden railway, planned to operate from the Aegean to the Red Sea, gained new credibility.[38] East Africa and the Congo had long been regular destinations for economic migrants in the mining sector, especially among the islands' Jewish communities, and Ameglio and his allies believed that the presence of Dodecanese "Italians" in these settings might facilitate the construction of new railroads.[39] Emigration at the turn of the century, when droves of Dodecanese relocated to the United States, had led to a decline in the population by almost half, but it had also created a new source of income for those who remained on the islands, in the form of remittances.[40] Emigration had been curtailed during World War I due to maritime traffic restrictions, then ceased almost entirely in 1921 with the US quota. By the time that the Italian state had installed itself officially in the Aegean, many Dodecanese natives had begun to return to the islands from abroad. Italian Aegean citizenship represented a new passport that could enable Dodecanesians to circulate throughout the eastern Mediterranean—between Alexandria, the islands, and the coastal cities of the eastern Aegean—and to obtain again the wealth that Dodecanese emigrants had steadily been able to accumulate in a previous era of open borders. Such emigration had constituted, in the words of one observer, "a notable economic resource for the population."[41]

The decree of Italian citizenship resulted in protests in the island of Kalymnos as well as an attempt by islanders to form their own government and declare themselves autonomous from Italian rule. A correspondent from

38   AUSSME, "Libia," L.8 N.62.
39   Diane Perelsztein, Willy Perelsztein, and John Boyle, dirs. *Rhodes Forever* (Brussels: Les films de Memoire, 1995), film, 59 mins.
40   Emanuel Cassotis, *The Karpathian (Dodecanese) Presence in America* (Rhodes: Stegi Grammaton ke Technon Dodecanesou, 2012).
41   Alhadeff, *L'ordinamento giuridico*, 43.

a Berlin newspaper, there to cover these events, compared it to the project to integrate the German-speaking areas of the Alto Adige in northwest Italy.[42] But the policy in the Dodecanese remained distinct from the one in the Alto Adige, where the Italian government began a massive campaign to Italianize the German-speaking population shortly after annexation. In the Dodecanese, new language policies mandated only five hours per week of instruction in the Italian language, and until 1937, these five hours were offset by instruction in the mother tongue in schools organized according to ethnic confession. From 1926 to 1936, the Italian government encountered little resistance to integrating most of the inhabitants of the islands as Italian nationals holding Aegean citizenship. A cable from the Ministry of Foreign Affairs enthusiastically declared that Italian Aegean citizenship was a policy feat that was helping to bring about the esteem and loyalty of local subjects: "the most efficient and useful form of propaganda that we can make for the Italian regime in the Aegean islands [...] [it] demonstrates to our sympathetic *Dodecannesini* the moral advantage of belonging to a nation like Italy and of being in its patronage."[43]

In many ways, Aegean citizenship resembled the old regime of the capitulations by allowing locals to maintain independence in civil affairs and encouraging the communities to self-organize according to "cult" or religion. Yet though citizenship was not meant as a proxy for ethnic assimilation, as was arguably the case in Alto Adige, it did imply an introduction of Italian nationalism and brought Dodecanese subjects into a new form of patronage with the Italian nation-state. Italy's form of citizenship in the Aegean was almost unique among ex-Ottoman subjects. Most other former subjects of the Ottoman Empire—including Syrians, Palestinians, and Iraqis—did not immediately acquire some form of metropolitan citizenship from their respective new rulers. While Aegean citizenship did make them quite similar to Cypriots who, according to the Second Treaty of Lausanne, became imperial subjects of the English crown while still organized according to religion,

---

42   Correspondence collected by the Italian Ministry of Foreign Affairs, appearing in the *Berliner Tageblatt* on December 13, 1925. ASMAE, 988/1925 (Busta: Decreto Cittadinanza).

43   "*Dimostrare cioè ai Dodecanesini sudditi nostri simpatizzanti la convenienza morale di appartenere ad una grande Nazione come l'Italia o di goderne il favore. È ciò che fanno la R. Legazione ed i RR. Consolati, proteggendo e aiutando gli uni e gli altri. Il riconoscimento della cittadinanza italiana dodecanesina, ottenuto recentemente dalla R. Legazione, è certamente la più efficace ed utile propaganda che possiamo fare per il regime italiano delle Isole Egee.*" 23 April 1929, ASMAE, 998/1929.

the Italian administration of the Dodecanese had a much more "national" character than the one in Cyprus. As Alexis Rappas has documented, the British Empire closely watched the Italian administration in the Aegean and the recognition of Italy's success in the Aegean led the British Empire to adopt a more aggressive policy of inclusion of Cypriot subjects into the British national empire.[44]

Having firmly positioned itself as the heir to the Ottoman Empire in the Dodecanese, the Italian state began aggressively to apply Italian nationality to refugees of Ottoman collapse throughout the wider Aegean region. As a result of their location in a central sea corridor of the eastern Mediterranean, the islands were deeply connected through trade and migration to widespread outposts across the Mediterranean and Africa. The terms of the population exchange between the Greek and Turkish population according to the Lausanne Treaty had stipulated a two-year window in which locals could elect their nationality, and tacitly accept to migrate to either Greece or Tukey. Dodecanese subjects who opted for either Turkish or Greek nationality were supposed to emigrate from the islands, but no expulsions took place at this time. Instead, the administration committed to applying Italian nationality generously to persons who were seeking to return or immigrate to the islands in order to ensure that the number of residents who had held either Greek or Turkish nationality was minimal. Italy chose to be flexible on the two-year window within which a person was supposed to opt for a nationality, as well as on the treaty's definition of *établi*, understanding it to indicate that the person was domiciled in the islands—that is, propertied there—rather than resident in them. This ensured that all emigrant persons who were away at the time of annexation, 1924, were able to naturalize to Italian nationality upon return—even if their residence was intended as a temporary one before emigrating again—well after the two-year statute of limitations had ended.

The most frequent explanation given in naturalization applications by persons petitioning after the two-year window had expired was that they had "forgotten" to opt for Italian citizenship or had been "unaware" of the 1924 annexation of the islands to Italy. Such language reveals how citizenship, while it certainly did not imply *consenso*—neither consent nor consensus— did ensure some level of acquiescence from locals: applications for Italian Aegean nationality were often peppered with declarations of "obedience" and

44   See Alexis Rappas, "The Transnational Formation of Imperial Rule on the Margins of Europe: British Cyprus and the Italian Dodecanese in the Interwar Period," *European History Quarterly* 45, no. 3 (2015): 467–505.

"devotion" to Italy. Successful applications for Aegean citizenship painted the applicant as either politically disinterested or outright loyal to the Italian state. A Bulgarian who had immigrated to Rhodes in 1925—and who had no obvious ties to the archipelago—was able to obtain Italian Aegean citizenship in 1932 with the patriotic exclamation that he had "always been unquestioningly obedient to Italian laws and devoted to the glorious Italian regime that I admire and the glorious tricolor flag that has protected me now for twelve years."[45] Precisely because Aegean natives claimed Italian nationality while not being ethnically Italian, their loyalty and attitude toward the Italian state became paramount, and often, the final arbiter as to whether they would be allowed to reside in the islands. In some instances, the local administration granted Italian nationality even when aware that the applicant had clearly fabricated a connection to the islands, as was the case, for example, with Michele Albagli, a rabbi for the synagogue of Rhodes, who provided a birth certificate stating he was born in Rhodes that the Italian administration recognized as falsified—*un trucco*. But the administration chose to renew his residency permit and Italian Aegean nationality in 1935 anyway because "he speaks Italian and demonstrates favourable sentiments toward us" (*"conosce la lingua italiana e dimostra setimenti a noi favorevoli"*). Following the introduction of the 1938 race laws, however, the recognition of Albagli's false claim to have been born in Rhodes would be used to revoke his Italian nationality; he was eventually forced to leave the island together with his family in 1939.[46]

These case-by-case basis determinations about Italian naturalization did exclude many people—the vast majority of them Greek men—from returning to reside or reclaim property in the islands. The public *bolletino* of the Italian administration of the islands annually announced the names of Dodecanese residents who, because they had obtained Greek nationality, had lost their status as Italian nationals. Persons with Greek nationality were still allowed to reside in the islands, but they were often labeled as potential *schedati* or political dissidents. Although Venizelos and Mussolini reached a rapprochement in 1928, a community of exiled Dodecanesians continued to seek the support of the League of Nations for the cause of liberating the islands from Italian rule, citing the gross violation of the will of the local ethnic majority for union with Greece. In ways that were not dissimilar from Italian

---

45   *"Sono stato sempre ossequiente alle leggi Italiane e devoto al Regime Italiano che ammiro le sue glorie e la gloriosa bandiera tricolore che da 12 anni mi protegge"*; Nicola Vergof, N. 1758/39–1932, Rhodes, March 5, 1937, GAK, 323/1935.
46   GAK CCRR, "ALBAGLI Michele."

colonial rule in Libya, where the Italian state monitored the entrances and exits of Italians between Italy and Libya, Aegean nationals drew the attention and energies of the administration and revealed the way mobility presented both imperial possibilities and anxieties about sovereignty.[47] Some persons inevitably slipped through the cracks of Italian surveillance, and, often, it was the porous borders of the Mediterranean Sea that disrupted attempts to establish Aegean subjects as Italian nationals. Dodecanese natives suddenly appeared on the lists of the Greek army: "it's the usual story of a Dodecanese sailor whose mother is from Crete" ("*è la solita storia dei marittimi dodecannesini la cui madre è cretese*"), remarked an administrator in a file about one such case.[48] Crete's vicinity to the Dodecanese, with the resulting proximity of Greek citizenship, was a persistent thorn in the administration's side. But the comment also reveals Italian concerns about how Greek citizenship, which was acquired on the basis of both maternity or paternity—unlike Italian citizenship, which could only be inherited through the paternal line— had the potential to undermine Italian efforts to naturalize all resident ethnic Greeks to Italian Aegean citizenship.

During this period the Ministry of Foreign Affairs evaluated a variety of situations that challenged whether Italian nationality for Aegean natives could be used to consolidate Italian politics abroad. It assessed, for example, whether to provide Italian passports to Dodecanese refugees of World War I who had fled to Russia and now sought to leave the Union of Soviet Socialist Republics (USSR). Despite the fact that, as an official remarked in the case notes, to do so would have helped to save these applicants from the perils of communism, the Ministry of Foreign Affairs determined that to liberally grant Italian Aegean citizenship to whoever petitioned for it abroad would risk the prestige and integrity of the citizenship project.[49] In cases like these, when political objectives stood in tension with the politics of nationalism, Italy chose to naturalize only Dodecanese subjects who could potentially become loyal subjects of the empire by having contact with the local population. Dodecanese natives would have to demonstrate a combination of familial ties, private property, and an intention of residing permanently in the islands. Such decisions ensured that this form of citizenship continued to

---

47   Pam Ballinger, "Colonial Twilight: Italian Settlers and the Long Decolonization of Libya," *Journal of Contemporary History* 15, no. 4 (2016): 813–38.

48   GAK DOD, 323/1936.

49   Diplomatic Cable, November 29, 1929, III.B.1, ASMAE, Political Affairs, "Dodecanneso," 993/1929.

serve as a means toward consolidating *italianità* and national identity, even at the expense of Fascist ideological goals like anti-communism. Yet in all of these cases class was also a factor and "the regime valorized certain forms of mobility as indices of modernity," as Pamela Ballinger has described of the situation among Italian colonists in Libya.[50] Persons could acquire Italian Aegean citizenship with an expressed intent of emigrating, for example, if they were of significant financial means.[51]

Although it was possible to return to and reside in the islands without Italian Aegean citizenship, naturalizing to it was the only means for returning Dodecanese subjects to reclaim property. In one such case, Paolo Candilafti had left the islands for Australia in 1919 but had returned to Europe two years later after finding work in France. In 1936 he returned to Kastellorizo from Marseilles and sought to reclaim a small piece of property he had received through dowry. Candilafti explained that in 1919, the year that he had emigrated, Kastellorizo had been under French sovereignty and it was solely for this reason that he had a French passport and not because he had been "insubordinate." After his paperwork was cleared through the Ministry of Foreign Affairs in Rome, Candilafti was granted ad hoc Italian Aegean citizenship on the basis that since he was born an Ottoman subject, by virtue of the Second Treaty of Lausanne, he retained his option of claiming Italian nationality. At the same time, Rome affirmed that Candilafti's demonstrated humility warranted his Italian citizenship—"the interested party is a merit-worthy and able person, he could be considered one of our subjects because he was only absent [...] for reasons of work."[52] By ensuring that all returning emigrants like Candilafti assumed Italian Aegean citizenship in exchange for the right to claim their property, the administration made residents who held another nationality into a minority.

Dodecanese natives who obtained Greek nationality—or who had completed Greek military service—could not be naturalized to Italian Aegean citizenship without inciting diplomatic tensions. But many returning Dodecanese emigrants were coming from imperial regimes in which their status as workers or temporary migrants meant they had avoided conscription

---

50   Ballinger, "Colonial Twilight," 824.
51   "Cittadinanza dei Dodecannesini," Circular no. 78, October 2, 1925, GAK, 93/1927/163.
52   *"L'interessato sia persona meritevole di agevolazione, si potrebbe considerarlo nostro suddito, perchè assente dall'isola a scopo di lavoro."* N. 1556/3, Kastellorizo (Castelrosso), December 29, 1936, GAK, 323:1935.

in the Greek army and effectively had never obtained Greek national status. Returning emigrants from Australia, for example, who had acquired a form of English colonial citizenship while abroad could be repatriated to the archipelago and naturalized to Italian nationality on the basis that Australia was at this time still an English dominion. The Italian state maintained that whatever civil status Dodecanese workers had obtained abroad was inferior as compared to an Italian Aegean nationality, and that it could be easily exchanged for a form of Italian nationality, since it was unlikely to produce diplomatic tension with other nation-states. The age of great transatlantic migrations having led Dodecanese natives to move for work to the United States, South America, and Australia, as well as other European colonial regions such as East Africa and the Belgian Congo, the worldwide diaspora of Dodecanese locals continued to present the Italian government with occasions for exploiting the indeterminacy of national identity that existed in the new age of empire that had followed the World War I.

But the indeterminacy of national identity that existed in the Aegean also existed in Egypt, where in the early 1930s the Fascist state was also engaged in an active program to foster "national" sentiment. The Italian presence in Egypt went back to well before the British invasion of Egypt in 1882, and though the Italian community in Egypt had supported the British at that time, it also temporarily made them into stateless refugees.[53] Among the notable artists of Italian origin who emerged from the vibrant and cosmopolitan atmosphere of Alexandria were several well-known figures of Italian nationalism, including the poet and literary critic Giuseppe Ungaretti, and the poet and futurist Filippo Tomaso Marinetti, both of whom were eventually linked to the Fascist regime and its cultural revolution. Recent studies of Egypt have emphasized that the Fascist regime paid close attention to the Italian community at this time and, in some instances, sought to entice unemployed Italians in Egypt to relocate to East Africa. It also continued to aggressively use the European capitulations to maintain its ties with this community. As Marta Petricioli has demonstrated, so many persons in Egypt were already in possession of some form of Italian diplomatic protection that by the 1930s Italy was unable to define clearly just who constituted its Italian community in Egypt, and, in turn, to construct a coherent educational policy

---

53 Alexander Kazamias, "Between Language, Land and Empire: Humanist and Orientalist Perspectives on Egyptian Greek Identity," in *Greek Diaspora and Migration since 1700: Society, Politics and Culture*, edited by Dimitris Tziovas, 177–92 (London: Taylor & Francis, 2016).

to align with its expansionist goals in Egypt.[54] Against this backdrop, a 1933 reform in which the Italian state guaranteed all Dodecanese persons residing abroad the right to acquire Italian Aegean nationality no doubt intended to dispel such confusion and to strengthen Italy's imperial program in Egypt. Mussolini declared that the law "responds to an urgent matter: because numerous communities of persons originating in the Dodecanese, residing abroad, especially in Egypt, had requested Italian citizenship, and they could not receive consular support until the condition of their citizenship had been resolved."[55] By affirming that Italian Aegean nationality was valid in Egypt, the Fascist state further advanced an ambitious program to encourage the presence of Italian Aegean nationality in British imperial Egypt and to expand the Italian Empire into another Mediterranean country with which it had longtime diasporic ties.

Mussolini's stance on Italians abroad—as "custodians of Italian culture" charged with a "mission to civilize the world"—is well known and has always been a part of the critical literature on Italian Empire.[56] What is novel here is that the mission of exporting *italianità* to the world was entrusted to the hands of Italian Aegean nationals as well as Italians. The expansion of Italian Aegean nationality to nonresidents—in this case, growing the Italian state through the Dodecanese diaspora—closely reproduced reforms that Italy had made to its own citizenship two decades earlier. In 1912, not coincidentally the same year that Italy had launched its empire in the Mediterranean with the

---

54   Marta Petricioli, "Italian Schools in Egypt," *British Journal of Middle Eastern Studies* 24, no. 2 (1997): 179–91. See also Annalaura Turiano and Joseph Viscomi, "From Immigrants to Emigrants: Salesian Education and the Failed Integration of Italians in Egypt, 1937–1960," *Modern Italy* 23, no. 1 (2018): 1–17; Joseph Viscomi, "Mediterranean Futures: Historical Time and the Departure of Italians from Egypt," *Journal of Modern History* 91, no. 2 (2019): 341–79. See also, Andre Aciman's memoir, *Out of Egypt*, in which he describes his uncle Vili obtaining Italian citizenship in Istanbul by establishing a remote connection to a branch of his family that left Livorno for the Ottoman Empire in the sixteenth century. Andre Aciman, *Out of Egypt* (London: Tauris Parke, 2019).

55   "*Risponde ad un motivo d'urgenza, poiché numerosi nuclei di originari del Dodecanneso, residenti all'estero, e specialmente in Egitto, avevano richiesto la cittadinanza italiana, e non potevano essere convenientemente tutelati da rappresentati italiani, finché la loro condizione di cittadinanza non fosse esattamente fissata.*" Historical Archive of the Italian House of Deputies (Archivio Storico della Camera dei Deputati), Disegno di Legge, 1379.

56   Anne-Marie Fortier, "The Politics of 'Italians Abroad': Nation, Diaspora, and New Geographies of Identity," *Diaspora: A Journal of Transnational Studies* 7, no. 2 (1998): 197–224.

invasion of Libya and the Dodecanese, the Italian state undertook to reform its citizenship laws in order to enable emigrants to retain Italian citizenship while living abroad, thus encouraging a constitutive link between emigration and empire. The 1933 reform similarly simplified the process for reintegrating Dodecanese subjects who had emigrated away from the islands but who wished to reenter and reside there, by establishing patrilineal connection to the islands as the main rationale for issuing Italian Aegean citizenship. The articles of the Lausanne convention, with their emphasis on residence, now became secondary to the principle that it was possible to inherit or pass on Italian nationality to one's descendants. Italian Aegean citizenship thus became an even broader and more flexible form of nationality. By 1934, when the 1933 law went into effect, even someone born outside the Dodecanese who had never set foot in the islands could become an Italian national by virtue of a hereditary relationship to a Dodecanese native. The local administration seized upon the new flexibility of the law to make a handful of Greek Dodecanese persons born in Egypt and residing in Alexandria into Italian nationals on the grounds that their fathers had emigrated there as "Italians" when the Dodecanese were already under Italian rule.[57] The irony is that while reforms to Italian citizenship in 1912 had enabled dual citizenship and reinforced the normative principle of acquisition of Italian identity on the basis of ethnicity or race—that is, the principle of *jus sanguinis*—the same strategies were now ostensibly leading to the expansion of Italian citizenship to non-ethnic Italians in the Mediterranean.

The 1933 reforms further introduced the option of *"grande naturalizzazione,"* or naturalization to full metropolitan citizenship after military service. Becoming a full Italian citizen at this time also implied joining the Fascist party. The intent was not to turn as many Italian Aegean locals as possible into Italian citizens but to grant naturalization to full Italian citizenship "restrictively," so as to strengthen the image of Italian nationality abroad through the creation of a colonial elite. The poor, for example, were automatically excluded from the category of people who could naturalize to full Italian citizenship.[58] An article about the reform appearing in *The Messenger of Rhodes* explained that the option of naturalizing to Italian citizenship was meant for those persons who, for reasons of business, were often away from the islands and living abroad, but who were eager in any

---

57 GAK, Envelope 323:1935.
58 "Decreto sul riconoscimento della piena cittadinanza italiana," Protocol 2/22/17, GAK CCRR.

case to be a part of the "national life" of Italy.[59] A certain class of elite and "Italianized" subjects were to have full rights of mobility and be able to emigrate abroad and move freely among Italian colonial spaces. The reform also anticipated the new politics of race that were to emerge in the aftermath of the invasion of Ethiopia. Although officially the option of full Italian citizenship had no racial definitions and, like the Italian Aegean nationality that had preceded it, was open to all ethnicities in the archipelago, internal memos show that the administration was pleased to see that the Greek Orthodox community was applying for Italian citizenship in large numbers.[60]

The reform fundamentally undermined the sense of cultural difference that had initially defined Italian Aegean nationality—the belief that while Aegean subjects were not a colonized they still could not be included in the Italian nation-state either—and arguably marked the apotheosis of the belief in *mediterraneità*, and in the cultural and ethnic commonalities that Sergi had championed in 1895. It gave Aegean subjects the same rights of inclusion and belonging to Italy that ethnic Italians possessed. Mario Lago, who championed the reform, also warned the Ministry of Foreign Affairs in Rome that Italian national identity would deteriorate if applicants were to qualify for *grande naturalizzazione* after completing their military service outside of Italy proper.[61] Yet this is exactly what was to happen and on an increasing basis. A young physician from Rhodes, Giorgio Peridi, as an example, obtained full Italian citizenship in Alexandria. The remarks in his file said that Giorgio Peridi "had [during his residency on Rhodes] nourished Hellenic sentiment but he did not make obvious political propaganda and he behaved well toward the authorities." After medical school in Athens, he had moved to Alexandria where he gained employment at the Italian hospital, named after Benito Mussolini, and demonstrated his loyalty to the regime by "assiduously attending, and obtaining good results in, lessons in Italian culture and literature that are given at the Fascist Center." Since he had

59   "Il Decreto sulla cittadinanza," *Messaggero di Rodi* (242), 29 November 1933.
60   Decreto sul riconoscimento della piena cittadinanza italiana," Protocol 2/22/17, GAK CCRR.
61   Lago wrote that Dodecanese natives should complete military service in Italy "[s]o that they may form an exact understanding of the power and greatness of the *patria* [...] for this reason they should spend their period of military service in vaster environments where they will find themselves exclusively in contact with the metropolitan element." Telespresso n.1885, Mario Lago to the Ministry of Foreign Affairs (Uffici Trattati), 13 January 1935, MAE, 988/1935.

already signed up for the required military service in colonial Eritrea, Rome affirmed his accelerated naturalization to Italian citizenship.[62]

The 1933 reforms to Aegean citizenship were prescient of a larger ideological shift that was about to take place; within a year, Italy would launch its brutal invasion of Ethiopia. The empire as largely a project of growth of Italian economic markets and the spread of national identity abroad—that is, the empire as it had been conceived by the Liberal nationalists—was being subtly supplanted by the empire that served to fully consolidate the Fascist dictatorship, and to no small extent, Mussolini's totalitarianism. Indeed, unbeknownst to Lago, he was being surveilled at this time and all his private correspondence was being intercepted and sent to Rome; by 1936, he was asked to resign from his position as governor of the Aegean. Although Lago's vision of the Italian mission on the islands had been linked to the ideals of Fascism, his ideas of Italy's expansion were still entwined with Liberal-era notions of empire as revitalizing Italian nationalism, a nostalgic recuperation of Italy's Mediterranean past in which Italian culture had been fertilized by cross-cultural creolizations. As Lago explained in a personal note when he sent to Mussolini a copy of his novel *E intanto lavoriamo*, which he wrote in his retirement from public service after 1936, "Following your directives, I governed while always keeping in mind the Levantine tradition of Italy, so now, evoking in a novel [...] I have exalted the eternal Mediterranean vocation of the Italian people."[63]

While Italian governance in the Dodecanese in the previous decade had relied on the idea of *mediterraneità* as a subtle means of inclusion while still inscribing difference on Italy's citizen-subjects in the Aegean, by 1934 the Fascist state in Rome had begun to chart another path. It had begun to campaign for assimilation—not to *italianità*, however, but to the Fascist dictatorship and its imperatives of labor, conquest, and resettlement in the African colonies. Following the invasion of Ethiopia, the idea of *romanità*, or Romanness, would sustain not only biological racism but also a set of measures aimed at revising and controlling the political identifications of the population.

---

62   GAK, Envelope 323/1935.

63   *"Come—seguendo le vostre dirretive—ho governorato avendo costantantemente la visione della tradizione levantina dell'Italia, così ora, rievocando in un romanzo ('E intanto lavoriamo' Editore Mondadori) le opera realizzata laggiù del regime e gli avvenimenti che, culminando nella conquista dell'Impero, ebbero a Rodi l'eco più appasionata, ho esaltato l'eterna vocazione mediterranea degli italiani."* ACS: SPD CO (Segretario Particolare del Duce Carteggio Ordinario) 527.1935.

The Jewish Communities of Rhodes and Kos

If the Italian administration considered diasporic Greeks in Egypt desirable for acquiring Italian citizenship, it also held, for at least a decade, the Jewish communities of Rhodes and Kos to be strong allies in the project of the advancement of the Italian Empire. The 1933 reform built upon existing practices of applying Italian Aegean nationality to refugees of Ottoman collapse, especially Jewish ones, who, as neither Greek nor Turkish, were not treated in the population exchange that had resolved the collapse of the Ottoman Empire in the Aegean region. Full Italian citizenship, when it became available, provided them with a means for mobility and circulation throughout the Mediterranean region and notable members of the Aegean Jewish communities were some of the first to acquire full Italian citizenship when the option became available.

The origins of the Jewish communities of Rhodes and Kos extend into antiquity; records of a small settlement in the islands occur as early as the first century BC. The small community of Greek-speaking Romaniote Jews was integral to commerce in the life of the Byzantine Mediterranean. After the Ottoman Empire's capture of the islands in 1522, the community changed shape dramatically, as the Aegean islands began to absorb the diaspora of Jews expelled by the Spanish sovereigns. The Jewish refugees from Spain brought with them a new Judeo-Spanish language, Ladino, as well as the religious rites of Sephardim. By the turn of the twentieth century, almost one-quarter of the local population in the town of Rhodes was Jewish. This remained the case until globalization and the draw of new sources of wealth and labor led the community to emigrate in large numbers beginning at the turn of the twentieth century, as the Greek community had. The Jewish community maintained cohesion through kinship, establishing new communities of Rhodes and Kos-originating Jews, often called Rhodeslis, in their destination cities.[64] It was common practice for members of the Jewish

---

64   Renée Hirschon, "Jews from Rhodes in Central and South Africa," in *Encyclopedia of Diasporas: Immigrant and Refugee Cultures Around the World*, , vol. 2, edited by Melvin Ember, 925–34 (New York: Springer, 2007); Keretz Yitzchak, "The Migration of Rhodian Jews to Africa and the Americas, 1900–1914: The Beginning of New Sephardic Communities," in *Patterns of Migration, 1850–1914: Proceedings of the International Academic Conference*, edited by Aubrey Newman and Stephen Massil (London: The Jewish Historical Society of England and the Institute of Jewish Studies, University College, London, 1996), 321–34.

community to return home to choose spouses from their extended family, leading to significant endogamy, as well as the legendary "bride bazaars" in which men who had returned to the island chose wives from members of their community. A sense of the islands as a storied "home" grew in parallel to the increased mobility of the community's emigrants.

Rhodesli communities were therefore already a transnational community, with enclaves established from Los Angeles to the Belgian Congo, when the Italian state took the islands by fiat in 1912 from a weakening Ottoman Empire. Up until the late 1930s, the Italian state liberally granted Italian Aegean nationality to any Jewish person who was a returning emigrant or refugee of Ottoman collapse and desired residence in the islands—provided they were of "good moral and political conduct" and did not espouse anti-Italian sentiment. Moreover, for the first decade of Italian rule, the Jewish and Turkish minority communities and the Greek Orthodox majority had equal rights to naturalize to Italian citizenship. Early propaganda celebrated the diversity of the ethnicities that were contained within the small space of the islands of Rhodes and Kos, and as discussed in chapter 2, pictured Italian rule as a glorious reclamation of the microcosms of the Levant. Under the Lago administration, initiatives aimed at reviving the "cosmopolitan" and "Mediterranean" culture of the islands for the purpose of tourism reinforced the Liberal era's nationalist adoption of the capitulations as a means of diplomatic protection for the local population, and also notably supported Jewish communities in not only Rhodes and Kos but also the wider Aegean region. Because of the annexation of the islands to Italy, the Dodecanese did not experience the exchange of approximately 1.5 million people between Greece and the newly formed nation of Turkey at the end of World War I—famously referred to the "un-mixing of the peoples," by British foreign minister Lord Curzon—in what was the death knell of the cosmopolitan way of life in the region.[65]

Unlike Greeks and Turks in the Aegean, who had the option to claim Greek or Turkish citizenship, the path toward national belonging and identity in the aftermath of Ottoman collapse was less clear for Jews. Mussolini even affirmed in a special directive that extra consideration should be paid to naturalizing Jewish persons who petitioned for Italian Aegean nationality

---

65 Renée Hirschon, ed., *Crossing the Aegean: An Appraisal of the 1923 Compulsory Population Exchange between Greece and Turkey* (New York: Berghahn Books, 2003). See also Bruce Clark, *Twice a Stranger: The Mass Expulsions that Forged Modern Greece and Turkey* (Cambridge, MA: Harvard University Press, 2009).

since, because they were neither Greeks nor Turks, no other nation-state would intervene to contest their Italian nationality. He added that Italian Aegean nationality should be applied to those persons who were "desirable" as a result of being financially well off, and that Jewish refugees represented a potential asset to the Italian state's rule in the islands.[66]

Alongside citizenship petitions, the Italian government also assessed numerous applications from Jewish persons for positions within the local administration. Requests were sometimes from natives of the islands, but other requests came from Jewish persons residing elsewhere in the Mediterranean—some even hailed originally from Italian merchant cities such as Livorno. Many desired to relocate to Rhodes and be a part of the new Italian administration. Because some of these Jewish applicants had a high level of education and possessed skills such as accounting and competency in four or even five languages of the Mediterranean, the Italian government often found positions for such Jewish persons in the nascent Italian adminis-tration.[67] Under these favorable conditions, a sizable community of wealthy Jewish refugees of the Greco-Turkish War assimilated into the islands from the Anatolian coast and naturalized as Italian Aegean citizens, increasing the total number of Jewish persons residing in the islands to roughly four thousand persons. Migration briefly reversed the trend toward the decline of the Jewish population through emigration and bringing the community to a size it had not seen since the turn of the century.[68]

The increase in the size of the Jewish community may also have helped Italy to undermine the opposition of the Greek Orthodox community, in what some scholars have speculated was a divide and conquer strategy.[69] Since the era of Liberal occupation of the islands, the Jewish community had supported the Italian presence and, as described earlier in this chapter, the opening of the Dante Alighieri school in 1915, had been enthusias-tically received by the Jewish minority community in Rhodes. But it was not only that the Jewish community admired the Italian state both before

---

66 "Cittadinanza dei Dodecannesini," Circular no. 78, 2 October 1925, GAK, 93/1927/163.

67 GAK DOD, Box 30, Series B, F.3/1918, "Forze Armate."

68 See Esther Fintz Menasce, *Gli ebrei a Rodi: Storia di un'antica comunità annientata dai nazisti* (Milan: Guerini, 1992).

69 See Cesare Marongiù Buonaiuti, *La politica religiosa del fascismo nel Dodecanneso* (Naples: Giannini, 1979), a study of Fascist Italy's religious policy in the islands and the so-called *autocephalia* or dismantling of the structure of the local Greek Orthodox Church and its ties with the patriarchate in Constantinople.

and during Fascism. It was also that the Jewish community of Rhodes and Kos constituted an important link between the metropole and the overseas territories and embodied the possibility of what might be termed an exclusive inclusion for the Aegean—that is, the possibility of expanding Italian national identity to the margins while still maintaining an exclusionary regime of difference with locals.

Italy's rising star in the Aegean under Italian rule attracted many notable members of the Jewish community in the Balkans and Aegean as well as many intellectuals from other Mediterranean and European cities. Permanent and semi-permanent notable Jewish residents in the islands included Marcus Berger, Vitalis Strumza, Davide Gaon, Michele Albagli, and Isaiah Sonne—the latter was a major Judaica scholar who went on to have an illustrious career. The Italian administration drew these Jewish notables into a project to establish a rabbinical college in Rhodes in order to provide higher education to young Jewish men in the islands. Although the project was suspended in 1938 during the deployment of the anti-Semitic race laws, the Italian government initially saw this project as supporting not only the local Jewish community but also the Italian state's larger interests in the region, as graduated rabbis of the program would eventually service other Italian-speaking Jewish communities in the eastern Mediterranean. The rabbinical college would thus deepen links between the Jewish communities of the Italian Peninsula and Italian Aegean communities of the empire in Rhodes and Kos. Lago, who was seen as presiding over a "Renaissance" of the Jewish community, privately hoped that the Jewish community in Rome would help lend financial support to the public works of the Italian administration for the benefit the Jewish communities of Rhodes and Kos.[70]

When the option to assimilate to full Italian citizenship became available to Italian Aegean subjects through the 1933 reform, the Jewish community immediately began to take advantage of it. Many of the island's most prominent Jewish subjects applied for and acquired full Italian citizenship after the 1933 reforms went into effect. But there were exclusions as well. Poor Jewish natives from Rhodes—even those who had also assiduously attended the Italian schools and professed devotion to the Fascist regime— were still denied Italian citizenship on the grounds that they were too poor for such an elevated status. This pattern of denials, present even in

70   ASMAE Affari Politici 1931-45 14 (36–7), Fasc. 7, "Scuole."

the period of greatest expansionist enthusiasm, foreshadowed the way that local governance and the system of citizenship and naturalizations were already viewed as regimes of exclusion as much as of inclusion; this pattern of denials would be exacerbated by the introduction of the anti-Semitic race laws in 1938.

Vitalis Strumza is an interesting and exemplary illustration of the path of Jewish notables who found their way into the island of Rhodes and sought full Italian citizenship. A Jewish notable who had been an Ottoman bureaucrat—at one point even a candidate for local representation of his Jewish community in Salonica—Strumza moved to Rhodes in the aftermath of Ottoman collapse, in 1921, and promptly began a career of service to the Italian administration; reportedly his appointment was in part due to his close friendship with Felice Maissa, the acting governor in the islands at this time.[71] Strumza worked closely with Isaiah Sonne, who stayed on Rhodes between 1935 and 1938 as a professor at the rabbinical college, to complete a short monograph about the history of the Jewish communities in Rhodes.[72] Strumza regularly communicated with the *gran rabbi* in Rome, Davide Prato, about developing the international profile of the rabbinical college in Rhodes. In 1934, Strumza applied successfully for full Italian citizenship, which enabled him to travel freely back and forth between Italy and Rhodes. At one point, he was even named by the Italian governor a *cavaliere della corona*, a member of the Order of the Crown of Italy, an honorific established by Vittorio Emanuele, the first king of Italy, to commemorate national unification. But Strumza had to leave the islands just a few years later, when the anti-Semitic race laws nullified Italian citizenship for all Jews who had acquired it after 1919. Italian surveillance documents capture the bitterness of the situation for Strumza in 1938. As he wrote to Davide Prato in Rome, "It's useless that I should describe to you our mood here. I am getting ready to leave, my heart heavy with bitterness at the thought of abandoning this island and this environment for which I have worked passionately and with love over the past eighteen years."[73]

71 Notes in Strumza's surveillance file suggest that his appointment was partly due to the fact that he was a personal friend of Maissa. "Strumza," GAK CCRR.

72 Interestingly, this monograph includes the history of the Jews of Rhodes under the category of the history of Italian Jews; Vitalis Strumza, *Alcuni cenni storici sugli Ebrei di Rodi* (Bologna: L. Capelli, 1936).

73 "Strumza," GAK CCRR.

Strumza's story illustrates the ambivalences that characterized the Italian Empire's attitude towards the Rhodesli Jewish community. On the one hand, Jews, especially notables and intellectuals, stood to become an important class of imperial subjects and, given their location at an important nexus of Italian imperial interests, could be viewed as key actors in the advancement of Italy's broader imperial interests in the region. On the other hand, the Italian view of the native population as fundamentally a "Levantine" and ultimately a "subject" population was present in policies toward the Jewish community even under Mario Lago. The arc of the Fascist dictatorship's motivation for at first privileging and then persecuting the Jewish community was not always discernible among the community, however, and the Jewish communities of Rhodes and Kos regularly sought to accommodate the Italian Fascist regime. A surveilled 1935 letter to the president of the Jewish community at the time, Hizkià Franco, for example, tells how a local, pro-Italian teacher had recently been fired for proselytizing Betar Zionism to his students. In his defense, the teacher pointed out the similarities between Mussolini's Fascist revolution and Betar Zionism (which, like Fascism, was also oriented as a youth movement).[74] The administration offered no clemency and the teacher, Alberto Hassan, was fired permanently from his post, in a move that heralded an imminent crackdown on education in religious schools, one that would commence with the arrival of Cesare De Vecchi in the islands in 1937.

In 1938, when the Italian administration oversaw the deployment of the anti-Semitic race laws against all Jews residing in the Aegean, close to one thousand Jewish persons, almost a quarter of the Jewish population of Rhodes at the time, were affected. De Vecchi interpreted the race laws to mean, first, the stripping of any form of Italian citizenship—including Italian Aegean citizenship—from any Jewish person who had naturalized to the Aegean after 1919. But he also went further. About 350 of the affected Jewish persons were in possession of Turkish nationality but the rest were among those who had naturalized as refugees of the Ottoman collapse and the Greco-Turkish War, the so-called Asia Minor catastrophe.[75] De Vecchi, an original member of the quadrumvirate that had organized the Fascist march on Rome, chose to follow the nullification of citizenship with an edict of expulsion for all Jews who had arrived in the islands after 1919.

---

74 GAK DOD, k.49/series B/1938/837.
75 See Fintz-Menasce, *Gli ebrei a Rodi,* and Hirschon, *Crossing the Aegean.*

Many of the affected Jewish persons petitioned the Italian government in Rome directly to have their expulsion sentences reversed, either by pleading that they held Italian nationality as naturalized Italian Aegean citizens, or by showing certificates of Italian protection that classified them as domiciled (*établis*) and therefore protected by the 1924 Treaty of Lausanne. But De Vecchi was categorical in his response that persons who had arrived in the Dodecanese Islands as refugees of the Asia Minor catastrophe had only resided in the islands "in passing" (*"di passaggio"*) and had obtained Italian passports only "given the procedures agreed on at the time about the Hebrew element" (*"date le facilitazioni accordate in quel tempo all'elemento ebraico"*).[76] As the Italian government had already done previously on several occasions when expelling "undesirable" minority residents of Rhodes and Kos, De Vecchi invoked the principle of the ethnic minority that the Lausanne negotiations had introduced to resolve the Greco-Turkish War, and stated that, given that the islands' ethnic majority was of Greek "race and religion," Jewish persons had no recourse to the protections of the 1924 Lausanne Treaty.[77] De Vecchi affirmed their status as *apolidi* or stateless persons.[78]

This implementation of ideological racism was particularly striking given the fact that, as we have seen, Jewish Dodecanesians, both those in the islands and those abroad, had previously enjoyed status as non-Muslim Europeans in the Ottoman regime of the capitulations, then had, under Italian rule, obtained first Italian consular protection then Italian citizenship. There was in fact dissent within the Italian administration about whether new anti-Semitic priorities invalidated the status of Jews who held Italian Aegean citizenship or full Italian citizenship. Galeazzo Ciano, minister of foreign affairs and close confident of Mussolini, supported some of the petitions of Levantine Jews who argued that their "small citizenship" protected them from expulsion and also wrote to De Vecchi to point out that *piccola cittadinanza*

---

76   "*La revoca della cittadinanza ha effetto soltanto per gli ebrei che avessero ottenuto la cittadinanza medesima in base ad un provvedimento formale di concessione, adottato nell'esercizio di un potere discrezionale, con facoltà, quindi, di accogliere o respingere le domande degli interessati*"; "Provvedimenti per la difesa della razza," GAK DOD, 725/1938.

77   "*É stato solo di passaggio, non può neppure considerarsi suddito italiano di diritto a norma dell'art.30 del trattato di Losanna. Né aveva diritto ad opzione—di cui del resto non esiste traccia—perché non appartenente alla maggioranza etnica della popolazione del Possedimento (art.32 trattato di Losanna)*"; GAK DOD, f. 725/1938.

78   GAK DOD, f. 725/1938.

was a nonrevocable status. De Vecchi replied that members of the Jewish community of Rhodes and Kos who were being expelled had a status that was much lower, that is, *cittadinanza italiana egea*, and that such a discretional citizenship could be revoked at will.[79]

The anti-Semitic race laws have been widely treated in the historiography of Fascist Italy, and for this reason it is not necessary here to go into the multiple factors—not least of them being Mussolini's alliance with Nazi Germany—that went into the regime's decision to adopt an official politics of race against its own Jewish communities, and the effects of these on Italian Jews.[80] I will therefore confine my comments to the motivations for and the impact on the race laws as seen from the perspective of the Jewish communities living in the Dodecanese at this time (in a moment, I will address their impact on other communities in the islands). Given the longstanding ambivalences that the Italian administration had maintained about the local Dodecanese population—whether it could be integrated into the national body politic or had to be held as entirely foreign—the race laws permitted the administration to enact both of these ideas in a more aggressive way, and to affirm its sovereignty as rooted in its own imperial ambitions rather than in the powers awarded it by virtue of the Lausanne Treaty. Indeed, De Vecchi's reinterpretation of the Lausanne Treaty during the deployment of the anti-Semitic race laws is revealing of the ways in which a lack of clarity had always existed about the juridical construction of Dodecanese inhabitants. Were Dodecanese subjects Italian nationals or were they colonial subjects receiving some form of diplomatic protection from the

---

79   "*Agli ebrei immigrati nel Possedimento dopo il 1 gennaio 1919, non la piccola cittadinanza è stata concessa (ciò che per l'articolo 1 del R.D.L. 10 settembre 1922 avrebbe dovuto essere concessa per Decreto Reale) ma la cittadinanza egea*"; "Provvedimenti per la difesa della razza," GAK DOD, f. 725/1938.

80   Savero Gentile, *Le leggi razioni: Scienza giuridica, norme, circolari* (Milan: EDUCatt, 2010); Aron Gillette, *Racial Theories in Fascist Italy* (London: Routledge, 2002); Michele Sarfatti, *The Jews in Mussolini's Italy: From Equality to Persecution* (Madison, WI: University of Wisconsin Press, 2006); Susan Zuccotti, *The Italians and the Holocaust: Persecution, Rescue and Survival* (London: Halban, 1987); Renzo de Felice, *The Jews in Fascist Italy: A History*, translated by Robert Miller (New York: Enigma, 2001); Alberto Burgio, *Nel nome della razza: Il razzismo nella storia d'Italia 1870–1945* (Bologna: Il mulino, 2000); Joshua Zimmerman, *Jews in Italy under Fascist and Nazi Rule, 1922–45* (Cambridge: Cambridge University Press, 2005); Olindo de Napoli, "The Origin of the Racist Laws Under Fascism: A Problem of Historiography," *Journal of Modern Italian Studies* 17, no. 1 (2002): 106–22.

Italian state? By revoking the citizenship of a large portion of the Jewish community, and subjecting the rest of it to the same persecutory measures as the rest of Italy's Jewish communities (in both Italy and Libya), De Vecchi affirmed the idea that the Italian mandate in the Aegean was a form of national empire in the Mediterranean. The deployment of the anti-Semitic race laws made it clear that Italian Aegean citizens did not enjoy a form of diplomatic protection—nor any other form of *piccola naturalizzazione*— that might entitle them to live in the Aegean as foreigners and members of an ethnic minority, as they had under the Ottoman state in the Aegean. Given this framework, the "inclusive" decision to expand the possibilities linked with Italian Aegean citizenship in 1933 was not as antithetical as it might appear to the "exclusive" decision, in 1938, to expel nonnative Jews in the Aegean, and to aggressively carry out other measures against Jews in the islands. In both cases, the Fascist state moved to more fully align its policies in the colonies with its policies at home. This perspective not only illustrates the fundamental entanglement of nation-state and empire in Italy, but also the ways in which race was an essential, not just rhetorical, category within the regime's colonial policies. As Esmonde Robertson has observed, when Italy adopted the race laws, there were almost as many Jews in Italian imperial territories as there were in the peninsula, and the former were already registered as "Oriental" Jews.[81] The symbolic and real demarcation of difference between the Mediterranean and the Levant provided an ideological framework for race and nation, both at home and in the overseas colonies.

Within the local memory and historiography, however, the deployment of the anti-Semitic race laws has sometimes been linked to the personality of De Vecchi—an authoritarian who ruled with an iron fist, the equivalent in the Aegean of Mussolini's heinous conquest of Ethiopia. In fact, the anti-Semitic racist measures expressed wider ideological shifts within the Fascist state. The Jewish communities of the broader Aegean, not just from the islands of Rhodes and Kos, had constituted an important link between the metropole and the overseas territories and within the project to reinforce the identity of the nation-state in Italy's imperial projects abroad. In the earlier phase of Italian presence in the Dodecanese, the geographical extent of the Jewish community, which mirrored the broader diffusion of the Italian nation throughout the Mediterranean and that called up associations with the great

81   Esmonde Robertson, "Race as a Factor in Mussolini's Policy in Africa and Europe," *Journal of Contemporary European History* 23, no. 1 (1988): 37–58, 45.

merchant age, had made them seem ideal citizens. Moreover, while much of the Jewish community of the Dodecanese had arrived in the sixteenth century fleeing the persecution of the Spanish Inquisition and finding protection in the Ottoman Empire, some of them were so-called Levantines, or Italian descendants of the famous Genoese and Venetian merchant empire. Mario Lago had seen the Jewish communities of Rhodes and Kos—with their transnational networks and ties with the Jewish communities in peninsular Italy—as vital instruments for the project of *mediterraneità*, of a Mediterranean Empire that supported the unity, wealth, and prestige of the Italian nation-state. Yet these very same transnational links—with their potential to reinforce Italian sovereignty on a wider regional level—were no longer necessary once the empire had been officially "enacted" and achieved through the conquest of Ethiopia. As Cristina Lombardi-Diop and Gaia Giuliani have suggested, the Ethiopian invasion marked a "resolution" to longstanding anxieties about racial difference with Southern Italians, and while "whitening" the character of Southern Italians, it marked Jews out instead as Italy's remaining internal other.[82]

Those Jewish persons who remained in the archipelago because they had retained Italian Aegean citizenship—that is, because they were natives or residents of the archipelago prior to the collapse of the Ottoman Empire—suffered the same humiliations as Jews in peninsular Italy did. Jewish persons could not be teachers or caregivers to any minor who was not Jewish; could not run or own a business or possess property of significant value (more than five thousand *lire*); could not have any domestic help that was Italian; could not be part of a civil or military administration or hold any kind of public office; and all members of the Jewish community were required to report to the local civil registry and register their religion. Survivors from this period particularly remember the closing of Jewish private schools and the expulsion of Jewish children from Italian public schools: the Italian support of education and literacy among the Jewish community had been a special source of positive relations between community leaders and the Italian administration. Given these conditions of persecution, many members of the Jewish community voluntarily emigrated. Italy's early adoption of anti-Semitism therefore paradoxically saved many members of the community from the fate of deportation in 1944 during the Nazi occupation of the islands.

---

82 Gaia Giuliani and Cristina Lombardi-Diop, *Bianco e Nero: Storia dell'identità razziale degli italiani* (Florence: Le Monnier, 2013), 24.

But the deployment of the anti-Semitic race laws in Rhodes and Kos nevertheless represents an important development toward the community's eventual demise during World War II. By affirming that Jewish subjects in the Aegean had no right to protection under the Lausanne Treaty, the Italian state participated in the process of making European Jewish people into refugees or stateless persons—in the language of the day, *apolidi*—who had no legal protection. The stripping of the citizenship of Jewish persons is widely recognized as one of the key mechanisms that enabled the Holocaust—the reduction of Jewish persons to "bare life" serving as a juridical precursor to their annihilation in the camps.[83] The recent cataloguing of the special surveillance archive in Rhodes has also revealed that there was definitely Italian collaboration with the Nazi deportations of Jewish islanders that took place in 1944, and that some parts of the action may have been carried out by the de facto Italian government at the time. This government, while admittedly under the oversight of the Nazi command, was not Fascist, but Liberal, since the 1943 signing of the armistice had passed the islands over to the administration of Admiral Innigo Campioni.[84]

During the war itself, Rhodes became a temporary home for many stateless Jews, including refugees from Central Europe who arrived in Rhodes by shipwreck as they attempted to escape to Palestine (the famous Pentcho refugee ship).[85] But Jews from the Aegean, who had recently been considered Italian Jews, were now effectively stateless, even as the refugee crisis swelled in Europe and expanded into the Mediterranean. Stories like that of Mose Varon illustrate how unlucky it was to have opted for Italian citizenship in the 1930s. Varon had been born in Smyrna in 1922, just one year before the collapse of the Ottoman Empire, and had naturalized to Rhodes and to Italian Aegean citizenship in the 1930s, and therefore was a victim of the Italian anti-Semitic race laws. He made multiple attempts to escape from Rhodes to Palestine, one of which included a close shave with death by drowning when he swam out to meet a ferry boat as it departed from the harbor of Rhodes, but he had always been turned back in

---

83   Giorgio Agamben, *Means without End: Notes on Politics* (Minneapolis: University of Minnesota, 2000).

84   GAK CCRR, "Varon." On the deportations in Rhodes, see also Anthony McElligott, "The Deportation of the Jews of Rhodes, 1944: An Integrated History" in *The Holocaust in Greece,* edited by Giorgos Antoniou and Dirk Moses, 58–86 (Cambridge: Cambridge University Press, 2018), 72.

85   See John Bierman, *Odyssey* (New York: Simon & Schuster, 1984).

Palestine. Varon was one of eighteen hundred Jewish subjects in the islands in July 1944, all of them established as stateless persons and therefore beyond the protection of international treaty. All were deported to concentration camps in Poland in what was the last deportation of the war. There were only one hundred survivors from the camps and none of them returned to the islands after the war.[86]

As at all sites of the Holocaust in Europe, questions remain about how the atrocity of the deportations could occur. But in the case of the Jewish communities of Rhodes and Kos, such questions are complicated by further ones about the community's identity, and how their experience during their last resident phase in the islands, during Italian occupation, impacted them both during the Holocaust and after. As we have seen, the community's last phase of residency in the islands of Rhodes and Kos was intimately bound up with the idea and memory of Italian culture and identity, of both *italianità* and *mediterraneità*. Prior to its alignment with Nazi ideology, Italy's Fascist administration sought, with some success, to enlist the Jewish community of the islands in the Fascist project to rebuild the islands into a center of "Levantine" culture. At times, the community viewed Fascist ideology as aligning with Zionism, and even when faced with patent racism and persecution, they turned to their Italian nationality as an important form of belonging that might protect them from anti-Semitism elsewhere. To be sure, the fact that Italy eventually adopted an anti-Semitic policy, and that Fascist Italy aligned itself with Hitler's Nazi ideology, is not absent from collective memories of Italian rule. But memoirs by survivors of the deportations, some historical accounts, and local history insist upon the Italian rule in the islands as a golden age during which the community thrived and prospered.[87]

---

86   In contrast to Jewish persons who were former Italian Aegean citizens, those Jewish persons who still held Turkish nationality were saved from the deportations through the intervention of the consulate in Istanbul. On the issue of Italian collaboration with the Nazi regime, see Marco Clementi, "The Italian Occupation of the Balkans and the Jewish Question during WWII," *Vestnik of Saint Petersburg University, History* 63, no. 1 (2018): 174–86.

87   Survivors of the period have completed a number of memoirs and works of history. The following texts all touch upon the Italian period in the islands though to greater and lesser degrees: Esther Fintz Menascé, *Gli Ebrei a Rodi: Storia di un'antica communità annientata dai nazisti* (Milan: Guerrini, 1991); Hizkia M. Franco, *The Jewish Martyrs of Rhodes and Cos,* translated by Joseph Franco (Los Angeles: Rhodes Jewish Historical Foundation, 2009); Haham Solomon Gaon and Mitchell Serels, eds., *Del Fuego:*

This ambiguity and complexity persists into the present in the regimes of citizenship available to the Rhodesli diaspora. One of the little-known legacies of Italian sovereignty in the Dodecanese is that it today enables members of the Rhodesli diaspora to acquire Italian citizenship by demonstrating their Dodecanese heritage. The large Dodecanese Jewish community in Zimbabwe, for example, maintains its Italian passports to this day with very few exceptions. Many Rhodesli Jews from there and elsewhere have carried forward their "Italian" heritage into present-day regimes of European citizenship. And as Europe shifts uneasily between ideas of nationalism and globalization, their patterns of migration often no longer follow metropole-colony lines. As one person interviewed for this book explained, his father chose to give up his Italian citizenship—which he held by virtue of heredity through his own father, who was born in Rhodes in 1926—when Zimbabwe nationalized; but he was able to acquire it for himself later, in 2011, through his patrilineal relationship to his grandfather.[88]

In another legacy of Italy's imperial experiences, following the hierarchies of race that set white colonial subjects of the Mediterranean above African colonial subjects, today's norms about citizenship enable mobility and inclusion for some former Italian colonial subjects, while others are excluded. As will be discussed in more detail below, the legend that Italians and Dodecanese natives were like "one face, one race" has mostly implied ethnic bonds among Greeks and Italians that were reinforced by the biological racism that Italy adopted following the invasion of Ethiopia. But it is worth observing that the persistence of this phrase may also be thanks to the ways that Italy initially constructed its governance on the islands as the renewal of the Ottoman state in the Mediterranean—that is an idea of "one face, one race" among Italians, Greeks, Turks, and Jews. The idea of a Mediterranean ethnic unity seems to be at least partially borne out in contemporary legal practices and in the continuing maintenance and acquisition of Italian citizenship among the Rhodesli community.

Sephardim and the Holocaust (New York: Sepher-Hermon Press, 1995); Isaac Jack Lévy, *Jewish Rhodes: A Lost Culture* (Berkeley: Magnes Museum, 1998); Rebecca Amato Levy, *I Remember Rhodes* (New York: Sepher-Hermon Press for Sephardic House at Congregation Shearith Israel, 1987); and Laura Varon, *The Juderia: A Holocaust Survivor's Tribute to the Jewish Community of Rhodes* (Westport, CT: Praeger, 1999).
88   Joey Hasson of the Rhodesian (Zimbabwe) Rhodesli community kindly gave me an interview about his experience acquiring second-generation Italian citizenship through his patrilineal links to Rhodes. Interview on December 13, 2016.

One Face, One Race: *Romanità* in the Aegean

On the eve of Italy's 1935 invasion of Ethiopia, Italy moved to repatriate about two hundred Dodecanese Greeks who were residing in East Africa at this time. Lago initially protested Rome's request for repatriation on the grounds that the situation in the Aegean was economically too unstable for the repatriation of Dodecanese Greeks and suggested instead that they be relocated to Eritrea. But his view changed after the arrival of this community in the island and enthusiastic reports about the "political and moral conduct" of the repatriating Greeks, who demonstrated "enthusiasm for the upcoming Italian action in Ethiopia."[89] The case notes vividly recount how the arrival of the community had attracted the attention of the Greek population. One Greek refugee reportedly shouted to a crowd gathered around him,

> If I knew how to write I would publish who the Greeks are because you don't know them, but once you know them you will hate them as I do because they are as barbaric as the Abyssinians [Ethiopians]. The Italians are in contrast civil, good and human and if it weren't for the [governor of Ethiopia] saving us, we would have been lost. So why not love the Italians? And why not want to be Italian?[90]

The case notes went on to describe why this peasant had become so loyal: in Ethiopia, he had sought the protection of a certain Greek rebel, but Zervo, as the nationalist was called, had betrayed him and he had suffered several injuries while being held as a prisoner of the Ethiopian state. The Italian foreign ministry eventually intervened, which led to his repatriation to the Dodecanese. In Rhodes, the Italian authorities now urged Rome to grant Italian Aegean citizenship to him and others like him who "have not been brainwashed by anti-Italian rhetoric, for all that the propaganda has been so thorough in Abyssinia."[91] At a time when Italy's international image was being discredited due to the violent and illegal invasion of Ethiopia, these new arrivals represented hope for a spread of imperial fervor among the Greek community.[92]

---

89   GAK DOD, f. 1493/1935.
90   GAK DOD, f. 1493/1935.
91   *"Non siano imbevuti della retorica antitaliana per non essere stata la propaganda molto efficace in Abissinia"*; GAK, Envelope 1493/1935.
92   See Bruce Strang, *Collision of Empires: Italy's Invasion of Ethiopia and its International Impact* (New York: Routledge, 2017).

This documentation not only underscores the diasporic ties among Ethiopian Greeks and Dodecanese ones, but it also speaks volumes about the larger ideological turn that the Fascist state was making and how it was to impact the Italian administration of the Dodecanese. The suggestion that this Greek was illiterate ("If I knew how to write") aligned with Mussolini's claim that the war in Ethiopia had to be waged for Italy's peasant class to prosper. This idea had been heralded in the *strapaese* artistic movement discussed in the previous chapter and it became central to the demographic campaign to conquer a "vital space" for Italy's growing unemployed and peasant class. As Gaia Giuliani and Cristina Lombardi-Diop have shown, the Ethiopian conquest ensured that the South could represent the cradle of a new Mediterranean civilization.[93] The anecdote provided by the archive suggests that the Italian state imagined such racialization to extend to Greeks, with the Ethiopian invasion having the potential to "whiten" the character of Dodecanese Greeks as well as at that of Italians. In Ethiopia, the Italian army was still facing resistance to its invasion and the administration now equated Greek irredentism—embodied in figures like the nationalist Zervo—with the anticolonial movements of the uncivilized and "barbaric" African populations over which it now sought sovereignty.

The "whiteness" of the local population would soon be affirmed by Lago as he began asking questions about whether the new provisions against mixed marriages and mixed unions in the Italian colonies in East Africa applied to natives in the Aegean.[94] The episode reveals the way that the Italian administration was moving toward the view that the islands had the potential to become an Italian and ethnic Greek space. Within a year's time, the government began organizing the resettlement of Italian foresters to agricultural colonies

---

93   *"A mio avviso, infatti, il concetto di stirpe italica—e la sua intercambialità con razza, civilizzazione, nazione e popolo—nello spostare e posizionare la nerezza al di fuori dei confine nazionali, ebbe la capacità di fissare, dal punto di vista discorsivo, il significato di italianità-come mediterraneità in modo da distinguerla dall'identità razziale dei colonizzati (mediterranei ma africani) facendo altresì appello ad una romanità (biologico-storico-culturale) che ne sbiancava il carattere. Questa operazione permise, da un lato, l'inclusione discorsiva di tutte le cosiddette differenze razziali interne al popolo italiano in un'unica identità razziale nazionale e, dall'altro, al Meridione di divenire più di una semplice parte costitutiva di tale unità, ma la culla stessa del nuovo cittadino modello"*; Giuliani and Lombardi-Diop, *Bianco e nero*, 24.*

94   See Alexis Rappas, "The Domestic Foundations of Imperial Sovereignty: Mixed Marriages in the Fascist Aegean," in *New Perspectives on the History of Gender and Empire: Comparative and Global Approaches,* edited by Ulrike Lindner and Dörte Lerp, 31–58 (London: Bloomsbury Academic Press, 2018).

in Rhodes and Kos. A further set of laws against the Greek minority in Turkey meant that the Italian state was also integrating and assimilating a number of new ethnic Greek arrivals from Turkey alongside those from Ethiopia. It was clear that the Greek Dodecanese inhabitants ultimately belonged in the Mediterranean, thanks to the logic of a "Roman" race. The imperial state viewed the Turkish and Jewish minorities, on the other hand, as no longer in possession of the rights of inclusion granted to their Greek counterparts.

If the 1935–36 conquest of Ethiopia was a watershed moment for the Fascist state and the Italian Empire, it also constituted a turning point in Italian views about citizenship in the Dodecanese. The policies of inclusion, exclusion, and Mediterranean belonging that had governed the archipelago for the first decade of Italian sovereignty were revised as Italy brought the Dodecanese into ideological alignment with Italy's other colonies. From the invasion of Ethiopia until the German occupation of the islands in 1943, the Italian state instituted a set of repressive measures that dovetailed with a new politics of race and racialization emanating from fears about the degeneration of the Italian race given Italy's vast territorial enlargement in East Africa. In 1937, the Italian state banned instruction of all native languages in both Italian and private and religious schools, began closing places of worship that were linked to resistance to the Italian state, and initiated a politics of assimilation to "make" Aegean Greeks into Italians. These repressive, assimilationist measures were coupled with expulsions of Turkish and Jewish minorities, who, as non-members of the ethnic majority, were deemed unprotected by the Lausanne Treaty. The Italian state, revising its earlier position toward refugees, now determined it had no diplomatic or legal obligation to allow nonnative minority communities to reside in the archipelago. Likewise, by 1937–39, under the authority of Cesare De Vecchi, the most common recipients of naturalization to full Italian citizenship in the Aegean would be members of the local population who were serving as adjunct *carabinieri*.

De Vecchi had ruled ferociously in Italian Somaliland from 1923 to 1928. As minister of education in Italy from 1935 to 1936, he had further overhauled the Italian education system to make it reflect the ideals of the Fascist regime, advocating an educational program that inculcated a wider sense of Roman and Savoy imperial history and imparted "true notions of military culture to the youth."[95] His installation, in 1937 and at Mussolini's

---

95   Cesare Maria De Vecchi di Val Cismon, "Cultura e Discipline Militari negli Istituti Civili di Istruzione," Discourse of March 1935, in *Bonifica Fascista della Cultura* (Milan: Mondadori, 1937), 188.

order, as the governor of the Italian administration of the Dodecanese joined the repressive policies of colonialism in Somalia together with an aggressive transformation of the school system into a laboratory for educating a model Fascist citizen. Under his rule, Dodecanese youth were invited to join Fascist youth organizations, such as the Opera Nazionale Ballila, and recruited to attend summer colonies in the interior of Rhodes where they were to learn the values of hard work and sacrifice to the regime. The response to these reforms, which also included the banning of instruction in native languages, was staggering: almost all children stopped attending school at this point following an uptick in local nationalist sentiment. As the next chapter will show, De Vecchi's strategy largely backfired because locals proved adept at avoiding school attendance and at creatively reworking the lessons they did learn at school.

Legends about De Vecchi's firebrand personality tend to help to bracket him as an aberration within the culture of Italian rule. His arrival in the Dodecanese is remembered as an attempt by Mussolini to exile the wingnuts in his party (the suggestion that De Vecchi be "banished" to Rhodes was allegedly launched by Luigi Federzoni, minister of the colonies at the time).[96] But in this same time period, in a 1937 visit to Libya that followed the Ethiopian conquest, Mussolini presented himself in Libya as the "founder of the Empire" and "defender of the prestige of Rome, the common mother of all Mediterranean peoples."[97] Protests in Rhodes against a proposed visit may have prevented Mussolini from traveling there in that same year.[98] De Vecchi became well known for similar spectacles in which he attempted to draw massive crowds to listen to him declaiming the Fascist state's preeminence in the Mediterranean. Like Mussolini, De Vecchi also went to special lengths to ensure that the local community viewed a healthy dose of Italian propaganda films about the empire. In fact, contrary to the popular perception that he was one of the party's wingnuts, De Vecchi's presence in the islands was very much in line with the wider cultural transformation of the Fascist state.

With De Vecchi's arrival, the notion that Italian Empire marked the expansion of an Italian nation-state in the Mediterranean—a notion

---

96   Alexander De Grand, "Mussolini's Follies: Fascism in Its Imperial and Racist Phase, 1935–40," *Contemporary European History* 13, no. 2 (2004): 127–47, 132.

97   See John L. Wright, "Mussolini, Libya, and the Sword of Islam," in *Italian Colonialism*, edited by Ruth Ben-Ghiat and Mia Fuller, 121–30 (New York: Palgrave and MacMillan, 2005).

98   ACS: Divisione Polizia Politica, 1927–44 "Dodecanneso," B.9.

that, as chapter 1 detailed, had its roots in the Risorgimento era itself—came into sharp conflict with Fascist policies of race that defined the Italian Empire after the Ethiopian conquest. The conquest of Ethiopia brought more than nine million Muslims under Italian colonial rule and engendered new demands for racial distinctions between Italian settlers and subject populations. As Giulia Barerra has argued in her study of state–settler relations in Italian colonial East Africa, a surge in concubinage and mixed relationships occurred in East Africa after the invasion and in the context of massive unrest and resistance to Italian rule.[99] From 1883 (the establishment of Eritrea) until 1936, Italian East African colonies had been small-scale settlement communities, accompanied by concubinage with local Eritrean women (*madamismo*) as well as mixed marriages in which Italian settlers recognized their relationships with Eritrean women; in many cases, mixed-race children were also recognized as Italians and received Italian nationality. As Barrera points out, these relationships were common but constituted a minimal part of the fabric of Eritrea under Italian, colonial rule given the relatively small size of the Italian settler community at this time. After the 1935 invasion of Ethiopia, however, there was an outbreak of concubinage among Italian settlers and local East African women that threatened to upset colonial hierarchies. In response, the first Italian antimiscegenation laws appeared in East Africa, making mixed marriages illegal and punishable by up to five years in prison. These provisions against mixed-marriage and *métissage* were, in effect, the first "laws for the defense of the race" (*proveddimenti per la difesa della razza*). As scholars have pointed out, these first provisions to protect the Italian race anticipate the anti-Semitic race laws that appeared in 1938 after Mussolini's alliance with Hitler and show that the investment in biological racism was inherent to Italy's own policies of nation and empire.[100]

Italy introduced the category of *romanità* in order to define its own ideological racism as distinct from that of the Third Reich in the midst of that unstable alliance.[101] The Ethiopian invasion isolated Italy from the League of Nations and cemented the alliance with Nazi Germany, but Mussolini

---

99   Barrera, "Sessualità e segregazione."

100   Robertson, "Race as a Factor"; De Grand, "Mussolini's Follies"; Olindo De Napoli, "The Origin of the Racist Laws under Fascism: A Problem of Historiography," *Journal of Modern Italian Studies* 17, no. 1 (2012): 106–22.

101   See Fabrizio de Donno, "La Razza Ario-Mediterranea," *Interventions: International Journal of Postcolonial Studies* 8, no. 3 (2006): 394–412.

and Hitler were strange bedfellows. Both had long nourished a bitter rivalry over outstanding issues such as Germany's designs on Austria, Italy's siding with the Entente during World War I, and the territorial dispute over the Alto Adige. But *romanità* did more than define an ideological distance from Hitler—it also disavowed racial theories from the Liberal nationalist era. As chapter 1 described, earlier strains of racial theory upheld the view of Italians as belonging to a Mediterranean race, and Sergi went as far as to ascribe its origins, however prehistoric, to East Africa. But these views were fundamentally linked to the view that Italy's diasporic identities could advance the project for national empire; they were also linked to nostalgia for Italy's ties with a Levantine world. Diaspora and emigration were at odds with Mussolini's commitment to demographic empire and to the state-orchestrated resettlement of Italians in the colonies.

Mussolini's introduction of the term *mare nostrum*, our sea, in 1936 clearly harkened back to the nationalist rhetoric of empire as well as to the campaign for empire in North Africa and the Balkans that had been championed by the Italian Nationalist Association decades earlier. Yet Mussolini's ideas of Eurafrica and a *communità imperiale* in the Mediterranean affirmed colonial hierarchies and the rule of difference with colonial populations in order to ensure that Italian resettlement in the Mediterranean would not be accompanied by racial degeneration. In the Aegean, the introduction of *romanità* as a term can be understood, then, as the end of the older Liberal-nationalist idea of Mediterranean Empire, of *mediterraneità*, as a great multicultural project that created inclusion through the partial exclusion, or the holding of difference, with the Levantine. In this second-generation, Fascist style of empire, *romanità* was able to retain the unity and consanguinity of an Italo-Greek stock— the memory of the *italogreci* in the words of Sergi—while simultaneously establishing the Turkish and Jewish parts of the population as dangerous Others. This move resolved the ambiguities that had characterized Italy's initial mandate in the islands and paved the way for a day when the islands—with only ethnic Italian and Greek residents—might constitute a distant province of Italy.

Similar to the ways that the antimiscegenation laws in East Africa anticipated the 1938 introduction of the anti-Semitic race laws in Italy, a race politics in the Dodecanese that interpreted the Lausanne convention's provision on ethnic minorities as a means to expel "undesirables" now began to make itself felt, most significantly by the islands' Turkish Muslim minority. The Muslim population of the Dodecanese had been under scrutiny and threat of expulsion for almost a decade before Italy introduced an official politics of race into its governance of citizenship. Archival records show that as early as 1929, for example, Rome had refused the extradition of Yousef Soleiman, a Muslim subject, on the basis that he "did not belong to the ethnic majority of the islands, well known to be of the Greek Orthodox race and language."[102] Soleiman had immigrated to the United States with an Italian passport, but in Pennsylvania had been convicted of running a brothel. Soleiman clearly embodied the crime, vice, and lack of hygiene that ran counter to the social utopia of Fascism. But it was Soleiman's status as an ethnic minority Muslim and as a "foreigner" that Italy invoked to legally prevent his return to the islands.

While there were relatively few instances of Turkish petitions for resident permits or Aegean citizenship, Muslims who did apply were less likely than their Greek counterparts to receive residency or citizenship, and the Italian state frequently noting, in its response to such petitions, that this community was unprotected by the Lausanne Treaty. In 1934, Bilal Terzioglu, a Turkish islander, was denied his request to join his relatives in Rhodes, although he essentially was pleading for asylum, as he was a deserter of the Ataturk army and therefore unable to return to Turkey.[103] Terzioglu was not alone. There were also instances of Muslims who wished to retain the Turkish citizenship they had acquired while in Turkey, while continuing to reside in the islands, a desire that the administration flatly refused. Given the proximity of Rhodes and Kos (where the Turkish minority resided) to mainland Turkey, the denial of residency or citizenship mean that Turkish locals often chose to leave the islands and emigrate permanently to Turkey on local caiques under the cover of night.

The same racialized criteria applied to persons viewed as having been contaminated by Turkish elements and as therefore socially degenerate. When the local administration determined that the Greek Orthodox Filizza Psaltu not only was a prostitute but also had been living with her presumed pimp, a Turk, for several years, she was deemed of "horrible moral conduct" and therefore denied even a residence permit for Rhodes.[104] The administration's decision about Psaltu ran counter to its policy on prostitution, which tended toward normalization and regulation. The decision to expel Psaltu

---

102   Archivio Storico del Ministero degli Affari Esteri, ASMAE, Affari Politici: 993/1929.
103   28 December 1934; GAK, 323/1935.
104   Petition for Filizza Psaltu, GAK DOD, f.323/1935.

clearly aligns with Ann Stoler's observations on colonial concubinage—that it "worked" as long as mixed relationships did not upset and invert racial and colonial hierarchies.[105] The idea that a Greek Orthodox resident was in the clutches of a Turkish local challenged an underlying commitment to Greco-Roman racial supremacy over Levantine others.

What is also striking, however, is the way that the Italian state did not ultimately abide by its racist policies at this time, but continued to view Aegean locals in the original terms of its mandate there—as "not a population of color," which could not therefore be subjected to the same ideologies of race as in Italy's other African colonies. After the departure of De Vecchi from Rhodes, the Italian administration softened its position on the expulsion, in Rhodes and Kos, of Jews originating from Turkey.[106] The administration also accepted declarations of "Aryan" race from Turkish persons. To take one example, a Turkish national, Zecrà Cuzeta, produced a declaration that both himself and his future wife, both Muslim, were of "Aryan race," and he successfully petitioned for the administration's approval to marry an ethnically Turkish, Italian Aegean citizen.[107]

Similarly, when a Muslim subject, Giovanna Boni, claimed that the father of the first of her three children was an Italian marshal ("*un certo Luciano Vincenzo*"), the authorities' main concern was that the child be registered properly as an Italian subject.[108]

By the late 1930s mixed marriages were in some cases further viewed as part of a Catholicization project. When an Italian citizen, Francesco De Savio, wanted to marry an Orthodox woman who held Italian Aegean citizenship, the administration supported his desire even in the face of opposition to the marriage from the bride's father, who had requested that De Savio be repatriated so as to prevent the affair from going forward. The administration responded that the bride could freely choose because she was an "Italian

105   Ann Stoler, "Carnal Knowledge and Imperial Power: Gender, Race and Morality in Colonial Asia," in *Gender at the Crossroads of Knowledge: Feminist Anthropology in the Postmodern Era*, edited by Micaela di Leonardo, 6–67 (Berkeley: University of California Press, 1991).

106   A document dated August 1, 1942, from the Civil Registry and Statistics Department (Dipartimento di Anagrafe e Statistici) of the local government of the Dodecanese Islands stated, "*vennero erroneamente compresi anche gli ebrei già sudditi turchi, i quali essendo stabiliti nel Possedimento all'entrata in vigore del Trattato di Losanna (6 agosto 1924) acquistarono di diritto o per opzione, la cittadinanza egea.*"

107   GAK DOD, 1939/649 Mixed Marriages. Petition dated September 6, 1939.

108   GAK DOD, 1939/649 Mixed Marriages. Petition dated January 12, 1938.

subject and not Greek, and because she has already decided to celebrate the matrimony with a Catholic rite."[109]

In fact, the disavowal of racial differences with the local population continued to be a facet of Fascist governance despite the adoption of an official politics of race. As late as 1939, a surveillance file, today archived in Rhodes, made copious remarks about the character of an Italian marine, Giuseppe Franco, who was on his way to Leros for deployment. Among a list of positive traits that the secret police in Rome enumerated to assure the local authorities that he could be trusted not to betray state secrets—although he was not a member of the Fascist party—was the marine's apparent disregard for his Italianness: "he ignores his race and religion since he was born in Castellammare di Stabia (Naples)."[110] The idea that Italy's project of empire was culturally and even ethnically expansive, intent on nullifying race, persisted in the Aegean. If one result of the Ethiopian invasion was that it finally ensured the "whiteness" of the Italian nation, it also transformed the very definition of nation at the core of the Fascist state.[111] What Giuseppe Franco's blithe denial of his race suggested was that he could carry forward the ideology of the new imperial man: the investment in Fascist conquest, and *romanità*—rather than in *italianità*—that were central to the project of Fascist nation-building in the Mediterranean.

That Franco was from Naples affirms the fact that discourses of colonial conquest following the invasion of Ethiopia had succeeded in reframing the South as pivotal to a new Roman Empire.[112] As chapter 1 discussed, the cradle of Italian civilization had been linked to the Mediterranean since the late nineteenth century and nationalists had long seen an expansion in the Mediterranean as both a logical effect of Italian unity and a resolution to the crisis of cultural and economic fragmentation that had been a result of the unification. The official politics of race that the Fascist state adopted following its vast expansion into East Africa in 1936 was an attempt to encode this goal of a great Mediterranean expansion into its colonial policies, and to no small extent, it reshaped Italian governance and the administration of

---

109   GAK DOD, 1939/649 Mixed Marriages.

110   *"Si ignora la razza cui appartiene e la religione che professa, siccome nato a Castellamare di Stabia"*; GAK CCRR, "FRANCO Giuseppe fu Alonso."

111   See David Forgacs, *Italy's Margins: Social Exclusion and Nation Formation since 1861* (Cambridge: Cambridge University Press, 2016); and Giuliani and Lombardi-Diop, *Bianco e Nero*.

112   Giuliani and Lombardi-Diop, *Bianco e Nero*, 24–25.

Rhodes and the other Dodecanese islands. This chapter has further suggested the possibility that the administration of the Dodecanese, and the ambiguity that surrounded it, may have also helped to produce the anti-Semitic policies that specifically targeted "Oriental" or "Levantine" Jews who had been assimilated to the Italian state at the end of World War I.

Conclusion

Giuseppe Franco's apparent disregard for nation and race might also well be understood vis-à-vis the expression, "*una faccia, una razza*" or "one face, one race," the tagline that has characterized popular representations as well as one of the most significant studies of Italian rule in the Dodecanese.[113] It has been linked to an observed nostalgia for Italian rule as well as to the myth of *Italiani brava gente,* or the idea that Italians were soft and gentle—even in the context of colonialism and wartime occupation—and has much less often been considered with regard to Italian concepts of race. But recuperating Italy's vast project to form Italian Aegean citizens makes clear that ideologies and hierarchies of race were core concerns of Italian governance well before the adoption of an official stance on race after 1936. Between 1912 and 1934, the idea that the natives were privileged subjects of the empire not only compelled development and nation-building in the Aegean, but also produced incremental reforms to citizenship policies, until finally there existed only a very fine distinction between Italian diaspora communities outside of the peninsula and Italian Levantine communities in the Aegean and broader eastern Mediterranean region. And even as anticolonial movements in East Africa—as well as in the Dodecanese—began to threaten and undermine Italy's imperial sovereignty, the local administration strengthened its project to imagine at least the Greek Dodecanese part of its national peripheries. It was at this juncture that the phrase *una faccia, una razza* took on its full semantic meaning, indicating Fascist plans to remake the Dodecanese islands in the image of Roman Empire. While new policies in education responded to growing fears of anticolonial revolt among the empire's occupied subjects from the Dodecanese to East Africa,

---

113 The locution emphasized in Nicholas Doumanis's wonderful study *Myth and Memory in the Mediterranean: Remembering Fascism's Empire* (New York: St. Martin's Press, 1997) and in its Italian translation, *Una faccia una razza: Le colonie nell'Egeo,* translated by M. Cupellaro (Bologna: Il mulino, 2003).

an easing of these policies also supported the continued pacification of the local population. As Mia Fuller has argued, "Italians displayed a partial indifference to difference."[114]

Serious questions therefore remain about what the Dodecanese would have looked like had Italy remained in power there in the postwar period. Understanding some part of the full scope of Italy's citizenship projects in the Dodecanese is today possible because of the availability of provincial archives in Rhodes—archives that Italy would have culled and then burned had World War II not broken out. For most of the postwar period these archives remained closed and the wider consequences of Italian rule were subsumed into larger narratives of World War II. The German occupation led to a de facto loss of Italy's control of the islands, and popular narratives of the war have tended to emphasize the period of 1943–45 as a period of German atrocities, in which the Italian army became victims of their former co-belligerents—although the period also featured ongoing collaboration between the Nazis and Fascists who refused to recognize Italy's armistice with the Allies. It is possible, on the other hand, to speculate about an alternative history in which, had Italy instead remained with its traditional allies, France and Britain, it might have been able to retain its mandate in the Dodecanese after World War II and a much more protracted process of transforming Italian rule during the postwar period might have ensued. Recent studies of citizenship in the French Empire have argued, for example, that imperial belonging was far more flexible than has generally been recognized, with the result that subjects under colonial rule often sought to revise and transform their status, seeking to become equals in the hope of abolishing the hierarchies of the colonial system just as much as they sought to resist it through nationalist movements.[115]

As the next chapter discusses, Italy's state- and nation-building projects were often reworked by locals in such a way as to redefine colonial institutions and to reject the Italianization that issued from these citizenship projects. Many locals were also very eager to attend Italian public schools and benefit from education and public sector jobs offered by the Fascist state. It is therefore safe to say that the 1945 liberation of the islands, followed by an eventual integration with Greece in 1947, which was hailed as the result of more than a century of resistance on the part of the local population, obscures

---

114   Mia Fuller, *Moderns Abroad* (New York: Routledge, 2007), 58.
115   Frederick Cooper, *Citizenship between Empire and Nation: Remaking France and French Africa, 1945–1960* (Princeton, NJ: Princeton University Press, 2014).

the breadth and the extent to which the period of the 1920s and 1930s, when Italy expanded citizenship to include the Aegean, brought the local population into unusual but nevertheless important forms of belonging in an imperial Mediterranean.

CHAPTER FOUR

Everyday Fascism in the Aegean

The previous two chapters considered how the ideological shift that occurred in the Fascist dictatorship after the invasion of Ethiopia (1935–36) changed both representations (chapter 2) and rule in (chapter 3) the Dodecanese.[1] This chapter will consider how and why local history, memories, and archival records of everyday life have often personified the ideological differences of the Fascist state, characterizing some Italians as "good" and others as "bad." This dichotomy is most frequently evident in the characterization of Cesare De Vecchi, who governed the islands after 1936, as an "insane" man in comparison to Lago, who was "συνετό," or clear-headed and rational.[2] De Vecchi has frequently embodied, in the minds of Dodecanese locals, everything that was "bad" or "Fascist" about Italian rule, while Lago has embodied everything that was "good" and "Italian."[3] While it's clear that the two governors strongly align with different phases of the Fascist regime, the different possible meanings of "good" and "bad" are not only ambiguous but they also suggest similarities with memories of Fascism and anti-Fascism (and Fascism as anti-Fascism) in Italy. Given the extent to which the Italian Empire invested in assimilating the local population to Italian and Fascist culture, this chapter assesses whether locals engaged in "tactics" of resistance

---

1   Historiography has also tended to perpetuate this periodization, and in some instances nostalgia for Italian rule; as an example, see Ettore Vittorini, *Le isole dimenticate: Il Dodecaneso da Giolitti al massacro del 1943* (Florence: Le Lettere, 2002); as is clear from the title, the golden age of the Italian period of the islands ended in the 1943 massacre by the Germans.

2   See G.M. Sakellaridi, "Antonio Ritelli," in *Kalymniaká Chronika*, vol. 6 (Athens, 1986), 151–68; a longer discussion of this text is later in the chapter.

3   On this issue of Dodecanese perceptions of Italian character and the personification of Italians versus Fascists through the Lago-De Vecchi dichotomy, see also Nicholas Doumanis, *Myth and Memory in the Mediterranean: Remembering Fascism's Empire* (New York: St. Martin's Press, 1997), 163–97.

and evasion in everyday life similar to the ways that Italians in the Italian Peninsula did in the same era.

From the perspective of policy, differences between the two governments of Lago and De Vecchi are less clear cut. Many policies enacted starting in 1937 were the realization of assimilation programs already underway during Lago's tenure (1923–36)—and as the previous chapter discussed, Lago's administration built upon structures that the Italian state had put in place before the end of World War I and the annexation of the islands to Italy. One important example of this were Italian education projects, which had roots in the period of "temporary" occupation under the Giolitti government and that were highly popular with much of the local population despite opposition to the Italian state. The 1936 invasion of Ethiopia was a crucial turning point in the Fascist dictatorship in terms of discourse: it marked the height of Mussolini's popularity, the introduction of a biological politics of race unified around *romanità*, and the Axis alliance between Mussolini and Hitler. The myth of national regeneration through colonial expansion reached a fever pitch in 1936, as did Fascism's pretensions to have created a new "imperial" man, one who was both virile and racist.[4] It is fitting, then, that local memories about Italian rule after the invasion of Ethiopia tend to emphasize the outlandish demagoguery of De Vecchi—his notorious tours through the city in a luxury automobile furiously honking the horn, and his calls for mass rallies on the Foro Italico in Rhodes. What was less extraordinary—and less often narrated—is that the administration under Lago also engaged in propaganda to assimilate and court the loyalty of the local population.

When explaining the era to persons unfamiliar with it, locals will describe the first decades as "Italian" rule, until 1936, when "Fascist" rule began. This is, of course, erroneous. The islands had been under Fascist rule since 1923, and Mario Lago was clearly a member of the Fascist party. But locals will assert that under "Italian" rule the islands experienced Italian culture, urban renovation, and modernization in infrastructure, and the development of tourism and Italian citizenship. Meanwhile during "Fascist" rule there was

---

4   See Ruth Ben-Ghiat, *Fascist Modernities* (Berkeley: University of California Press, 2001); Lorenzo Benadusi, *The Enemy of the New Man: Homosexuality in Fascist Italy* (Madison, WI: University of Wisconsin Press, 2012); Valeria Galimi, "The 'New Racist Man,'" in *In the Society of Fascists: Acclamation, Acquiescence and Agency in Mussolini's Italy*, edited by Giulia Albanese and Roberta Pergher, 149–68 (New York: Palgrave MacMillan, 2012).

political repression and an attempt to remake Greek national and ethnic identity. This bifurcation of the twenty years of Fascist rule is also presented in their interpretation of the "character" of Italians. Locals underscore that though there were indeed threatening officials present—identifiable by their "black shirts"—such officials were outnumbered by countless "Italians" who showed themselves to be peaceful and humane. The dichotomy between "Italians" and "Fascists" thus raises critical questions about the politics of postcolonial memory in the Aegean, and the degree to which the local community is activating, in its assessment of the interwar years, the myth of *Italiani brava gente*, or Italians as "good people."

This trope has been observed throughout Europe and is often invoked alongside a larger perception that totalitarianism in Italy was either a failure or a "soft" dictatorship—one that was doubtless less evil than Italy's vicious Axis partner. But this is less true for Greece on the whole where, with the exception of the Dodecanese, the myth of *Italiani brava gente* is much less present. Like Poland, which endured a double occupation of both the German and Russian armies, parts of Northern Greece experienced occupation by the Italian and then German armies during 1940 and 1941. History and memory there have tended to resist any tendency to paint a black-and-white picture of Germans as "evil" and Italians as "soft" dictators—or as lovers who preferred to serenade local women and play the mandolin than to stage invasions and make war, as romanticized in the bestselling work of fiction, *Captain Corelli's Mandolin*.[5] The presence of the myth of *Italiani brava gente* among survivors in the Dodecanese thus seems, interestingly, to hew more closely to a larger European memory of the war than to the collective memory of World War II in Greece.

In his groundbreaking study, Nicholas Doumanis has explored this unique and fascinating collective Dodecanese memory of the Italian era. His study shows that locals are quick to speak of Italians as "good people" or to remember a time when Italians and Greeks traded claims that they were "one face, one race." Doumanis argues that the presence of these tropes might be read as a critique of the Greek nation-state as well as the ethnonationalist

5   See the work of Lidia Santarelli, *The Hidden Pages of Contemporary Italian History: War Crimes, War Guilt, Collective Memory* (London: Routledge, 2004); and "Muted Violence: Italian War Crimes in Occupied Greece," *Journal of Modern Italian Studies* 9, no. 3 (2004): 280–99. The popular and critically acclaimed 1994 novel *Captain Corelli's Mandolin* by the British author Louis de Bernières is an excellent example of how Italian Fascism has emerged in postwar European culture as a laughable parody of dictatorship and empire when compared with Nazi Germany.

tradition of Greek historiography: if locals have suggested that, when it came to some aspects, such as modernization and infrastructure, they might have lived better under Italian rule than they have since the integration of the islands into Greece, it is a fine example, argues Doumanis, of the defects of the history of modern Greece as it has been written, mostly by Greeks within Greece. That is to say Greek historiography has discounted the numerous transnational and arguably "Mediterranean" histories and influences of Greece, both before and after Ottoman rule, and has taken as axiomatic the idea that Greece's modern history has been one of resistance against foreign rule and an inevitable and almost teleological process toward the establishment of a sovereign and ethnically Greek nation-state.

This chapter intends to offer a different interpretation of these so-called positive memories of Italian rule by setting them into dialogue with the wider problem of memories of Italian Fascism as studied by many historians of everyday life more recently. In what follows, I analyze both oral testimonies and archival documentation using the tools of *Alltagsgeschichte,* the history of everyday life, an analytical frame that has been used in a variety of contexts, for example, within studies of Nazi Germany, but that has been an especially fruitful strategy for overcoming some of the problems associated with the modern historiography of Italian Fascism. The historiography of Fascist Italy has frequently been undercut by the idea that Mussolini's totalitarianism was "imperfect" and that if Mussolini invented a provocative formula for dictatorship that later dictators followed—best encapsulated by his statement, "Everything in the State, nothing outside the State, nothing against the State"—the historical memory of Fascism has mostly registered the failure of Mussolini to accomplish its stated goals.[6] Seen from this perspective, some of the positive memories of Fascist rule in the Dodecanese may in fact speak to the recognition of such an ideology alongside a further desire to confirm that ideology's failure. The dichotomy between "Fascists" and "Italians" may, in fact, signify, respectively, the attempt to enforce a statist ideology and the failure of both Italians and locals in the Aegean to fully comply with those directives.

As historians of everyday life have further argued, the Fascist state's failure to achieve these (ultimately unsustainable) ambitions elides the ways that "ordinary" people may have experienced these "extraordinary" times, and

---

6   As Arthurs, Ferris, and Ebner note, this dismissive point of view of Fascism has been held by "no less an authority than Hannah Arendt," who claimed that Italian Fascism was "just an ordinary nationalist dictatorship." Josh Arthurs, Kate Ferris, and Michael Ebner, *The Politics of Everyday Life in Fascist Italy* (New York: Palgrave MacMillan, 2017), 2.

that they nevertheless faced dilemmas and difficulties, moments of resilience and times of defeat. As Josh Arthurs, Michael Ebner, and Kate Ferris further point out, the downgrading of the dramatic hold of the dictatorship has been exacerbated by a rift in postwar Italian historiography created, on the one hand, by the anti-Fascist narrative, which suggests Italians were fundamentally against Fascism and resisted it, and on the other by a more critical approach that has tended to emphasize the ways in which Italians were "co-opted" by the dictatorship and the numerous strategies both the party and the Fascist state used to obtain *consenso* (in Italian, both consent and consensus). These very different tendencies in the historiography have reinforced the cliché that Italian Fascism was fundamentally an ideological vacuum that left open the possibility of resistance and disobedience on a systemic level: "daily life under Mussolini has been presented in 'indulgent,' 'colorblind,' or 'humanizing' terms, permeated with nostalgia for shared cultural reference points and, supposedly, a simpler and more innocent time."[7]

In light of a wide body of criticism that has shown that the myth of the "good" Italian is just that—especially in the case of Italian colonial empire, where some of Fascism's worst crimes were perpetrated—this chapter aims to develop a picture of everyday life under Fascist rule that examines the ways locals recognized, resisted, but also accommodated and subtly undermined the top-down directives of the Italian state.[8] In what follows, my aim is not to arrive at any conclusion about whether the Italian state presented a government that was either "good" or "bad" for the local community in the Dodecanese, but rather, to use such notions to give a more attentive reading of sources "from below," and to reveal the inevitable fissures in the overly neat dichotomy between "good" Italians and "bad" Fascists. The chapter brings further archival evidence to demonstrate the ways in which "Fascist" concerns may often have overlapped with "Italian" ones, and finally, considers the ways in which such a dichotomy may speak to local perceptions of "extraordinary" times when, as ordinary people, they coped with and "made do" under the apparatus of an Italian Fascist state.

As described in the previous chapter, the Italian administration believed that Italian Aegean citizenship could help to assimilate locals in the islands,

---

7   Arthurs, Ferris and Ebner, *Politics of Everyday Life in Fascist Italy,* 4.

8   David Bidussa, *Il mito del bravo italiano* (Milan: Il Saggiatore, 1994); Angelo Del Boca, *Italiani, brava gente: Un mito duro a morire* (Vicenza: Neri Pozza, 2005); Nicola Labanca, "Colonial Rule, Colonial Repression and War Crimes in the Italian Colonies," *Journal of Modern Italian Studies* 9, no. 3 (2004): 300–13.

and petitioners for citizenship were certainly forced into compliance with the system of patronage that belief implied. Petitions contained obsequious gestures and pleading statements to suggest that, rhetorically at least, petitioners were willing to simulate an infantilized position and suggest that they saw Italy as the father figure of the strong state. But this does not mean that they did not see through such a system: applicants wittingly falsified information, attempted to exploit the mutability and ambivalences of Italian colonial discourse, and crafted novel ways to retain their local practices and customs. In other words, local acquiescence to the Fascist dictatorship does not mean that locals were accepting of it; but nor does their ability, on some occasions, to have obtained advantages from, to have creatively reworked, carefully defied, or resiliently accommodated the regime mean that the Italian state in the Aegean was any less a significant influence on their lives.

If locals experienced De Vecchi as bombastic, "Fascistic," and the archetype of the "blackshirts," they were also sometimes keen to preserve the benefits that supposedly came from "Italian" industry and activity. This chapter further explores whether Dodecanese locals may designate these two "faces" of Fascist rule, embodied in the images of Lago and De Vecchi, not only as a sign that they recognized key ideological shifts in the Italian administration, but also as a sign of their own ambivalent attitudes toward their occupiers. This dichotomy may thus testify both to an increasing recognition of the fragility of the Fascist regime, despite its authoritarian measures, as well as to a desire to recuperate the benefits of the Fascist state in the face of its authoritarian measures. As Paul Corner has argued, the very notion of "consent" for the Fascist regime can be reframed when one accounts for the agency of Italian citizens under Fascist rule and considers that many Italians were aware of the deterioration of the Fascist party, especially as Mussolini's state became increasingly leveraged by its wars of conquest.[9] If we restore such agency to locals in the Dodecanese under Fascist rule, can we also find ambivalent acts of both compliance and resistance?

As an imperial context, there may seem to be no ambiguity in the Dodecanese about consent for the regime, and historians in Greece have typically ruled out the presence of consent for the Italian state in the islands, as Italy represented a foreign power that repressed the ethnic identity of

9   Paul Corner, "Everyday Fascism in the 1930s: Centre and Periphery in the Decline of Mussolini's Dictatorship," *Contemporary European History* 15, no. 2 (2006): 195–222; see also, Giulia Albanese and Roberta Pergher, eds., *In the Society of Fascists: Acclamation, Acquiescence and Agency in Mussolini's Italy* (New York: Palgrave MacMillan, 2012).

the local population. But as the previous chapters have demonstrated, the Italian administration maintained a position of both inclusion and difference with the local population, carefully navigating its authority in the region vis-à-vis the prior Ottoman administration, and the islands occupied a special position within Italy's national-imperial discourse of Mediterraneanism. The project to assimilate locals may have shared some features with the projects to Italianize populations in the Alto Adige and the Adriatic region, while in other ways assimilation projects sought to leverage the possibilities of shared histories. Moreover, even if the local population did not consent to Fascist rule, this does not mean that the Fascist dictatorship did not use many of the same strategies that it used at home to court *consenso,* in its double meaning of both consent and consensus. It's possible to consider a complex set of strategies that the Fascist state used to integrate and assimilate the local population, as well as an equally complex set of tactics that the local population used to respond to such strategies. Fascist state-building projects were lived by locals in myriad ways, interpreted, negotiated, redefined, and reimagined, and have accrued further new meanings later when the period was remembered and narrated.

To access this view "from below," this chapter introduces a combination of archival documents and oral histories that throw light onto everyday life under Italian rule and to interrogate the relations between occupiers and occupied under Fascist rule. As Alessandro Portelli has demonstrated, archival and oral sources analyzed together stand the best chance of revealing not only the past but the ways that past becomes embedded in people's myths, subjective dreams, and collective memories of history.[10] In this sense, analyzing how Fascism was experienced in everyday life also helps to frame and articulate questions about what have been the enduring legacies of Italian Empire in the Dodecanese, during the postwar period, and within new historical contexts moments, such as the expansion of the European Union, and the role of Greece to help manage its borders. I collected these oral testimonies over the course of several years between 2009 and 2013. The advanced age of the population by the early twenty-first century meant that most of the informants had been children or young adults at the time of Italian rule; to compensate for this I also questioned them about their parents' experiences of and opinions about the regime. As young persons during the years 1937–43, my interviewees had experienced some of the Fascist regime's

---

10　Alessandro Portelli, *The Death of Luigi Trastulli and Other Stories: Form and Meaning in Oral History* (Albany, NY: State University Press of New York, 2001).

most forceful attempts at assimilation of its Dodecanese subjects, which, as in Italy, was directed especially at the youth, meant to instill admiration and loyalty for the regime and mold them into Fascists.

Using a "snowball" method, in which interviewees suggested new persons to interview, I was able to interview more than forty persons, either former or current residents of all of the islands (only Patmos and Astypalaia were not represented). Interviews were conducted in a combination of English, Greek, and Italian, and, in an echo of what the Italian state wished for its empire in the Aegean, Italian proved consistently to be the lingua franca in which we were best able and felt most comfortable communicating; many interviewees were keen to find someone with whom they might speak Italian. The level of Italian possessed by all interviewees—especially those who grew up in either Rhodes or Kos—is a strong testament to the success of the Italian state in its program to educate an entire generation in Italian culture and language. Given the space available to me here, it is not possible to include all of the insights, perceptions, and outrages, as well as humorous anecdotes and love stories, that interviewees shared with me. What follows instead is a discussion of the trends, tropes, and ideas that proved both recurring and meaningful as examples of locals negotiating the institutions, economies, and projects of Fascist Empire.

My analysis considers how locals embraced tactics so as to enact what Michel de Certeau has called "the art of making-do." As de Certeau describes it, the art of making-do entails *"ways of using* the constraining order of the place or of language. Without leaving the place where he has no choice but to live and which lays down its laws for him, he establishes within it a degree of *plurality* and creativity. By an art of being in between, he draws unexpected results from his situation."[11] This combination of archival documents and oral testimonies offers a striking account of how locals used their agency to reap the benefits of modernization and developmentalism—embracing the idea that Italy was a beacon of culture and Europe—as well as to distance the assimilation project and political repression that Fascism also implied. Further, they provide an avenue into the questions of how and to what degree Dodecanese subjects subscribed to the Mediterraneanism that this book has so far described as the most salient and recurring discourse within Italy's rule in the islands. As the previous two chapters discussed, Mediterraneanism enabled Italy to secure its sovereignty but was also in conflict with rigid

---

11   Michel de Certeau, *The Practice of Everyday Life* (Berkeley: University of California Press, 1984), 30.

hierarchies of difference, and later, after the invasion of Ethiopia, with Fascist politics of nation and race. This chapter continues this discussion, considering how such a conflict may have manifested itself in the civil administration of the islands and within further state-building projects such as education and the state's intervention into local religious practices.

The chapter further discusses to what extent the local Dodecanese colonial subject was able to evade and resist the invasion of Fascist state into their everyday lives, while not discounting either the possibility there may have been decisive benefits to be drawn from Fascist rule, too. Italian education was probably the most salient example of the conflict between, on the one hand, the socio-cultural and economic advantages that the Fascist state provided, and on the other, the idea that an everyday act could also imply cooperation with Fascist imperialism. Many interviewees suggested that, even as children, they were fully aware of the fact that Italian education was a dangerous expression of the Fascist state's projects of assimilation, but that the arrival of an Italian school in their village was often a novel and welcome addition to their rural life (this was especially the case in some of the more sparsely populated areas of the islands). Such a conflict was felt in many other facets of everyday life—from accepting a public sector job, to joining the OND (Organizzazione Nazionale Dopolavoro), to expressing typically "Fascist" behaviors such as racism and anti-Semitism.

In the analysis that follows the large majority of interviewees were men. Unfortunately, my invitations to interview were often rebuffed by women with assertions that they knew "nothing" about history and of fear regarding the light that my research might shine on them. The discussion of the involvement of women in female-led protests in the Dodecanese—for example, the famous "rock wars," which both David Sutton and Nicholas Doumanis have commented on—therefore relies heavily on archival documentation.[12] Adopting Luisa Passerini's concept of women as "mediators" of protest helps to reveal how women, while not the focus of the Italian state's energies and concerns with regard to assimilation, mobilized and organized resistance against the Italian state.[13]

12 Nicholas Doumanis, *Myth and Memory in the Mediterranean*, 66–80; David Sutton, *Memories Cast in Stone: The Relevance of the Past in Everyday Life* (New York: Berg, 1998), 79–98.

13 Luisa Passerini, *Fascism in Popular Memory: The Cultural Experience of the Turin Working Class* (Cambridge: Cambridge University Press, 1987), 138–49.

Education, Assimilation, and Cultural *Bonifica*

Lago's cultural initiatives were by design complementary to the tourism
program and the larger desire to preserve the Oriental aspect of the islands,
as chapter 2 discussed. And as noted above, both historiography and local
memory have tended to register Lago's rule as one of benign intervention
and even cultural patronage. The cultural initiatives promoted by Lago to
preserve the Levantine way of life followed the same course as regulation of
citizenship and civil status: that is, they were a ruse that partly masked the
assimilation policy also underway, but they also acted as an effective means
for promoting Fascist colonial modernity as a form of anti-modernity in which
the homelessness of modernism was countered by an emphasis on the rural,
the traditional, and the folkloric. Legitimized by a colonial gaze, the lively
presence of religious activities and festivals expressed the Mediterranean
modernity of the Italian colonizers. What's more, this vision relied on the
foreclosure of other modernities and effectively shored up Fascist Italy's
narrative about restoring Italian vitality through colonization in the Orient. A
poem by a German visitor to the island of Rhodes in 1934 sums up the stereotypical view of Lago's tenure as a benevolent period of Italian philanthropy:

> Without a Ministry, and without a Parliament
> An artist governs, commands this island
> And makes it into an incomparable jewel.
> The Governor, to whom Mussolini has entrusted this throne
> He is called Mario Lago

König, the poem's author, describes the island of Rhodes' romanticism as
in direct connection to its picturesque Levantine aspect, which the tourism
program had succeeded in privileging. Lago, the artist, governs with wisdom
by promoting customs and sacred traditions:

> He governs with magnificence and dominates with wisdom
> Cultural center of the Levant, worthy of being visited
> Here reign tranquility and romanticism
> The color of the Levant ... and of the Orient
> Here the richness of customs can be admired,
> The abundance of mosques and the sacred tradition.[14]

---

14   "*Senza Ministero, e senza Parlamento/Un artista governa, comanda quest'isola/E ne
fa un gioiello impareggiabili/Il Governatore, al quale Mussolini ha confidato questo trono/Si*

König's encomium to Lago's rule underscores how the "Oriental" customs of the local population were inserted into a larger tableau of touristic "color" meant for consumption by visitors. But the poem also reveals how Fascist dictatorship in the islands entered into everyday life by intervening into local religious practices.

The Lago administration spent significant time and energy on projects such as the effort to recuperate the so-called Filiremo Madonna, a Byzantine icon that had disappeared at some point after the 1522 sack of Rhodes by the Turks. Reports of the icon throughout the Middle East and Russia streamed into the Ministry of Foreign Affairs as the regime embarked on a wild goose chase to locate this prized religious relic. Although the icon was never found, the search encapsulates the administration's desire to preserve religious symbolism, in this case literally an icon of Oriental exoticism. Meanwhile, it undertook to dismember the Greek Orthodox church's structure and power. The *autocefalia,* or project to sever the local Greek patriarchate from the main patriarchate in Constantinople, was a major effort during the Lago tenure.[15]

The administration's commitment to retaining "traditional" and "Oriental" culture is revealing of the way that preserving the local was often a means of deflecting the potential for broader nationalisms to reach daily life. A telling example of the administration's commitment to local traditions—one that kept the archipelago, literally, behind the times—was the decision to have the large Ottoman clock tower chime the "ancient" hour, that is, the time as it was recorded in Mecca. The clock itself was part of the property of a prominent Turkish family's *waqf,* or trust, and in 1935, a family member had visited the island and reset the clock to the standard hour, as was also the case in nearby Turkey at that time. The local administration declared that the clock clearly belonged to the city and not to the *waqf;* for more than a century and a half it had signaled to its Muslim citizens the hour of prayer. At first, a secretary recommended that they verify that the Muslim community agreed to this change, but, ultimately, the administration intervened to change the clock back to signaling the Meccan hour. In a discussion of the issue, the general

chiama Mario Lago/Egli governa con magnificenza e domina con saggezza/Centro culturale del Levante, degno di essere visitato,/Qui regnano la tranquillità ed il romanticismo,/Il colore del Levante ... dell'Oriente/Qui si ammirano la ricchezza dei costumi,/L'abbondanza delle moschee e la sacra tradizione." GAK DOD, 216/1935/1.

15   Its scope (and eventual failure) is outside the bounds of this study. Cesare Marongiù Buonaiuti has admirably dealt with this topic in *La politica religiosa del fascismo nel Dodecanneso* (Naples: Giannini, 1979).

secretary added, "the local Muslim contingent, naturally *with the exception of the fanatical modernizers,* remained very satisfied with the provision taken by the Government, and the old clock, placed within the tower of Piazza Solimano, went back to chiming the traditional hour yesterday at five o'clock."[16] Not only was the Italian government opposed to Kemalist nationalism, but its sense of colonial modernity pivoted on notions of "returning" to an older way of life. Such a paradoxical attitude was also felt in other programs that aimed to weed out all nationalist activity by virtue of state surveillance.[17]

Locals were not particularly aware of the *autocephalia* program or the administration's extensive surveillance over the Greek Orthodox Church. They remained acutely aware, on the other hand, of the changes that De Vecchi institutionalized after taking office when, because of the failure of the *autocephalia,* De Vecchi moved to close all Greek Orthodox churches. The decision that set off an outbreak of protests. Similarly, what locals have registered was not the administration's encouragement of local festivals, but the new holidays that Italy later provided them. As Haralambo Stamatis of Kos remembers, much more notable for him than the administration's attitude to local celebrations was the fact that the Italian state gave all workers employed in state jobs an annual paid holiday when Italy commemorated its invasion of Ethiopia.[18]

It was, in effect, the later practices of *bonifica,* and the attempt to remake local identity through an aggressive propaganda campaign, which elicited

---

16   "*L'elemento mussulmano locale, ad eccezione naturalmente dei fanatici modernizzanti è rimasto molto sodisfatto del provvedimento preso dal R.Governo perchè l'orologio vecchio, collocato nella torre di Piazza Solimano, riprendesse a segnalare l'ora all'antica, cosa che è avvenuta ieri alle 17*"; GAK, Envelope 746[1]/1936; emphasis mine.

17   As a cable concerning Greek irredentism described, "church and school are the most effective instruments for the defense of Dodecanese ethnicity, and they are being used by our regime with determination—in some cases according to the arrogant and the Jesuit, but we remain audacious—we must apply ourselves and undermine their national strength. Because of this, the school reform, which each year is giving us greater and greater results; we must reach the *autocefalia* at all costs." The full text of the diplomatic cable from the local government to the Ministry of Foreign Affairs, dated December 7, 1929, regarding "*propaganda irredentista,*" reads: "*chiesa e scuola sono gli strumenti più efficaci della difesa etnica dodecanesina, e sono usati dal nostro regime con determinazione—a seconda dei casi arrogante e gesuitica, ma sempre audacissima—noi dobbiamo applicarci a smussarne l'efficacia nazionale. Da qui l'ordinamento scolastico, che dà risultati ogni anno più evidenti e soddisfacenti; da qui l'autocefalia che dobbiamo a tutti costi raggiungere*"; ASMAE, 998/1929/irredentism.

18   Interview with Haralambo Stamatis (Χαραλαμπο Στατματτις), March 31, 2013.

the strongest emotions and reactions among locals. To take an example prominent with interviewees, the infrastructure and organization of an effective school system, which was established under Lago, is much less discussed by locals than De Vecchi's 1937 overhaul of the schools. And yet, when queried, it's clear that Italian public schools also constituted a major event in many people's lives on the island. The Italian government had mandated that children attend school until at least the third grade—what was a dramatic insistence on the education of young children who would have otherwise been forced into labor to support their parents in agricultural work. Under Lago, all schools in the islands had eventually included from two to five hours of instruction in the Italian language. Instruction in Italian was often led by local schoolteachers after they had received training in Rhodes, making local education also translate into jobs for locals. Many interviewees recalled that going to school also meant being provided with textbooks, sometimes even a first pair of shoes.

But these memories pale in comparison with the day they were told to quit going to school by their parents in protest for De Vecchi's Fascist reforms. After taking office in July 1937, Cesare De Vecchi eliminated the teaching of Greek, Hebrew, and Turkish in Italian schools and closed all private or religious schools, effectively banning any language apart from Italian for instruction. Because the reform led to an outbreak of protests it backfired entirely in its apparent objective to forcing a rapid and total assimilation of the entire population. People who therefore recall that Lago "wanted to make us all into Italians," tend to point to this as an example of how Lago was much more effective in his strategies than his replacement was; they gloss over the significance and impact that Italian public schools and Italian language education may have had on them.[19]

What's also elided in these memories of resilience and protest is the fact that the changes undertaken by De Vecchi were not a radical rupture with the previous decade of imperial rule but the result of longstanding discussions about the most effective way to assimilate Dodecanese youth and obtain their loyalty for Italy and the Fascist regime. Lago's administration had wrestled with the problem of language and its inherent capacity to create a sense of Italian belonging, and he had debated whether to ban native languages from schools—as De Vecchi eventually did. The first government had eventually put into place a program that suppressed other languages only in the final

19   Interview with Leonidas Diakoyiannis, Kefalos, Kos, March 30, 2013.

years of high school. But one of Lago's last efforts as governor was to urge the Ministry of Foreign Affairs to undertake a scholastic reform that might more effectively assimilate the local population. Lago had called for more urgency concerning the matter of local assimilation in the aftermath of the invasion of Ethiopia, which had led to international condemnation of Italy's Fascist state.[20] Lago's parting words for educational reform, targeted Dodecanese youth ages fifteen to eighteen and recommended steering this demographic away from Hellenistic propaganda by forcing them to enroll in Italian public schools after junior high (*ginnasio*) and requiring them to pass the Italian *esame di maturità*. These measures would have had the final result of sending more Dodecanese youth to study in Pisa, "where—as experience tells us— they return completely imprinted with the Fascist mentality, and proud of their Italian citizenship."

Lago's parting words to the Ministry of Foreign Affairs emphasized that Italy should focus on the education of the elite youth that would attend post-secondary education: "the leavened ideals of the Empire also germinate in our beautiful Aegean islands; we should make it possible for our youth to receive these in their hearts: they will soon bear us excellent fruits."[21] But the Ministry of Foreign Affairs responded negatively to Lago's idea, concluding that if high-school-aged Dodecanese studied in Pisa, they were likely to immigrate to Athens afterward, where they would be even more susceptible to Greek nationalist propaganda. Given the backdraft of anti-Italian sentiments that the Italian invasion of Ethiopia had caused, the Fascist government chose to realign its educational policy in the islands, focusing on an even younger age, and installing, not coincidentally, a recent minister of education from Italy, Cesare de Vecchi.[22]

20   On the international fallout of the Ethiopian invasion, see Bruce Strang, *Collision of Empires: Italy's Invasion of Ethiopia and Its International Impact* (New York: Routledge, 2017); Neelam Srivastava, *Italian Colonialism and Resistance to Empire, 1930–1970* (London: Palgrave MacMillan, 2018).
21   "*Donde—come l'esperienza ha dimostrato già all'evidenza—ci ritornano perfet- tamente inquadrati nella mentalità fascista, fieri della cittadinanza Italiana. I fermenti ideali dell'Impero germinano anche nelle nostre belle Isole Egee: facciamo che i giovani li ricevano nel cuore: daranno in breve frutti eccellenti*"; Lago to the Minister of Foreign Affairs, letter dated July 12, 1936 in reference to scholastic reform, ASMAE, AP 1931–45, b.14 "Dodecanneso."
22   On Ethiopia, Lago had lamented the loss of loyalty among the local population in the following way: "*Durante il periodo sanzionista e la minaccia di conflitto bellico derivante dal concentramento in Mediterraneo della flotta Britannica e dagli accordi militari marittimi*

As Lago's replacement, De Vecchi's administration seemed to bring together his prior experiences as the ferocious colonial governor of Italian Somalia from 1923 to 1928 with his ideologically driven policies as Italy's education minister in 1935–36. His educational reform was targeted at strengthening Fascist recruitment to the Dopolavoro trade unions by first recruiting Dodecanese youth into members of the Opera Nazionale Ballila, the Fascist youth organization. As minister of education, De Vecchi had appropriated the concept of *bonifica* in his numerous speeches on the special role of education and youth in the Fascist state. The concept of *bonifica,* which originated with Mussolini's program to drain the swampland of the Pontine Marshes and encapsulated his plan to regenerate the region as Italian farmland for Italians, eventually became the symbol of the ideological revolution that Mussolini claimed his dictatorship was putting into effect in politics, culture, and everyday life; after 1938, *bonifica,* or the commitment to "regenerate" the Italian race also signified the regime's adoption of an official position on race.[23] De Vecchi's speeches as minister of education in Italy were prescient of the policies he later implemented in the Dodecanese and foreshadowed the role of recuperating Roman imperial history as a means toward an assimilation that was not "Italian" in orientation, but "Fascist." As De Vecchi declared in 1936, "Our national pride, our imperial thirst, the whole Roman tradition that is in our blood, that permeates our spirit, that constitutes the springboard for our every movement at the orders of the genius that saw how to guide us, are a function of the strong State."[24]

De Vecchi maintained that scholastic reform was the surest means of cultivating ideal Fascist youth, believing that in the school setting it was possible to cultivate the austerity of youth and to guide young people to

tra l'Inghilterra ed alcuni Stati Mediterranei, il Possedimento ha dovuto sottoporre ad una severa revisione, non solamente i suoi apprezzamenti militari, ma anche le condizioni di convivenza delle popolazioni indigene, la loro fedeltà, grado di assimilazione: in una parola, il loro lealismo."

23   Ruth Ben-Ghiat, *Fascist Modernities* (Berkeley: University of California Press, 2004); Claudia Montavani, *Rigenerare la società: L'eugenetica italiana dalle origini ottocentesche agli anni trenta* (Soveria Mannelli: Rubbettino, 2004).

24   "Il nostro orgoglio nazionale, la nostra sete di imperio, tutta la tradizione romana che è nel nostro sangue, che pervade il nostro spirito, che costituisce la molla di ogni nostro movimento agli ordini del genio che ha veduto e che ci guida, sono in funzione dello Stato forte"; Cesare Maria De Vecchi di Val Cismon, *Bonifica Fascista della cultura* (Milan: Mondadori, 1937), 63.

embody the ideals of the strong state.[25] The bombastic forms of elementary education introduced by De Vecchi produced in the local population not only a greater awareness and a rejection of assimilationism, but also offered ways for re-appropriation and reworking. Ippokrates Logothetis remembered that while there was no Greek history taught in his elementary school, the discussions of Roman Empire in his textbook, *Il Risorgimento dell'Ovest*, nevertheless affirmed his own Greek identity and showed him that "everything that the Romans knew it was because we Greeks had taught them it."[26]

In some cases, such reworking of Italian education invited novel linguistic tactics. Manoles Despotakis of Rhodes, for example, attended elementary school for one year under De Vecchi's administration (he quit later to help his parents with agricultural work). One of his strongest memories was of learning a Latin aphorism, "*ibis redibis nunquan in bello moriries*" ("you will go, you will return, never in war will you perish"). The ingeniousness of this phrase, Despotakis explained, is that depending on whether you use a comma, the aphorism can mean the exact opposite (i.e., "you will go, you will never return, in the war you will perish"). The expression thus illustrates a duplicitous economy of expression alongside the entire drama of valor and warfare. Within the setting he learned it, the phrase certainly spoke of the impressive Fascist commitment to conquest and revolution and it doubtless instilled in Despotakis an enormous admiration for Roman Empire and culture.[27] But Despotakis was also able to creatively rework this lesson by further asserting that the aphorism originally came from the Oracle of Delphi. In a gesture that resembles the tactics identified by oral historians and some scholars in postcolonial literature, that of "code-switching," Despotakis appropriated the Italian colonial rhetoric for a lesson in Greek culture. In ways that mirrored the double-entendre of the phrase that so inspired him, he showed himself equally able to be duplicitous. When telling me this alternative interpretation of the Latin, Despotakis further shifted from Italian into speaking Greek. This was not just a simple act of translation, but implied

---

25   "*Il fanciullo deve presentarsi alla così detta istruzione di primo grado già formato per accogliere alcune vere nozioni di cultura militare che non rappresentano d'altra parte misteri eleusini e che nella loro austerità ed essenza di retorica costituiscono da sole elementi effica- cemente concorrenti alla formazione del carattere.*" "Cultura e Discipline Militari negli Istituti Civili di Istruzione," discourse of March 1935, in De Vecchi, *Bonifica Fascista della cultura*, 188.

26   Interview with Manoles Despotakis, Rhodes, July 24, 2009.

27   Interview with Manoles Despotakis, Rhodes, July 24, 2009.

untranslatability, and emphasized how he saw the other possible meanings of the phrase as relating to his Greek identity.[28]

Seen from this perspective of re-appropriation and reworking, De Vecchi's scholastic overhaul in 1937 in fact says volumes about more subtle strategies of local resistance that had also worked to undermine the Fascist state's technologies of empire during the era of Lago's rule. As Cesare Buonaiuti has suggested in a singular study, De Vecchi's turn to his focus to the school system and the institutionalization of the Italian language came about after the failure of the *autocephalia*, or the project to assimilate locals in the islands through the dismemberment of the Greek Orthodox church.[29] His decree in July 1937, moreover, which established that schools on the Dodecanese were to have methods and schedules identical to metropolitan ones had several purposes apart from just legislating that the hours spent on native language could not exceed those spent on Italian. Many instructors were fired and replaced with Italian ones and those who remained employed, a desirable position, had to be demonstrably pro-Fascist. In addition, in this new school system the religious instruction had to be Catholic.[30] The regime reserved the right to shut down private religious schools for noncompliance with these new measures, and by June 1939 (Decree 163) it had permanently closed all the private schools. But this decree also responded to the fact that private schools had been a source of frustration and subterfuge against the expansion of the state's authority over education during the Lago period. Private schools had often sought to appropriate state subsidies while continuing to teach their own didactic material and teachers in these private schools had frustrated Italian authorities on more than one occasion by attempting to collect pensions from both Italy and Greece.[31]

Programs of cultural and educational *bonifica* in the islands in the late 1930s were also the realization of one of the Italian state's goals for its rule in the islands from the outset: making Italian into the official language of the Aegean. Orazio Pedrazzi, for example, had remarked that establishing the Italian language on Rhodes was an a priori necessity for all other cultural

---

28   On code-switching in Italian postcolonial writing, see Alessandro Portelli, "Fingerprints Stained with Ink: Notes on 'Migrant Writing' in Italy," *Interventions* 8, no. 3 (2007): 472–83; Emma Bond, *Writing Migration through the Body* (New York: Palgrave Macmillan, 2018), 197–237. See also, Emily Apter, *Against World Literature: The Politics of Untranslatability* (London: Verso, 2014).

29   Marongiù Buonaiuti, *La politica religiosa*, 84–100.

30   Marongiù Buonaiuti, *La politica religiosa*, 99.

31   Telespresso N.250, March 5, 1937, ASMAE, AP 1931–45, b.14 Dodecanneso.

programs of the regime: "first we must institute on the islands the necessary ordinances to render our language dominant."[32] Ideologues like Franco Ciarlantini had similarly observed that Italy's lamentable lack of empire had produced the linguistic dominance of French in the Mediterranean. Ciarlantini, a founding editor of the nationalist journal *Il grido della stirpe,* claimed that the Italian language would easily have been dominant in the region as a result of its maritime empires: "At one time our language was nearly official, especially in Egypt and Turkey."[33] According to Ciarlantini, Italy's lack of empire meant the Italian language did not correspond to its "real" cultural hegemony in the Mediterranean: "nations that feel themselves to be hegemonic and to have a mission to fulfill speak only their own language and they impose it in all forms of traffic, from spiritual to political and economic," he wrote.[34] Ciarlantini had argued that the Italian language could once again be "hegemonic" with the expansion of the empire in the Levant and institutionalization of Italian public schools, and this project started with sovereignty and educational reform in the Dodecanese.

Such ideas doubtless influenced Fascist educational programs that were undertaken by Lago who oversaw the creation of new school curriculum. During this period, the idea of shared maritime histories was brought to bear on pedagogical materials. When familiarizing Greek schoolchildren with the Latin alphabet, for example, a phoneme like *"na"* could be illustrated with the word *na-ve,* and an image of ship, in an obvious reference to a shared Mediterranean culture (see figure 4.1, an Italian-era syllabarium, or phonics textbook).

While it was only later, under the administration of De Vecchi, that the goal of Italian as the official language in the islands was achieved within the framework of state schools and policy, the desire to make Italian dominant in the Aegean had also been expressed under Lago's administration. The goal had been clearly expressed among the Jewish communities of Rhodes and

---

32   "*Nel Dodecanneso il problema è quindi duplice: prima istituire nelle nostre isole gli ordinamenti necessari a rendere la nostra lingua dominante, e poi fare di Rodi un faro di cultura nazionale che vada oltre ai confini delle isole ed illumini anche i paesi dove vivono i nostri emigranti,*" Orazio Pedrazzi, *Il Levante Mediterraneo e l'Italia* (Milan: Alpes, 1925), 56–57.

33   "*Un tempo la nostra lingua era pressochè ufficiale, specie in Egitto e in Turchia.*"; Franco Ciarlantini, *Viaggio nell'Oriente Mediterraneo* (Milan: Mondadori, 1936), 52.

34   "*I popoli che sentono di essere egemonici e di avere una missione da assolvere parlano soltanto la loro lingua e la impongono in tutte le forme del traffico, da quelle spirituali a quelle politiche ed economiche.*" Ciarlantini, *Viaggio nell'Oriente Mediterraneo,* 56.

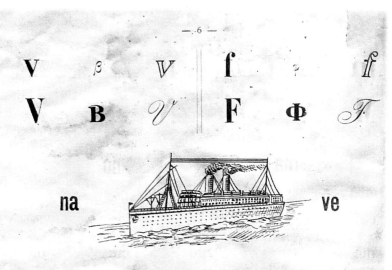

SILLABE (Leggere verticalmente, poi orizzontalmente)
ΣΥΛΛΑΒΑΙ ('Ανάγνωσον καθέτως, κατόπιν ὁριζοντίως)

va	av	vu	vo	af	uf	ev	if	fu
fon	nev	uf	fin	ven	vι	fan	of	fa
vio	*via*	*vie*	*viu*	*vuo*	*fiu*	*fia*	*fie*	*fio*	*fuo*

APPLICAZIONE - 'Εφαρμογὴ

1 - Ni no à no ve na vi ma io ne ò
u na 2 - Non ò · fa me 3 - U na na ve
fu ma 4 - Mi a non na non vie ne 5 - Vi no
nuo vo 6 - Un uo vo 7 - Fiu me 8 - Ni no à
no ve an ni 9 - Vie ni 10 - Io ò fa me
11 - Fam mi u na na ve 12 - Fan no u na
vi a nuo va 13 - Eu fe mio e An na non
àn no fa me 14 - I fiu mi 15 - Ev vi va

Figure 4.1: Page from a syllabarium, Vittorio Mancus. *I miei primi passi:
Sillabario illustrato e Prime letture ed essercizi ad uso delle scuole delle Isole Egee.*
Rodi: Tipografia "Rodia," 1926.

Kos who were clear supporters of the regime. The Italian state's replacement of the Alliance Israélite Universelle system with Italian private schools presaged a further emphasis on new Italian culture programs within the Jewish community that occurred during the first decade of Fascist rule.[35] By 1925, the regime had intervened to reform an existing Hebrew private school "so as to give that Italian culture which enables them to come closer to the homeland and reinforces the sentiments of affection and gratitude that the Jews profess over there."[36] As Aron Rodrigue has demonstrated, Lago's project to establish a rabbinical school in Rhodes profited from a vacuum of Sephardic institutions created by the collapse of the Ottoman Empire.[37] It also embraced a curriculum that included Italian language and literature, and certainly invested less in spreading the values of Sephardim than it did in the diffusion of the linguistic and cultural prestige of Italy throughout the Levant and greater Middle East.

The inclusion of secular subjects relating to Italian language and culture reached its apogee after the arrival of Riccardo Pacifici, a classically trained rabbi from the prominent Jewish community of Florence. Pacifici was brought from Venice to direct the rabbinical school in Rhodes in 1930 and he remained there until 1936, when he returned to Genoa to serve as chief rabbi there (he was ultimately deported in 1943 from Italy and perished at Auschwitz). By 1938, the school had attained international prestige and had recruited and graduated at least a decade of prestigious alumni, an international class of rabbis, who would very likely have gone on to disseminate the importance of Italian culture had it not been for the Holocaust that in a few years' time swept up many of the school's graduates. The school itself was forced to close in 1938 because the anti-Semitic race laws made it unviable for attracting students. But as Rodrigue shows, De Vecchi sought to keep the school open, even as he enforced the expulsion of Jewish persons who had naturalized to the islands after the end of World War I. De Vecchi recognized the rabbinical

---

35   On the role of the Alliance Israélite Universelle in shaping French Empire in the eastern Mediterranean, see Aron Rodrigue, *French Jews, Turkish Jews: The Alliance Israélite Universelle and the Politics of Jewish Schooling in Turkey, 1860–1925* (Bloomington: Indiana University Press, 1990).

36   "*Per poter dare [...] quella cultura italiana che la avvicinasse alla Patria e che rafforzzasse in essa quei sentimenti di affezione e riconoscenza che gli Ebrei laggiù professano*"; memo dated December 2, 1925, ASMAE, AP, "Dodecanneso," 988/1925.

37   Aron Rodrigue, "The Rabbinical Seminary in Italian Rhodes, 1928–38: An Italian Fascist Project," *Jewish Social Studies* 25, no. 1 (2019): 1–19.

school's important contribution to the project of Italian Empire in the eastern Mediterranean.

Stella Levi, one of 150 survivors of the 1944 Jewish deportations from Rhodes, recalled how the rabbinical school had served the community in much bigger ways than just to trained rabbis. The school offered enrichment lessons in Italian culture to the entire Jewish community. After the Rabbinical school's closure, and her own expulsion from Catholic school due to the 1938 anti-Semitic race laws, she had continued her education in Italian literature and culture. She connected, through a local bookstore, with several Italian schoolteachers who, for the love of culture, agreed to give free lessons to Jewish children in Rhodes. At least one of the teachers, as she recalled, had been a member of the Communist party and an anti-Fascist.[38]

Admiration and thirst for Italian culture were not limited to the Jewish community and many Greek interviewees were passionate about their fondness for both their lessons and their teachers from Italy. Their love for Italian culture, however, was clearly separate in their minds from the problem of Fascist state-building projects. Interviewees expressed the idea that the ideology that accompanied this education was all spectacle, and that if the De Vecchi tenure was attached to the idea of imposing a "Roman way of life," it was a testimonial to the regime's fundamentally weak sovereignty at that time. In this regard, Manoles Despotakis's memories of evading the ideology at work in his elementary education suggest neither nationalism nor anti-Fascism but the ability to "make do" or to draw unexpected results from his situation. He recalled with pride, for example, being singled out by his Italian instructors as a bright young man with a keen memory for Roman history, but putting off their invitations to join the Balilla, the Fascist youth organization. He told his teachers that his mother needed him at home and help with household and field work.[39] As Despotakis explained, this was a calculated excuse: had he said that it was his father who opposed his participation in the Balilla, he would have indicated a potentially dangerous opposition to the regime; instead, Despotakis banked correctly on the presumption that the Fascist state saw local women as apolitical (about which more in a moment). In truth, neither his mother nor his father had strongly opposed Despotakis joining the Balilla. The anecdote thus emphasizes Despotakis's cleverness, how he was able both to benefit from the system—learning Roman history, Italian, and Latin—and

38   Interview with Stella Levi, New York City, February 20, 2012.
39   Interview with Manoles Despotakis, Rhodes, July 24, 2009.

to evade its intention of engaging him in deeper propaganda and remaking his identity and national consciousness.

De Vecchi's educational reform seems finally to have helped promote Greek national identity rather than to have stymied it, and to have brought the Dodecanese Greek community into line with other Greek national movements in the Aegean.[40] As Mihales Katzinikolas recalled, his mother took him out of school at this point because the scholastic reform was a direct attack on his Greek identity.[41] Some interviewees even remembered that De Vecchi's educational reform led to the creation of "secret schools" that continued instruction in the mother tongue.[42] "Secret schools" (κρυφό σκολειό) had been a widespread phenomenon in Greece under Ottoman rule from the fifteenth through nineteenth centuries, and were central to the development of Greek nationalist sentiment.[43] How widespread "secret schools" were in the Dodecanese—or how much, on the other hand, testimonies to them reflect the fact that memory of Italian rule has been woven into the fabric of the larger narrative of Greece under occupation—is unclear. As Katzinikolas remembered, his education in Italian made much more of an impression on him than any lessons he continued after he stopped attending school.

What he did remember is the night school that he enrolled in after the war, ostensibly to make up for the missing years of his education; he eventually graduated in medicine and became a physician. Because educational reform occurred in the years leading up to the outbreak of the war, in many cases, the fact that it led to a premature conclusion of their primary education was much more memorable than the idea that it made them more "Greek" or more "nationalist" than they had been before the reforms. It is worth remembering, too, that linguistic diversity was already part of life in the Dodecanese archipelago, even prior to Italian rule; Jewish and Greek persons, for example, knew Turkish because it was the language of commerce, and Turkish and Jewish communities also knew some Greek. That Italian should

---

40   As Alexis Rappas also notes, having recourse to Greekness was one of the main ways in which Greek elites in the Aegean asserted their entitlement to independence from colonial rule in both Cyprus and the Dodecanese. Alexis Rappas, "Greeks under European Colonial Rule: National Allegiance and Imperial Loyalty," *Byzantine and Modern Greek Studies* 34, no. 2 (2010): 201–18, 204.

41   Interview with Mihales Katzinikolas, Rhodes July 15, 2009.

42   See also Doumanis, *Myth and Memory*, 85.

43   Theodore G. Zervas, *The Making of a Modern Greek Identity: Education, Nationalism, and the Teaching of a Greek National Past* (Boulder, CO: East European Monographs, 2012).

become an additional language of communication was not novel or disruptive. The strategies of adaptation and linguistic code-switching that they adopted in the face of Fascist ideology may be seen, with hindsight, as both an act of resilience as well as an indicator of the human hunger for culture and knowledge.

However, it is also clear that these tactics were born out of necessity and were employed in reaction to the increasingly repressive atmosphere in the islands after 1936. The archive, for example, records how a young Jewish man, Ezra Hanan, a local vendor in Rhodes, briefly landed in jail when he reproached a young Greek who refused to accept an ice cream from him (because Hanan was Jewish). Hanan had not just reproached the Greek but had shouted loudly in Italian, "Speak the language of your father!"[44] The police ultimately accepted Hanan's justification that he only wanted to know whether he was speaking to an Orthodox Greek or a Muslim, and given Hanan's "good moral, penal, and political precedents" chose to let the young man go with only a reprimand. In all likelihood, however, Hanan would easily have distinguished between a Greek and a Turk. Hanan's retort seems, rather, to have aimed at shaming the Greek, who by speaking to him in Italian had revealed his co-option by the Fascist state. In fact, the police report described the young Greek as a *"giovane fascista"* (young fascist). This apparently minor incident speaks to how an increased presence of bullying in everyday life was one of the main ways that Fascism operated in its supposed ideological vacuum. As Michael Ebner has shown, bullying was commonplace in the 1930s in Italy, such that violence permeated "personal relationships and social interactions became political. The threat of physical attacks, institutional confinement, and financial ruin loomed over even the most mundane events." The incident reveals the depth to which cultural and linguistic *bonifica*— the mandate to make Italian into the official language of the Aegean—had overtaken everyday life and begun to contaminate intercommunal relations and infiltrate "public spaces, the work place, and even the family home," as it was also doing in the Italian Peninsula at the time.[45]

44 *"Parla la lingua di tuo padre."* GAK DOD, f. 662/ 1938.
45 Michael Ebner, *Ordinary Violence in Mussolini's Italy* (New York: Cambridge University Press, 2011), 216.

Women as Mediators: Gender, Resistance, and Mixed Matrimonies

Moments of even more visible resistance, ones that have traditionally been recalled as demonstrations of Greek nationalism, might similarly be reconsidered in the light of everyday tactics to resist Fascism. Perhaps one of the most remembered displays of local "nationalism" is the so-called Rock War on Kalymnos. When a group of women gathered to protest the *autocephalia*, they continued to throw rocks at the local carabinieri until a male member of the community, a goatherd, joined the protest, and was shot at and killed. The Rock War has been a revered legend in Kalymnos, a testimonial to the will and impetuous spirit of the Kalymnian people, proof of their riotous and devious nature and the fact that their ardently "Greek" character led them to resist Italian rule more than any other islanders in the archipelago did. It has also been taken to attest to the fierce character of Kalymnian women and the strongly matrilocal orientation of the insular microsocieties of the Dodecanese.[46] As Dimitris Roditis, grandson of a Kalymnian woman who participated in the Rock War protest, suggested, no Kalymnian woman who recalls the Rock War can help but wear an amused smile.[47]

The Kalymnos Rock War can also be reconsidered from the perspective of "tactics," that is the tools of ordinary people in the face of restricted options for more organized forms of dissent. In Doumanis's discussion of the Kalymnos Rock War he has linked it to the presence of the myth of the "good" Italian in the islands with locals remembering how the carabinieri respected a (gendered) code of honor and did not shoot at anyone until a man joined the protest.[48] In Roditis's telling, however, it was not so much gender mores that the carabinieri respected: in fact, they fired because the goatherd was adroit with a slingshot and had begun to launch boulders of a dangerous size. The Rock War of Kalymnos is therefore also a good example of how even small instances of resistance could meet with significant brutality and force by the Italian state, and how women, in particular, could sometimes act as mediators of organized protest in order to shield the community from the risks inherent in any kind of dissent.

---

46   See David Sutton, *Memories Cast in Stone: The Relevance of the Past in Everyday Life* (New York: Berg, 1998).
47   Interview with Dimitris Roditis, Kalymnos, July 28, 2010.
48   On the common occurence of protests with rocks, see also Doumanis, *Myth and Memory*, 67–85.

The Kalymnos Rock War was not the only instance in the catalog of Dodecanese evasion and resistance to the Fascist state in which women were the architects. The involvement of women in protests may in fact have been a frequent phenomenon. So-called rock wars occurred on multiple islands and occasions. This was especially the case in the outlying islands, which since the creation of the Greek state in 1821 had enjoyed "privileges" and been free from taxation and interference from the Ottoman state. A 1936 report by a local Italian officer describes how an attempt to carry out the census in Olympos, a far-flung village on the northern edge of the island of Karpathos, was frustrated when the entire village, especially its female component, organized against the officers commissioned to take the census.[49] The reporting Italian officer described a series of obstacles created by the local population that testify to a variety of tactics that a village could deploy to resist the Fascist state's expansion into their lives. First, the mayor and local teachers of Olympos had refused to carry out the census. The local teachers and the mayor had offered the excuse that it was the village women who were refusing based on their belief it would lead to further taxes and to the conscription of Karpathian men into the Italian military. The latter notion would have been highly unlikely since military service was linked to and reserved for those who desired full Italian citizenship—and was therefore only available to persons who had been heavily surveilled and shown themselves to be Fascists. The Italian officers made some further unsuccessful attempts to coerce the local elite to convince the villagers, especially the women, who were presented as the most obstinate faction, by reminding them that the census had a purely statistical scope. The Italian officers next attempted to conduct the census themselves, dividing the village into two parts. As they walked through the village of Olympos, which has a casbah-like design in which rooftops may be used for household activities and for communication between households, they found that half of it was abandoned and that women had gathered on the rooftops, where they threw rocks down at the Italian officers amid violent screaming— the famous funerary ululation of Olymbos women (said to be linked with the frequent loss of male family members at sea). The resulting scene of screaming, rock-throwing, and chaos was recorded by the Italian officer on commission. In response, the Italians committed to "restoring order" and undertaking the census themselves.

49 GAK DOD, f. 639 (1)/1936.

This incident reveals how involved local women were in shaping attitudes toward and responses to Fascism. As Luisa Passerini has shown in her discussion of everyday life under Fascist rule, it was very often women who acted as "mediators, sometimes accepting and other times evading, the obligations imposed by the regime."[50] What the Italian officers failed to recognize was that the women were mediating a broader form of political protest and putting that protest in a form that the authorities would have difficulty knowing how to control. As the officers reported, after deciding that they should conduct the census themselves, they called on the local mayor to come, but when the mayor was a few meters from the main square, they witnessed a hundred women stream in from the surrounding alleys to block his passage. The Italian carabinieri again "reestablished order" but meanwhile the mayor had disappeared yet again. He eventually sent a message that he was under house arrest and surrounded by an all-female blockade. He further reminded them of his difficult position, as a local mayor—or *podestà*, as in the Fascist parlance—to liaise between the Fascist state and the local community. His hands were tied: if he supported the census it would irritate his party and prevent him from winning the upcoming local elections. The Italian officers replied by proceeding to the mayor's home, which they did find surrounded by a group of fifty women; but these women, they noted, were mostly from the mayor's family or relatives of other members of his party. This led the Italian commander to believe that the women were *with*, rather than *against*, the mayor. Later in the afternoon, the Italians heard screams coming from the mayor and rumors that the women were threatening to kill him, further convincing the Italian officers that his "arrest" had been a staged event. The police discounted completely the idea that the women may in fact have organized a swift movement of dissent against the census in the face of the mayor's apparent position of compliance with the Fascist state.

The resolution of this episode is further revealing of how the regime intervened into everyday life and handled organized political dissent when it occurred. The census was at last carried out, and the Italian authorities concluded that the "instigator" of the opposition had been the mayor's brother, a *"schedato politico"* or person with a political file, who had been previously expelled from the islands in 1922 (also for resistance to the census). The mayor, his brother, and three involved teachers were fired

---

50   Luisa Passerini, *Fascism in Popular Memory: The Cultural Experience of the Turin Working Class* (Cambridge: Cambridge University Press, 1987), 139.

from their civil posts and replaced by other local persons, and the former mayor from the opposing political party was restored to power. Yet the Italian report remarked that, although they had interrogated them, not one woman in the village had been willing to point out a culprit; they had therefore assigned blame and punishment based on previous records and assumptions. Such expulsions of Greek patriots were later cited by the Dodecanese diaspora abroad in their letter-writing campaign to the League of Nations, helping the event to acquire the nationalist tenor that it eventually carried in local memory.[51] The episode underscores the repressive order that the Fascist state used in its rule in the islands. But it also emphasizes how frequently women could be mediators, of both organized dissent, and of the assimilationist policies of the Fascist state. Recalling Manoles Despotakis's choice to blame his refusal to join the Balilla to his mother's will (as opposed to his father's), also points to a commonplace of memories of everyday life, that is, that sometimes it was women, even more than men, that objected to the Fascist state. Multiple interviewees suggested that it was their mothers, more than their fathers, who opposed their attendance at the Italian schools, as they were more upset than their fathers by the underlying policy of assimilation, what was a direct attack on a maternal prerogative to educate their children.

The role of women as mediators and as opinion-makers regarding broader attitudes toward the Fascist state was also present as the local population navigated the delicate question of mixed matrimonies. The Italian state's attitudes toward matrimony in the Dodecanese islands eventually contrasted with its stance towards "mixed-race" unions in other Italian colonies, which were made illegal after the first set of laws in 1937 for the "defense of the race." After 1938, a prohibition against mixed marriage did go into effect in the islands, but because of the whiteness of the Dodecanese subject, and because difference with the locals was constructed along the terms of religion rather than race—with conversion to Catholicism always a possibility—the policy allowed mixed marriages between Italians and locals (with the exception of Jewish Dodecanese ones), even as Italy adopted a broad set of provisions for surveilling and regulating marriages in Italian colonies. Prior to 1937–38, a permissive, arguably sometimes even encouraging, attitude had prevailed regarding such marriages. This contrasted with the British attitude toward mixed marriages in nearby Cyprus, but aligns with Italian permissiveness

---

51   See Emanuel Cassotis, *The Karpathian (Dodecanese) Presence in America* (Rhodes: Stegi Grammaton ke Technon Dodecanesou, 2012).

toward mixed marriages in Italian East Africa prior to the Ethiopian war.[52] As Giulia Barrera has demonstrated, marriages and concubinage were often acceptable there because they reproduced the larger power dynamics of colonialism; in instances of *madamismo*, or concubinage, women in sexual relationships with Italian colonizers were usually domestic servants and even when these relationships were normalized through marriage, the gender hierarchies ultimately reinforced colonial ones.

Concubinage, or *madamismo* was not a typical facet of Dodecanese life under Italian rule. Most mixed relationships resulted in marriage and followed a different set of codes based on local customs and dowry practices. But it was still the case that mixed marriage may have served to reinforce the colonial order, and, indeed, the "moderate" techniques of assimilation and empire that were adopted under Lago. A noteworthy instance of a mixed marriage, for example, was the one between Giulio Jacopi, the superintendent of archaeology and monuments on Rhodes, and a local Greek woman. The marriage was celebrated in a 1935 issue of *The Messenger of Rhodes*, as part of an internal spread that reported on the massive public works and urban renovations that had been established during Lago's ten-year tenure. In fact, it was no accident that the two stories should have appeared together— the marriage was perhaps being celebrated because it embodied the Mediterraneanism that Fascist Italy claimed to be enacting, particularly in its continued emphasis on "local" traditions and customs, as discussed earlier in this chapter. The two photographs of husband and wife, he in suit and tie, she in the traditional peasant costume of Astypalea, celebrated a larger marriage of sorts, one between the Fascist state and the "local" peasant culture, which Mussolini, within a year's time, would be claiming to revitalize through land reclamation schemes in the islands of Rhodes and Kos.

Yet, much as with citizenship, marriage between Italians and Greeks never became normative or a simple affair regarded lightly by the Italian state. A case-by-case monitoring of it enabled the Fascist regime to exercise multiple levels of control. Such surveillance was justified in part on the basis that, as in Italy, marriage between Italian men and Greek women made Italian citizenship possible for wives and any offspring, making marriage a proxy for larger questions about the inclusion, allegiance, and identity of Italian

---

52   As Alexis Rappas observes, "In Cyprus the British strongly discouraged it, as it was generally thought that local marriage compromised the impartiality of British civil servants; and usually an official who had married locally could expect to be transferred imminently to another colony." Rappas, "Greeks under European Colonial Rule," 208.

imperial subjects in Aegean. Second, the need to preserve the individual religious statute of each of the communities on the island had been one of the main criteria for the nonintegration of the islands into metropolitan Italy—that is, its annexation as a *possedimento* as opposed to a province of Italy. But this paradoxically meant that the state could also intervene on matters of "byzantine" marriage practices, to ensure that the local traditions became imbricated with new Fascist regulations and institutions. This initial "preservation" of local marriage practices became a means for the Italian government to enter into the daily life of inhabitants; meanwhile the regime touted it as one way in which Italians demonstrated "respect" for Dodecanese inhabitants. But locals proved equally adept at finding clever ways of exploiting and evading the complex system Italy put into place so as to monitor closely the habits of social reproduction within the local community.

Generally speaking, both history and local memory record marriages between Italians and local Greek subjects as having been frequent, but the meanings assigned to this phenomenon are often divergent. Nicholas Doumanis has argued that many locals accepted these marriages, despite some reticence, with poor families recognizing that marrying an Italian often offered a good opportunity for a daughter.[53] But some locals interviewed took the reverse point of view, describing the distinct advantage that marrying their local women offered to Italian colonizers. One interviewee, Ippokrates Logothetis, a native of Tilos, recalled how Italians often married the "best" women during their occupation of the islands, and that the Italian skill at courting and then marrying respectable women had the potential to encourage Italian integration into the community, especially in the eyes of Dodecanese subjects who were wary of the Italian state intervening in their affairs. While it is hard to ascertain what Logothetis might have meant by his reference to the women that Italian men married as the "best," one possible meaning is that they were from prosperous families. Traditional dowry practices were still very much in place in the islands at the time of Italian rule, and marriage to a Dodecanese woman meant that an Italian official or soldier would receive a plot of land. Indeed, to help justify his

---

53   Doumanis suggests further that the one defining trait of the Italians, in the eyes of Dodecanese locals, was their willingness to marry outside of these traditional dowry practices, thus providing a solution for poor women. "What distinguished the Italians was their preparedness to marry women without any concern for dowry. They were admired because of their willingness to 'take' brides from poor families." Doumanis, *Myth and Memory*, 171.

atypical point of view that mixed marriages had sometimes benefited Italians even more than locals, Logothetis later introduced me to a grandson of one of these marriages, explaining that the Italian man was there on his annual holiday, enjoying the very piece of property that his grandfather had acquired through dowry more than fifty years ago.[54]

Aegean locals thus seem to remember mixed matrimony as sign of Italian integration into their community and a reflection of their own strength and appeal as a community. A favorite legend among oral informants is about Italians who married local women then ultimately stayed in the islands even after the war had ended.[55] And it remained a point of pride, of course, that Dodecanese women were "beautiful" and appealing to Italian colonizers. These notions of "beauty" were of course linked to ideas of race.[56] One interviewee, Angela Morfou, had, at age seventeen, married an Italian soldier whom she recalls as handsome and elegant, a typical description of Italian soldiers by Dodecanese locals. She also remembered Italian "benevolence," citing an instance when soldiers distributed food to the poor of Rhodes. Yet soon after her Italian husband died, early in the war, she rebaptized her son as a Greek Orthodox Christian, changing his name from Benedetto to Nikos. She taciturnly observed that the son from her first marriage could be recognized as not Greek "from twenty meters away" and had the "light" features of a European. When she remarried to a Greek later, she concealed from her community the true story of her son's father. However, she described secretly holding the knowledge that her son was Italian, especially during her years as a chambermaid in hotels catering to European tourists in Rhodes, when the memory of her "Italian" son helped her to feel more European herself.[57]

The Italian colonial administration's views of mixed matrimonies grew increasingly guarded over time and reflected the Fascist state's shifting positions on race after the invasion of Ethiopia. Yet ambivalence about mixed matrimonies was at the core of Italian attitudes about mixed marriage in the Aegean: on the one hand, mixed marriage would help to bring Italian "modernity" to the islands, but on the other, it had the power to encourage the

---

54   Interview with Ippokrates Logothetis, Tilos, August 20, 2009.
55   Interview with Manoles Despotakis and Mihales Katzinikolas, Rhodes, July 21, 2009.
56   On the entanglement of beauty and race, especially in the context of interethnic identities and relationships see Kym Ragusa, *The Skin Between Us: A Memoir of Race, Beauty and Belonging* (New York: Norton and Co., 2006).
57   Interview with Angela Morfou, Rhodes, August 12, 2010.

social and moral degeneration of the Italian community. The entanglement of mixed marriage with Catholicization was also an important factor in Italian views about mixed marriage. Corrado Prodomi, an early Italian missionary in the islands, declared that "of course in general the fair sex loved the Italians more than the Greeks. Because they certainly saw that Italians were less depraved and very well educated, generous, and respectful. It's understandable that affection was born and hence a few mixed matrimonies."[58] If Greek women were eager to marry Italians, according to Prodomi, it was also because by doing so, they guaranteed the sanctity and durability of their marriage. Marrying an Italian man meant an Aegean woman became Catholic, and Catholicism did not admit divorce. In shades of the Orientalism that have been discussed in previous chapters, Prodomi described Greek Orthodox marriage as a spectacle and ritual devoid of real meaning. He recounted a Greek joke that he felt was emblematic of the lightness with which marriage was viewed: "We take one hour to marry and you Catholics do it in three minutes—but the next day we get divorced while you are married your whole life." He went on at length about the poor character of Greek men who effectively victimized women and made a mockery of marriage.[59] From the point of view of Catholic doctrine, then, mixed matrimony was beneficial and could be sanctioned as a means to improve the overall moral standards of the local community.

At the same time, conversion to Catholicism was rare and, in the absence of a radical program to assimilate locals, state intervention into local marriage practices offered a route toward undermining the power of the Greek Orthodox Church. A complex system was therefore born to enable the Fascist state to intervene and manage matrimony. These Fascist interventions into the civil administration and to issues such as matrimony proved far from simple. Chief among the difficulties was negotiating its commitment to the personal statute, the preservation of which had been the main rationale for creating a special form of citizenship for Dodecanese locals. The commitment to the personal statute forced Italy to recognize and even to arbitrate customs that

---

58 Corrado Prodomi, *Memorie di un missionario di Rodi-egeo, 1913–1920* (Verona: A. Bettinelli, 1937), 142.

59 "Given the false and devious character of the Greek, that it is not difficult to find an excuse and force a loophole to get a divorce. The victims are always the women, anyone can understand, especially if they are not rich or beautiful or fertile. Generally, the Greek is capricious and even as an old man marries a girl of fourteen or fifteen." Prodomi, *Memorie di un missionario di Rodi-egeo*, 142.

it found backward, reprehensible, and antithetical to the state's commitment to integration and assimilation, such as divorce, which was legal among all of the local communities. As Prodomi stated, no Italian would ever recognize divorce as sane, since "each divorce brings with it at a minimum either the dissolution of the family, which is the first organization of man on Earth, or the total unhappiness of the husband and wife and therefore is a betrayal, a terrible action, an abominable fact."[60] But when two Jewish Dodecanese subjects decided to file for divorce, their requests were duly processed on the basis that to do so was in accordance with Hebrew law. The divorce was eventually registered with the Civil Registry in Milan, where in this instance, the marriage had originally been recorded.[61]

On the other hand, preservation of the civil statute mobilized further state surveillance and reform, with mixed matrimony becoming one of the main ways in which the Fascist state claimed sovereignty over local religious customs and surveiled the private lives of the population. It was possible, for example, that a resident of the archipelago might have Turkish or Hellenic citizenship, which they had acquired either prior to the Lausanne Treaty or thereafter. As described in the previous chapter, the regime naturalized as many Aegean subjects as possible into Italian citizens; however, many Hellenic and Turkish nationals continued nonetheless to reside in one of the islands. Mixed marriages (*matrimoni misti*) therefore occurred not only for unions between Italians and Aegean citizens, but when any Italian Aegean citizen married a person of a different national sovereignty. Under Ottoman rule, all marriages had been handled within the different religious communities and were events that invested religious heads with considerable power. Prodomi, for example, referred to the local Greek religious authorities as "despots" who were uncooperative, dogmatic, and usurious, eager to collect taxes from these traditions, and using their power to assert their authority against the Italian state. In order to marry someone of a different religion or nationality, a woman needed to obtain both her birth certificate and a certificate of "*stato libero*," that is to say, her status as an unwed woman. Prodomi lamented that Greek Orthodox bishops were especially obstinate when they had to issue such a certificate for marriage between an Italian man and a Greek woman:

---

60   "*Ogni divorzio porta sempre almeno, o la dissoluzione della famiglia che è la prima società dell'uomo sopra la terra, o la completa infelicità degli sposi quindi è un tradimento, un'azione difettosa, un fatto abominevole.*" Prodomi, *Memorie di un missionario*, 146.

61   Domanda di Marcel Menascè e Amelia Alhadeff, 2 novembre 1935, GAK DOD: 1936/639/2.

When a certificate for an unmarried woman is required, one must go to the despot, that is to say, the bishop. Only he can give such a document. However, it is very difficult to obtain it. In cases of a mixed marriage it is necessary to procure a certificate of baptism and the unwed state of the girl. Greek baptism is not recognized by us, but we have to have the certificate of it, and only the Greek bishop can give such a document, after paying a tax of sixty *lire*—and the Bishop must not be aware that the girl is marrying a Catholic, otherwise he won't give it to us.[62]

Prodomi's words suggest how Greek Orthodox bishops presented the clearest obstruction to the state's policies to encourage these marriages. In 1929, Italy therefore introduced a process for civil matrimony that divested the Greek Church of its power to oversee mixed marriage between Italians and Greeks as well as other cross-communal or cross-national marriages. The reform also curtailed the practice of collecting taxes related to the civil administration of marriage (although local Greek bishops eventually proved adroit at evading this practice). Local Italian *podestàs* (mayors) in outlying villages and on other islands had to report these civil matrimonies to the central administration on Rhodes; in instances where the mayor was not Italian but Greek, the extensive administrative paperwork and petitions documented local compliance with the Fascist state.

The establishment of civil matrimony had ensured that Italy could maintain surveillance over marriages between people of different religious communities as well as those between people of different national sovereignties. But by 1936, such mixed marriages were also an issue that needed to be thought about in the context of increasing anxieties about race within Italy's African colonial contexts. Lago weighed carefully whether "color" and "racial mixing" were issues that needed to be factored when evaluating the Fascist state's policies on mixed matrimonies. His words on the matter reveal that racism among Italians toward Aegean subjects was present, but that allowing mixed matrimony to occur in the previous decade had been part of a broader strategy of political pragmatism in the archipelago:

---

62   "*Quando si vuole un certificato di stato libero si deve andare dal Despote cioè dal Vescovo. Solo lui può dare tale documento. È però molto difficile ottenerlo. Nei matrimoni misti è necessario il certificato di Battesimo e di stato libero della ragazza. Il Battesimo greco da noi è riconosciuto, ma dobbiamo averne il certificato, il Vescovo greco solo può dare tale documento, dietro la tassa di 60 lire italiane al mio tempo—e il Vescovo non deve accorgersi che la ragazza sposa un cattolico, altrimenti non ce lo dà.*" Prodomi, *Memorie di un missionario*, 147.

Mixed marriages among Italians and Dodecanese should not be encouraged: but they cannot be impeded either. Dodecanese women are not women of color. Impeding or prohibiting systematically mixed marriages would be politically disastrous. In other words, we have to desire that our men marry in Italy, and that they bring to Rhodes their wives and families. There is greater guarantee of harmony and conjugal morality; the pure race is preferable to the mixing of races. But if it gets out that the government opposes mixed marriages, holding "Greeks" inferior to "Italians," we will create a dangerous and unjustified atmosphere of racial hatred.[63]

Although Lago's views align with earlier ones that the Dodecanese was not "a population of color" (see chapter 3), his words still presaged increasing concerns about the "moral" integrity of Italian colonial population, which at this same juncture, was growing thanks to the introduction of resettlement programs. He added that mixed marriages could still be a concern when "circumstances of deficient morality of the bride or her family are also present."[64] The latter kind of union, between a colonizer and a woman of low status were "the most deplorable and the most deplored cases, and unfortunately, they are numerous."[65] Fears about "moral" degeneration among the Italian community show how racism certainly impacted Italian views of mixed marriage, and that it was seen as not problematic only when compared with unions among Italians and African woman.

But an important role of women to act as both mediators of and to maintain colonial hierarchies remained. As mediators, women found new power and autonomy, and on occasion, a women would make use of the civil matrimony process to obtain a mixed marriage when her family objected to it.[66]

---

63   "*I matrimoni misti, tra Italiani e Dodecanesini non debbono essere favoriti: ma non si possono nemmeno impedire. Le Dodecanesine non sono donne di colore. Un impedimento o un contrasto sistematico ai matrimoni misti sarebbe politicamente disastroso. In altre parole, dobbiamo desiderare che i nostri uomini si sposino in Italia, e portino a Rodi moglie e famiglia. V'è più garanzia di armonia e moralità coniugale; la razza pura è preferibile ai vantaggi dell'avvicinamento delle due razze. Ma se si diffonde la convinzione che il Governo avversa i matrimoni misti, ritenendo i 'greci' inferiori agli 'italiani', creiamo un'atmosfera di odio di razza pericolosa e ingiustificata.*" Memo dated September 21, 1936. GAK DOD, 639/1936.
64   "*Concorrono ragioni di moralità deficiente della sposa o dell'ambiente familiare.*"
65   "*Questi sono i casi più deplorabili e più deplorati e purtroppo numerosi.*"
66   See Alexis Rappas, "The Domestic Foundations of Imperial Sovereignty: Mixed Marriages in the Fascist Aegean," in *New Perspectives on the History of Gender and Empire:*

Lago's choice to admit that mixed marriage was an inevitable fact of imperial life ensured the colonial order, because it was, of course, Italian men who married Aegean women, ultimately transmitting their Italian citizenship and identity to both the woman and the children that resulted from that marriage. To some observers, both local and Italian, the Italian state's position was ultimately one of encouragement of mixed marriage. Lago's call for the administration to exercise caution concerning mixed marriages was a far cry from prohibiting them. In fact, his reflection on the matter followed a specific incident: the father of an Italian soldier had learned of his engagement to a local woman on Rhodes and, to prevent the marriage, had contacted the Italian military and succeeded in repatriating his son. Lago inveighed against this outcome, remarking that "in regard to the special case of Scalzotto, it is worth remarking that it is best, 'to leave it in the private domain.' The bad part is this is not what happened. That is, the authorities intervened and had the young man leave at the request of the father. And that should not have happened."[67] Lago's words may seem to point mainly to his dismay at the loss of local military manpower via the soldier's return to Italy. But reading between the lines, they clearly point to how the Italian policy was to tacitly accept mixed marriage while wanting it to remain a "private" affair about which Italian citizens at home were to remain unwitting. This situation aligned the Aegean very closely with the policy in Italian East Africa before the invasion of Ethiopia.

Yet ambivalence remained the central attitude toward mixed marriage and corresponded to the ambivalent views that Italy had about its imperial project in the islands. As Alexis Rappas has remarked: "Not of colour, and yet racially different, 'almost the same, but not quite,' the Dodecanese woman embodies here the point of balance of colonial rule between rapprochement and distancing."[68] The Fascist state's policies on mixed matrimonies revealed its unresolvable conundrum about its project for the islands: on the one hand, the administration could not be seen to espouse colonial and openly racist policies, but on the other hand, it could not go so far as to imagine the Aegean as an extension of Italy either. Although Lago's reaction underscored

---

Comparative and Global Approaches, edited by Ulrike Lindner and Dörte Lerp, 31–58 (London: Bloomsbury Academic Press, 2018).

67   *"Quanto al caso speciale Scalzotto, dice bene che conviene 'lasciare la cosa nel campo privato'. Il male è che non è stato fatto. Si è cioè intervenuti allontanando di autorità il giovane su richiesta del padre. È ciò non si doveva fare."*

68   Rappas, "Greeks under European Colonial Rule," 7. "Almost the same, but not quite," is from Homi Bhabha, "Of Mimicry and Man: The Ambivalence of Colonial Discourse," *October* 28, no. 2 (1984): 125–33, 126.

that mixed marriages in the Dodecanese did not present the same problem as ones in East Africa, the "solution" he proposed for this issue followed the same route as other Italian colonies where resettlement helped to mitigate questions of race and colonial sovereignty.[69] Such a proposal coordinated with the resettlement projects and the establishment of agricultural colonies in Rhodes, which commenced under his rule and were grown by De Vecchi's administration. When a mixed relationship did occur, the administration moved to ensure it resulted in marriage, which inevitably implied an Aegean woman's conversion to Catholicism, and also helped to ensure that any children of these marriages were raised as Italians and not Greeks. In an abundance of instances, this negotiation seems to have resulted in a happy arrangement for locals. Italian men could aim to have relationships with women from respected families; they had children who, as Italian citizens, may have also promoted the subtle politics of assimilation that Lago wished to see. But by maintaining its traditional dowry practices, which included the provision of a plot of land to a recently wed couple, locals also acted to ensure that with Aegean women secured traditional and respectable situations and that they did not enter into an arrangement of concubinage.

If the Dodecanese woman embodied the ambivalent political discourse that Italy had toward the Aegean, then she also mediated the Italian state's negotiation of moral and cultural boundaries between Italians and their white and racially similar Aegean subjects. The legend that the Italians tended to choose and marry the "best women" may also point at the subtle colonial hierarchies that were at work within such a negotiation. As Logothetis recalled, a mixed marriage also sometimes meant that an Italian integrated himself into their community, altering the dynamics of assimilation that were evident in other areas of Italian rule. Indeed, it was only later, with the repatriation of Italians during and after the war, that women who married Italians emigrated to Italy. Given that the local communities were also often what anthropologists refer to as "matrilocal," with the mother of the family exerting an enormous power to shape her household and to raise children, the local community also perhaps stood assured that their "best" women would be powerful mediators of the regime's politics. Even if most women who married Italians converted to Catholicism, newlywed couples often settled nearby, under the watchful eye of the bride's family. To be sure, mixed

69 On the relationship between sovereignty and settlement, see Roberta Pergher, *Mussolini's Nation-Empire: Sovereignty and Settlement in Italy's Borderlands, 1922–43* (Cambridge: Cambridge University Press, 2019).

matrimony was still regarded with trepidation by many locals. When probed on the matter, one interviewee, Giorgos Glynatsis, in the village of Emborios on Kalymnos, admitted that though they did on occasion talk about Italians and Greeks as "one face, one race"—mostly because it rhymed—they never would have used that phrase when discussing the much more sensitive topic of mixed marriage.[70]

The way a mixed marriage could also be an occasion for tactical reversal and resilient accommodation of the Fascist state is also evident in local responses to the numerous reforms that Italy eventually put into place concerning local marriage practices. In 1938, Italy extended a new civil code regarding marriage and effectively reneged on its stated commitment to preserve in entirety the civil statute of each of the ethnic communities on the islands. This reform was intended to bring mixed marriage into line with Catholic doctrine. The basic tenets of the law were cohabitation and the rule of patriarchy (*il marito è il capo della famiglia*), but it also prohibited bigamy, a heading under which some authorities included multiple remarriages, and marriage between cousins, or endogamy, a not uncommon occurrence in the Aegean. The reform also clearly meant to undermine the power of local religious institutions and especially Greek Orthodox bishops. Yet the archive documents how locals attempted to revise and resist these reforms. A local *podestà* (mayor) from the village of Istrio (Rhodes), for example, managed to evade the new law when his brother sought to marry a woman who was three times a widow—making it her fourth marriage and the ecclesiastical sin of "quadrigamy." He suggested that the couple pursue a civil matrimony instead, officiated all the same by the local patriarch, whose idea it was.[71] When no authority intervened upon publication of the wedding banns in the local newspaper, the *podestà* allowed the marriage to take place. In this instance, an additional source of anger by the Italian administration, when the marriage eventually came to its attention, lay in the fact that in using the civil ceremony to undertake a marriage that was now, technically, illegal, the patriarch had somehow also managed to collect his usual tax. The local notable had defended his action by explaining that he was used to such civil matrimonies because of his experiences as an immigrant in Australia.

---

70   Interview with Giorgos Glynatsis, August 3, 2011.
71   "My brother told me that he knew of this ecclesiastic impediment and that's why he thought of a civil matrimony as a solution, and he had asked the village pastor, Father Elia Cotiadi, if it was possible to put into place a contract for a civil matrimony instead." GAK DOD, "Mixed Marriages," f. 649/1939.

De Vecchi ultimately agreed to the legitimacy of the marriage and the local *podestà* received no more than a mild slap on the wrist and the admonishment not to repeat such conduct. The absence of severe punishment speaks to the fact that De Vecchi showed himself to be as "liberal" as Lago about not interfering with local practices. But the incident also speaks volumes about the increasing dexterity of locals in evading these so-called "modernizations," which were little more than a pretext to force the state into the everyday life of Dodecanese locals. The response by these Dodecanese keenly exhibits what Certeau calls the "art of making do" and the ability to draw unexpected results from the colonial situation.[72] First, the locals resorted to a concept introduced by the regime itself—civil matrimony—in order to avoid the recently introduced civil code. Second, they then used the civil matrimony to enact the marriage as they might have under Ottoman rule, with the local patriarch collecting his usual tax. And, finally, when all of this came into question by the Fascist authorities, their defense was to refer to another colonial context, in Australia, as the explanation for their methods. This last response was indeed somewhat ingenious, as the Italians were to some degree, in their annexation of the islands as a *possedimento*, informed by the British model of the "dominion."[73] Not only were locals applying Italian laws as they wished, but they were exploiting the loopholes, paradoxes, and ambivalences of Italian rule and bending colonial law to their own economic and social advantage.

The 1938 anti-Semitic race laws also impacted how the Italian state handled the right to marry among other ethnicities and locals. As in East Africa, where, up until the 1935 invasion of Ethiopia, the Italian government had taken no official position on marriages or relationships between Italian settlers and local women, the local government in the Dodecanese had granted metropolitan citizenship to children of such relationships on the basis of patrilinearity, or transmission of citizenship according to fatherhood. But after 1938, in order to obtain a marriage license, it was necessary that both parties show certificates that proved each was of an "Aryan race" (*di razza ariana*). Marriages between Italian persons and foreign persons became

---

72   Michel de Certeau, *The Practice of Everyday Life*, 30.

73   Apart from the British commonwealth there may have been other models for the dominion type of rule closer to the Aegean. See Sally McKee, *Uncommon Dominion: Venetian Crete and the Myth of Ethnic Purity* (Philadelphia: University of Pennsylvania Press, 2000) and Thomas Gallant, *Experiencing Dominion: Culture, Identity, and Power in the British Mediterranean* (Notre Dame, IN: University of Notre Dame Press, 2002).

subject to the regulation and approval of the Interior Ministry in Rome, and the procedure for obtaining civil matrimony was altered, undermining the power of the local church and ensuring that the Interior Ministry in Rome had the right to approve or deny all mixed marriages.

By these measures Italy affirmed that Italian Aegean nationals were subject to new regulations on race while the "*jus connubii*, or right to marry, would not be denied them, only limited in its extent."[74] This treatment of civil statuses illustrates what Davide Rodogno has identified as the special role of the Dodecanese archipelago in the construction of Italian Empire, and the ways in which the islands may have served as a juridical model for later territorial conquests in Albania and the Dalmatian coast.[75] Rodogno's theory of the Aegean as a "small space," linked to the overarching idea of the empire as a *spazio vitale* for the Italian nation—the Fascist equivalent of the Nazi party's concept of Lebensraum—seems mostly based on the various suggestions, found in archival documents, put forward by Fascist ideologues as to how best to utilize the archipelago for imperial plans, not many of which were enacted. For example, Rodogno mentions the proposition of one ideologue that all of the local inhabitants of the Dodecanese be expelled in order to make space for Italian colonialists. Such an event never occurred, and its suggestion does not reflect the very limited scope of resettlement projects that eventually took place in the Aegean. As in other areas of its rule, Fascist ideologues presented ideas that were far more ambitious than practicable; and, clearly, many proposals were rooted in larger debates about the nature of Italian sovereignty in the Aegean and related to the extent to which the islands should be considered as part of national Italy.

The numerous instances of mixed marriage that did occur in the Dodecanese reveal that it was a complex site of negotiation, both on the part of the Italian state and on the part of the local population. Although the Italian state's policy was to endorse mixed marriages, every petition for a mixed matrimony generated new questions about the standing of the bride's family, as well as, on some occasions, the quality of the Italian soldier who wished to be groom. There was never at any point during Italian rule a simple

74 Davide Rodogno, *Fascism's European Empire: Italian Occupation during the Second World War* (Cambridge: Cambridge University Press, 2006), 66.
75 "Italy's colonial experiences in Libya, Africa Orientale Italiana (AOI, Italian East Africa), Albania and its Aegean possessions (the Dodecanese) determined the constitutional framework of the territories conquered after 1940 and influenced the organization of their governments and administrations"; Rodogno, *Fascism's European Empire*, 42.

formula for how to manage mixed marriage, and with more reforms came more complications. And questions about the effects of mixed marriage on the social fabric of the local environment remained an enduring feature of Italian rule.

Brava or *Cattiva Gente*: Italian and Fascist States

While resettlement and the expansion of the Fascist corporatist state in the Aegean was not originally envisioned for the islands, such projects inevitably emerged after the Ethiopian war, the resulting sanctions against Italy, and the Fascist state's subsequent ambition to achieve "autarchy" or independence of Italian production from international trade. As Nicola Labanca has observed, a defining trait of the Italian colonial project was its commitment to exporting the corporatist welfare state to its colonies abroad.[76] The Dodecanese were no exception and the regime made several efforts at promoting agriculture and industry on the islands. All local people employed in these new sectors of the economy were encouraged to join the Opera Nazionale Dopolavoro (OND). As Victoria De Grazia has shown, the OND was an important arm of the Fascist state and was instrumental to courting consent for the Fascist dictatorship and for drawing ordinary people into the Fascist state as a transformative revolution.[77]

Even as the islands became a theater for impending expansionist wars and witnessed a buildup of Italian armed forces, the regime attempted to promote industry and land-reclamation projects aimed at industrialization and sought to draw skilled and unskilled labor into these projects. Haralambo Stamatis, of Kos island, was thrilled at the opportunity to have paid work to support his family and he eventually became a card-carrying member of the OND, even though he was not yet eighteen years old.[78] On the other hand, Leonidas Diakoyiannis, also of the western end of Kos, refused to join the OND, seeing it as tantamount to joining the Fascist party. In his view, not

---

76   As Nicola Labanca describes, *"una definizione circolò negli ultimi anni del fascismo: quella del colonialismo italiano come 'impero di lavoro'. Per questa ragione, nella retorica del regime, quell'impero avrebbe dovuto essere diverso dagli altri, 'plutocratici' e 'rapaci', delle potenze liberali."* Nicola Labanca, *Oltremare: Storia dell'espansione coloniale italiana* (Bologna: Il mulino, 2002), 308.

77   Victoria De Grazia, *The Culture of Consent: Mass Organization of Leisure in Fascist Italy* (Cambridge: Cambridge University Press, 1981).

78   Interview with Haralambo Stamatis (Χαραλαμπο Στατματτις), March 31, 2013.

joining the Fascist party yet still working for the Italian government was something to be proud about—no doubt because it foregrounded his agency even in a situation of profound limitations. Diakoyiannis had specialized engineering training and he later worked as a lead engineer on the project to build an Italian navy base in Leros. During his interview, he expressed great satisfaction that in in this role he had been able to demonstrate to the Italian line management—a Sicilian, he specified—that he was both skilled and politically astute enough to work for and be paid by the Fascist state at the same time that he actively evaded it.[79]

The arrival of two major Italian companies, TEMI and CAIR, which produced tobacco and wine on the islands led to numerous jobs for local Dodecanese people; still others became employed in reforestation and agricultural projects.[80] By the mid-1930s, while the islands were under the administration of Lago, the Italian state began organizing the resettlement of foresters from Northern Italy into the agricultural regions of Rhodes.[81] Forced to reconcile their knowledge of the underlying cultural assimilation project that had characterized the Lago period with these newer schemes to make the Dodecanese a model for expanding corporatist empire in the Mediterranean, locals now faced questions about how they would deal with the extraordinary changes brought by industrialization, land reclamation, and resettlement of agricultural settlers from Italy. In effect, these changes intensified pressure on Dodecanese Greeks to become actors in the new imperial economy and put local persons who were benefiting from the regime in a much more difficult position, and one much more subject to scrutiny from their local community. Within this setting, the splitting in memory between "Italian" as opposed to "Fascist" rule, and between Italians as *brava* or *cattiva gente*, as "familiar" people or "others," seems to respond to these dilemmas and pressures, which increased in the late 1930s. In many ways, this binary mirrors back the Italian colonial gaze, which alternatively imagined Greeks as fraternal actors or "cousins" in the new colonial project and as strangers and Levantine others.

Locating Italians within such an ambivalent, if mirroring, discourse, suggests that for Aegean subjects, anger at and trepidation of Italians were

79   Interview with Leonidas Diakoyiannis, Kefalos, Kos, March 30, 2013.

80   TEMI stood for Tabacchi Egei Manifattura Italiana and CAIR stands for Compagnia Agricola Industriale Rodi. The latter company is still in business today as a local wine company in Rhodes.

81   See Renzo Groselli, *Gli uomini del legno sull'Isola delle rose: La vicenda storica del villaggio italiano di Campochiaro a Rodi: 1935–1947* (Trento: Curcu Genovese, 2018).

accompanied by desires to accommodate, benefit, and establish comfortable boundaries with Italian settlers and administrative actors. Locals are keen to emphasize that not all Italians were good, but stories about the "good" Italians often provide important narrative clues as to how Dodecanese Greeks were able to relate to their Italian colonists and, at times, to be successful in transcending cultural differences and the colonial hierarchies that informed Fascist rule.

The new economic policies brought not only reforestation and agricultural programs, but also many Italian agricultural workers from Bolzano and Trento to carry them out. These labor projects were important sites of contact and fraternization between Italian colonizers and Dodecanese subjects. Pinos Christos remembers that though there was some tension between Italian agricultural workers and Greek Dodecanese persons—because the Italians were enacting the regime's policy of land expropriation—residents were also able to establish certain qualities as familiar.[82] The rural ways of these Italian colonizers made them similar to Greek peasants. On the island of Kalymnos, Giorgos Glynatsis remembers how the Italians arrived in 1937 and prepared the land for extensive farming. The speed with which they accomplished their task was quite impressive to him and a sign of Italian ingenuity—he felt that his community in Kalymnos might be able to learn new farming strategies from their Italian colonists. Modernization is another important trope that counteracts negative memories of Fascist rule. Glynatsis, for example, remembers that his father had gone to Leros as a manual laborer for the construction of the port, and had returned telling of the impressive speed with which construction of an entirely new city had taken place there. Italians were builders and workers.[83]

In the words of Manoles Despotakis, "Italy tried to make Rhodes into something great." Even though he was aware of the repressive political machinery that propelled these attempts at development and assimilation, he nevertheless admitted to a degree of awe about the ambitious scale of the renovation and industrial projects.[84] Ippokrates Logothetis remembers how the Italian army reconfigured the island of Tilos by laying cement on one of its most beautiful beaches in order to ready the harbor for military operations. While this was a negative event in the history of Tilos, it was nevertheless another example of the way in which Italians were industrious. The same

---

82   Interview with Pinos Christos, Rhodes Island, July 26, 2010.
83   Interview with Giorgos Glynatsis, Kalymnos Island, August 10, 2010.
84   Interview with Manoles Despotakis, Rhodes Island, July 24, 2009.

Figure 4.2: The Empire of Work: Italian Fascists oversee construction of the port in the island of Kalymnos © Archive Touring Club Italiano.

sort of ambivalent discourse characterizes Logothetis's recollection of Mario Lago: "He was a great politician! So great that he was dangerous to us Greeks. With the mouth that he had, with the politics that he made, he convinced many to become Italians and to take Italian citizenship."[85]

Public narratives about the wartime period seem also to have helped shape narrative strategies for squaring the benefits of Italian rule with its repressive Fascist policies. The memoir of Giannis Sakellaridi, an enduring public figure of Kalymnos who had worked as an employee of the Italian tobacco firm TEMI, illustrates the ways in which many Dodecanese persons felt they had to justify their choices under Fascist rule and to distance any perception that they had been co-opted. In his memoir, published in a local history in 1986, Sakellaridi notes approvingly that under Lago's rule, the city of Rhodes was transformed into a cosmopolitan place with elegant buildings.[86] At the same time, Sakellaridi frames his employment for TEMI as at least potentially an act of resistance, since by working for the Italian government he was able

85   Interview with Ippokrates Logothetis, Tilos Island, August 9, 2009.
86   G.M. Sakellaridi, "Antonio Ritelli," in *Kalymniaká Chronika*, vol. 6 (Athens: Anagnōstērio Kalymnu Hai Musai, 1986), 151–69.

to remain in the archipelago instead of emigrating as many of his educated compatriots had done.[87] Sakellaridi's essay on Antonio Ritelli, one of the last Italian *podestàs* of the island of Kalymnos, is revealing of how distinctions between "good" and "bad" Italians were put to service to make the case for such internal resistance, as well as to distance the perception that, by working for the imperial state, a person had in any way been coopted or had acquiesced to the regime's political ideology. In his portrait of Ritelli, Sakellaridi seeks not only to create a "human" bond but also to construct Ritelli, a Fascist official at the time, as nevertheless an example of "light in the midst of the thick darkness of the Fascistic bestial force." His description of Ritelli mirrors his description of his own stance on Fascist rule as resisting it while remaining within it.[88]

In 1938 when Italy consolidated its corporatist empire and these companies underwent structural changes, all employees of the TEMI cooperative lost their shares in the company and were demoted to low-grade agricultural workers for the Italian monopoly. According to Sakellaridi, Ritelli was removed from his post in 1939 because of his attempt to rescue the local shareholders of the TEMI tobacco company. When Ritelli was forcibly removed from the island under the cover of night, it was his punishment, by the Fascists, for the "humanity" of these latter actions.[89] Interestingly, Sakelleridi's story of Antonio Ritelli seems to mirror many of the rhetorical strategies that ultimately defined memories of Fascism in Italy in later decades, with its emphasis on the "color blind" and "humanizing" nature of the regime.

Sakellaridi's portrait of Ritelli adopts the long history of nineteenth-century Italian nationalism, one that is well known in the islands, for the purpose of representing an anti-Fascist position in the 1930s. He recounts that just before Ritelli was forced off the islands, he gave Sakellaridi a copy of Silvio Pellico's *Le mie prigioni*, the story of the Italian resistance of the Austro-Hungarian dominance. The gift is emblematic of how Sakellaridi imagined his resistance as sometimes silently shared among Italians and Dodecanese locals. Sakellaridi recounts how, through this gift—concealed inside an envelope—Ritelli was able to communicate the "goodness" of his people, and

---

87   Nicholas Doumanis has argued that Sakellaridi formulated an idea of patriotism that consisted not in putting up formal resistance but in "foiling Italy's wish to rid the Dodecanese of its potential leaders." Doumanis, *Myth and Memory in the Mediterranean*, 120.

88   "φωτεινό σημάδι μέσα στο πυκνό σκολάδι της φασιστικής κτηνωδοθς βιας"; Sakellaridi, "Antonio Ritelli."

89   Sakellaridi, "Antonio Ritelli."

his understanding of the situation at that time being lived by the Kalymnian people: "I thought that I was living in a dream. Ritelli was incarnating the human being in its most divine form. Ritelli was incarnating the good sides of his country that had managed to understand deeply the resistant behavior of the Kalymnians, their irredentist behavior. The Kalymnian defiance of authority, their mood and behavior of the wild horse." The symbolism of Sakellaridi's narrative is clear: Ritelli's parting gift conveyed not only that Sakellaridi should know his desire to resist the Fascist state internally was a noble one, but also that even the Fascists were fundamentally anti-Fascists. Sakellaridi seems to echo the way the Fascist past was transformed, in Italy, into an aberration in Italian culture, along the lines of Benedetto Croce's famous assertion that Fascism was merely a "parenthesis" between the Risorgimento and the Resistance.[90] Sakelleridi also notes that Kalymnians had nourished many Italian cultural gifts prior to the Fascist state, describing the 1904 establishment of a reading group called the Café Italia, and the efforts of a certain Alekos Andreis, a Kalymnian who had fought alongside Garibaldi, to bring Italian theater to the island.[91] By describing Ritelli's acts of "internal" humanity, Sakellaridi also subtly deflects attention in his memoir from his own position as someone who worked for and cooperated with the Fascist state, suggesting an alibi of "internal resistance" for the political cooption that such employment probably suggested to others.

Following patterns that similarly recall the memory of Fascism in Italy, some of Sakellaridi's anecdotes about the Italian era in the island of Kalymnos show support of Italian Fascism's cultural and social values, while marking these as separate from Fascism as a political and imperial project in the islands—although scholarship has made clear that the cultural and social

---

90 For some interesting discussions of the temporality of Benedetto Croce's claim that Fascism was a "parentheses" and the way it directs back to the more humane form of nationalism that preceded it, see Angela Dalle Vacche, *The Body in the Mirror: Shapes of History in Italian Cinema* (Princeton, NJ: Princeton University Press, 1992); Claudio Fogu, *The Historic Imaginary: Politics of History in Fascist Italy* (Toronto: University of Toronto Press, 2003); and Philip Morgan, *Fascism in Europe, 1919–45* (Abingdon, VA: Routledge, 2007).

91 While it is outside the bounds of this study, Dodecanesians' knowledge about Italy's nineteenth-century nationalist movements is certainly worth acknowledging; it speaks both to the inherently transnational and global dimensions of nineteenth-century nationalism, and to the particular ebb and flow of these movements within the Mediterranean region. Maurizio Isabella and Konstantina Zanou, *Mediterranean Diasporas: Politics and Ideas in the Long Nineteenth Century* (London: Bloomsbury, 2016)

values of Italian Fascism were deeply entwined with its political objectives. Rather than consider Fascism's broad stranglehold on culture and society during the dictatorship, Sakellaridi describes how Ritelli, as *podestà*, carried out policies that aimed to reinforce local traditions and stringent local gender mores. One example concerns the custom in Kalymnos that men and women should bathe in the sea separately, with a wall separating their bathing areas; when some eager men climbed the wall so as to spy on the women's beach and a local doctor complained about this breach of local custom, Ritelli authorized the police to apprehend anyone who violated this rule. While Sakellaridi relates this story to show how Ritelli had "made a real effort to understand the local culture," and hints at a favorable view of the Fascist regime of law and order. Declaring that Ritelli "put administrative weight behind enforcing local customs," Sakellaridi concludes that the island was therefore better off for having such a *podestà*.

Sakellaridi ultimately enjoins his readers to engage in a selective memory of the Fascist past: the "good" Italians, like Ritelli, must be kept alive in Dodecanese memory, in comparison with the "blackshirts," who, he suggests, should be forgotten. The binary between "Italian," as a signifier of the positive virtues of nationalism—that is, culture and progress—and "Fascist," as a signifier of violence and colonial domination over Greek identity and culture has in these ways been important to creating a selective memory of Italian rule in the islands. For the most part, while many locals may seek to narrate the period with balance, the aspects of the period that were useful and beneficial to them are referred to as "Italian," while those that were culturally repressive were "Fascist." Locals refer to "Italian" buildings, for example, but "Fascist" politics. They are also more than willing to differentiate between "good" and "bad" Italians. The idea of the "good" Italian can include culture, modernization, and sometimes cosmopolitanism but is just as often vague and mutable.

To be sure, not all Italians were "good," but those that were "bad" have additional labels. Oral informants speak of "Italians with a tail" (*Italiani con la coda"*), who collaborated and cooperated closely with the Fascist state. This derogative expression indicated the "Latin" or Italophone population that did not directly hail from Italy, but from other parts of the Mediterranean, and who had found beneficial positions in the regime, the so-called Franco-Levantine community, that is, the wealthy European merchant class of the nineteenth-century Ottoman state, especially those hailing from Egypt and Turkey, who took part in the Fascist state in the islands. Manoles Despotakis remembers that "there was not one good Franco-Levantine" and that, at the end of the war, a certain Franco-Levantine named Mario was made by the village of Archangelos to wear a Greek flag and to march through the main square shouting, *"Viva la Grecia!"*[92] While such "bad" Italians are still alive and well in some cases, narratives tend to use distinct language to refer to them, variously invoking the terms "Fascist," "Levantine," or an "Italian with a tail." In invoking the little-studied community of Franco-Levantines, Despotakis also hints at the fact that the Italian Empire overlapped with Italy's own history of emigration in the Mediterranean region—thus destabilizing many of its best efforts to construct a homogeneous idea of Italian national identity or *italianità*. In some instances, Greek patterns of migration that overlapped with Italian ones also contributed to this softening of Italian culture and its distance from Fascism. Haralambo Stamatis of Kos, for example, explained that his father already spoke some Italian because he had migrated to Argentina at the turn of the century, and was therefore more inclined to accept the idea that his son would learn Italian at school.[93]

In a similar vein, much of the discussion about familiarity and fraternization with Italian soldiers or administrators—the legend that Italians and Greeks were like "one face, one race"—might be reframed as a means by which the occupied were able to narrate their recognition of the weakening of the Fascist state. Mihales Katzinikolas's version of a commonplace about fraternization among Italians and Greeks shows how imagining friendship often helped diminish the potential threat of the occupying army: "Poor soldiers. They were not so loved by the local population because they were foreigners, but every so often they arrived at the café to have some conversation. We were almost friends. We saw that these soldiers were Mediterranean people like us. We shared ouzo and wine, and we sang."[94] Katzinikolas carefully tempers his description: it was not so much that Italians and Greeks were friends as that they were *almost* friends (*"eravamo quasi amici"*), and this enabled Greeks to demystify the strangeness of these foreigners. There were also definite limits to this friendship and, if early in the war on occasion they were to speak of politics, after Italy declared war on Greece in 1940, all such fraternization ended.

---

92 Interview with Manoles Despotakis, Rhodes Island, July 24, 2009.
93 Interview with Haralambo Stamatis (Χαράλαμπο Στατματτις), March 31, 2013.
94 *"Poveri soldati. Non erano tanto amati dalla popolazione perché erano stranieri, ma ogni tanto arrivano al caffè per fare qualche conversazione. Eravamo quasi amici. Abbiamo visto che questi soldati era gente mediterranea come noi, abbiamo diviso dell'ouzo, vino, cantavamo."* Interview in Italian with Mihales Katzinikolas, Rhodes Island, July 26, 2009.

Katzinikolas nevertheless invokes an idea of *"gente mediterranea"* when speaking of the Italian occupiers—that cliché of the Mediterranean as a site of shared histories and traditions. While the idea of *"gente mediterranea"* that Katzinikolas invokes is certainly not the Mediterranean Empire that Italy had sought to construct during its twenty-year rule of the archipelago, his allusion to a social (and often socialist) Mediterranean is not entirely adrift from some of the meanings that the Fascists ascribed to the word. By imagining their colonizers as similar to them, locals implicitly placed Italians in the same subaltern group—that is, Southern, emigrant, or even Levantine—that they felt themselves to be in with respect to the idea of Europe. It is also true that Dodecanese locals believed themselves keen observers of the histrionics and rhetoric of Fascist rule and remain proud, for example, of the fact that they were able to discern between Fascist officials and members of the *fanteria*, or army. As Katzinikolas describes, it was easy to tell a Fascist by his uniform, his beret, and his boots. An Italian, on the other hand, was recognizable by his powerlessness with respect to the Fascist state.

Yet as much as Dodecanese residents are keen to tell stories about Italian rule, there is still silence and sensitivity about the era. Popular myths of fraternization among Italian occupiers and Dodecanese occupied may obscure more sinister undertones. In the context of one interview, in which I showed a photograph of a road being built on Kalymnos in the mid-1930s, an informant pointed to one man and said "he was very Fascist," then immediately asked that I redact this statement, as people concerned are still alive. Do popular myths like "one face, one race" serve to conceal other, more difficult discussions about consent and consensus for Fascist rule on the islands? When probed, locals were sometimes more willing to abandon pretenses to Greek patriotism and said more about how relations between Italians and locals navigated shifting political alliances as well as about the complex legacies of Fascism that unfolded after the war. Ippokrates Logothetis remembered that his schoolteacher, a certain Nicholas Morphopos, had gone to Pisa to study Italian language and culture and eventually acquired full Italian citizenship after completing military service on the island of Leros. Logothetis believed himself "lucky" to have had a teacher with so much knowledge of Italian culture, but he also reflected that some of Morphopos's behavior constituted collaboration, or at a minimum, opportunism. His admiration for Morphopos was mixed with contempt, in what is a typical expression of ambivalence in local judgments of Fascist rule.

Logothetis also recalled how during the military operations of 1939 Morphopos helped the Fascist army to secure the island. Yet later, after the Italian armistice with the Allies and the eventual English invasion, Morphopos also assisted the British in learning where the Fascists had held their arsenals around the island—weapons that could now be used against the Germans.[95] Whether it was because he ultimately shifted to the cause of the victors, or because there was simply an absence of discussion about the Fascist period on the islands, Morphopos retained his position of prestige in the postwar context and obtained a coveted position in local government with a guaranteed salary and pension. Logothetis remembered with some acrimony that his uncle, who did not at any point benefit from paid jobs provided by the regime and had not collaborated, was passed over for the same job. Logothetis's memory is a counternarrative to the one that says that teachers during the period of Italian rule became petty bourgeois patriots who guided Dodecanesians toward discovering their national consciousness.[96] This anecdote also invites more serious study of how the German, then British (Allied) occupation, and the ensuing Greek civil war have impacted and reshaped the memory of Italian Fascist rule in the islands.

We must also concede that, as in Italy, the Fascist regime may have been impressive to locals at some moments—despite its clearly colonial and repressive apparatus. It is not uncommon to hear Dodecanese locals talk about the awe they felt when watching airplanes land on the water in the harbor of Rhodes or attending the elaborate parades that marked the Ethiopian invasion. Dodecanese residents often recall how the Italian period was one when "things were accomplished" or even more frequently, "περάσαμε καλά," meaning, "we lived well." Such beliefs are not receding with the passing of the generation that lived under Fascist rule; on the contrary, they have regained social currency in the current climate of prolonged economic and political crisis in Greece. Locals will frequently explain that, while there were both "good" and "bad" Italians, the general conditions were certainly better in comparison to today, when taxes are paid to the Greek state and no subsidies

---

95   As was also true in Italy, a parallel civil war between Fascists and Italian forces who had changed sides after the armistice occurred within the islands in 1943–45. See Luca Pignataro, "Le isole italiane dell'Egeo dall'8 settembre 1943 al termine della seconda guerra mondiale," *Clio, rivista trimestrale di studi storici* 37, no. 3 (2001): 465–552.

96   Doumanis claims that "from 1912 to 1943, after their [uppermost echelons of Dodecanesian society's] efforts had completely failed, the nationalist struggle was carried on by petit bourgeois patriots, particularly primary school teachers. Their patriotic duty was to provide leadership and inculcate political awareness among the common folk"; Doumanis, *Myth and Memory in the Mediterranean*, 101.

or support are seen in return. In 2013, as part of a broad slate of reforms Greece required to undertake by the EU in exchange for the restructuring of part of their sovereign debt, the entire country of Greece, with the exception of the Dodecanese prefecture, began the painstaking process of establishing property titles. Thanks to the Italians, locals in the Dodecanese explained at that time, the Dodecanese prefecture had a cadaster in place and, for once, this periphery was *ahead of* and not *behind* the rest of Greece.[97] This positive view of the modernization undertaken by the Italians is also echoed in discussions of tourism, the one healthy economy in the islands. Yet each time such innovations are indicated, it is the "Italians" who were authors, never the "Fascists." Praise for the innovations of the regime can thus exist on the same plane as heroic narratives about local nationalism and the patriotic spirit that resisted attempts to assimilate locals through an occlusion of the Fascist nature of occupation. The silences and omissions required to maintain this duality are striking.

And yet, as this chapter has demonstrated, there were also many small but verifiable cases of resistance to the Fascist state. Locals did eventually find numerous ways of evading and creatively reworking assimilation projects and the attempt of the Fascist state to root itself in their daily lives—in religious and civil matters, in their education, and in questions of labor and livelihood. If stereotypes about Mediterranean cultural unity were essential to the ways in which Italian Empire sought to reinforce Italian nationalism and fascism, these same stereotypes of cultural, and to a certain extent, racial familiarity were apprehended, questioned, revised, accommodated, and appropriated by locals. Italian policies and local attitudes toward mixed marriage offer a revealing example of how the statist intervention into life in the Aegean was always complex. While the Italian administration was still wary of the moral, and later, the racial degradation that might result from the proliferation of mixed matrimonies, it sought a course in policy that might legitimize mixed marriages, and in turn, promote the continuing program of cultural imperialism in the Aegean. At the same time, the local community's acceptance of these mixed marriages speaks to the ways in which locals dealt with the Fascist state not only by resisting, but also sometimes by accommo-dating, while striving to maintain their own cultural identities and traditions within the framework of Italian rule. If the imperial fantasy of cultural unity has persisted in popular memory, we can only presume that this owes itself,

97   Suzanne Daley, "Who Owns This Land? In Greece, Who Knows?" *The New York Times*, May 26, 2013.

at least partly, to the success of Fascist state-building projects to draw the local population into the nationalist and nostalgic character of its rule. On the other hand, as numerous interviewees attested, such Mediterraneanism lent itself to creative reworking and inspired novel ways of evading the relentless expansion of the Fascist state. These tactical reversals, as this book's conclusion will next discuss, have formed the basis of an enduring memory of Fascism that emerged in the Aegean in the decades after the war.

Conclusion: Postcolonial Returns

Italy overcame formidable barriers to forging an overseas empire—belated nationhood, internal fragmentation, and low standing within circles of international diplomacy, but the abrupt loss of most of this empire, a little-remarked result of Italy's 1943 armistice with the Allies, in some ways has proven one of its most consequential legacies. If the postwar period in Italy gave rise to a *rimozione,* or repression, and a reframing of Fascism as a period when all Italians were anti-Fascists (even those who were Fascists), a similar dynamic is often found at work in the cultural memory of Italian Empire. The myth of *Italiani brava gente,* or Italians as "good people," has not only shaped Italian memory of Fascism, but also seems to have influenced a wider, transnational recollection of it within its former colonial settings.[1]

Notions of Italian-style European Fascism have helped to soft-pedal the Italian Empire. Even before it was established in scholarship that Italy had a significant empire, that project had come to be understood as different from other empires, as having a "national" character, and as so idiosyncratic as to resist all ordinary memorialization. Some observers have called this

---

1   See Daniela Baratieri, *Memories and Silences Haunted by Fascism: Italian Colonialism MCMXXX–MCMLX* (Bern: Peter Lang, 2001); Cristina Lombardi-Diop and Caterina Romeo, "Italy's Postcolonial 'Question': Views from the Southern Frontier of Europe," *Postcolonial Studies* 18, no. 4 (2015): 367–83; Nicola Labanca, "Colonial Rule, Colonial Repression and War Crimes in the Italian Colonies," *Journal of Modern Italian Studies* 9, no. 3 (2004): 300–13; Irma Taddia, *La memoria dell'Impero: Autobiografie d'Africa Orientale* (Manduria: P. Lacaita, 1998); David Bidussa, *Il mito del bravo italiano* (Milan: Il Saggiatore, 1994); Angelo Del Boca, *Italiani, brava gente: Un mito duro a morire* (Vicenza: Neri Pozza, 2005); Pam Ballinger, "Borders of the Nation, Borders of Citizenship: Italian Repatriation and the Redefinition of National Identity after World War II," *Comparative Studies in Society and History* 49, no. 3 (2007): 713–41; and Stephanie Malia Hom, *Empire's Mobius Strip: Historical Echoes in Italy's Crisis of Migration and Detention* (Ithaca, NY: Cornell University Press, 2019).

phenomenon an "amnesia" about Italy's colonial past, but it might more rightly be understood as a selective memory.[2] As the last chapter showed, in the Aegean, memories of Italian Empire attempt to accommodate the ways in which Italian Empire was an important (indeed, extraordinary) part of their history. Such a point of view operates in the face of the perception that Italy never even had an empire to begin with. It is in this sense—a defiance of the idea that Italy was not a colonial power—that one might contextualize what there is of a memory of Italian imperialism in Italy as well. Signs of the imperial past are everywhere in Italian urban spaces and culture, from the chillingly rationalist "square coliseum" in the EUR district of Rome, built to commemorate the conquest of Ethiopia, to the horribly racist song "Facetta Nera" ("Little Black Face"), whose tune can still be caught as a cellphone ringtone. Italian colonies in Eritrea, Libya, and Albania—and last but not least, the Dodecanese—are present within popular culture while being conspicuously absent from the history of modern Italy that is commonly taught in school.

Italy's continuous rule in the Aegean Sea may appear as one of the most glaring examples of "memory loss" in the historical memory of empire; on the other hand, the Aegean has returned within the cultural memory of Italian Empire within the context of new postcolonial conditions.

For most of the postwar period, Italian ambitions in the Balkans were comparatively much better known than Italian rule in the Aegean. Mussolini's notorious 1939 call to *"spezzare i reni della Grecia"* (to break the kidneys of Greece), which encapsulates these, shows how the memory of Italian designs for expansion in the Balkans is often knit together with the larger, much more dramatic memory of World War II. Perhaps as a consequence of this, studies of the Italian annexation of the Balkans focus more on the links between expansion in Italy's borderlands and the Balkans, and tend to overlook how a major colonization in the southeast Aegean anticipated the Fascist state's 1940 advance on Greece.[3] As chapter 1 showed, a similar deficit can be found

---

2   Michele Battini and Stanislao Pugliese, *The Missing Italian Nuremberg: Cultural Amnesia and Postwar Politics* (New York: Palgrave MacMillan, 2007); and Karen Pinkus, "Empty Spaces: Decolonization in Italy," in *A Place in the Sun: Africa in Italian Colonial Culture from Post-unification to the Present,* edited by Patrizia Palumbo, 299–320 (Berkeley: University of California Press, 2003).

3   See, for example, Glenda Sluga, *The Problem of Trieste and the Italo-Yugoslav Border: Difference, Identity and Sovereignty in 20th Century Europe* (Albany, NY: State University Press, 2001). An exception to this tradition of linking the Balkans with Northeastern Italy is the more recent research that ties the Balkans to the Aegean, see Andreas Guidi,

in studies of the Italian colonization in Africa in the nineteenth century; although recent scholars have offered rich new perspectives on how the issues of nation and race that defined the Liberal-era's project of colonization may anticipate those that defined the Fascist state's colonization of Africa, they have not examined in much detail how the "scramble for Africa" occurred alongside another scramble, that is, the ambition for territories in the Balkans and North Africa under Ottoman decline.

A further problem of the historical memory of the Aegean relates to the way in which the islands are today part of Greece but were not so at the time of Italian rule. The islands were integrated with Greece in 1947, after two years of nominal control by the British Empire. The unusual, post-Ottoman (but still Ottoman-like) quality of this insular setting makes it difficult to include as part of the history of the Italian occupation of the Balkans and Greece. Using Greek national history as a frame of reference elides how, in 1912, a multiethnic population of Greeks, Turks, and Jews inhabited the islands and conjured up fantasies that Italians had inadvertently stumbled onto an old Levantine world. To acknowledge that complex imaginary challenges widespread conventions of the writing of history according to the boundaries of the nation-state.

If Italian rule in the Dodecanese is thus especially absent from history of European Empire or Europe during World War II, the contours of Italian history certainly have not helped to remedy this gap. With the exception of Luca Pignataro's recent studies, the Dodecanese is not automatically viewed as part of Italy's colonial history; by the same token when included as part of Italy's wartime history, it enjoys the status of being a little-known and obscure chapter.[4] Tellingly, one Italian language history of the occupation is titled *Isole dimenticate* (Forgotten Islands). This book focuses on how part of the Italian army was "massacred" during the German occupation of the islands after 1943.[5] It fails to seriously consider how the islands were brought into an ambitious Italian agenda of empire in the Mediterranean, how rule in the islands aligned with issues of emigration and diaspora in Italian culture, and

"Youth and Generations between Two Empires: Changing Sociabilities from Ottoman to Italian Rule in Rhodes," PhD diss., Paris: Université Paris Sciences et Letters, 2018.

4   Luca Pignataro, *Il Dodecaneso italiano, 1912–1947* (Chieti: Solfanelli, 2011). Nicola Labanca also dedicates one chapter to the Aegean in *Oltremare* (Bologna: Il mulino, 2007).

5   Ettore Vittorini, *Isole dimenticate: Il Dodecaneso da Giolitti al massacro del 1943* (Florence: Le Lettere, 2002).

the extent to which Italy invested in the local economy and culture so as to reproduce its own nationalist and Fascist narratives of national regeneration.

In contrast with this lack of historical inquiry, well-known representations of Italian rule have made the Aegean into somewhat of a fixture within Italian popular culture. Gabriele Salvatores's hit film *Mediterraneo* is doubtless the most well-known one. The film, which won the Academy Award for best foreign film for its revival of the genre of Italian film comedy in 1990, is about a platoon of inept Italian soldiers who, marooned on a Greek island "of zero strategic importance," lose all touch with World War II. The film's plot therefore seems to rehearse the very "forgetting" that has been so central to the creation of a selective memory of the Italian colonial empire. As Clarissa Clò has observed, adopting the Dodecanese as a setting at that time provided a timely frame of reference, as Italy had just begun to confront the first waves of immigration from the Balkans.[6] Shot on location in Kastellorizo, the postage stamp-size island off the coast of Turkey, the film also engages viewers as an advertisement for touring the Greek islands. The film has eventually inspired a veritable boom in the local Kastellorizan economy of tourism, with travelers, especially Italian ones, arriving by the droves, hoping to connect with the "authenticity" of the landscape as portrayed in the film.[7]

Much as hundreds of thousands of Italian travelers were primed for a "cinematic" encounter with Rhodes (to use the words of Maria Benzoni who traveled to the island in 1935), thanks to the careful ways in which the Italian state had crafted markers of "Levantineness" into the built environment, Italian viewers are likely to recognize the film's plot as "authentic," thanks to the ways in which it draws on familiar markers about Italian national identity, especially that of the *inetto*, or the inept Italian. As Millicent Marcus has written in her essay on the film, *Mediterraneo* "builds a bridge between the 1990s generation and its predecessor."[8] It is, in other words, a very strong testimonial of the revising of Italian wartime history in the 1990s. Salvatores drew clearly on the familiar narrative that Italians were anti-Fascists. Based on Renzo Biasion's anti-Fascist, neorealist novel about the Italian

---

6   Clarissa Clò, "Mediterraneaneo Interrupted: Perils and Potentials of Representing Italy's Occupations in Greece and Libya Through Film," *Italian Culture* 27, no. 2 (2009): 99–115.

7   See Angelina Carpovich, "Theoretical Approaches to Film-Motivated Tourism," *Journal of Tourism and Hospitality Planning and Development* 7, no. 1 (2010): 7–20.

8   Millicent Marcus, *After Fellini: National Cinema in the Postmodern Age* (Baltimore: Johns Hopkins Press, 2002), 76–93, 86.

occupation of Crete in 1941–43, *The Army I Love You (Sagapò)*, the film offers its characters a choice between staying committed to the state or dropping out and "resisting from within"; all of the characters ultimately choose the latter and adopt the position of making love and not war. One protagonist even takes to painting watercolors of the Greek landscape to pass the time in a manner that recalls Carlo Levi during his internment as an anti-Fascist in Lucania, immortalized in his memoir, *Cristo si è fermato a Eboli*. If much of the film's success seems to reside in its ability to draw on familiar tropes of Italian national history and identity, another part of its appeal certainly resides in its celebration of Italy's colonial past. The film's suggestion of a Mediterranean brotherhood—invoking and reminding Italian audiences of the *una faccia, una razza* cliché—fits in with the way that contemporary Italians, as they confront immigration, tends to deny the fact that race is part of Italian culture.[9]

As I have argued in this book, the "one face, one race" tagline is a historical formation, one that spoke at the time to the subtle and often unstable ideas about nation and race that accompanied the imperial era in Italy. It expressed the belief that Italians were rooted in the Mediterranean, as in the anthropological investigations of Giuseppe Sergi, with his assertion that a Greco-Roman "stock" settled in (or colonized) the Italian Peninsula. Salvatores's film constitutes not so much a "repression" or an "amnesia" about Italy's colonial past, then, as an important return to cultural and ideological formations that were at the core of the Italian state's ideas about its empire in Africa and the Mediterranean. Although Italian rule in the Aegean is conspicuously absent from the history books, its cultural accretions nevertheless seem to remain potent actors within contemporary Italian, and perhaps larger European and even global identities.

Sites of Selective Memory

This study grew out of a rich field of postcolonial scholarship that has reconsidered the importance of understanding Italy's colonial past, as a means of understanding its transition from an "emigrant" to an "immigrant"

---

9   On the disavowal of Italian race in contemporary Italian culture, see in particular, Cristina Lombardi-Diop, "Postracial/Postcolonial Italy," in *Postcolonial Italy: Challenging National Homogeneity*, edited by Cristina Lombardi-Diop and Caterina Romeo, 175–90 (New York: Palgrave Macmillan, 2012).

nation. But what about the rhetorical uses of the Mediterranean Sea and their impact on such postcolonial transitions? Revisiting the historical and cultural underpinnings of the Italian state in the Aegean has helped to reveal not only how the Mediterranean was imagined as the "natural" homeland of the Italian nation, but also how it was an "imaginative geography," to borrow Edward Said's turn of phrase, of unity against a backdrop of internal fragmentation, disunity, and disappointment with the unification. Seen from this perspective, the so-called *questione meridionale*, or Southern Question, both a problem of national stability, and a discourse about the "otherness" of the South, was also present in a nationalist empire in the Mediterranean.

Looking at this discursive framework of the Mediterranean, that is, the Southern Question from a transnational and transcultural perspective, it becomes clear that colonization in the Aegean was bound to take on an increasingly "nationalist" character and to link nation building at home, especially in the South, with nation building in the overseas empire. As Italy struggled to craft a coherent national identity at home, that struggle defined its increasingly expansive imperial state. As chapters 1 and 2 showed, romantic and nostalgic beliefs about Italy's Greco-Roman roots conditioned Italians to believe that modernity implied a return to fabled histories about Mediterranean regional unity. Chapter 3 discussed how this imaginative geography both shaped colonial imaginaries of hegemony and dictated the ways that Italy ruled its subjects and defined the categories of nation and race. And the final chapter considered how these Mediterraneanist colonial policies were perceptible in everyday life, redefined, and subtly undermined by the local population via tactics of resistance to Fascist rule. But what of how Mediterraneanism has interacted, and continues to interact, with the southeast Aegean's own troubles with diaspora, nation, and inclusion into Europe? If the Southern Problem was also an imperial one it may not be unique to the Italian case; it may also apply to all of Europe's peripheries, holding them in continued postimperial formation. Put simply, can we speak about a European Southern Question? And if so, is it important to consider it for bettering our understanding of European postcolonial identities?

Today restoration efforts to Italian architectural and infrastructural modernity in the islands highlight such questions. Under the aegis of improving tourism and the local economy of the Dodecanese islands, the European Union has recently made investments in public funds to restore the massive architectural legacy of Italian rule. As an example, Lakkhi, the port city of Leros island (described in the Introduction) has been restored as a European cultural heritage project—rather than a local or a national one. The campaign for it pivoted on the same severing of "Italian" from "Fascist" that, as chapter 4 discussed, is characteristic of local historiography and oral narratives of Italian rule. As an Italian architect interviewed for the online version of the English-language Greek newspaper *Ekathimerini* described: "Until recently, there were some reservations about all that in Italy because these buildings were constructed during Fascist rule. However, these buildings were never symbols of the party, while Rationalism, although originating in Italy, became an international style. Lakki is precious to Leros. It is a jewel which could, under proper management, attract quality tourism to the island."[10]

These calls for funding to restore Italian architecture in the Dodecanese reproduce clichés that the Italian state embraced in the interwar period—as chapter 2 showed, the Italian state was heavily invested in the vision that the Dodecanese could have an international, even cosmopolitan tourism economy. More dangerously, they disavow the very Fascist project that sustained these massive architectural interventions. The desire both to maintain in the islands an urban redesign that resembles the timeless cosmopolitanism the Italian state imagined for its rule, and, at the same time, to uncouple that project from the Fascist state that produced it speaks to larger questions about the future legacies of Italian Empire in Italy and the Mediterranean.

To be sure, the Dodecanese are not unique in their preservation of the Italian architectural built environment. In Asmara (Eritrea), the urban intervention of the Italians remains intact and looks almost exactly as it was designed in the 1930s. As Mia Fuller has eloquently observed, the contemporary built environment of postcolonial Asmara presents the visitor with a verifiable "colonial inertia," one that begs the question, "What have been the ruptures and continuities, *there*?" If scholars have puzzled over the conflicting and selective memories surrounding Italian colonialism, fewer have wondered, in Fuller's words, "How do the formerly colonized remember their time as colonial subjects; what do they prefer to forget; and in what ways are their memories relevant to their future—if at all?"[11]

As in Italy, troubles with remembering the Fascist past in the islands go back to 1943 and to the complicated ways in which Italy's loss of its colonies was subsumed into the larger history of World War II. The Italian signing of the armistice led to a Nazi advance into areas of Greece that Italy

---

10   Giorgos Lialios, "Lakki: Architectural Gem on Island of Leros, Finally Gets Due attention," *Ekathimerini*, September 19, 2014.
11   Mia Fuller, "Italy's Colonial Futures: Colonial Inertia and Postcolonial Capital in Asmara," *California Italian Studies* 2, no. 1 (2011): 5–6.

had held militarily, which included the Aegean and the Dodecanese. In the Dodecanese, the period of Nazi occupation is registered as the most dramatic part of the war, and, in some ways, it overshadows the period of Italian rule, even though the latter lasted considerably longer and left significantly more imprint in terms of culture, infrastructure, and institutions. But the period of Nazi occupation helps to unite the Dodecanese memory among Greeks with the larger national memory. Like other areas of Greece, the Dodecanese experienced massive famine during World War II due to the Allied strategy of blockade, which coincided with the devastating Nazi occupation and a refugee crisis of mobility between islands.[12] The memory of this period among Dodecanese Greeks thus not only resembles the memory of the period in mainland Greece, but also, in oral narratives, cuts across communal fissures and tends to bring the fragmented memories of Greeks and Turks into a collective memory about the wartime famine.[13] Oral narratives among the Jewish community tend to gloss over the widespread famine and naturally center on the deportations of July 1944.[14] Throughout all the islands in the Dodecanese, the wartime period is variously commemorated in local monuments and museums as well as in a cottage industry of local memoirs, many of which are self-published. In Rhodes and Kos, monuments to the deported Jewish communities can be found at central points in the historic center, where they join Greek and Turkish memorials to Nazi occupation as well as to soldiers who fell during World Wars I and II. Collectively, these monuments and museums operate as what Pierre Nora might call *lieux de memoire*: spaces of memory and heritage by means of which the local community attempts to secure its own identity.[15]

However, if the wartime period is commemorated in *lieux de memoire* that gesture at the possibility of cross-communal memories and multicultural histories of the war, these sites of memory also seem to be doing work to revise the past and rewrite more difficult emotions and memories related to

12   Sheila Lecour, dir. *A Basket of Food: Greece in the 1940s* (2013). See also Sheila Lecour, *Mussolini's Greek Island: Fascism and the Italian Occupation of Syros in World War Two* (London: Bloomsbury, 2009).

13   Hazal Papuccular, "Fragmented Memories: The Dodecanese during World War II," in *Heritage and Memory of War: Responses from Small Islands*, edited by Gilly Carr and Keir Reeves (New York: Routledge, 2014), 36–54.

14   Nathan Shachar, *The Lost World of Rhodes: Greeks, Italians, Jews and Turks between Tradition and Modernity* (Brighton: Sussex Academic Press, 2013), 217–19.

15   Pierre Nora, "Between Memory and History: *Les Lieux de Memoire*," *Representations* 26 (Spring 1989): 7–24.

the period of Italian rule. As chapter 4 described, the local Greek community takes great pride in the idea that they resisted Fascist Italy's civilizing projects and attempts by Fascist authorities to remake their ethnic, religious, and linguistic identities. More difficult questions about cooperation and collaboration with the Fascist state are bracketed and downplayed in comparison with the experience of perseverance and triumph over adversity during wartime occupation. A frequent, almost ubiquitous trope is to recall that soldiers in the Italian army who were targeted by the Nazi–Fascist alliance suffered a fate even worse than that of the locals. The part of the Italian army that stayed loyal to the Italian state's armistice with the Allies was left to starve, and, under threat of death if they were caught stealing foodstuffs in abandoned properties, they sought refuge in hidden caves where they waited out the end of the war, "abandoned completely like wild men."[16]

These experiences look not unlike Greek resistance to Nazi-Fascism in mainland Greece and further help to connect the Dodecanese to the larger metanarratives of World War II. In Italy, the experience of civil war and the Resistenza, or the armed resistance to the Nazi–Fascist alliance after 1943, significantly reshaped historical narratives about the Fascist past. Such experiences of heroic victimhood have doubtless helped to rehabilitate postwar Italy and are present not only in *lieux de memoire* but also in neorealist films, popular culture, historiography, and across media as well as in oral narratives. As Claudio Fogu has aptly remarked, "to study the Italian memorialization of the war and Nazi Fascism means primarily to probe the subtle negotiations between the politics governing the institutionalization of memory events and the poetics that absorb them into metahistorical narratives; it also means, in the process, to expose the continuities between Fascist and post-Fascist historical imaginaries."[17] One cannot help but wonder to what degree the memory of the period of the resistance might be doing, if not the same, at least similar work in the Dodecanese as it has done in Italy. Are memories of the Nazi occupation helpful in sidestepping questions about local collaboration with the Italian state? While there are plenty of signs and historical markers of wartime occupation in the islands, no such equivalents exist indicating the Fascist origins of much of the architecture.

16   Fotis Varelis, *Kitala* (Athens: Fotis Varelis, 1977), 647–53.
17   Claudio Fogu, "*Italiani brava gente*: The Legacy of Fascist Historical Culture on Italian Politics of Memory," in *Politics of Memory in Postwar Europe*, edited by Richard Ned Lebow, Wulf Kansteiner, and Claudio Fogu, 147–76 (Durham, NC: Duke University Press, 2006), 147–48.

Historical and poetic narratives that bring the period of Italian rule into alignment with the larger narrative of Greece under occupation also conceal the fact that the historical memory of Italian rule is put to use to negotiate the complex and contested transition from empire to nation-state in the Aegean. Within Greek narratives, the Italian period is brought into the history of Greece in association with the prior four centuries of Ottoman rule. The word for the period of Italian sovereignty in the Dodecanese, *Italokratia*, strongly intimates the *Turkokratia*, the word used throughout Greece for Ottoman domination. The tradition of writing about Greece in an ethnonationalist vein, one that narrates a teleological history toward the independence of Greece from Ottoman rule, has long been criticized by scholars of modern Greece.[18] But similar poetics of resisting Ottoman rule also underpins narratives about the Italian Empire. An eight-hundred-page tome of local history, focused on the Italian period, in Kitala, a small village located in inland Rhodes, begins by stating that the village's existence has been recorded since just after the fall of Constantinople to the Turks in 1421, but that the history of Kitala proper began in 1908 when the Young Turks rose to power and Ottoman dominion in the Aegean began to draw to its end; the 1912 landing of Italians in Rhodes is thus drawn as less important than the ending of the Ottoman rule.[19] The perspective on the Italian Empire that this local history offers is therefore not of contested encounter and resistance against the Fascist state, but instead is a parenthesis within the village's long and storied struggle for Greek national identity.

The current emphasis on the restoration of Italian architecture helps to draw the islands back into a European project, and to distance the legacies of the Ottoman past in the islands. As Molly Greene has demonstrated, during the period of Ottoman rule in Greece, the history of Greeks was deeply entwined with the Ottoman state, its institutions and its other subjects, but this is not a narrative commonly adopted in Greece.[20] Since the integration

---

18   See Alexis Rappas, "Greeks under European Colonial Rule: National Allegiance and Imperial Loyalty," *Byzantine and Modern Greek Studies* 34, no. 2 (2010): 201–18; Nicholas Doumanis, *Myth and Memory in the Mediterranean: Remembering Fascism's Empire* (New York: St. Martin's Press, 1997); Anna Triandafyllidou, *Immigrants and National Identity in Europe* (London: Routledge, 2001); Mark Mazower, "The Messiah and the Bourgeoisie: Venizelos and Politics in Greece, 1909–1912," *The Historical Journal* 35, no. 4 (1992): 885–904.

19   Varelis, *Kitala*, 1–108.

20   Molly Greene, *The Edinburgh History of the Greeks, 1453–1774: The Ottoman Empire* (Edinburgh: Edinburgh University Press, 2015) and Molly Greene, *A Shared World:*

of the Dodecanese into Greece in 1947, the municipality of Rhodes has embarked on undoing many of the islands' Ottoman interventions: Byzantine churches that had been converted into mosques by the Turkish rulers have been restored to their original function, and Ottoman elements have been removed from many civil buildings.[21] Vestiges of the Ottoman presence in the islands are today notably deemphasized, in both their Turkish and Jewish manifestations. At present, many of the most important Turkish monuments are not currently open to the public. This includes the Mosque of Suleymaniye, originally built in 1522 to commemorate the Turkish conquest of the islands, considered one of Rhodes' most important Ottoman landmarks and one of the Ottoman Empire's most important mosques outside of Istanbul. Either through deliberate restoration programs, or because of a lack of collaboration with the local Turkish community, traces of the Ottoman past on the island are slowly being wiped away.[22]

This erasure mirrors that of the islands' Turkish community itself. Alongside the one in Thrace, the Turkish communities of Rhodes and Kos constitute an officially recognized minority in Greece. But while statistics place the community at almost five thousand people, its presence is minimally felt. Many of the properties in the historic centers of Rhodes and Kos are held in Turkish ownership, but these are often rented out and their owners reside in neighboring Turkey. Turkish is not included in bureaucratic documents and it is rarely if ever heard. There have been calls for the Turkish community's greater visibility, including instruction in Turkish in local schools and greater openness and comfort concerning public displays of religion and worship.[23] An increase in tension between the Turkish minority in Rhodes and Kos and the Greek majority has often been linked to the ongoing conflict in Cyprus, which has divided Turkish and Greek Cypriots since the early 1960s. The small and uninhabited islets situated between the Dodecanese in so-called "grey zones," Imia and Kardak, have also sparked tension and flare-up in Greco-Turkish relations, and continue to serve as

Christians and Muslims in the Early Modern Mediterranean (Princeton, NJ: Princeton University Press, 2000).

21   See Georgios Karatzas, "Representing Historical Narratives in the Urban Space: The Making of a Heritage Space in Urban Rhodes, 1912–1950," The Mediated City Conference, London, April 1–3, 2014.

22   See Mia Fuller, "Utopia Europe: Making Rhodes Greek," *Traditional Dwellings and Settlements Review* 22, no. 1 (2010): 15.

23   Kira Kaurinkoski, "The Muslim Communities in Kos and Rhodes: Reflections on Social Identities in Contemporary Greece," *Slavica Helsingiensia* 41 (2012): 47–78.

reminders that armed conflict between Greece and Turkey is still not an impossibility and that maintaining diplomatic relations between the two countries is paramount.[24]

Given these ongoing Greco-Turkish tensions and the minority's silent presence within the islands, the period of Italian rule under the administration of Mario Lago is often remembered by local Turks as comparatively a better one.[25] But as chapter 3 discussed, reprisals against the Turkish community were certainly not unheard of during the interwar period. As the Italian state, successively rereading the Lausanne Treaty's provision for the exchange of minority populations, gradually moved to legally expel much of the Turkish community, it encouraged for a second time since the collapse of the Ottoman Empire the emigration of Turks in the Aegean into Turkey.[26] Ironically, with a few important exceptions, there has been little consideration of how Italy's policies of race, introduced in 1938, aligned with processes of ethnic cleansing that had broadly been underway in the Aegean region since the decline and collapse of the Ottoman Empire and how it helped to usher in postwar arrangements that have almost uniformly favored Greek claims on the Aegean.[27] The few Ottoman monuments that have been restored in the postwar period, on the other hand, are those that were part of the Italian commitment to retain the exotic and Oriental aspect of the heritage landscape, including several minarets and ablution fountains that were depicted in postcards in the 1930s.[28]

Such fond remembrances of the Italian past also live on in the postwar and postcolonial remnants of the once-thriving Jewish communities of Rhodes and Kos. World War II ultimately marked the end of Rhodes' resident Jewish minority; the community currently has only thirty year-round residents. This transformation reflects the fact that, although the Jewish community

---

24   See Michael Robert Hick, "The Imia/Kardak Affair, 1995–6: A Case of Inadvertent Conflict," *European Security* 7, no. 4 (1998): 118–36.

25   Papuccular, "Fragmented Memories."

26   See also Sahizer Samuk and Hazal Papuccular, "Aegean in Motion: The Reasons, Consequences and Tragedies of Four Distinct Phases of Migration in the Aegean Sea," *Journal of Izmir Mediterranean Academy*, no. 3 (2018): 56–74.

27   See Hazal Papuccular, "Fragile Balances: Turkish Foreign Policy on the Sovereignty of the Dodecanese Islands, 1940–1947," *Journal of Balkan and Near Eastern Studies* 20, no. 5 (2018): 405–19.

28   Emma Maglio, "The Changing Role of Historic Town of Rhodes in the Scenario of Ottoman and Italian Rules in the Light of the Iconographic Sources," *Eikonocity* 1, no. 1 (2016): 75–88.

was integral to the development of the islands and at one point made up a significant percent of the population of Rhodes, its destruction prior to the islands' transfer to Greece meant that its members were never part of the Greek state. Since the islands were not officially part of Greece at the time of World War II, the Jewish community of the islands has not been entitled to the Greek state's reparations to survivors of the Holocaust.[29] The old Jewish quarters in the two islands now have Greek toponymy and Greeks have resided in the former Jewish houses since the 1944 deportations. The difficulty of rectifying the loss of Jewish property in the islands has certainly contributed to a certain "insularity" within Jewish memories of Italian rule, such that they seem to intersect very little with the Greek or Turkish memories of the same period.[30]

But the Italian past serves the Jewish community for another purpose— that of maintaining a Mediterranean, or Sephardic but still European, identity. Much as Greek memories of the Italian Empire help to elide the Ottoman past, the Italian period helps to shuttle the Rhodesli Jewish community into the present. The Rhodesli diaspora gathers annually in July, on the date of the deportations, in the Djuderia, or old Jewish quarters of Rhodes and Kos. Their visits to the islands coincide with the peak of summer travel to the islands, which helps to bring visibility to the Jewish history in the islands. As chapter 3 described, the Rhodesli diaspora preserves the right to Italian citizenship on the basis of heritage. In the context of EU integration, their patterns of migration often no longer follow metropole-colony lines, but may traverse borders that ironically replicate the old routes of empire; one interviewee explained that he used his Italian heritage citizenship (via a Rhodesli connection) to immigrate from South Africa to the United Kingdom; this fact was all the more ironic when one considers that the two

29   Rhodes and Kos fell outside of the purview of the official Organization for the Welfare and Reparation of Israelites of Greece (Οργανισμός Περιθάλψεως και Αποκατάστασης Ισραηλιτών Ελλάδος); see Alexis Rappas, "Memory and Property in Insular Spaces: The Case of Postcolonial Rhodes," working paper presented at "Islands in the Mediterranean: New Theorisations of Insularity," European University Institute, Florence, May 2014. For a description of how the Jewish quarter, the Djuderia, has been changed entirely to Greek toponymy, leaving little trace of the Jewish quarter as it once was, see Esther Fintz Menascé, *Buio nell'Isola: Rodi 1943–1945: La tragedia dei militari italiani e l'annientamento degli ebrei* (Milan: Mimesis, 2014), 141–46.
30   Alexis Rappas, "Memorial Soliloquies in Post-colonial Rhodes and the Ghost of Mediterranean Cosmopolitanism," *Mediterranean Historical Review* 33, no. 1 (2018): 89–110.

countries were once tied together through the British commonwealth.[31] The Rhodesli diaspora therefore maintains a deterritorialized link to the island that is explicitly mediated through their Italian identity and citizenship. If the Italian Empire marks the Jewish community's last phase of residency in the islands, Italian identity is also a means to connect with the future of the Mediterranean in a new age of "postnational" globalization.

Recent restoration efforts have also focused on reviving Italian modernist buildings that valorized the islands as a place of Mediterraneanness. As chapter 2 discussed at length, the Kalithea Baths offer a prime example of how Italy regrafted the Ottoman past in order to promote the islands as a site of national regeneration and rejuvenation. With their deliberate elision of Byzantine elements in favor of Arabic ones as well as their evocation of ancient Rome, the baths were enlisted by Italian architects in an argument about the Mediterranean as a site of both exotic otherness and imperial renewal. Today the Kalithea Baths have been partially restored, and are once again advertised to tourists visiting Rhodes, promoted as a convenient detour on the typical itinerary between the port and city of Rhodes and the archaeological excavations at Lindos. Similarly, after a long debate about whether the New Market should be offered up to private investors in order to pay for restorations, the municipality recently reclaimed the building for public uses. And a full restoration of the Italian-era cinema in the island of Leros was completed, in 2004, through EU subsidies.

In 2011, the Dodecanese guild of civil engineers launched a further campaign to fund the preservation of several buildings connected to Italy's development of industry and agriculture, while calling for complete conservation of all the buildings constructed under Italy's 1926 master plan: "The industrial heritage is part of the architectural and cultural heritage of a place," the petitioners claim, "which as a whole is an integral part of local history and the memory of a people."[32] The call to "conserve as a whole" the remnants of Italian Empire may be part of a broader nationwide erosion of the myth of modern Greece.[33] But it is also worth reflecting that the choices being made about how to preserve local memory and local heritage

---

31   See also Guido Tintori, "The Transnational Political Practices of 'Latin American Italians,'" *International Migration* 49, no. 3 (2011): 168–88.

32   Petition to Save Samica Flour Mill, http://savesamica.blogspot.gr, accessed 10 October 2019.

33   See Vangelis Calotychos, *Modern Greece: A Cultural Poetics* (London: Bloomsbury, 2003).

are increasingly connected not to reflecting on the nature of Italian Empire or Italy's colonial modernity, but to restoring its syncretizations of the Mediterranean. Maintaining such Mediterranean syncretizations also seem alive and well in Italian policies of citizenship, however unofficial, toward the Rhodesli diaspora, which are in striking contrast with policies toward second-generation migrants who, although born in Italy, are not automatically considered Italians and are able to acquire Italian citizenship only by applying for it once they reach age eighteen.

Following the hierarchies of race that set white colonial subjects of the Mediterranean "above" African colonial subjects, such norms about citizenship enable some former Italian colonial subjects to have the right to mobility and inclusion, while others are excluded. The ideological project to make inhabitants of the Aegean imperial citizens of the Mediterranean Empire, alongside the politics of race and empire that underpinned Italy's citizenship project, has been consigned to oblivion. The expression *mia fatsa, mia ratsa* (a loose Greek translation of the Italian, *"una faccia, una razza"*), has helped to trivialize and bracket Italian rule; it would seem to be a way not only of soft-pedaling the Fascist past, but also of encouraging locals in the Dodecanese to both selectively remember intercommunal life and to negate contemporary legacies of them.

If Italian rule provides new ways of imagining intercommunal tensions as seemingly multicultural topographies, such imaginaries also help to bring the islands more closely to the concept of Europe today. One must in turn ask, is the endurance of the currency of the Italian past purely an expedient? Or is it that Italy's ambition to craft an empire that is Mediterranean and imperial—rather than Southern and provincial—that has provided the Aegean with a touchstone for contemporary ideas about Europeanness and belonging in Europe? Meanwhile, the rose-tinted version of the Italian state in the Aegean lives on.

Bibliography

Archival Sources

Central Archive of the State, Rome (ACS)
General State Archives of Greece, Prefecture of the Dodecanese, Rhodes (GAK DOD)
General State Archives of Greece, Special Surveillance Archive of the Royal Carabinieri, Rhodes (GAK RCCR)
Historical Archive of the Italian Chamber of Deputies
Historical Archive of the Ministry of Foreign Affairs, Rome (ASMAE)
Historical Archive of the State Army, Rome (AUSSME)
Touring Club Italiano, Milan (TCI)

Secondary Sources

Abulafia, David. *The Mediterranean in History*. New York: Oxford University Press, 2003.
Aciman, Andre. *Out of Egypt*. London: Tauris Parke, 2019.
Agamben, Giorgio. *Means without End: Notes on Politics*. Minneapolis: University of Minnesota, 2000.
Ahmida, Ali Abdullatif. *Forgotten Voices: Power and Agency in Postcolonial Libya*. Hoboken, NJ: Taylor & Francis, 2013.
Alatri, Paolo. *D'Annunzio*. Turin: Unione Tipografico-Editrice Torinese, 1983.
Albahari, Maurizio. *Crimes of Peace: Mediterranean Migrations at the World's Deadliest Border*. Philadelphia: University of Pennsylvania Press, 2015.
Albanese, Giulia, and Roberta Pergher, eds. *In the Society of Fascists: Acclamation, Acquiescence and Agency in Mussolini's Italy*. New York: Palgrave MacMillan, 2012.
Alhadeff, Vittorio. *L'ordinamento giuridico di Rodi e delle altre isole italiane dell'Egeo*. Milan: Istituto editoriale scientifico, 1927.

Allen, Beverly, and Mary J. Russo. *Revisioning Italy: National Identity and Global Culture*. Minneapolis: University of Minnesota Press, 1997.

Andall, Jacqueline, and Derek Duncan. *National Belongings: Hybridity in Italian Colonial and Postcolonial Cultures*. New York: Peter Lang, 2010.

Anderson, Benedict. *Imagined Communities: Reflections on the Origins and Spread of Nationalism*. New York: Verso, 1991.

Anderson, Sean. "The Light and the Line: Florestano di Fausto and the Politics of *Mediterraneanità*." *California Italian Studies Journal* 1, no. 1 (2010): 1–13.

Antoniades, Anthony. "Italian Architecture in the Dodecanese: A Preliminary Assessment." *Journal of Architectural Education* 38, no. 1 (1984): 18–25.

Apter, Emily. *Against World Literature: The Politics of Untranslatability*. London: Verso, 2014.

Arthurs, Josh. "The Excavatory Intervention: Archaeology and the Chronopolitics of Fascist Italy." *Journal of Modern European History* 13, no. 1 (2015): 44–58.

—. *Excavating Modernity: The Roman Past in Fascist Italy*. Ithaca, NY: Cornell University Press, 2016.

Arthurs, Josh, Kate Ferris, and Michael Ebner. *The Politics of Everyday Life in Fascist Italy*. New York: Palgrave MacMillan, 2017.

Aymes, Marc. *A Provincial History of the Ottoman Empire*. London: Routledge, 2013.

Balducci, Hermes. *Architettura turca a Rodi*. Milan: Ulrico Hoepli, 1932.

Ballinger, Pam. "Rewriting the Text of the Nation: D'Annunzio at Fiume." *Quaderni* 11 (1997): 117–55.

—. *History in Exile: Memory and Identity at the Borders of the Balkans*. Princeton, NJ: Princeton University Press, 2003.

—. "Borders of the Nation, Borders of Citizenship: Italian Repatriation and the Redefinition of National Identity after World War II." *Comparative Studies in Society and History* 49, no. 3 (2007): 713–41.

—. "Colonial Twilight: Italian Settlers and the Long Decolonization of Libya." *Journal of Contemporary History* 15, no. 4 (2016): 813–38.

—. *The World Refugees Made*. Ithaca, NY: Cornell University Press, 2020.

Bandini, Giovanna. *Lettere dall'Egeo: Archaeologhe italiane tra 1900–1950*. Florence: Giunti, 2003.

Baratieri, Daniela. *Memories and Silences Haunted by Fascism: Italian Colonialism MCMXXX–MCMLX*. Bern: Peter Lang, 2001.

Barrera, Giulia. "Mussolini's Colonial Race Laws and State-Settler Relations in Africa Orientale Italiana, 1935–41." *Journal of Modern Italian Studies* 8, no. 3 (2003): 425–43.

—. "Sessualità e segregazione nelle terre dell'Impero." In *L'Impero fascista: Italia ed Etiopia (1935–41)*, edited by Riccardo Bottoni, 393–414. Milan: Il mulino, 2008.

Battini, Michele, and Stanislao Pugliese. *The Missing Italian Nuremberg: Cultural Amnesia and Postwar Politics*. New York: Palgrave MacMillan, 2007.

Baudi di Vesme, Carlo. *Rodi e il problema del Levante*. Padova: La Garangola, 1934.

Becker, Jared M. *Nationalism and Culture: Gabriele D'Annunzio and Italy after the Risorgimento*. New York: Peter Lang, 1994.

Bedhad, Ali. *Belated Travelers: Orientalism in the Age of Colonial Dissolution*. Durham, NC: Duke University Press, 1994.

Benadusi, Lorenzo. *The Enemy of the New Man: Homosexuality in Fascist Italy*. Madison, WI: University of Wisconsin Press, 2012.

Ben-Ghiat, Ruth. *Fascist Modernities*. Berkeley: University of California Press, 2004.

—. "Modernity Is Just Over There: Colonialism and Italian National Identity." *Interventions* 8, no. 3 (2006): 380–93.

—. *Italian Fascism's Empire Cinema*. Bloomington: Indiana University Press, 2015.

Ben-Ghiat, Ruth, and Mia Fuller, eds. *Italian Colonialism*. New York: Palgrave and MacMillan, 2005.

Ben-Ghiat, Ruth, and Stephanie Malia Hom. *Italian Mobilities*. Abingdon: Routledge, 2016.

Ben-Yehoyada, Naor. *The Mediterranean Incarnate: Region Formation between Sicily and Tunisia since World War Two*. Chicago: Chicago University Press, 2018.

Benzoni, Maria. *Oriente Mediterraneo: Memorie di una crociera*. Milan: La Prora, 1935.

Bernal, Martin. *Black Athena: The Afroasiatic Roots of Classical Civilization*. New Brunswick, NJ: Rutgers University Press, 1987.

Bernheimer, Charles. "Fetishism and Decadence: Salome's Severed Heads." In *Fetishism as Cultural Discourse*, edited by Emily Apter and William Pietz, 62–83. Ithaca, NY: Cornell University Press, 1993.

Bertelli, L.V., ed. *Guida delle Colonie e Possedimenti*. Milan: Touring Club Italiano, 1929.

Bhabha, Homi. "Of Mimicry and Man: The Ambivalence of Colonial Discourse." *October* 28, no. 2 (1984): 125–33.

—. *The Location of Culture*. New York: Routledge, 1994.

Bhabha, Homi, ed. *Nation and Narration*. New York: Routledge, 1990.

Bidussa, David. *Il mito del bravo italiano*. Milan: Il Saggiatore, 1994.

Bierman, John. *Odyssey*. New York: Simon & Schuster, 1984.

Birtek, Faruk, and Thalia Dragonas, eds. *Citizenship and the Nation-State in Greece and Turkey*. New York: Routledge, 2005.

Blumi, Isa. *Ottoman Refugees, 1878–1939: Migration in a Post-Imperial World*. London: Bloomsbury, 2015.

Bocquet, Denis. "Rhodes 1912: Les mésaventures du Général d'Ameglio." *Cahiers de la Méditerranée*, no. 68 (2004): 133–52.

Bond, Emma. "Toward a Trans-national Turn in Italian Studies?" *Italian Studies* 69, no. 3 (2014): 415–24.

—. *Writing Migration through the Body*. New York: Palgrave Macmillan, 2018.

Bond, Emma, and Guido Bonsaver, Federico Faloppa. *Destination Italy: Representing Migration in Contemporary Media and Narrative*. Bern: Peter Lang, 2015.

Booth, C.D., and Isabelle Bridge. *Italy's Aegean Possessions*. London: Arrowsmith, 1928.

Borelli, Elena. *Giovanni Pascoli, Gabriele D'Annunzio, and the Ethics of Desire between Action and Contemplation*. Madison, WI: Fairleigh Dickinson Press, 2017.

Borutta, Manuel, and Sakis Gekas. "A Colonial Sea: The Mediterranean, 1798–1956." *European Review of History* 19, no. 1 (2012): 1–13.

Bosworth, Richard. "Britain and Italy's Acquisition of the Dodecanese, 1912–1915." *The Historical Journal* 13, no. 4 (1970): 683–705.

—. *Italy, the Least of the Great Powers: Italian Foreign Policy before the First World War*. Cambridge: Cambridge University Press, 1979.

—. *Italy and the Wider World, 1860–1960*. New York: Routledge, 1996.

Bosworth, Richard, and Patrizia Dogliani. *Italian Fascism: History, Memory and Representation*. London: Macmillan, 1999.

Braudel, Fernand. *The Mediterranean and the Mediterranean World in the Age of Philip II*. Translated by Sian Reynolds. New York: Harper & Row, 1976.

British Naval Intelligence Division, *Dodecanese*, 2nd Edition. London: Geographical Handbook Series, 1943.

Burdett, Charles. *Journeys through Fascism: Italian Travel Writing between the Wars*. New York: Berghahn, 2007.

Burdett, Charles, and Derek Duncan. *Cultural Encounters: European Travel Writing in the 1930s*. New York: Bergahn Books, 2002.

Burgio, Alberto. *Nel nome della razza: Il razzismo nella storia d'Italia 1870–1945*. Bologna: Il mulino, 2000.

Burke, Edmund, and David Prochaska. *Genealogies of Orientalism: History, Theory and Politics*. Lincoln, NE: University of Nebraska Press, 2008.

Cacciari, Massimo. *Arcipelago*. Milan: Adelphi, 1997.

Calotychos, Vangelis. *Modern Greece: A Cultural Poetics*. London: Bloomsbury, 2003.

Campbell, Timothy, and Anna Paparcone. "Interview with Roberto Esposito." *Diacritics* 36, no. 2 (2006): 49–56.

Caponetto, Rosetta Giuliani. *Fascist Hybridities: Representations of Racial Mixing and Diaspora Cultures under Mussolini*. New York: Palgrave MacMillan, 2015.

Carabott, Phillip John. "The Temporary Occupation of the Dodecanese Islands: A Prelude to Permanency." *Diplomacy and Statecraft* 4, no. 2 (1993): 285–312.

Caraci, Ilaria Luzzana, and Mario Pozzi, eds. *Scopritori e viaggiatori del cinquecento e del seicento*. Milan: Riccardi, 1991.

Carpovich, Angelina. "Theoretical Approaches to Film-Motivated Tourism." *Journal of Tourism and Hospitality Planning and Development* 7, no. 1 (2010): 7–20.

Carrera, Alessandro. "Idola mediterranei." In "Il mondo visto da sud e *La prima volta*: Una conversazione con Franco Cassano." Edited by Massimo Lollini. Special issue, *California Italian Studies* 4, no. 2 (2013): 9–14.

Cassano, Franco. *Il pensiero meridiano*. Bari: Laterza, 2005.

Cassotis, Emanuel. *The Karpathian (Dodecanese) Presence in America*. Rhodes: Stegi Grammaton ke Technon Dodecanesou, 2012.

Cavazza, Stefano. *Piccole patrie: feste popolari tra regione e nazione durante il fascismo*. Bologna: Il mulino, 2003.

Cecchi, Emilio. *Et in Arcadia ego*. Milan: Mondadori, 1960.

Celik, Zeynep. *Urban Forms and Colonial Confrontations: Algiers under French Rule*. Berkeley: University of California Press, 1997.

Centro nazionale di studi dannunziani e della cultura in Abruzzo, ed. *Verso l'Ellade: Dalla Città morta a Maia: 18. Convegno internazionale: Pescara, 11–12 maggio 1995*. Pescara: Ediars, 1995.

Chakrabarty, Dipesh. *Provincializing Europe: Postcolonial Thought and Historical Difference*. Princeton, NJ: Princeton University Press, 2000.

Chambers, Iain. *Mediterranean Crossings: The Politics of an Interrupted Modernity*. Durham, NC: Duke University Press, 2008.

Choate, Mark. *Emigrant Nation: The Making of Italy Abroad*. Cambridge, MA: Harvard University Press, 2008.

—. "Tunisia, Contested: Italian Nationalism, French Imperial Rule, and Migration in the Mediterranean Basin." *California Italian Studies* 1, no. 1 (2010): 1–20.

Ciacci, Leonardo. *Rodi italiana, 1912–23: Come si inventa una città*. Venice: Marsilio, 1991.

Ciarlantini, Franco. *Viaggio nell'Oriente Mediterraneo*. Milan: Mondadori, 1936.

Cixous, Hélène. "Fiction and Its Phantoms: A Reading of Freud's *Das Unheimliche* (The Uncanny)." *New Literary History* 7, no. 3 (1976): 525–46, 619–45.

Clark, Bruce. *Twice a Stranger: The Mass Expulsions that Forged Modern Greece and Turkey*. Cambridge, MA: Harvard University Press, 2009.

Clementi, Marco. "The Italian Occupation of the Balkans and the Jewish Question during WWII." *Vestnik of Saint Petersburg University, History* 63, no. 1 (2018): 174–86.

Clementi, Marco, and Ireni Toliou. *Gli ultimi ebrei di Rodi: Leggi raziali e deportazioni nel Dodecaneso italiano, 1938–1948*. Rome: DeriveApprodi, 2015.

Clò, Clarissa. "Mediterraneo Interrupted: Perils and Potentials of Representing Italy's Occupations in Greece and Libya Through Film." *Italian Culture* 27, no. 2 (2009): 99–115.

Clogg, Richard. *A Concise History of Greece*. Cambridge: Cambridge University Press, 2013.

Colonas, Vassilis. *Italian Architecture in the Dodecanese Islands, 1912–1943*. Athens: Olkos, 2002.

Cooper, Frederick. *Colonialism in Question: Theory, Knowledge, History.* Berkeley: University of California Press, 2005.

—. *Citizenship between Empire and Nation: Remaking France and French Africa, 1945–1960.* Princeton, NJ: Princeton University Press, 2014.

Cooper, Frederick, and Ann Laura Stoler. *Tensions of Empire: Colonial Cultures in a Bourgeois World.* Berkeley: University of California Press, 1997.

Corner, Paul. "Everyday Fascism in the 1930s: Centre and Periphery in the Decline of Mussolini's Dictatorship." *Contemporary European History* 15, no. 2 (2006): 195–222.

—. *The Fascist Party and Popular Opinion in Mussolini's Italy.* Oxford: Oxford University Press, 2012.

Corradini, Enrico. *Sopra le vie del nuovo impero: Dall'emigrazione in Tunisia alla guerra nell'Egeo.* Milan: Fratelli Treves, 1912.

Culler, Jonathan. *Framing the Sign: Criticism and Its Institutions.* Norman, OK: University of Oklahoma Press, 1988.

Dainelli, Giotto. "Rodi dei cavalieri." *Le vie d'Italia: Rivista mensile del Touring Club Italiano,* no. 3 (1922): 234–40.

Dainotto, Roberto. *Europe (in Theory).* Durham, NC: Duke University Press, 2007.

Dalle Vacche, Angela. *The Body in the Mirror: Shapes of History in Italian Cinema.* Princeton, NJ: Princeton University Press, 1992.

D'Annunzio, Gabriele. *Taccuini.* Edited by Enrica Bianchetti and Roberto Forcella. Milan: Mondadori, 1965.

—. "La vergine Anna." In *Tutte le novelle,* edited by Annamaria Andreoli and Marina de Marco, 133–77. Milan: Mondadori, 1992.

—. *Pleasure.* Translated by Lara Gochin Raffaeli. New York: Penguin, 2013.

De Amicis, Edmondo. *Constantinopoli.* Milan: Fratelli Treves, 1881.

—. *Constantinople.* Translated by Stephen Parkin. London: Hesperus Classics, 2005.

de Bernières, Louis. *Captain Corelli's Mandolin.* London: Vintage Books, 2016 [1994].

de Certeau, Michel. *The Practice of Everyday Life.* Berkeley: University of California Press, 1984.

De Donno, Fabrizio. "La Razza Ario-Mediterranea." *Interventions: International Journal of Postcolonial Studies* 8, no. 3 (2006): 394–412.

—. "Routes to Modernity: Orientalism and Mediterraneanism in Italian Culture, 1810–1910." *California Italian Studies Journal* 1, no. 1 (2010): 1–23.

—. *Italian Orientalism: Nationhood, Cosmopolitanism, and the Cultural Politics of Identity.* New York: Peter Lang, 2019.

de Felice, Renzo. *The Jews in Fascist Italy: A History.* Translated by Robert Miller. New York: Enigma, 2001.

De Grand, Alexander. *The Italian Nationalist Association and the Rise of Fascism in Italy.* Lincoln, NE: University of Nebraska Press, 1978.

—. "Mussolini's Follies: Fascism in Its Imperial Racist Phase, 1935–1940." *Journal of Contemporary European History* 13, no. 2 (2004): 127–47.

De Grazia, Victoria. *The Culture of Consent: Mass Organization of Leisure in Fascist Italy*. New York: Cambridge University Press, 1981.

—. *How Fascism Ruled Women, 1922–45*. Berkeley: University of California Press, 1992.

de Lauretis, Teresa. *Technologies of Gender: Essays on Theory, Film, and Fiction*. Bloomington: Indiana University Press, 1987.

Del Boca, Angelo. *Gli italiani in Africa orientale*. Rome: Laterza, 1976.

—. *Italiani, brava gente: Un mito duro a morire*. Vicenza: Neri Pozza, 2005.

Demoule, Jean-Paul. *Mais où sont passés les Indo-Européens: Le mythe d'Origine de l' Occident*. Paris: Editions du Seuill, 2014.

De Napoli, Olindo. "The Origin of the Racist Laws under Fascism: A Problem of Historiography." *Journal of Modern Italian Studies* 17, no. 1 (2012): 106–22.

Deplano, Valeria. *L'Africa in casa: propaganda e cultura nell'Italia fascista*. Florence: Le Monnier, 2015.

—. "Within and Outside the Nation: Former Colonial Subjects in Post-war Italy," *Modern Italy* 23, no. 4 (2018): 395–410.

Derrida, Jacques, and Anne Dufourmantelle. *Of Hospitality*. Translated by Rachel Rowlby. Stanford, CA: Stanford University Press, 2000.

Desio, Ardito, and Giuseppe Stefanini. *Le colonie, Rodi, e le isole italiane dell'Egeo*. Turin: Unione Tipografico Editrice, 1928.

De Vecchi di Val Cismon, Cesare Maria. *Bonifica Fascista della cultura*. Milan: Mondadori, 1937.

Di Carmine, Roberta. *Italy Meets Africa: Colonial Discourses in Italian Cinema*. New York: Peter Lang, 2011.

Dickie, John. *Darkest Italy: The Nation and Stereotypes of the Mezzogiorno, 1860–1900*. New York: Palgrave MacMillan, 2016.

Di Meo, Alessandro. *Tientsin: La concessione italiana, Storia delle relazione tra Regno d'Italia e Cina, 1886–1947*. Rome: Ginevra Bentivoglio Editoria, 2015.

Divani, Lena, and Photini Constantopoulou. *The Dodecanese: The Long Road to Union with Greece: Diplomatic Documents from the Historical Archives of the Ministry of Foreign Affairs*. Athens: Kastaniotis Editions, 1997 [in Greek and English].

Donati, Sabina. "'Statutis Civitatis' and 'Italianità': Origins and Historical Evolution of Citizenship in Italy (1861–1950)." PhD diss., Geneva: University of Geneva, 2007.

—. *A Political History of National Citizenship and Identity in Italy, 1861–1950*. Stanford, CA: Stanford University Press, 2013.

—. "Italy's Informal Imperialism in Tienjin during the Liberal Epoch, 1902–22." *The Historical Journal* 52, no. 2 (2016): 447–68.

Doumanis, Nicholas. *Myth and Memory in the Mediterranean: Remembering Fascism's Empire*. New York: St. Martin's Press, 1997.

—. *Una faccia una razza: Le colonie nell'Egeo*. Translated by M. Cupellaro. Bologna: Il mulino, 2003.

Durrell, Lawrence. *Reflections on a Marine Venus*. London: Faber and Faber, 1963.

Dyson, Stephen. *In Pursuit of Ancient Pasts: A History of Classical Archaeology in the Nineteenth and Twentieth Centuries*. New Haven, CT: Yale University Press, 2006.

Ebner, Michael. *Ordinary Violence in Mussolini's Italy*. New York: Cambridge University Press, 2011.

Einaudi, Luigi. *Un principe mercante: Storia dell'espansione italiana*. Turin: Bocca, 1900.

El Houssi, Leila. *L'urlo contro il regime: Gli antifascisti italiani in Tunisia tra le due guerre*. Rome: Carocci editore, 2014.

Ente naz. ind. turistiche/Governo delle isole italiane nell'Egeo. *Calitea: Rodi* [Édition français]. Rome: Tip. Novissima, 1930.

Fabian, Johannes. *Time and the Other: How Anthropology Makes its Object*. New York: Columbia University Press, 1983.

Falasca-Zamponi, Simonetta. *Fascist Spectacle: The Aesthetics of Power in Mussolini's Italy*. Berkeley: University of California Press, 2000.

Fanon, Frantz. "Algeria Unveiled." In *Decolonization: Perspectives from Now and Then*, edited by Prasenjit Duara, 42–55. London and New York: Routledge, 2004.

Federzoni, Luigi [Giulio De Frenzi, pseud.]. *L'Italia nell'Egeo*. Rome: G. Garzoni Provenzani, 1913.

Ferris, Kate. *Everyday Life in Fascist Venice, 1929-40*. Basingstoke: Palgrave Macmillan, 2012.

Finaldi, Giuseppe Maria. *Italian National Identity in the Scramble for Africa: Italy's African Wars in the Era of Nation-building, 1870–1900*. Oxford: Peter Lang, 2009.

Fintz Menascé, Esther. *Gli ebrei a Rodi: Storia di un'antica communità annientata dai nazisti*. Milan: Guerini, 1992.

—. *Buio nell'Isola: Rodi 1943–1945: La tragedia dei militari italiani e l'annientamento degli ebrei*. Milan: Mimesis, 2014.

Fiore, Teresa. *Pre-occupied Spaces: Remapping Italy's Transnational Migrations and Colonial Legacies*. New York: Fordham University Press, 2018.

Flandini, Eugenio. *L'Isola di Rodi e le Sporadi*. Milan: Fratelli Treves, 1912.

Flaubert, Gustave. "Rhodes." In *Voyage en Orient*, 320–26. 1850. Reprint, Saint-Amand: Gallimard, 2006.

Fogu, Claudio. *The Historic Imaginary: Politics of History in Fascist Italy*. Toronto: University of Toronto Press, 2003.

—. *"Italiani brava gente*: The Legacy of Fascist Historical Culture on Italian Politics of Memory." In *Politics of Memory in Postwar Europe,* edited by Richard Ned Lebow, Wulf Kansteiner, and Claudio Fogu, 147–76. Durham, NC: Duke University Press, 2006.

—. "Futurist Mediterraneità: Between Emporium and Imperium." *Modernism/ Modernity* 15, no. 1 (2008): 25–43.

—. "From Mare Nostrum to Mare Aliorum: Mediterranean Theory and Mediterraneanism in Contemporary Italian Thought." *California Italian Studies* 1, no. 1 (2010): 1–23.

Foot, John. *The Archipelago: Italy since 1945.* London: Bloomsbury, 2019.

Forgacs, David. *Italy's Margins: Social Exclusion and Nation Formation since 1861.* Cambridge: Cambridge University Press, 2016.

Fortier, Anne-Marie. "The Politics of 'Italians Abroad': Nation, Diaspora, and New Geographies of Identity." *Diaspora: A Journal of Transnational Studies* 7, no. 2 (1998): 197–224.

Franco, Hizkia M. *The Jewish Martyrs of Rhodes and Cos.* Translated by Joseph Franco. Zimbabwe: HarperCollins, 1994.

Freud, Sigmund. "The Uncanny." In *The Standard Edition of the Complete Works of Sigmund Freud,* vol. 17, 217–56. Stanford, CA: Stanford University Press, 2001; first published in 1919.

Fromkin, David. *A Peace to End All Peace: Creating the Modern Middle East, 1914–1922.* New York: Holt, 1989.

Fuller, Mia. "Mediterraneanism." In *Environmental Design: Presence of Italy in the Architecture of the Islamic Mediterranean,* edited by Attilio Petruccioli, 8–9. Rome: Carucci Editore, 1990.

—. "Building Power: Italy's Colonial Architecture and Urbanism." *Cultural Anthropology* 3, no. 4 (1998): 455–87.

—. "Preservation and Self-Absorption: Italian Colonization and the Walled City of Tripoli, Libya." In *Italian Colonialism,* edited by Ruth Ben-Ghiat and Mia Fuller, 131–42. New York: Palgrave and MacMillan, 2005.

—. *Moderns Abroad.* New York: Routledge, 2007.

—. "Laying Claim: On Italy's Internal and External Colonies." In *A Moving Border: Alpine Cartographies of Climate Change,* edited by Marco Ferrari, Elisa Pasqual, and Andrea Bagnato, 99–111. New York: Columbia University Press, 2008.

—. "Utopia Europe: Making Rhodes Greek." *Traditional Dwellings and Settlements Review* 22, no. 1 (2010): 15.

—. "Italy's Colonial Futures: Colonial Inertia and Postcolonial Capital in Asmara." *California Italian Studies* 2, no. 1 (2011).

Gabaccia, Donna. *Italy's Many Diasporas.* New York: Routledge, 2013.

Gadda, Carlo Emilio. "Approdo alle zattere." In *Il Castello di Udine,* 141–49. Florence: Edizione Solaria, 1931.

Galimi, Valeria. "The 'New Racist Man.'" In *In the Society of Fascists: Acclamation, Acquiescence and Agency in Mussolini's Italy*, edited by Giulia Albanese and Roberta Pergher, 149–68. New York: Palgrave MacMillan, 2012.

Gallant, Thomas. *Experiencing Dominion: Culture, Identity, and Power in the British Mediterranean*. Notre Dame, IN: University of Notre Dame Press, 2002.

Gaon, Haham Solomon, and Mitchell Serels, eds. *Del Fuego, Sephardim and the Holocaust*. New York: Sepher-Hermon Press, 1995.

Garber, Marjorie B., and Nancy Vickers. *The Medusa Reader*. New York: Routledge, 2003.

Gentile, Emilio. *The Sacralization of Politics in Fascist Italy*. Cambridge, MA: Harvard University Press, 1996.

—. *The Struggle for Modernity: Nationalism, Futurism and Fascism*. Westport, CT: Praeger, 2003.

Gentile, Savero. *Le leggi razioni: Scienza giuridica, norme, circolari*. Milan: EDUCatt, 2010.

Geppert, Dominic, William Mulligan, and Andreas Rose, eds. *The Wars before the Great War: Conflict and International Politics before the Outbreak of the First World War*. Cambridge: Cambridge University Press, 2016.

Gere, Cathy. *Knossos and the Prophets of Modernism*. Chicago: University of Chicago Press, 2009.

Gerwarth, Robert. "The Axis: Germany, Japan and Italy on the Road to War." In *The Cambridge History of the Second World War, Vol 2: Politics and Ideology*, edited by Richard Bosworth and Joseph Maiolo, 21–42. Cambridge: Cambridge University Press, 2015.

Gibson, Mary. "Biology or Environment? Race or Southern 'Deviancy' in the Writings of Italian Criminologists, 1880–1920." In *Italy's "Southern Question": Orientalism in One Country*, edited by Jane Schneider, 99–115. Oxford: Berg, 1998.

Giglio, Annalisa. *Città del Mediterraneo: Kos: Architetture italiane nel Dodecaneso, 1912–43*. Bari: Poliba, 2009.

Giglio, Raffaele. *Per la storia di un'amicizia: d'Annunzio, Hérelle, Scarfoglio, Serao: documenti inediti*. Naples: Lofredo, 1977.

Gillette, Aron. *Racial Theories in Fascist Italy*. London: Routledge, 2002.

Giuliani, Gaia, and Cristina Lombardi-Diop. *Bianco e nero: Storia dell'identità razziale degli italiani*. Florence: Le Monnier, 2013.

Giuliani, Gaia. "L'Italiano Negro: The Politics of Colour in Early Twentieth-Century Italy." *Interventions* 16, no. 4 (2014): 572–87.

Goeschel, Christian. "Staging Friendship: Mussolini and Hitler in 1937." *Journal of Modern History* 6, no. 1 (2017): 149–72.

Goglia, Luigi, and Fabio Grassi. *Il colonialismo italiano da Adua all'impero*. Rome-Bari: Laterza, 1981.

Gori, Fernando. *Egeo Fascista*. Rome: Unione Ed. D'Italia, 1941.

Gorman, Daniel. *Imperial Citizenship: Empire and the Question of Belonging.* Manchester: Manchester University Press, 2013.

Gramsci, Antonio. *La questione meridionale.* Rome: Editori Riuniti, 2005.

Greenblatt, Stephen. *Marvelous Possessions: The Wonder of the New World.* Chicago: University of Chicago Press, 1991.

Greene, Molly. *A Shared World: Christians and Muslims in the Early Modern Mediterranean.* Princeton, NJ: Princeton University Press, 2000.

—. *The Edinburgh History of the Greeks, 1453–1774: The Ottoman Empire.* Edinburgh: Edinburgh University Press, 2015.

Groselli, Renzo. *Gli uomini del legno sull'Isola delle rose: La vicenda storica del villaggio italiano di Campochiaro a Rodi: 1935–1947.* Trento: Curcu Genovese, 2018.

Guidi, Andreas. "Defining Inter-Communality between Documents, Tradition, and Collective Memory: Jewish and Non-Jewish Capital and Labor in Early Twentieth Century Rhodes." *Southeast European and Black Sea Studies* 17, no. 2 (2017): 165–80.

—. "Youth and Generations between Two Empires: Changing Sociabilities from Ottoman to Italian Rule in Rhodes." PhD diss., Paris: Université Paris Sciences et Lettres, 2018.

Hadjikyriacou, Antonis. *Islands of the Ottoman Empire.* Princeton, NJ: Markus Wiener Publishers, 2019.

Hametz, Maura. "Replacing Venice in the Adriatic: Tourism and Italian Irredentism, 1880–1936." *Journal of Tourism History* 6, nos. 2–3 (2014): 107–201.

Helmmreich, Paul. *From Paris to Sèvres: The Partition of the Ottoman Empire at the Peace Conference of 1919–1920.* Columbus: Ohio University Press, 1974.

Hérelle, Georges. *Notolette Dannunziane: Ricordi, Aneddotti, Pettegolezzi.* Edited by Guy Tosi. Pescara: Centro Nazionale di Studi Dannunziani, 1984.

Herzfeld, Michael. "The Horns of the Mediterraneanist Dilemma." *American Ethnologist* 11, no. 3 (1984): 439–54.

—. "Practical Mediterraneanism: Excuses for Everything from Epistemology to Eating." In *Rethinking the Mediterranean*, edited by W.V. Harris, 45–63. Oxford: Oxford University Press, 2005.

Hester, Natalie. *Literature and Identity in Italian Baroque Writing.* Burlington, VT: Ashgate, 2008.

Hick, Michael Robert. "The Imia/Kardak Affair, 1995–6: A Case of Inadvertent Conflict." *European Security* 7, no. 4 (1998): 118–36.

Hirschon, Renée. "The Jews of Rhodes: The Decline and Extinction of an Ancient Community." In *The Last Ottoman Century and Beyond: The Jews in Turkey and the Balkans, 1808–1945,* edited by Minna Rozen, 291–307. Tel Aviv: Tel Aviv University, 2002.

—. "Jews from Rhodes in Central and South Africa." In *Encyclopedia of Diasporas: Immigrant and Refugee Cultures Around the World,* vol. 2, edited by Melvin Ember, 925–34. New York: Springer, 2007.

—. "Cosmopolitans in the Old Town: The Jews of Rhodes: A Story of Extinction and Survival." Paper presented at Deportation of Jews and Rhodes and Cos: 1944–2014, Commemorative International Symposium on the Holocaust in the Aegean, Rhodes, Greece, July 22, 2014.

Hirschon, Renée, ed. *Crossing the Aegean: An Appraisal of the 1923 Compulsory Population Exchange between Greece and Turkey.* New York: Berghahn Books, 2003.

Hom, Stephanie Malia. "Empires of Tourism: Travel and Italian Colonial Rhetoric in Libya and Albania, 1911–43." *Journal of Tourism History* 4, no. 3 (2012): 281–300.

—. *The Beautiful Country: Tourism and the Impossible State of Destination Italy.* Toronto: University of Toronto Press, 2015.

—. *Empire's Mobius Strip: Historical Echoes in Italy's Crisis of Migration and Detention.* Ithaca, NY: Cornell University Press, 2019.

Hom Cary, Stephanie. "The Tourist Moment." *Annals of Tourism Research* 31, no. 1 (2004): 61–77.

—. "Destination Italy: Tourism, Colonialism, and the Modern Italian Nation-State, 1861–1947." PhD diss., Berkeley: University of California, 2007.

Horden, Peregrine, and Nicholas Purcell. *The Corrupting Sea: A Study of Mediterranean History.* Malden, MA: Blackwell, 2000.

Hughes-Hallett, Lucy. *Gabriele D'Annunzio: Poet, Seducer, and Preacher of War.* New York: Alfred A. Knopf, 2013.

Ilbert, Robert, and Ilios Yanakakis, *Alexandria, 1860–1960: The Brief Life of a Cosmopolitan Community.* Alexandria: Harpocrates, 1997.

Ipsen, Carl. *Dictating Demography: The Problem of Population in Fascist Italy.* Cambridge: Cambridge University Press, 1996.

Isabella, Maurizio. "Liberalism and Empires in the Mediterranean: The Viewpoint of the Risorgimento." In *The Risorgimento Revisited,* edited by Silvana Patriarca and Lucy Riall, 232–54. New York: Palgrave Macmillan, 2012.

Isabella, Maurizio, and Konstantina Zanou. *Mediterranean Diasporas: Politics and Ideas in the Long Nineteenth Century.* London: Bloomsbury, 2016.

Jaja, Goffredo. *L'Isola di Rodi.* Rome: Società Geografica Italiana, 1912.

Jensen, Peter. "The Greco-Turkish War, 1920–1922." *International Journal of Middle East Studies* 10, no. 4 (1979): 553–65.

Kanz, Christine, and Adam Cmiel. "Ex-Corporation: On Male Birth Fantasies." *Imaginations* 2, no. 11 (2011): 54–67.

Karatzas, Georgios. "Representing Historical Narratives in the Urban Space: The Making of a Heritage Space in Urban Rhodes, 1912–1950." The Mediated City Conference, London, April 1–3, 2014.

Kaurinkoski, Kira. "The Muslim Communities in Kos and Rhodes: Reflections on Social Identities in Contemporary Greece." *Slavica Helsingiensia* 41 (2012): 47–78.

Kazamias, Alexander. "Between Language, Land and Empire: Humanist and Orientalist Perspectives on Egyptian Greek Identity." In *Greek Diaspora and Migration since 1700: Society, Politics and Culture*, edited by Dimitris Tziovas, 177–92. London: Taylor & Francis, 2016.

Khuri-Makdisi, Ilham. *Eastern Mediterranean and the Making of Global Radicalism.* Berkeley: University of California Press, 2010.

Kirschenblatt-Gimblett, Barbara. *Destination Culture: Tourism, Museums, and Heritage.* Berkeley: University of California Press, 1998.

Kitrolimides, Paschalis. *Eleftheros Venizelos: The Trials of Statesmanship.* Cambridge: Cambridge University Press, 2013.

Knepper, Paul. "Lombroso's Jewish Identity and its Implications for Criminology." *Australian and New Zealand Journal of Criminology* 44, no. 3 (2011): 355–69.

Labanca, Nicola. *Oltremare: Storia dell'espansione coloniale italiana.* Bologna: Il mulino, 2002.

—. "Colonial Rule, Colonial Repression and War Crimes in the Italian Colonies." *Journal of Modern Italian Studies* 9, no. 3 (2004): 300–13.

—. *La guerra italiana per la Libia, 1911–31.* Bologna: Il mulino, 2012.

—. "The Italian Front." In *The First World War*, edited by Jay Winter, 266–96. Cambridge: Cambridge University Press, 2013.

Lago, Mario. *E intanto lavoriamo.* Milan: Mondadori, 1941.

Lasansky, Medina. *The Renaissance Perfected: Architecture, Spectacle and Tourism in Fascist Italy.* University Park, PA: Pennsylvania State University, 2004.

Lazzarini, Mario. *Le colonie d'Italia: Somalia, Libia, Eritrea, Etiopia, Dodecaneso.* Foggia: Italia Editrice, 2007.

Le Corbusier. *Towards a New Architecture.* London: Architectural Press, 1946.

Lecour, Sheila. *Mussolini's Greek Island: Fascism and the Italian Occupation of Syros in World War Two.* London: Bloomsbury, 2009.

— dir. *A Basket of Food: Greece in the 1940s.* 2013.

Lévy, Isaac Jack. *Jewish Rhodes: A Lost Culture.* Berkeley: Magnes Museum, 1998.

Levy, Rebecca Amato. *I Remember Rhodes.* New York: Sepher-Hermon Press for Sephardic House at Congregation Shearith Israel, 1987.

Lewis, Mary Dewhurst. "Geographies of Power: The Tunisian Civic Order, Jurisdictional Politics, and Imperial Rivalry in the Mediterranean, 1881–1935." *Journal of Modern History* 80, no. 4 (2008): 791–830.

—. *Divided Rule: Sovereignty and Empire in French Tunisia, 1881–1938.* Berkeley: University of California Press, 2014.

Livadiotti, Monica. *La presenza italiana nel Dodecaneso tra il 1912 e il 1948: La ricerca archeologica, la conservazione, la scelte progettuali.* Catania: Edizioni del Prisma, 1996.

Lombardi-Diop, Cristina. "Postracial/Postcolonial Italy." In *Postcolonial Italy: Challenging National Homogeneity*, edited by Cristina Lombardi-Diop and Caterina Romeo, 175–90. New York: Palgrave Macmillan, 2012.

Lombardi-Diop, Cristina, and Caterina Romeo. "The Italian Postcolonial: A Manifesto," *Italian Studies* 69, no. 3 (2014): 424–33.

—. "Italy's Postcolonial 'Question': Views from the Southern Frontier of Europe." *Postcolonial Studies* 18, no. 4 (2015): 367–83.

Lombardi-Diop, Cristina, and Caterina Romeo, eds. *Postcolonial Italy: Challenging National Homogeneity.* New York: Palgrave Macmillan, 2012.

Loomba, Ania. *Colonialism/Postcolonialism: The New Critical Idiom,* 2nd ed. New York: Routledge, 1998.

—. *Colonialism/Postcolonialism: The New Critical Idiom,* 2nd ed. New York: Routledge, 2007.

Lumley, Robert, and Jonathan Morris. *A New History of the Italian South: The Mezzogiorno Revisited.* Exeter: Exeter University Press, 1997.

Luzzi, Joseph. *Romantic Europe and the Ghost of Italy.* New Haven, CT: Yale University Press, 2008.

MacCannell, Dean. *The Tourist: A New Theory of the Leisure Class.* New York: Schocken Books, 1976.

Maglio, Emma. "The Changing Role of Historic Town of Rhodes in the Scenario of Ottoman and Italian Rules in the Light of the Iconographic Sources." *Eikonocity* 1, no. 1 (2016): 75–88.

Malette, Karla. *European Modernity and the Arab Mediterranean: Toward a New Philology and a Counter-Orientalism.* Philadelphia: University of Pennsylvania Press, 2010.

Maravigna, Pietro. *Gli italiani nell'Oriente balcanico, in Russia e in Palestina, 1915–19.* Rome: Stab. Poligrafico per l'amministrazione della guerra, 1923.

Marcus, Millicent. *After Fellini: National Cinema in the Postmodern Age.* Baltimore: Johns Hopkins Press, 2002.

Marongiù Buonaiuti, Cesare. *La politica religiosa del fascismo nel Dodecanneso.* Naples: Giannini, 1979.

Martinoli, Simona. "Il ruolo del Touring." In *Architettura coloniale italiana nel Dodecaneso, 1912–1943,* edited by Simona Martinoli and Eliana Perotti, 43–57. Turin: Fondazione Giovanni Agnelli, 1999.

Martinoli, Simona, and Eliana Perotti. *Architettura coloniale italiana nel Dodecaneso, 1912–1943.* Turin: Fondazione Giovanni Agnelli, 1999.

Mavris, Nicholas. *Sforza vs. Sforza: The Free Movement and the Foreign Policy of Its Leader.* New York: Dodecanesian League of America, 1943.

Mazower, Mark. "The Messiah and the Bourgeoisie: Venizelos and Politics in Greece, 1909–1912." *The Historical Journal* 35, no. 4 (1992): 885–904.

—. *Inside Hitler's Greece: The Experience of Occupation, 1941–44.* New Haven, CT: Yale University Press, 1993.

—. "Travellers and the Oriental City, c. 1840–1920." *Transactions of the Royal Historical Society* 6, no. 2 (2002): 59–111.

—. *Salonica, City of Ghosts: Christians, Muslims, and Jews, 1430–1950.* New York: Alfred A. Knopf, 2005.

McClintock, Ann. *Imperial Leather: Race, Gender and Sexuality in the Colonial Contest.* New York: Routledge, 1995.

McClure, William Kidston. *Italy in North Africa: An Account of the Tripoli Enterprise.* London: Constable, 1913.

McElligott, Anthony. "The Deportation of the Jews of Rhodes, 1944: An Integrated History." In *The Holocaust in Greece,* edited by Giorgos Antoniou and Dirk Moses, 58–86. Cambridge: Cambridge University Press, 2018.

McGuire, Valerie. "An Imperial Education for Times of Transition: Conquest, Occupation, and Civil Administration of the Southeast Aegean." In *Italy in the Era of the Great War,* edited by Vanda Wilcox, 145–63. Leiden: Brill, 2018.

—. "Italian Identity, Global Mediterranean: Heritage and the Cultural Politics of Tourism in the Aegean." In *Transcultural Italies: Mobility, Memory and Translation,* edited by Charles Burdett, Loredana Polezzi, and Barbara Spadaro, 75–99. Liverpool: University of Liverpool Press, 2020.

McKee, Sally. *Uncommon Dominion: Venetian Crete and the Myth of Ethnic Purity.* Philadelphia: University of Pennsylvania Press, 2000.

McLaren, Brian. *Architecture and Tourism in Italian Colonial Libya: An Ambivalent Modernism.* Seattle: University of Washington Press, 2006.

Mitchell, Timothy. *Colonising Egypt.* Berkeley: University of California Press, 1988.

Moe, Nelson. *The View from Vesuvius: Italian Culture and the Southern Question.* Berkeley: University of California Press, 2002.

Monina, Giancarlo. *Il consenso coloniale: Le società geografiche e l'Istituto coloniale italiano: 1896–1914.* Rome: Carocci, 2002.

Montalbano, Gabriele. "The Making of Italians in Tunisia: A Biopolitical Colonial Project, 1881–1911," *California Italian Studies* 9, vol. 1 (2019): 1–21.

Montavani, Claudia. *Rigenerare la società: L'eugenetica italiana dalle origini ottocentesche agli anni trenta.* Soveria Manelli: Rubbettino, 2004.

Morgan, Philip. *Italian Fascism, 1915–1945.* New York: Palgrave MacMillan, 2004.

—. *Fascism in Europe, 1919–45.* Abingdon, VA: Routledge, 2007.

Moses, Dirk A. "Cutting out the Ulcer and Washing away the Incubus of the Past: Genocide Prevention Through Population Transfer." In *Decolonization, Self-Determination, and the Rise of Global Human Rights Politics,* edited by A. Dirk Moses, Marco Duranti, and Roland Burke, 153–78. Cambridge: Cambridge University Press, 2020.

Mussolini, Benito. *Opera omnia.* Florence: La Fenice, 1951–63.

Nardelli, Federico Vittore. *L'Arcangelo.* Rome: Alberto Stock, 1931.

Negash, Tekeste. *Italian Colonialism in Eritrea: Policy, Praxis, and Impact, 1844–1941.* Uppsala: Uppsala University Press, 1987.

Noel-Welch, Rhiannon. *Vital Subjects: Race and Biopolitics in Italy.* Liverpool: Liverpool University Press, 2016.

Nora, Pierre. "Between Memory and History: *Les Lieux de Memoire.*" *Representations* 26 (Spring 1989): 7–24.

Omero. *Odissea.* A cura di Maria Grazia Ciani. Venice: Tascabili Marsilio, 2000.

Oriani, Alfredo. *Fino a Dogali.* Bologna: Garagagni, 1912.

Orlandi, Luca. "An Italian Pioneer on Ottoman Architecture Studies in the Dodecanese Islands: Hermes Balducci (1904–1938)." In *Proceedings of the 14ᵗʰ International Congress of Turkish Art,* edited by Frédéric Hitzel, 531–41. Paris: Collège de France, 2013.

Orlandi, Rosita. *Le isole italiane dell'Egeo, 1912–1947.* Bari: Levante, 1994.

Pagano, Tullio. "From Diaspora to Empire: Enrico Corradini's Nationalist Novels." *Modern Language Notes* 119, no. 1 (2004): 67–83.

Palumbo, Patrizia. *A Place in the Sun: Africa in Italian Colonial Culture from Post-unification to the Present.* Berkeley: University of California Press, 2003.

Pankhurst, Richard. *Education in Ethiopia during the Italian Fascist Occupation.* New York: African Publishers, 1972.

Pannuti, Alessandro. *La comunita italiana di Istanbul nel XX secolo: Ambiente e persone.* Istanbul: Edizioni ISIS, 2006.

Paoletti, Emanuela. *The Migration of Power and North–South Inequalities.* Basingstoke: Palgrave MacMillan, 2011.

Papuccular, Hazal. "Fragmented Memories: The Dodecanese during World War II." In *Heritage and Memory of War: Responses from Small Islands,* edited by Gilly Carr and Keir Reeves. New York: Routledge, 2015.

—. "Fragile Balances: Turkish Foreign Policy on the Sovereignty of the Dodecanese Islands, 1940–1947." *Journal of Balkan and Near Eastern Studies* 20, no. 5 (2018): 405–19.

Pasqualini, Maria-Gabriella. *L'esercito Italiano nel Dodecaneso, 1912–43: Speranze e realtà i documenti dell'Ufficio Storico dello Stato maggiore dell'Esercito.* Rome: Ufficio Storico SME, 2005.

Passerini, Luisa. *Fascism in Popular Memory: The Cultural Experience of the Turin Working Class.* Cambridge: Cambridge University Press, 1987.

—. *Memory and Utopia: The Primacy of Intersubjectivity.* London: Equinox, 2007.

Patriarca, Silvana. *Italian Vices: Nation and Character from the Risorgimento to the Republic.* New York: Cambridge University Press, 2010.

Patriarca, Silvana, and Lucy Riall. *The Risorgimento Revisited: Nationalism and Culture in the Nineteenth Century.* Basingstoke: Palgrave and MacMillan, 2011.

Pedrazzi, Orazio. *Dalla Cirenaica all'Egeo.* Rocca San Casciano: L. Cappelli, 1913.

—. *Il Levante Mediterraneo e l'Italia.* Milan: Alpes, 1925.

Pellegrino, Angelo. *Verso oriente: Viaggi e letteratura degli scrittori italiani orientali, 1912–1982.* Milan: La vita felice, 2018.

Perelsztein, Diane, Willy Perelsztein, and John Boyle, dirs. *Rhodes Forever.* Brussels: Les films de Memoire, 1995.

Pergher, Roberta. *Borderlines in the Borderlands: Defining Difference through History, "Race," and Citizenship in Fascist Italy.* Florence: European University Institute, 2009.

—. *Mussolini's Nation-Empire: Sovereignty and Settlement in Italy's Borderlands, 1922–1943.* Cambridge: Cambridge University Press, 2019.

Pergher, Roberta and Marcus Payek, eds. *Beyond Versailles: Sovereignty, Legitimacy, and the Formation of New Polities after the Great War.* Bloomington: Indiana University Press, 2019.

Peri, Massimo, ed. *La politica culturale del fascismo nel Dodecaneso: Atti di convegno.* Padova: Esedra, 2009.

Petrakis, Marina. *The Metaxas Myth: Dictatorship and Propaganda in Greece.* New York: Tauris Academic Studies, 2006.

Petricioli, Marta. *Archeologia e mare nostrum: Le missioni archeologiche nella politica mediterraneo dell'Italia, 1898–1943.* Rome: Valerio Levi, 1990.

—. "Italian Schools in Egypt." *British Journal of Middle Eastern Studies* 24, no. 2 (1997): 179–91.

—. *L'Europe méditerranéenne/ Mediterranean Europe.* Bruxelles, Belgique: Peter Lang, 2008.

Petrucci, Marcella, ed. *Atlante geostorico di Rodi: Territorialità, attori, pratiche e rappresentazioni, 1912–1947.* Rome: Gangemi Editore, 2009.

Petrusecwiz, Maria. *Come il meridione divenne una questione.* Soveria Monelli: Rubettino, 1998.

Pignataro, Luca. "The End of the Italian Dodecanese, 1945–50." *Clio* 37, no. 4 (2001): 649–87.

—. "Le isole italiane dell'Egeo dall'8 settembre 1943 al termine della seconda guerra mondiale." *Clio* 37, no. 3 (2001): 465–552.

—. *Il Dodecaneso italiano, 1912–1947.* Chieti: Solfanelli, 2011.

Pinkus, Karen. *Bodily Regimes: Italian Advertising under Fascism.* Minneapolis: University of Minnesota Press, 1995.

—. "Empty Spaces: Decolonization in Italy." In *A Place in the Sun: Africa in Italian Colonial Culture from Post-unification to the Present,* edited by Patrizia Palumbo, 299–320. Berkeley: University of California Press, 2003.

Pongiluppi, Francesco. *La Rassegna Italiana: Organo degli interessi italiani in Oriente: Giornale Ufficiale della Camera di Commercio Italiana di Constantinopoli.* Istanbul: Edizioni ISIS, 2015.

Portelli, Alessandro. *The Battle of Valle Giulia: Oral History and the Art of Dialogue.* Madison, WI: University of Wisconsin Press, 1997.

—. *The Death of Luigi Trastulli and Other Stories: Form and Meaning in Oral History*. Albany, NY: State University Press of New York, 2001.

—. "Fingerprints Stained with Ink: Notes on 'Migrant Writing' in Italy." *Interventions* 8, no. 3 (2007): 472–83.

Porter, Dennis. *Desire and Transgression in European Travel Writing*. Princeton, NJ: Princeton University Press, 1991.

—. "Orientalism and Its Problems." In *Colonial Discourse and Post-Colonial Theory: A Reader*, edited by Patrick Williams and Laura Chrisman, 150–62. New York: Columbia University Press, 1994.

Pratt, Mary Louise. *Imperial Eyes: Travel Writing and Transculturation*. New York: Routledge, 2008.

Pretelli, Matteo. "Education in the Italian Colonies during the Interwar Period." *Modern Italy* 16, no. 3 (2011): 275–93.

Prodomi, Corrado. *Memorie di un missionario di Rodi-egeo, 1913–1920*. Verona: A. Bettinelli, 1937.

Pucci, Lara. "Remapping the Rural." In *Film, Art, New Media: Museum Without Walls?*, edited by Angela Dalle Vacche, 178–95. New York: Palgrave MacMillan, 2012.

Ragusa, Kym. *The Skin Between Us: A Memoir of Race, Beauty and Belonging*. New York: Norton and Co., 2006.

Rappas, Alexis. "Greeks under European Colonial Rule: National Allegiance and Imperial Loyalty." *Byzantine and Modern Greek Studies* 34, no. 2 (2010): 201–18.

—. "Memory and Property in Insular Spaces: The Case of Postcolonial Rhodes." Working paper, presented at "Islands in the Mediterranean: New Theorisations of Insularity," European University Institute, Florence, May 2014.

—. "The Transnational Formation of Imperial Rule on the Margins of Europe: British Cyprus and the Italian Dodecanese in the Interwar Period." *European History Quarterly* 45, no. 3 (2015): 467–505.

—. "The Domestic Foundations of Imperial Sovereignty: Mixed Marriages in the Fascist Aegean." In *New Perspectives on the History of Gender and Empire: Comparative and Global Approaches*, edited by Ulrike Lindner and Dörte Lerp, 31–58. London: Bloomsbury Academic Press, 2018.

—. "Memorial Soliloquies in Post-colonial Rhodes and the Ghost of Mediterranean Cosmopolitanism." *Mediterranean Historical Review* 33, no. 1 (2018): 89–110.

Re, Lucia. "Alexandria Revisited: Colonialism and the Egyptian Works of Enrico Pea and Giuseppe Ungaretti." In *A Place in the Sun: Africa in Italian Culture from the Post-unification to the Present*, edited by Patrizia Palumbo, 163–96. Berkeley: University of California Press, 2003.

—. "Italians and the Invention of Race: The Poetics and Politics of Difference in the Struggle for Libya, 1890–1913." *California Italian Studies* 1, no. 1 (2010): 1–59.

Renucci, Florence. "La strumentalizzazione del concetto di cittadinanza in Libia negli anni Trenta." *Quaderni Fiorentini Per La Storia Del Pensiero Giuridico Moderno,* nos. 33–34 (2005): 319–42.

Riall, Lucy. *Garibaldi: Invention of a Hero.* New Haven, CT: Yale University Press, 2007.

Robertson, Esmonde. "Race as a Factor in Mussolini's Policy in Africa and Europe." *Journal of Contemporary European History* 23, no. 1 (1988): 37–58.

Rochat, Giorgio. *Il colonialismo italiano.* Turin: Loescher, 1973.

Rodogno, Davide. *Fascism's European Empire: Italian Occupation during the Second World War.* Cambridge: Cambridge University Press, 2006.

Rodrigue, Aron. *French Jews, Turkish Jews: The Alliance Israélite Universelle and the Politics of Jewish Schooling in Turkey, 1860–1925.* Bloomington: Indiana University Press, 1990.

—. *Images of Sephardi and Eastern Jewries in Transition: The Teachers of the Alliance Israélite Universelle, 1860–1939.* Seattle: University of Washington Press, 1993.

—. "The Rabbinical Seminary in Italian Rhodes, 1928–38: An Italian Fascist Project." *Jewish Social Studies* 25, no. 1 (2019): 1–19.

Roletto, Giorgio. *Rodi: La funzione imperiale nel Mediterraneo Orientale.* Milan: Istituto Fascista dell'Africa Orientale, 1939.

Roumeni, Maurice. *The Jews of Libya: Coexistence, Persecution, Rehabilitation.* Brighton: Sussex Academic University Press, 2008.

Said, Edward. *Orientalism.* New York: Vintage Books, 1978.

Sakellaridi, G.M. "Antonio Ritelli." In *Kalymniaká Chronika,* vol. 6, 151–69. Athens: Anagnōstērio Kalymnu Hai Musai, 1986.

Samuk, Sahizer, and Hazal Papuccular. "Aegean in Motion: The Reasons, Consequences and Tragedies of Four Distinct Phases of Migration in the Aegean Sea." *Journal of Izmir Mediterranean Academy* no. 3 (2018): 56–74.

Santarelli, Lidia. *The Hidden Pages of Contemporary Italian History: War Crimes, War Guilt, Collective Memory.* London: Routledge, 2004.

—. "Muted Violence: Italian War Crimes in Occupied Greece." *Journal of Modern Italian Studies* 9, no. 3 (2004): 280–99.

Sarfatti, Michele. *The Jews in Mussolini's Italy: From Equality to Persecution.* Madison, WI: University of Wisconsin Press, 2006.

Sarti, Camillo. *Un viaggio in Oriente.* Varese: Nuova Italia, 1936.

Sbachi, Alberto. *Toward the Recognition of the Italian Empire: Franco-Italian Negotiations, 1936–1940.* Rome: Istituto Italo-africano, 1975.

Schayegh, Cyrus, and Andrew Arsen, eds. *The Routledge Handbook of the History of the Middle East Mandates.* London: Routledge, 2015.

Schnapp, Jeffery. "Epic Demonstrations: Fascist Modernity and the 1932 Exhibition of the Fascist Revolution." In *Fascism, Aesthetics, and Culture,* edited by Richard Golsan, 1–31. Hanover, NH: University Press of New England, 1992.

Schneider, Jane. *Italy's "Southern Question": Orientalism in One Country.* Oxford: Berg, 1998.

Segre, Claudio. *Fourth Shore: The Italian Colonization of Libya.* Chicago: University of Chicago Press, 1974.

Sergi, Giuseppe. *Etruschi e Pelasgi.* Rome: Nuova Antologia, 1893.

—. *Origine e diffusione della stirpe mediterranea.* Rome: Dante Alighieri Society, 1895.

—. *The Mediterranean Race: A Study of the Origins of European People.* Edited by Philip Lamantia. New York: Scribner and Sons, 1909.

Seton-Watson, Christopher. *Italy from Liberalism to Fascism, 1870–1925.* London: Meuthen, 1967.

Shachar, Nathan. *The Lost World of Rhodes: Greeks, Italians, Jews and Turks between Tradition and Modernity.* Brighton: Sussex Academic Press, 2013.

Sluga, Glenda. *The Problem of Trieste and the Italo-Yugoslav Border: Difference, Identity and Sovereignty in 20th Century Europe.* Albany, NY: State University Press, 2001.

Smith, Denis Mack. *Mussolini's Roman Empire.* New York: Viking, 1976.

Smith, Julia Clancy. *Mediterraneans: North Africa and Europe in an Age of Migration, c. 1800–1900.* Berkeley: University of California Press, 2013.

Smythe, S.A. "The Black Mediterranean and the Politics of Imagination." *Middle East Report*, no. 286 (2018): 3–9.

Spackman, Barbara. *Decadent Genealogies: The Rhetoric of Sickness from Baudelaire to D'Annunzio.* Ithaca, NY: Cornell University Press, 1989.

—. *Fascist Virilities: Rhetoric, Ideology and Social Fantasy in Italy.* Minneapolis: University of Minnesota Press, 1996.

—. *Accidental Orientalists: Modern Italian Travelers in Ottoman Lands.* Liverpool: Liverpool University Press, 2017.

Spadaro, Barbara. *Una colonia italiana: Incontri, memorie, e rappresentazioni tra Italia e Libia.* Milan: Mondadori, 2013.

Srivastava, Neelam. *Italian Colonialism and Resistance to Empire, 1930–1970.* London: Palgrave MacMillan, 2018.

Stigliano, Marco. *Modernità d'esportazione: Florestano di Fausto e lo stile del costruire nei territori italiani d'oltremare.* Bari: Poliba, 2009.

Stoler, Ann. "Carnal Knowledge and Imperial Power: Gender, Race and Morality in Colonial Asia." In *Gender at the Crossroads of Knowledge: Feminist Anthropology in the Postmodern Era*, edited by Micaela di Leonardo, 6–67. Berkeley: University of California Press, 1991.

—. "Colonial Archives and the Arts of Governance." *Archival Science* 2 (2002): 87–109.

Stora, Benjamin. *Algeria, 1830–2000.* Ithaca, NY: Cornell University Press, 2001.

Strang, Bruce. *Collision of Empires: Italy's Invasion of Ethiopia and Its International Impact.* New York: Routledge, 2017.

Strumza, Vitalis. *Alcuni cenni storici sugli Ebrei di Rodi*. Bologna: L. Capelli, 1936.

Sutton, David. *Memories Cast in Stone: The Relevance of the Past in Everyday Life*. New York: Berg, 1998.

Taddia, Irma. *La memoria dell'Impero: Autobiografie d'Africa Orientale*. Manduria: P. Lacaita, 1998.

Terre, Ingrid. "Managing Colonial Recollections: Italian–Libyan Contentions." *Interventions: International Journal of Postcolonial Studies* 17, no. 3 (2015): 452–67.

Tintori, Guido. "The Transnational Political Practices of 'Latin American Italians.'" *International Migration* 49, no. 3 (2011): 168–88.

Todorova, Maria. *Imagining the Balkans*. New York: Oxford University Press, 1997.

—. *Balkan Identities: Nation and Memory*. New York: New York University Press, 2004.

Tomasello, Giovanna. *La letteratura coloniale italiana dalle avanguardie al fascismo*. Palermo: Sellerio Editore, 1984.

—. *L'Africa tra mito e realtà: Storia della letteratura coloniale italiana*. Palermo: Sellerio Editore, 2004.

Touring Club Italiano. *Rodi: Guida del turista*. Milan: Bestetti e Tuminelli, 1928.

—. *Guida delle colonie e possedimenti*. Edited by L.V. Bertelli. Milan: Touring Club Italia, 1929.

Trento, Giovanna. "From Marinetti to Pasolini: Massawa, the Red Sea, and the Construction of 'Mediterranean Africa' in Italian Literature and Cinema." *Northeast African Studies* 12, no. 1 (2012): 273–307.

Triandafyllidou, Anna. *Immigrants and National Identity in Europe*. London: Routledge, 2001.

Tripodi, Paolo. *The Colonial Legacy in Somalia: Rome and Mogadishu, from Colonial Administration to Operation Restore Hope*. New York: St. Martin's Press, 1999.

Troilo, Simona. "'A Gust of Cleansing Wind': Italian Archaeology on Rhodes and in Libya in the Early Years of Occupation, 1911–14." *Journal of Modern Italian Studies* 17, no. 1 (2012): 45–69.

—. "Pratiche coloniali. La tutela tra musealizzazione e monumentalizzazione nella Rodi 'italian' (1912–1926)." *Passato e Presente* 87 (2012): 80–104.

Tsirpanlēs, Zacharias N. *Italokratia sta Dōdekanēsa, 1912–1943: Allotriōsē tou anthrōpou kai tou perivallonto*, prologos Ēlia E. Kollia. Rodos: Ekdosē Grapheiou Mesaiōnikēs Polēs Rodou, 1998.

Tumiati, Domenico. *Una primavera in Grecia*. Milan: Fratelli Treves, 1907.

Turiano, Annalaura, and Joseph Viscomi. "From Immigrants to Emigrants: Salesian Education and the Failed Integration of Italians in Egypt, 1937–1960." *Modern Italy* 23, no. 1 (2018): 1–17.

Van den Abbeele, Georges. *Travel as Metaphor: From Montaigne to Rousseau*. Minneapolis: University of Minnesota Press, 1992.

Varelis, Fotis. *Kitala*. Athens: Fotis Varelis, 1977.

Varon, Laura. *The Juderia: A Holocaust Survivor's Tribute to the Jewish Community of Rhodes*. Westport, CT: Praeger, 1999.

Verdicchio, Pasquale. *Bound by Distance: Rethinking Nationalism through the Italian Diaspora*. Madison, NJ: Fairleigh Dickinson Press, 1997.

—. "The Preclusion of Postcolonial Discourse." In *Revisioning Italy: National Identity and Global Culture*, edited by Beverly Allen and Mary J. Russo, 191–212. Minneapolis: University of Minnesota Press, 1997.

—. "Introduction." In Antonio Gramsci, *The Southern Question*, 7–26. Translated by Pasquale Verdicchio. Toronto: Guernica, 2005.

Viscomi, Joseph. "Mediterranean Futures: Historical Time and the Departure of Italians from Egypt." *Journal of Modern History* 91, no. 2 (2019): 341–79.

Vittorini, Ettore. *Isole dimenticate: Il Dodecaneso da Giolitti al massacro del 1943*. Florence: Le Lettere, 2002.

Vizvizi-Dontas, Donna. "The Allied Powers and the Eastern Question, 1921–1923." *Balkan Studies* 17, no. 2 (1976): 331–57.

Wolff, Larry. *Inventing Eastern Europe: The Map of Civilization on the Mind of the Enlightenment*. Stanford, CA: Stanford University Press, 1994.

Woodhouse, John. *Gabriele D'Annunzio: Defiant Archangel*. Oxford: Clarendon Press, 1998.

Wright, Gwendolyn. *The Politics of Design in French Colonial Urbanism*. Chicago: University of Chicago Press, 1991.

Wright, John L. "Mussolini, Libya, and the Sword of Islam." In *Italian Colonialism*, edited by Ruth Ben-Ghiat and Mia Fuller, 121–30. New York: Palgrave and MacMillan, 2005.

Yitzchak, Keretz. "The Migration of Rhodian Jews to Africa and the Americas, 1900–1914: The Beginning of New Sephardic Communities." In *Patterns of Migration, 1850–1914: Proceedings of the International Academic Conference*, edited by Aubrey Newman and Stephen Massil, 321–34. London: The Jewish Historical Society of England and the Institute of Jewish Studies, University College, London, 1996.

Zahra, Tara. *Great Departure: Mass Migration from Eastern Europe and the Making of the Free World*. New York: W. W. Norton, 2017.

Zanou, Konstantina. *Transnational Patriotism in the Mediterranean, 1800–1850*. Oxford: Oxford University Press, 2018.

Zervas, Theodore G. *The Making of a Modern Greek Identity: Education, Nationalism, and the Teaching of a Greek National Past*. Boulder, CO: East European Monographs, 2012.

Zervos, S. *The Dodecanese and the British Press*. Paris: Roussos, 1919.

Zimmerman, Joshua. *Jews in Italy under Fascist and Nazi Rule, 1922–45*. Cambridge: Cambridge University Press, 2005.

Zuccotti, Susan. *The Italians and the Holocaust: Persecution, Rescue and Survival*. London: Halban, 1987.

Index

Page numbers in **bold** refer to figures.

Aegean, the 6
    Corradini on 77
    early representations 39–40
    as feminine 51–52
    as a frontier 46
    influence 31
    integrated with Greece 249
    Italian rule 10
    Italian sovereignty 4, 12
    occupation of 148–58, 252
    recovery of 38
    reworking 43
    significance 20–21
Aegean citizenship 141–42, 144–45,
        147–48, 157–58, 158–69
Aegean Islands
    administration 26, 28
    annexation 22
    historical background 22–29
Africa
    colonization of 249
    influence 69
Afro-Mediterraneanism 63–71
agricultural colonies 184–85
agricultural projects 235
Al Qaeda 14
Albagli, Michele 162
Albania 91, 97, 151
Algeria **106**
Algerian War of Independence 7
Alliance Israeïlite Universelle system 214
Ameglio, Giovanni 150

Anatolia 154
Andall, Jacqueline 31n56
Anderson, Sean 100
Andreis, Alekos 239
anticolonial movements 192
anti-Fascist narrative 199
antimiscegenation laws 187
anti-Semitism 10, 70–71, 139, 174, 176–80,
        188, 203, 232
archaeological activity 41–42, 130, 138–39
Archipelago, the 22
architecture 5, **5**, **6**, 93–94, 252–53
    Arabic motifs 101–02, 104
    heritage 260–61
    Kalithea Baths 108–12, **110**, 260
    mediterraneità aesthetic 100–03, **102**,
        103, 104–06, **105**, **106**
    New Market 104–06, **105**, **106**
    Palazzo del Governo 101–02, **103**
    restoration of 256–57, 260–61
archival material 28–29
armchair travellers 99
art 55
Arthurs, Josh 93, 199
Aryanism 59–63, 66
assimilation 35, 139, 146, 160, 173–74, 185,
        199–200, 210, 230
assimilation programs 195–96, 201, 203
    cultural initiatives 204–07, 211–12
    education 207–12, **213**, 214–17
Austro-Hungarian Empire 28, 151
autocephalia 206

backwardness 40, 42
Balducci, Hermes 97, 111, 136
Balkan question, the 75
Balkan Wars 39n7
Balkanism 28
Balkans, the 27, 39, 248
Ballinger, Pamela 164
Barerra, Giulia 187, 222
beauty, and race 224
Bedhad, Ali 99
belonging 126, 141–94
    Aegean citizenship 141, 144–45, 147–48,
        157–58
    and annexation 148–58
    citizenship 141–45, 156–57
    colonial citizenship 141, 142
    and diplomatic protection 153–54
    dissemination of Italianness 148–58
    Jewish community 170–82
    and military service 168–69
    naturalization 142, 157, 161–64, 167–68,
        185
    and obedience 161–62
    one face, one race 182, 183–92
Ben-Ghiat, Ruth 123–24
Benzoni, Maria 129, 130, 130–32, 133,
    133–34
Bernal, Martin 59
Bernheimer, Charles 55
Bhaba, Homi 32–33, 116
Biasion, Renzo 250–51
Boggiani, Guido 45, 50
bonifica 206–07, 211, 217
Bopp, Franz 62–63
border politics 14–16
Borutta, Manuel 7–8
Bossi-Fini legislation 13–14
Bosworth, Richard 9
Braudel, Fernand 7, 22
British Empire 32, 95, 143, 160–61
brutality 218
bullying 217
Buonaiuti, Cesare 211
Burdett, Charles 129n80

CAIR 235
Campioni, Admiral Innigo 180
Candilafti, Paolo 164

Caponetto, Rosetta Giuliani 17
Catholicism, conversion to 221, 225, 230
Catholicization 225
Chambers, Iain 15
Choate, Mark 18–19, 65
Christos, Pinos 236
chronopolitics 93, 126, 140
Ciano, Galeazzo 176–77
Ciarlantini, Franco 129, 130, 132, 133,
    134–35, 212
Cirenaica 25
citizenship 140, 141–45, 185, 199–200, 261
    Aegean 141, 144–45, 147–48, 157–58,
        158–69
    colonial 141, 142
    denial to Turks 189
    extension of 156–57
    Greek 163
    by heritage 143, 148, 182, 259–60
    Jewish community 170–82
    and marriage 229
    and military service 168–69
    and obedience 161–62
    reform, 1933 167–69, 170, 173–74, 192
    stripping of 147
citizenship laws, reform, 1933 167–69, 170,
    173–74, 192
civil matrimony 227–28, 231–33
civilization, origin of 59
collaboration 255
colonial citizenship 141, 142
colonial conquest 133
colonial difference 34, 126
colonial display 113, 115
colonial expansion 8
colonial hierarchy 86, 124
colonial identities 127
colonial inertia 36
colonial mimicry 116–17
colonial modernity 34, 106, 126, 204, 206,
    261
colonial studies 18–19
colonialism 7, 8–9, 9–10, 18–19, 27, 222
    internal 24
    pacific 65
    unwillingness to confront 17
concubinage 187, 222, 230
consent 200–01

Constantinople 22, 74–75
consumption 90
Corfu 128
Corner, Paul 200
Corradini, Enrico 33, 43, 44–45, 71, 72,
    76–82, 90
Correnti, Cesare 69
cosmopolitanism 36, 68–69, 126–35, 140,
    171
Crete 163, 251
crisis of origins 37, 40, 48, 60
Crispi, Francesco 38, 41, 46
Croce, Benedetto 239n90
cross-cultural fertilization 7, 61–62
cruises 126–33
Culler, Jonathan 107, 108
cultural capital projects, Rhodes 94–95,
    107–13, **110**, **111**, **114**, 115–19, **117**,
    120, 121
cultural conservation 90
cultural hegemony 212
cultural initiatives 204–07, 211–12
cultural landscape 133
cultural unity, imperial fantasy of 244–45
culture
    legitimizing effects of 32
    multiple levels of 30n54
Curzon, Lord George 31–32, 171
Cyprus 95, 132, 161, 221
Cyrenaica 22

D'Annunzio, Gabriele 33, 43, 44, 45–58,
    69–70, 75–76, 79, 85, 131, 135, 154
    and Fascism 48
    marital and extramarital crises 50
    political career 48, 49
    tour of the Aegean 45–47, 48–58, 133
Dante Alighieri Society 127, 151
De Amicis, Edmondo 33, 43, 74–75
decadence 53
de Certeau, Michel 202
decolonization 7, 15, 15n21, 32
De Grazia, Victoria 127, 234
Demoule, Jean-Paul 63
Derrida, Jacques 138
De Savio, Francesco 190–91
Despotakis, Manoles 210–11, 215–16, 221,
    236, 240–41

De Vecchi, Cesare Maria 28, 35, 136,
    139, 146, 176, 177, 178–79, 185–87,
    190, 195, 196, 200, 206–07, 208–11,
    214–16, 231–32
developmentalism 202
Dewhurst, Mary Lewis 153
Di Fausto, Florestano 100, 101–02,
    104–06, 108
di San Giuliano, Antonino 150
Diakoyiannis, Leonidas 234–35
diaspora, politics of empire through
    158–69
difference 201
    affirmation of 85–86
    hierarchies of 126, 203
    indifference to 193
    rule of 188
diplomatic protection 153–54
divorce 225, 226
Dodecanese diaspora 158–69, 221
Dodecanese islands 6
    annexation 72, 81, 143–44, 148–58, 159,
        171
    archival material 28–29
    European capitulations 153–54
    forgotten occupation 249–50
    historical background 3–6, 22–29
    integrated with Greece 249
    Jewish community 170–82
    Nazi occupation 179, 254
    Ottoman presence 257
    as possession 144–45
    sovereignty 155
Donno, Fabrizio De 40–41
Doumanis, Nicholas 29, 197–98, 203, 218,
    223
dowry practices 223–24
Duncan, Derek 31n56
Durrell, Lawrence 138

East Africa 12, 19, 38, 153
    colonial projects 8–9, 10
    colonization 41, 46
    Dodecanese Greeks repatriated 183–84
    and origin of civilization 59–60
    state–settler relations 187
Eastern Question, the 39
Ebner, Michael 199, 217

economic policies 236
education 207–12, **213**, 214–17
Egypt 7, 132, 142
    Italian community 165–66, 167
elections, 1994 16n22
Eleusi 56–57
emigration 34, 38, 93, 241
    1870–1924 72
    Corradini on 77
    and imperialism 9
    politics of empire through 158–69
    the South 65, 72, 74–75
    transatlantic 65, 159
    to Tunisia 152–53
empire films 122–26, **124**, **125**
employment 235, 237–38
Esposito, Roberto 19
Ethiopia, invasion of 10, 11, 34, 46, 67,
    70, 94, 135, 139, 147, 156, 169, 179,
    183–84, 187, 196, 208, 243
ethnic affinity 34
ethnic diversity 4–5
ethnic unity 182, 183–92
ethnicity, and race 117–19, **118**, **120**, 121
Etruscan civilization 59, 67
Eurafrica 25, 67, 188
Euro-Mediterranean landscape 4
European Central Bank 2
European Commission 2
European Union 1, 2–3, 252–53
Europeanness 21
Euroscepticism 14
Evans, Arthur 41
exclusion 174
exoticism 99, 129, 135–36
expansion, necessity of 69
expansionism 79
exploration 133

familiar others 33
Fanon, Frantz 125–26
Fascism
    binary memories of 35–36
    D'Annunzio and 48
    legacies of 3
    rise of 33
Fascist Colonial Institute 127
Fascist dictatorship, and Italian Empire 11

Fascist discourses, hybridity 17
Fascist rule, definition 196–97
Fascist state 10
Federzoni, Luigi 33, 43, 44–45, 71, 72, 74,
    75–76, 79, 149
Ferris, Kate 199
festivals 86, 115–17, **117**, 123, 206
fetishism 57, 58
Filiremo Madonna, the 205
Fiore, Teresa 17
Five Star Movement 14
Flandin, Eugenio 85
Flaubert, Gustave 107
France 7, 12, 193
    annexation of Tunisia 19, 23, 77–78, 153
Franco, Giuseppe 191, 192
Franco, Hizkià 176
Franco-Levantine community 240–41
fraternization 241, 242
Fuller, Mia 138, 193, 253

Gabaccia, Donna 23
Gadda, Carlo Emilio 98, 127–28, 129
Galata 74–75
Gekas, Sakis 7–8
Genoa 22
gente mediterranea 242
geographic poetics 74
Giuliani, Gaia 23, 65, 179, 184
global financial crisis 2
Glynatsis, Giorgos 231, 236
Gobineau, Arthur de 62
Gorman, Daniel 143
Gramsci, Antonio 24, 32
Grand Tour travellers 128
Gravina, Maria 50
Greco-Roman Empire 4
Greco-Roman racial supremacy 190
Greco-Turkish tensions 257–58
Greco-Turkish War 172
Greece 1, 2, 69–70, 129–30, 150, 241, 254
    critique of 197–98
    D'Annunzio and 52–57
    engagement with 44
    image of 43–44
    masculinity 53–54, 58
    nationalism 7, 21, 149–50, 218–21
    occupation 197, 255–56

Ottoman presence 256–57
Ottomanization 42, 57, 58, 82
Sergi and 61–62
setback in Anatolia 154
significance 20
sovereign debt crisis 244
weakness 75–76
Greek citizenship 163
Greek community
  education 215–17
  Pedrazzi on 82–87
  stereotypes 118
Greek historiography 198
Greek identity 31, 216, 240
Greek irredentism 206n17
Greek national status 164–65
Greek revolution, 1820 3
Greekness 216n40
Greene, Molly 256
Guardian, The (newspaper) 1–2
Guidebook of the Colonies and Possessions
  (TCI) 112–13, **114**

Hanan, Ezra 217
health tourism 108
hegemony 32, 252
Hellenic rebirth 53
Hérelle, Georges 45, 46, 52
Hermes 54–55
Hitler, Adolf 188, 196
Hobsbawm, Eric 26
Holocaust, the 28, 180, 181, 214, 259
Hom, Stephanie Malia 90, 91
Homer 44, 51, 60–61
hospitality 138
Hotel of the Roses, Rhodes town **137**
Hughes-Hallett, Lucy 47
hybridity 17

identity 6
  European 2–3
  Greek 31, 216, 240
  Italian 8, 31, 36, 146–47, 149
  local 31
  national 3, 8, 24, 27, 31, 36, 65, 164–66,
    168, 241
  and power 15
  remaking 206–07

Rhodes 99
  volatility of 41
ideological alignment 185
*Il Levante Mediterraneo e l'Italia (The
  Eastern Mediterranean and Italy)* 144
immigration 13–14
imperial contexts 12
imperial heritage 130
imperial modernity 5
imperial past, signs of 248
imperialism 8, 9, 10–11, 19, 26–27, 90, 135,
  248
Indo-Europeanism 59–63
industrialization 234, 235
interdisciplinary approach 30–33
internal colonialism 24
International Monetary Fund 2
interwar period, zeitgeist of 6
Istituto Nazionale LUCE, Rhodes
  documentary 122–26, **124**, **125**
Italia turrita 75
Italian Empire 6, 8, 12, 21, 27, 32, 36, 70,
  166–67, 186–87, 256, 261
  amnesia about 247–48
  and Fascist dictatorship 11
  marginalization of 9
  need for 78
Italian Fascism 199
Italian Geographic Society 69, 131
Italian identity 8, 31, 36, 146–47, 149
Italian language 39, 207
  spread of 211–12, **213**, 214, 217
Italian nationalism 4, 12, 43
Italian Nationalist Association 22, 188
Italian rule, definition 196
Italian Tourism Company 127
Italiani brava gente myth 197, 199, 247
italianità 19–20, 65, 77, 78, 146–47,
  148–49, 164, 169, 241
Italianization 41, 193
Italianness 10, 24, 78, 146–47
  dissemination of 148–58
Italianness-as-Mediterraneanness 20
Italians, character of 197, 199, 238–43,
  247
Italians in the Orient 38–39
Italokratia 256
Italo-Turkish War 39n7, 71, 71–72, **73**, 74

Italy
  personification 75
  status 9
  unification 8, 11, 23, 24, 158

Jacopi, Giulio 222
Jewish community 28, 34, 35, 139, 146, 254
  assimilation 173–74
  citizenship 170–82
  deportations 180
  diaspora 259–60
  education 212, 214–15
  naturalization 171–72
  notables 173, 174–75
  origins 170–71
  persecution 176
  postcolonial remnants 258–59
  transnationalism 171, 179

Kalithea Baths, Rhodes 108–12, **110**, 260
Kalymnos 159–60, 236, **237**, 238–40, 242
Kalymnos Rock War, the 218
Karpathos 219–21
Katzinikolas, Mihales 216, 241–42
Knights of St. John 101, 136
Knossos 41
Kos 4, 138, 146, 151–52, 155, 190, 234–35
  agricultural colonies 184–85
  Jewish community 170–82, 214, 254,
    258–59
  minority populations 32
Kremastò 83–84

La Méditerranée 7, 12
Labanca, Nicola 92n12, 234
Lago, Mario 89, 108, 109–10, 116, 129, 148,
    150, 157, 158, 168, 169, 171, 173, 175,
    179, 183–84, 195, 196, 200, 204–05,
    207–08, 212, 222, 227–28, 229, 237,
    258
land-reclamation projects 234, 235
language 62–63, 139, 141, 185
  policies 160
  spread of Italian 151–52, 207, 211, 214,
    217
  suppression of others 207–08
Latin character 77
Latin renaissance 82

Lausanne, second treaty of 95, 147, 160–61,
    177, 180, 185, 189, 258
Law 189 13–14
Le colonie, Rodi, e le isole italiane dell'Egeo
    (Desio and Stefanini) 117–19, **118**
Le Corbusier 5, 104
League of Nations 162, 221
Lega, the 14, 16
Leros 1–3, 5, **5**, **6**, 104, 242–43, 252–53
Levant, the 12, 42, 74–75
Levantine otherness 32
Levantineness 93, 94, 107–12, 121, 136,
    250
Levi, Carlo 251
Levi, Stella 215
Liberal-era 10, 11
Libya 12, 19, 25, 27, 80, 97, 155, 163
  colonial citizenship 141, 142
  invasion of 44–45, 71, 72, 79
  Italian population 78
  tourism projects 91
L'illustrazione italiana (magazine) 89–140
Logothetis, Ippokrates 223–24, 230,
    236–37, 242–43
Lombardi, Pietro 108
Lombardi-Diop, Cristina 15n21, 23, 65,
    179, 184
Lombroso, Cesare 43, 59, 65, 66
London, treaty of 155–56
Loomba, Ania 30n54

madamismo 222
Magna Graecia 4, 57–58, 71, 130, 135
Marcus, Millicent 250
mare nostrum 58, 156, 188
Marinetti, Filippo Tomaso 165
marriage
  and citizenship 229
  civil 227–28, 231–33
  dowry practices 223–24
  laws 231–33
  licenses 232–33
  mixed 187, 190–91, 221–34, 244
  monitoring 222–23, 226
  regulations 223
  state intervention 225–26
  state policy 229–30
Mascantonio, Pasquale 45

masculinity 84
    anxieties about 40, 48, 49–58
    Greek 53–56, 58
Mazzini, Giuseppe 23
McClintock, Ann 37, 40, 46, 133
Mediterranean, the
    Aryan invasion 60–61
    as colonial/colonized sea 7–13, 39, 252
    in Italian nationalism 43
    as postcolonial sea 15–16, 17
Mediterranean culture 21–22
Mediterranean Empire, strategy of 25
Mediterranean race 20
Mediterranean Race, The (Sergi) 58–71
    Afro-Mediterraneanism 63–71
    and Aryanism 59
    and origin of civilization 59–60
    primordial unity 59
Mediterranean studies 7
Mediterranean unity 16–17
Mediterraneanism 35–36
    hierarchies 118–19, 202–03
    imperial formation of 30
Mediterraneanness 12, 20, 135–40, 147
mediterraneità 12, 20, 24, 34, 58–71, 91, 93,
      140, 146–47, 168, 179
    aesthetic 93–94, 96, 100–03, **102, 103,**
      104–06, **105, 106,** 136
    and Afro-Mediterraneanism 63–71
    and ethnic affinity 34
    goals 59
    replacement with *romanità* 94
    Rhodes 79–80
Mediterraneo (film) 250–51
Medusa 56–57
memorialization 247–48
memory
    politics of 197
    positive 169
    selective 240, 248, 251–61
memory loss 248
meridionalismo 15
methodology 30–33, 201–03
Michetti, Francesco Paolo 47–48
migrant literature 17–18
migration 12
    Afro-Mediterraneanism 63–71
    to North Africa 23

migration crisis 1–2, 13, 15
military service 168–69
Ministry of Foreign Affairs 26, 28, 145,
      154, 160, 163, 168, 208
Ministry of the Colonies 26, 145
minority communities 4, 32, 34, 80, 185
mixed marriages 187, 190–91, 221–34,
      244
    children 230
    and citizenship 229
    civil 227–28, 231–33
    dowry practices 223–24
    laws 231–33
    licenses 232–33
    monitoring 222–23, 226
    regulations 223
    state intervention 225–26
    state policy 229–30
modernism 5
modernity 91–92, 98, 130
    colonial 34, 106, 126, 204, 206, 261
modernization 24, 90, 98, 112, 140, 198,
      202, 244
Moe, Nelson 74
moral degeneration 225, 228, 244
moral superiority 42
Morfou, Angela 224
Morphopos, Nicholas 242–43
Movimento Cinque Stelle 14
multicultural identities 7
Muslim population 188–92
Mussolini, Benito
    alliance with Nazi Germany 177,
      187–88
    approach to modernity 91–92
    braggadocio 11
    and De Vecchi 186
    declares empire 70
    Eurafrica project 25, 67, 188
    first success 155–56
    imperialism 10–11, 27
    and Jewish community 171–72
    march on Rome 154
    mare nostrum 58
    Mediterranean strategy 1–2
    popularity 10, 196
    stance on Italians abroad 166
    totalitarianism 169, 198

Naples 131–32
nation building 252
national identity 3, 8, 24, 27, 31, 36, 65,
      168, 241
   indeterminacy of 164–66
national regeneration 126, 135, 196, 250
national resurgence 129
national unity, crisis of 37
nationalism 9, 12, 21, 35–36, 36, 66,
      169
   Greek 149–50, 218–21
   the Mediterranean in 43
   right-leaning swerve 33
nation-building 27, 145–46
naturalization 142, 157, 161–64, 167–68,
      171–72, 185, 226
Naval League 127
Nazi Germany 177, 179, 187–88, 193,
      198, 253–54
New Market, Rhodes 104–06, **105**,
      106, 260
Noel-Welch, Rhiannon 66
Nora, Pierre 254
North Africa 72
   conquest of 79
   migration to 23
North–South dualism 18
nostalgia 30, 36, 39–40, 43, 44, 49, 76–77,
      80, 192, 252

obedience 161–62
Olympia 53–56
one face, one race 182, 183–92, 231, 241,
      251
Opera Nazionale Ballila 186, 215, 221,
      234–35
oral testimonies 201–03
Organizzazione Nazionale Dopolavoro 34,
      126–27, 203
Oriani, Alfredo 25
Orient, the 12
Orientalism 12, 18, 32–33, 39, 40–41, 42,
      225
   Rhodes 34, 80–81, 107–12, **110**, **111**,
      125–26, **125**
Orientalization 41
Orsini, Luigi 131
Otherness 48, 146, 252

Ottoman Empire 3, 4, 22, 25, 28, 38–39,
      72, 77, 256
   collapse of 31–32, 39, 125, 171, 258
   colonialism 158
   and Greece 256–57
   refugees 161
   taxation 149, 152
   travel encounters with 41
Ottoman heritage, acceptance of 136
Ottomanization 42, 57, 58, 81, 82
Ouchy, Treaty of 45, 72

Pacifici, Riccardo 214–15
Palace of the Knights of St. John, Rhodes
      106, **106**, 215, 221
Palazzo del Governo, Rhodes 101–02, **103**
Pan-Arabian nationalism 7
Partriarca, Silvana 77
Passerini, Luisa 220
past, the, fetishism of 58
Patras 53
Patriarca, Silvana 19
patriotism 16
pax romana 156
Pedrazzi, Orazio 43, 44–45, 82–87, 115,
      143–44
Pelasgians, the 67–68
Pergher, Roberta 26–27, 32
Peridi, Giorgio 168–69
Pescara 50, 58
Petricioli, Marta 165–66
piccola cittadinanza 157–58, 177, 178
picturesque, the 115–16, 126, 133
Pignataro, Luca 29, 249
political recognition 39
population, islands 3
population exchange 31–32
Portelli, Alessandro 201
Porter, Dennis 32–33, 42n18
posing 82–87
postcolonial interpretive frameworks
      31n56
power, and identity 15
Prato, Davide 174, 175
Pratt, Mary Louise 113
Praxiteles 55–56
primordial unity 59
Prodomi, Corrado 225, 226, 226–27

protest 207, 218–21
public narratives 237–38
public works projects 159
Pucci, Lara 122
purification 136, **137**

race 33, 34, 68, 159
  Afro-Mediterraneanism 63–71
  Aryanism 59–63
  and beauty 224
  defence of 187, 221
  and ethnicity 117–19, **118**, **120**, 121
  hierarchies of 56, 182, 192, 261
  paradox of 43
  politics of 58, 144, 147, 168, 188–92,
    258
  positivist theories 59
  primordial unity 59
  Sergi's theory of 58–71
  stereotypes 118
  theories of 35
race laws 174, 176–80, 188–90, 232
racial differences, disavowal of 191
racial integrity 40
racial mixing 69
racialization 184
racism 187–88, 188–92, 203, 227–28
Rappas, Alexis 161, 216n40, 229
reforestation 235
regionalism 12, 23–24
Renzi, Matteo 16–17
representation, strategies of 113
resettlement 26, 235
resilience 207
resistance 195–96, 203, 216–17, 218–21,
  238–39, 244, 255
Rhodes 4, 28, 71–82, 190, 235, 236, 237
  agricultural colonies 184–85
  annexation 22, 71–72, 74, 81, 149–52
  archaeological projects 138–39
  Bath of Soliman 110–11, **111**, 112
  British rule 138
  Corradini and 76–82
  cosmopolitanism 140
  cultural landscape 81–82
  Dante Alighieri school 151–52
  elections 150
  ethnic diversity 134–35

  exoticism 99
  Federzoni on 75–76
  festivals 115–17, **117**, 123
  German occupation 193
  identity 99
  Jewish community 139, 146, 170–82,
    212, 214–15, 254, 258–59
  Kalithea Baths 108–12, **110**
  LUCE documentary 122–26, **124**, **125**
  Mediterraneanness 135–40
  mediterraneità 79–80
  minority populations 32, 80
  modernization 112, 140
  Orientalism 34, 80–81, 107–12, **110**,
    111, 125–26, **125**
  Ottoman heritage 136, 257
  Pedrazzi on 82–87
  purification 136, **137**, 138
  rabbinical school 214–15
  race and ethnicity 117–19, **118**, **120**,
    121
  reputation 92, 107
  state-sponsored tourism 126–35
  status 91
  tourism 34, 82
  travel literature 127–35
  Turkish community 124–26, **124**, **125**,
    155, 257–58
  urban renovation 76
Rhodes (city)
  conservation program 95
  esplanade 101
  Greek-inhabited area 96
  guidebooks 119
  Hospital of the Knights 94–95
  Hotel of the Roses **137**
  Jewish quarter **120**, 121, 133–34, 259
  Kalithea Baths 260
  medieval city 96, 98, 98–99
  mediterraneità aesthetic 100–03, **102**,
    103, 104–06, **105**, **106**
  New Market 104–06, **105**, **106**, 260
  Ottoman architecture 95, 96–97
  Palace of the Knights of St. John 106,
    106, 138
  Palazzo del Governo 101–02, **103**
  public buildings 101
  shoreline 101–02, **102**

signifiers 98
tourist zone 96, 101–02, 104
Turkish quarter 119, **120**, 121, 124–25
urban renovation 94–99
zoning laws 95–96
Rhodes tourism project 89–140, 136
  aesthetic harmony 90
  aesthetic vernacular 91
  conservation program 95
  cultural capital projects 94–95, 107–13,
    110, 111, 114, 115–19, **117**, 120, 121
  cultural conservation 90
  goals 90, 92–93
  and historical context 92
  inauguration 89
  and Levantineness 93, 94, 107–12,
    121
  master plan 89–90, 95–96, 98, 106,
    138
  and Mediterranean history 98
  mediterraneità 99
  mediterraneità aesthetic 100–03, **102,
    103**, 104–06, **105, 106**
  modernization 90, 140
  mosque restorations 109–10
  representation of Rhodes 99
  and rural life 121–26, **123, 124, 125**
  sense of the Oriental 97
  signifiers 98
  urban renovation 94–99
rimozione 247
Risorgimento, the 23
Ritelli, Antonio 238–40
Robertson, Esmonde 179
Rochat, 18
Rock War, the 218
Roditis, Dimitris 218
Rodogno, Davide 35, 233
Rodrigue, Aron 214
Roletto, Giorgio **xvii**
Roman Empire 24, 61–62, 139
Roman imperial lineage 20
romanità 58, 70, 91, 94, 97, 136, 139–40,
  146, 147, 169, 187–88, 191
Rome 13–14, 154
Romeo, Caterina 15n21
rural life, encounters with 121–26, **123,
  124, 125**

sagre 115
Said, Edward 7, 18, 31, 32–33, 39, 42, 62,
  85n116, 107, 252
Sakellaridi, Giannis 237–40
Salvini, Matteo 14, 16n22
Sarti, Camillo 130, 132–33
Scarfoglio, Edoardo 45, 46
Schnapp, Jeffrey 91–92
school attendance 186
Scramble for Africa 8
secret police archive 28
secret schools 216
selective memory 240, 248, 251–61
Sergi, Giuseppe 33, 43, 44, 130, 251
  Afro-Mediterraneanism 63–71
  anti-Semitism 70–71
  and Aryanism 59
  cosmopolitanism 68–69
  genealogy 59, 61–62
  goals 59
  idea of race 68
  and language 62–63
  and origin of civilization 59–60
  primordial unity 59
  racial theory 58–71
  rebuttal of the Indo-Europeanists
    61–63
  Southernism 66
sex tourism 52
shared past 5
social Darwinism 20
social engineering 2
social intimacy 124
Società Geografica Italiana 127
Society of Italian Navigation 127
Soleiman, Yousef 189
Somalia 10
sources 30–31
South, the 16–17, 45, 131–32
  backwardness 40
  economic collapse 37
  emigration 65, 72, 74–75
  Hellenized 57–58
  liberal humanist projects 66
  as *mediterraneità* 34
  representation of 75
  unemployment crisis 41
Southern problem, the 12–13, 19, 24

Southern Question, the 14, 24, 40, 252
Southernism 66
Southernness 27, 45
sovereignty 5, 16, 34–35, 113, 115, 135,
    144, 155
  anxieties about 163
  expansion of 158
  temporary 30
Spackman, Barbara 18, 41, 48, 82–87
spazio vitale 233
Stamatis, Haralambo 206, 234, 241
state-building 201, 234–45, **237**
stereotypes 35–36, 118, 244
Stoler, Ann 30–31
strapaese movement 121, 122
Strumza, Vitalis 174–75
Sutton, David 203
Syracuse 130

TEMI 235, 237–38
Terzioglu, Bilal 189
thalassological framework 8, 9, 11–12
Thucydides 57
Tilos 236
Todorova, Maria 28, 44
totalitarianism 169, 197, 198
Touring Club Italiano 112–13, **114**, 116,
    117, 121, 140
tourism 34, 82, 82–87, 138, 244, 253
  goals 92–93
  state-sponsored 34, 126–35
  strategies 128–29
  see also Rhodes tourism project
traditional dress 122, **123**
transatlantic migration 38, 65, 159
transnationalism 13–22
travel literature 33–34, 38, 42n18, 74–75,
    99, 127–35
Trento 25
Trieste 25
Triple Alliance, the 22
Tripoli 25, 80
Tripolitania 22
Tunisia
  French annexation 19, 23, 77, 153
  immigration 72
  Italian community 78, 152–53

Turkey 2, 31, 125, 149, 185, 189
Turkish community 34, 35
  stereotypes 118–19
Turkish nationalism 7

uncanny, the 51, 86–87
unemployment 41
Ungaretti, Giuseppe 165
Union of Soviet Socialist Republics (USSR)
    163
United States of America 21, 159
unredeemed lands, incorporation of 154

Varon, Mose 180–81
Venice 22, 93–94, 97, 102, **103**
Venizelos, Eleftheros 21
Verdicchio, Pasquale 24, 69n85
Verga, Giovanni 75
Versailles, treaty of 154
violence 217, 218
Virgil 68
virility, loss of 49–58

War on Terror 13–14, 15
welfare state 234
whiteness and whitening 20, 144, 184–85,
    191
Wilde, Oscar 55
Wilson, Woodrow 4, 148
women 218–34
  concubinage 187, 222
  as mediators 220, 221, 228–29
  mixed marriages 187, 190–91, 221–34
  protests 203, 218–21
  role of 130–32
Woodhouse, John 47
World War I 4, 8–9, 25, 26, 39n7, 150–51,
    153–54, 159, 163
World War II 3, 10, 19, 139, 179–81, 193,
    197, 248, 253–56, 259

Young Turks 149
youth organizations 186

Zanou, Konstantina 21
Zimbabwe 182
Zionism 181